Cambridge Imperial and Post-Colonial Studies Series

General Editors: **Megan Vaughan**, King's College, Cambridge and **Richard Drayton**, Corpus Christi College, Cambridge

This informative series covers the broad span of modern imperial history while also exploring the recent developments in former colonial states where residues of empire can still be found. The books provide in-depth examinations of empires as competing and complementary power structures encouraging the reader to reconsider their understanding of international and world history during recent centuries.

Titles include:

Sunil S. Amrith
DECOLONIZING INTERNATIONAL HEALTH
India and Southeast Asia, 1930–65

Tony Ballantyne
ORIENTALISM AND RACE
Aryanism in the British Empire

Anthony J. Barker
SLAVERY AND ANTI-SLAVERY IN MAURITIUS, 1810–33
The Conflict between Economic Expansion and Humanitarian Reform under British Rule

Robert J. Blyth
THE EMPIRE OF THE RAJ
Eastern Africa and the Middle East, 1858–1947

Roy Bridges *(editor)*
IMPERIALISM, DECOLONIZATION AND AFRICA
Studies Presented to John Hargreaves

T. J. Cribb *(editor)*
IMAGINED COMMONWEALTH
Cambridge Essays on Commonwealth and International Literature in English

Michael S. Dodson
ORIENTALISM, EMPIRE, AND NATIONAL CULTURE
India, 1770–1880

Ronald Hyam
BRITAIN'S IMPERIAL CENTURY, 1815–1914: A STUDY OF EMPIRE AND EXPANSION
Third Edition

Robin Jeffrey
POLITICS, WOMEN AND WELL-BEING
How Kerala became a 'Model'

Gerold Krozewski
MONEY AND THE END OF EMPIRE
British International Economic Policy and the Colonies, 1947–58

Javed Majeed
AUTOBIOGRAPHY, TRAVEL AND POST-NATIONAL IDENTITY

Ged Martin
BRITAIN AND THE ORIGINS OF CANADIAN CONFEDERATION, 1837–67

W. David McIntyre
BACKGROUND TO THE ANZUS PACT
Policy-Makers, Strategy and Diplomacy, 1945–55

Francine McKenzie
REDEFINING THE BONDS OF COMMONWEALTH 1939–1948
The Politics of Preference

John Singleton and Paul Robertson
ECONOMIC RELATIONS BETWEEN BRITAIN AND AUSTRALASIA 1945–1970

Cambridge Imperial and Post-Colonial Studies Series
Series Standing Order ISBN 0–333–91908–4
(*outside North America only*)

You can receive future titles in this series as they are published by placing a standing order. Please contact your bookseller or, in case of difficulty, write to us at the address below with your name and address, the title of the series and the ISBN quoted above.

Customer Services Department, Macmillan Distribution Ltd, Houndmills, Basingstoke, Hampshire RG21 6XS, England

Orientalism, Empire, and National Culture

India, 1770–1880

Michael S. Dodson

palgrave
macmillan

First published 2007 by
PALGRAVE MACMILLAN
Houndmills, Basingstoke, Hampshire RG21 6XS and
175 Fifth Avenue, New York, N. Y. 10010
Companies and representatives throughout the world

PALGRAVE MACMILLAN is the global academic imprint of the Palgrave Macmillan division of St. Martin's Press, LLC and of Palgrave Macmillan Ltd. Macmillan® is a registered trademark in the United States, United Kingdom and other countries. Palgrave is a registered trademark in the European Union and other countries.

ISBN-13: 978–1–4039–8645–0 hardback
ISBN-10: 1–4039–8645–2 hardback

This book is printed on paper suitable for recycling and made from fully managed and sustained forest sources.

A catalogue record for this book is available from the British Library.

Library of Congress Cataloging-in-Publication Data
Dodson, Michael S.,
Orientalism, empire, and national culture : India, 1770–1880 / Michael S. Dodson.
p. cm. – (Cambridge imperial and post-colonial studies series)
Includes bibliographical references and index.
ISBN-13: 978–1–4039–8645–0 (cloth)
ISBN-10: 1–4039–8645–2 (cloth)
1. India–Study and teaching–History–19th century. 2. Orientalism–England–History–19th century. 3. Sanskrit philology–Study and teaching–History–19th century. 4. India–Study and teaching–History–18th century. 5. Orientalism–England–History–18th century. 6. Sanskrit philology–Study and teaching–History–18th century. I. Title.
DS435.8.D63 2007
303.48'24205409034–dc22 2006051437

10 9 8 7 6 5 4 3 2 1
16 15 14 13 12 11 10 09 08 07

Printed and bound in Great Britain by
Antony Rowe Ltd, Chippenham and Eastbourne

For Tanja and Joshua

Contents

Preface

Benares, 11 January 1853, on a spacious, verdant site located approximately half way between the old city's congested alleys, waterfront *ghāṭ*s, and temples to the east, and the wide, planned streets of the European cantonment to the west. Here James Thomason, the Lieutenant-Governor of the North-Western Provinces, officially inaugurated the newly constructed home of the East India Company's Benares College. The building was a large and elaborate study in gothic revival architecture, replete with numerous towers, arches, and pinnacles, and, moreover, represented the first permanent base for the college which had been established by the Company six decades earlier, in 1791. Although seemingly at odds with the city's overwhelmingly 'Hindu' character, Thomason expressed a confidence that the new college building's 'architectural beauty' would undoubtedly produce a positive 'natural effect, upon the mind' of the college's Indian students.[1] Indeed, the building's 'surpassing magnificence' had also been characterised the previous day, in a parallel inaugural address given in Hindi, as representing a substantive testimony to the Company's commitment to the education, and intellectual improvement, of India's people.[2]

When, in the spring of 2000, I first spent some time on the site of Benares College (now part of Sampūrṇānanda Sanskrit University) to begin the research for this book, and managed to gain entry to the largely vacant original neo-gothic structure, I was impressed by its imposing, if now somewhat faded, grandeur. In particular, the physical similarities of the building to many of the Victorian churches in India, and at home in London, were instantly recognisable. Having walked through the large wooden double doors, the first thing I noticed was the light streaming through a stained-glass window high in the wall opposite. Along each side of the main hall were a series of small enclaves, resembling chantries, which had probably been used for teaching small groups of students in years previous. All were covered in a thick layer of dust. In many ways, it would have been easy then, at that first visit, to understand the building as a Victorian folly, a monument to the self-confidence of European civilisation and the imperial project. Yet over the course of the next several years, as I conducted the research for this book, it became clear to me that the educational programme pursued at Benares College during the mid-nineteenth century was far more ambitious, but also, ultimately far more ambiguous, than the inflated character of the building might at first suggest.

By the time of James Thomason's speech in 1853, the city of Benares had for many years represented an important outpost of the East India Company's government in northern India. During the late eighteenth century, for example, Benares served as a small buffer state between the Company's territory in Bengal and the hostile Mughal successor states to the west. The allied *rāja* of Benares, moreover, supplied the Company with much-needed intelligence on the movements of its various rivals.[3] Increasingly, however, as these rivals were subdued, it was the sacred character of Benares – its status as a place of pilgrimage for Hindus, its traditional standing as the fountainhead of all knowledge, and its reputation for Sanskrit learning – which had begun to best serve the Company's interests in its governance of India. In this regard, Thomason's inaugural speech that day specifically paid tribute to India's Sanskritic intellectual heritage, which he characterised as possessing 'a depth of thought, a precision of expression, and a subtlety of argument' which had 'excited the wonder of the learned in all countries of Europe'.[4]

Yet Benares College was then no longer wholly dedicated to education in the traditions of Sanskrit literature, which had been its founding mandate. Thomason was also celebrating that day the apparent successes of a new experimental pedagogy overseen by the college's superintendent, a Scotsman by the name of James R. Ballantyne, which advocated the recognition and appreciation of the 'gifts' of Hindu intellectual achievement, but in order to turn them to the 'highest purpose'. In a fundamental way, the very location of the new college building in the city – between the *ghāṭs* and the cantonment – reflected this new programme: Benares College was to act as a sort of 'common ground' for the comparison of the knowledges of East and West, which, it was hoped, would serve to demonstrate to Indians the ultimate truth of Western thought, thereby ushering in an age where 'a higher philosophy and a purer faith will pervade this land'.[5]

One of the most interesting features I found that first day inside the original college building is a series of aphorisms inscribed high upon the walls, above the heads of the Indian teachers and their students who would have sat on the floor beneath. Most appear in translation, in both English and Hindi, but have now largely been obscured by wear and vandalism. One, however, still left intact, has always caught my attention. It proclaims what, in the ideological context of the colonial nineteenth century, may be understood as a faith in the European monopoly upon 'truth', and an assurance that the utterances of Europeans held an ultimately transformative power:

> The lips of truth shall be established forever.
> A lying tongue is but for a moment.

Yet the accompanying Hindi version of this aphorism reveals a certain complexity and ambiguity worth dwelling upon:

> *Svarg satya teṃ hota hai, satya hi teṃ vyavahār*
> *Je te sukh samsār meṃ rahaiṃ, satya ādhār*

> Heaven comes from truth, and from truth itself comes good conduct.
> Whatever happiness one may find in the world, truth is its foundation.[6]

The role of colonial pedagogy and Western knowledge, its qualitative difference from the status of so much of the Sanskritic tradition, hinted at in the opposition of 'truth' and 'lie', is here fractured. Another claim to truth – a claim spoken in another language, and written in a distinct script – transgresses the norms of correspondence idealised in colonial translation to invoke heaven (*svarg*), happiness (*sukh*), good conduct (*vyavahār*), and a universality (truth as the foundation, *ādhār*) to undermine colonial claims of exclusivity.

What interested me then, and has formed the impetus behind this book, is the realisation, encapsulated in these aphorisms, of the potential of a complexity which lay behind an institution such as Benares College. It need not, in other words, simply be understood as an uncontested site for the production of colonial authority. Most prominently, a detailed attention paid to the features of the building itself has fuelled my curiosity about, and desire to take seriously, the activities of the *paṇḍit*s (Sanskrit scholars, or 'learned men') who worked as teachers, interlocutors, and translators in government employ. After all, in the context of Benares College, it was, ostensibly, their lips which communicated the 'truths' of Europe to the college's students. This relationship, between Indian *paṇḍit*s and the colonial government, within institutions such as Benares College, forms the central concern of this book. I ask after the cultural implications of their scholarship, produced in the context of colonial education. Thus, what are we to make of their personal letters, their legal decisions (*vyavasthā*), their essays and public lectures on science and religion? Can these too be characterised as being reducible to the figure of a lying tongue, or simply as born from a mimicry to a 'truth' represented in claims to Western civilisational superiority?

J. E. Saché *Benares College (Queen's College)* albumen print, 1868–69. Courtesy of the Alkazi Collection of Photography

Acknowledgements

I am indebted to numerous people across three continents for their help with this book. My first and foremost debt is to Chris Bayly, who acted as my Ph.D. supervisor at Cambridge. He has been incredibly generous with his time, knowledge, and good advice over the length of this project. Eivind Kahrs has read and commented on much of this work, and been most helpful in deciphering the intricacies and ambiguities of nineteenth-century Sanskrit, not to mention the intricacies of Norwegian jazz and French wine. Brian Hatcher has also read most of these chapters and has offered a great deal of very helpful suggestions. It has been a pleasure to find someone as enthusiastic about the issues discussed in this book as Brian is, and I look forward to his next book on Bengali *paṇḍits*. Javed Majeed offered invaluable criticism as examiner to the dissertation, and has since read and commented very helpfully on several later versions of the chapters. Tom Trautmann provided an insightful critique of the chapter on language and translation when it first went to *CSSH*, and since then has also read and commented on other parts of the book. Richard Drayton made several valuable suggestions, and most importantly, invited me to publish the book with Palgrave Macmillan. Thanks also to Gordon Johnson, Francesca Orsini for her support and Hindi tuition, John Smith for many coffees (and the strongest gin & tonic on the planet), and Tim Harper for his comments on the original dissertation, as well as David Arnold, Hayden Bellenoit, Mandakranta Bose, Kumkum Chatterjee, Vasudha Dalmia, Jeevan Deol, Sudeshna Guha, Maya Jasanoff, Shruti Kapila, Aishwarj Kumar, Peter Marshall, Michael McGerr, Polly O'Hanlon, Avril Powell, T. Robert Travers, and Jon Wilson.

In India, I am most grateful to several residents of the city of Varanasi, where the arguments presented in this book first took shape. My thanks especially to Sri Chandradhar Prasad Narayan Singh (Bhanu Babu), Dr Avadesh Kumar Chaube, Professor Anand Krishna, Dr Dhirendranath Singh, Virendra Singh, and Mahant Vir Bhadra Mishra, for their enthusiasm in discussing elements of the old city's history with me, and for their offers of help in navigating its remarkable resources.

The arguments in this book have been presented in a variety of forms to audiences in Cambridge, London, Cambridge (Mass.),

Washington DC, Vancouver, Minneapolis, Madison, and Bloomington. My thanks to all those who offered their questions and comments. I have also been fortunate to be able to discuss historiography at length with a series of very talented graduate students, and in particular those who took my cultural history colloquium in Bloomington around the time this manuscript was being revised, who seemed always ready to offer their criticism and insight.

Much of the research for this book was carried out with the financial assistance of the Cambridge Commonwealth Trust, the Smuts Memorial Fund (Cambridge), and the Rapson Fund (Cambridge). My thanks to their trustees, and especially to Dr Anil Seal for his generosity.

Thanks are also due to the very helpful librarians of the British Library, as well as the University Library, Centre of South Asian Studies Library, and Oriental Studies Faculty Library at Cambridge. The Government of West Bengal kindly granted me access to the records of the General Committee of Public Instruction in Calcutta. Thanks also to the staff of the West Bengal State Archive in Calcutta, the Uttar Pradesh Archives in both Allahabad and Lucknow, and the Royal Asiatic Society Library in London, for the assistance they provided. Sri Deomani Yagik, librarian of the exemplary Vishvanath Pustakalaya (also known as Goenka Library), which is hidden in the back alleys of Lalita Ghat in Varanasi, was particularly helpful in tracking down copies of some older printed works. The late HH Maharaja Vibhuti Narayan Singh generously permitted me to use the Ramnagar Palace Library. The staff of the Carmichael Library in Varanasi were always helpful, and thanks to Dr T. K. Biswas, the director of Bharat Kala Bhavan, BHU, for his assistance. Sophie Gordon and Stephanie Roy at the Alkazi Collection of Photography in London provided help with images.

Cambridge University Press has kindly permitted the republication of material in Chapter 4, which appeared in a much earlier form as 'Re-Presented for the Pandits: James Ballantyne, "Useful Knowledge," and Sanskrit Scholarship in Benares College during the Mid-Nineteenth Century' in *Modern Asian Studies*, 36, 2 (2002), 257–98; as well as material from Chapter 5, which appeared in an earlier form as 'Translating Science, Translating Empire: The Power of Language in Colonial North India' in *Comparative Studies in Society and History*, 47, 4 (2005), 809–35.

Finally, but most importantly, this book is dedicated to my wife Tanja, who has always been an incredible source of support and inspiration, and to our wonderful son Joshua.

A Note on Transliteration

The issue of transliteration is a difficult one for historians. To be certain, there are no generally accepted guidelines to follow in order to decide when to transliterate words from a different language, when to simply drop the use of diacritics, and when to offer anglicised versions of non-English words.

This book deals with a wide range of sources, which include printed and archival material not only written in English, but also in Sanskrit and Hindi. Persian words also tend to creep into these sources, especially in the eighteenth-century material. I have chosen to accurately transliterate, to the extent possible, all technical words, names, and titles appearing in South Asian language sources. I have done this because it appears to me to be consistent with the larger argument of the book, for diacritics serve to register within the text itself the presence of South Asian intellectual production.

For words common to both Hindi and Sanskrit, the most prevalent, or appropriate, form is usually adopted. Therefore, *paṇḍit* (not *paṇḍita*), *vyākaraṇa* (not *vyākaraṇ*), and *rāja* (rather than *rāj*, *rājā*, or *rājan*). The rendering of personal names is problematic, especially in instances where anglicised forms of Indian names have been used in the source material. In most cases, names are retained as written in South Asian language material, unless this is not known. Compounds (Bāpūdeva / Bāpū Deva) are generally left as found in the source material. Outdated diacritical marks in quotations are omitted. Place names have been left in their familiar, anglicised forms, however, as have words now common to English speakers. These include Sanskrit (and not *saṃskṛta*), Mughal, Benares, Avadh (but not Oudh), and Ganges. Persian transliteration has also been simplified so as to omit underlining.

I have not included a glossary of South Asian terminology used in this book, but have instead opted to offer rough equivalents to such terms within the text itself, whenever appropriate.

Introduction
Histories of Empire, Histories of Knowledge

This is a book about orientalism in India. It examines the varied manifestations of literary, historical, and linguistic scholarly practices which were utilised to constitute the object 'Indian civilisation' through the literature of Sanskrit, from about 1770 to 1880. Given this scope, the book is necessarily selective in its focus. Yet the subjects discussed are unified throughout by the argument that the practices of orientalism were necessarily double; that is, while, on the one hand, such practices were utilised by the colonial state to consolidate and authorise its rule over the subcontinent, on the other hand, orientalism also depended to a large extent upon the social standing and cultural expertise of one of the state's principal sets of Indian interlocutors, the Sanskrit *paṇḍit*s. This doubling, in which European authority was grounded upon forms of Indian authority, which simultaneously needed to be displaced, opens a field of enquiry in which the scholarship of orientalism becomes a much more ambiguous, and potentially subversive, set of practices. Thus, this book discusses three principal themes, grounded chronologically: from the late eighteenth century, in which the East India Company used orientalist knowledge, and the relationships forged with *paṇḍit*s, to underpin its burgeoning state in Bengal; to the uses made of orientalism's methodologies in 'constructive orientalist' educational initiatives in the nineteenth-century 'civilising mission'; and, finally, to the adaptation, by Indian Sanskrit scholars, of some of orientalism's principal discursive, institutional, and social constructs in the production of newly inflected Hindu identities.

The study of orientalism is, of course, an intellectual terrain first mapped in earnest by Edward Said. Without question, the publication of Said's *Orientalism* in 1978 changed the way in which historians must write about European researches into 'the Orient' and the rise of colonial governance. *Orientalism*'s central claim is that 'the West' has produced and managed – through a long history of literary production, academic scholarship, ethnography, and stereotyping – an image of the non-Western world as degenerate, exotic, despotic, essentially religious, effeminate, and weak. In short, the mirror image, or 'Other', of the West. European scholarship was conceived, moreover, to have produced a *powerful* representation of the Orient: by knowing the Orient, the West enabled itself to appropriate the Orient, speaking for it, and ruling over it. In a book that dealt largely with French literary sources and the Islamic regions of West Asia and North Africa, Said nevertheless moved outside his principal area of expertise to single out, within the Indian colonial context, the scholarship of the well-known British 'orientalists' William Jones and Henry Thomas Colebrooke. In doing so, Said made explicit that the deep connections he perceived between European 'rule' and European 'scholarship' held true in that context as well.[1]

Said's analysis served as a direct critique of a generation of academics whose work in the 1960s and 1970s idealised the role played by European scholar-administrators within an 'intercultural' (i.e. colonial) setting, and portrayed the European intervention into Asian historical and cultural analyses as essentially beneficial to Asian society. In the context of South Asia, Garland Cannon, for example, in 1964 characterised William Jones' scholarship as 'a humanistic exchange of material and cultural resources that maintains a deep respect for human rights and the brotherhood of man',[2] while in 1969, David Kopf lauded the cultural and civilisational regenerative effects which European orientalist researches had had upon early nineteenth-century Bengali society, characterising this era as a 'renaissance'.[3]

Since the publication of *Orientalism*, the terminology of its title has been utilised in a series of contradictory, but always pointed, political ways.[4] In many studies of eighteenth-century India, where William Jones had explicitly identified himself as an 'orientalist', the term continues to be inflected by some with a positive valuation, and reflects something of a lexical and ideological reclamation in the context of 'Saidian' postcolonial studies. This is especially so when historical scholarship in Asia is again invoked as an idealistic humanism to counter-weigh what is perceived as the domination of 'postmodern cynicism' within colonial discourse analysis. Several studies of the activities of the Asiatic Society of Bengal published during the 1980s and 1990s, for example, border on hagiography by virtue of the continued portrayal of William Jones and other orientalists as culturally sympathetic and politically disinterested scholars. In considering Jones as someone interested in Asia purely for its own sake, or for the sake of the furtherance of learning itself, the deep implications of eighteenth-century orientalist scholarship and the rise of imperial power have been marginalised.[5] This approach has also been reflected more recently by writers such as William Dalrymple, who in *White Mughals* seeks to portray in a largely positive light particular interracial sexual relationships, and by extension notes these to be indicative of the general character of Britain's early empire. Dalrymple points to a notion of eighteenth-century European cosmopolitanism, tolerance, and even 'multiculturalism' in India essentially to contrast the early empire with Victorian chauvinism, but also to invoke it as an idealised counterpoint to the current political context, dominated as it is by a perceived 'clash of civilisations' between Islam and the West.[6]

More frequently, recent studies of South Asia have invoked Said's work and the notion of 'Orientalism' as a more direct critique of British imperialism, focusing upon figures such as James Mill and Charles Trevelyan who held nothing but contempt for Jonesian-style orientalists. These studies have substantiated the role of European scholarship in producing forms of Indian 'other-ness' through characterisations of cultural degeneracy, social profligacy, and moral decay.[7] They have, moreover, tended to foreground the role of the colonial imaginary in such knowledgeable processes, and a relative disengagement with Indian social realities (not least because many such writers never visited India). Ronald Inden has argued that methodological Western scholarship on India has produced representations of Indian society as composed of, and regulated by, a variety of essences, including the social determinant of caste, a religion known as 'Hinduism', and the basic economic and social unit of the village. Inden asserts that Indian social and historical agency has been suppressed by such representations, for they have become part of a vision of Indian society as being regulated not by free will or individual human agency, but by an essential nature.[8] Interestingly, analyses which claim the most direct ideological affiliation to Said, including Lata Mani's work on representations of *satī* (widow burning)[9] and Gauri Viswanathan's study of the Company's educational policies[10] have tended to focus upon British evangelical and liberal-utilitarian writers of the early nineteenth century. In so doing, the notion of the eighteenth century's distinct status is also indirectly emphasised. Indeed, Inden has absolved William Jones of the charge of 'being an Orientalist' (in the Saidian sense), preferring to characterise James Mill and his *The History of British India* in this way, on the basis that Jones' texts never achieved the cultural hegemony which Mill's did.[11]

The term 'orientalism', therefore, has been used to characterise certain moments in British imperial history in both negative, and relatively positive, ways, as well as to draw distinctions between the eighteenth and nineteenth centuries, for example, on a similar foundation. In this book I question the viability of such broadly drawn contrasts, not least because they seem fundamentally inadequate to account for the range of relationships, institutions, and practices which composed the context of empire at any one time.[12] More immediately, this book strives to resituate the meaningfulness of the term 'orientalism' in historical analyses of South Asia, in the recognition that the current uses just noted obscure more than they reveal about the pursuit of knowledge within empire, and the range of orientalism's links to the projects of self-fashioning within the Indian empire. In other words, to describe a scholastic activity or a particular representation of Indian cultural forms as 'orientalist' should serve not as an ending point of analysis, but rather, as an initial point of entry, to prompt us to ask a series of questions regarding the social, cultural, and political context of such scholarship: How were instances of orientalist scholarship undertaken? What range of purposes did orientalist scholarship serve? Did these purposes evolve over time? Was orientalism always an unambiguous force in rendering the authority of the imperial state?

It is a principal argument of this book that orientalism in India is best understood as a shifting set of policy positions and localised practices, which were constantly adapted to changing circumstances in both the colonial context, and with respect to evolutions in metropolitan British thought, rather than a static *modus operandi*. For example, orientalist methodologies forged in the eighteenth century became an integral part of nineteenth-century educational policy which accepted the metropolitan British liberal preoccupation with the effecting of Indian 'progress' on a European model. As such, I will strive to use the terms 'orientalism' and 'orientalist' in a broadly conceived manner,[13] intended simply to invoke in this text a range of scholarly practices which were devoted to the explication of Indian history, cultural forms, and social structures, principally through the medium of Indian languages and texts, and through an association with recognised Indian learned elites, the *paṇḍits*. In downplaying a lexical focus upon valuation, whether a superfluous negative or an imagined positive one, this book proceeds then to substantiate the various ways in which orientalism worked within the context of the Indian empire, the goals and strategies which propelled it, the evolution of its practices, and the extent of its consequences, intended and unintended.

I accept Said's principal thesis that the practices of orientalism were devoted, first and foremost, to the advancement and empowerment of the colonial state. Said's study has demonstrated how orientalist scholarship provided Europeans with a vocabulary and imagery with which to justify the rule of colonised people.[14] Similarly, orientalism supplied the more mundane day-to-day cultural, social, and linguistic information to enable communication and governance. Warren Hastings, for example, the first Governor-General of British territories in India (1773–1785), clearly understood that the attainment of knowledge of Mughal and local forms of governance and land taxation practices, as well as of Indian languages and belief systems, provided the East India Company with the most basic tools with which British imperial administration in India was to be forged and maintained.[15] Yet it is an important element of the arguments presented in this book that orientalism was not directed solely at the construction of ruling authority upon European terms, but rather, was also a series of strategies to coopt, control and adapt elements of established Indian social, cultural, and political authority. For example, orientalist research into Indian history and language initiated in the eighteenth century through the employment of *paṇḍits* helped to naturalise the Company into India's accepted socio-political practices of religious and scholarly patronage. Similarly, British scholars invoked the assistance gained from *paṇḍits* to speak with authority on issues relating to a series of European debates over the status of 'oriental' civilisation, and the methodologies most appropriate to the proselytisation of Indians. In addition, an important part of the nineteenth-century liberal project of bringing improvement to India through rational education was the pursuit of a series of 'constructive orientalist'[16] strategies and practices which were devoted to utilising selected elements of respected Sanskrit texts, as well as the high social and cultural standing of the *paṇḍits*, to authorise specific visions of historical progress, civilisational hierarchy, and British superiority.

A further critical aspect of orientalism in India which needs to be underscored is that as a colonial enterprise, orientalism was inherently unstable. Certainly, it has been argued that orientalist representations embodied a range of internal complexity, and such complexity often rendered orientalist knowledge contradictory and problematic.[17] More pertinently, it is argued here that orientalist practices were unstable in the colonial context because the authority of so much orientalist research, and the representations of Indian history and society borne out of it, was predicated upon the relationships which Britons forged with their Indian intermediaries, the *paṇḍits*. Importantly, the authorisation of orientalist strategies in the furthering of the imperial state by reference to Indian forms of cultural authority also facilitated a variety of distinct cultural and political projects by Indian intellectuals. Indians could certainly make use of orientalism's principal discursive constructs, such as in the elaboration of a highly textualised version of Hinduism, ancient civilisational grandeur, and contemporary decline.[18] But more significantly, the institutionalised social and cultural underpinnings of the enterprises of orientalism and, in particular, constructive orientalist education, allowed *paṇḍits* to emerge more forcefully as cultural critics in the north Indian public sphere. In their engagement with Western knowledge, and concomitant construction of revived 'Hindu' identities potentially capable of subverting colonial imperatives, one can perceive that orientalism's claims could potentially be undone from within the very process of knowledge-making, or adapted to serve distinct aims never conceived by Europeans.

Histories of knowledge in the colonial context

Edward Said's body of scholarship recognised the centrality of knowledge to empire. The insight of *Orientalism*, in particular, has served to displace imperial histories based in high political narrative, social structures, and economic change. In their place, imperial histories of South Asia now largely take as their focus knowledge, and knowledgeable processes, whether as a tool to enable governance, a symbol of European superiority[19] and Asian difference,[20] or as the redemptive means to uplift and transform the minds and societies of the colonised into a semblance of 'modernity'.[21] While much of the historical work now being undertaken traces its historiographical genealogy to colonial discourse analysis, through Said and ultimately Foucault, it is also possible to perceive the increasingly important impact upon South Asian history of an alternative historiography, in the history of science and medicine.[22] Yet while seemingly being distinct, many of the basic characteristics which define these respective approaches have tended to a substantial convergence. The aim of the remainder of this introduction, primarily, is to enumerate and critique some of the principal features of both, in a manner homologous with the preceding discussion of O/orientalism, and to outline the theoretical practice followed in this book.

A principal feature of much of the work done on eighteenth- and nineteenth-century colonial discourse is an understanding of epistemological processes within the colonial sphere as being dominated by the apparatus of the 'colonial state'. It is Europeans, then, who are thought to possess nearly exclusively the power to create and mediate knowledge, and shape discursive meaning, and thus configure a rupture with the social and cultural forms of the pre-colonial.[23] Bernard Cohn, for example, in a series of essays which examine the institutionalisation of Indian languages, the processes of legal codification, and the museological display of Indian objects,[24] emphasises the role of the colonial state's institutions as the principal, or even sole, force in the 're-ordering' of Indian knowledge and cultural forms, and the 're-making' of their specific meanings. Much like Said's understanding of Orientalism, colonial discourse is fashioned from within European prerogatives and preconceptions, or from within a European way of knowing, which Cohn elaborates by reference to the 'investigative modalities' of European thought and scholarship. While bearing some little correspondence with Indian 'reality', colonial discourse nevertheless entered into a symbiotic and mutually constitutive relationship with European power in India. Similarly, Lata Mani argues that representations of *satī* were developed within a context of colonial domination, and by a particular, European, understanding of the place of Hindu scripture within the Indian normative world.[25] Indeed, her epistemology ultimately rejects the ability of Indian informants to mould or influence colonial knowledge, for they instead become simply conduits of information which is then interpreted according to a European framework.[26] Most recently, Nicholas Dirks' examination of caste has similarly highlighted the determining role of the power of the 'colonial leviathan', through its 'cultural technologies of rule', in the production of caste as the subcontinent's principal social determinant.[27] The conquest of India, therefore, is characterised in these studies as a wholesale 'conquest of knowledge'.[28]

Historiographies of science and empire have tended to reproduce a similar epistemological configuration, though often by reference to a dialectic of metropole and periphery, and a trope of the 'movement' of knowledge, rather than its 'construction'. In order to explain how 'science' was transplanted from the European metropolis and then flourished in the non-European periphery, George Basalla advanced a three-stage 'diffusionist' paradigm, which took as its foundation the distinction between a Europe which possesses scientific knowledge, and the 'non-scientific' realm of the overseas empire. Through its three stages, this model traces the dynamic of scientific progress through an 'extraction' of data from the periphery (we might take botany as our example), the subsequent 'transplantation' of Western science into the non-West, its mediation by European scientists, and, finally, the emergence of postcolonial national scientific traditions.[29] Certainly there are obvious parallels here with conceptions of the exportation of the 'nation' and 'nationalism' from Europe to Asia. Indeed, the diffusionist model is largely ahistorical in its generalising sweep, and Basalla, in particular, recalls imperial enlightenment paradigms by his equation of the scientific endeavours of modernity with the implied narrative of political independence.[30] Nevertheless, the diffusionist model has retained a surprising degree of currency in the historiography of 'colonial science', with elaborations and refinements being made to it into the early 1990s.[31] Roy MacLeod, for example, has enumerated not three stages, but rather, five 'passages', the early phases of which are dominated by the predominance of metropolitan 'control' over science.[32]

Through a conception of knowledge formation in the colonial 'periphery' which is coterminous with the movement of an intact body of knowledge ('science') from the metropole, the diffusionist model foregrounds a sense of epistemological isolation between coloniser and colonised, while also assuming a high degree of authoritativeness for 'scientific' knowledge. If the West is again endowed with a virtual monopoly of effective representational power, it is here couched in the language of the 'control' and 'co-ordination' of scientific enterprise, rather than the cultural 'Other-ing' of Orientalism and colonial discourse. What both of these approaches tend to neglect is a critical historical consideration of the status of particular knowledges, or representations, within a specific context, including details of knowledge-making processes, and the 'reception' or 'interpretation' of certain representations.[33] In this regard, many writers have attempted to destabilise perceptions of the representational authority of 'science' or colonial discourse, often through an acknowledgement of the importance of accounting for interpersonal 'contact' between formerly disparate socio-cultural groups, together with the need to define colonial encounters within the bounds of a specific historical-geographic locality.[34] Homi Bhabha's work, in particular, has foregrounded the inherent instability of colonial discourse when enunciated within the geographical space of colonialism.[35] His essay 'Signs Taken for Wonders', for example, argues that colonial discourse is inherently ambivalent, and as such, can never be as authoritative as it purports to be, for there is always a 'slip' in meaning, or a hybridisation, during its articulation and reception across socio-cultural boundaries, allowing for both a misunderstanding as well as a subversive redeployment. 'Resistance' is produced, in essence, through recognising a refusal to accept the subject positions inscribed for the colonised in colonial discourse, destroying the Self-Other dialectic which is fundamental to European domination.[36] Despite the many critiques of Bhabha's work,[37] the notion of 'hybridity' he deploys allows for a dynamicism in knowledge and culture, and, importantly, recognises meaning as negotiated and contested, rather than as a unilateral and authoritative imposition.

Other writers, often associated with a revisionist South Asian historiography, have attempted to invoke this sort of dynamicism by reference to the notion of 'dialogic' knowledge production in the colonial context (though often also eshewing Bhabha's 'postmodernism'). Gene Irschick, for example, in his *Dialogue and History* has stressed the 'cultural negotiations' which contributed to 'new formulations' of ideas of territory and identity in South India. Such new knowledge, or 'changed significations', are not produced unilaterally by the coloniser and then imposed upon Indian society, but rather are conceptualised as the unequal product of all groups in this context.[38] As well, C. A. Bayly, principal denizen of so-called 'Cambridge school' historiography, has noted the importance of accounting for the persistence of pre-colonial knowledges and institutions within colonial forms.[39] His recent study of the 'informational order', for example, has enumerated the process of its construction upon 'the foundations of its Indian precursors', the role which 'native informants' played in this process, and the ways in which Indian 'responses' to Western knowledge were informed through existent 'knowledge communities'.[40] Similarly, Norbert Peabody has argued that Indian informants made significant imprints upon colonial attempts to enumerate Indian social structures,[41] while Phillip Wagoner has asserted that 'far from being mere passive informants', Indian interlocutors 'contributed actively to the production of new epigraphic knowledge, and more fundamentally, even to the definition of epigraphy itself as a method for historical enquiry'.[42]

Within the history of science, as well, a focus upon a diversity of metropoles and peripheries in scientific undertakings has served, within the trope of the movement of knowledge, to complicate the genealogy of modern scientific practice. In particular, the breaking of the exclusive link between Europe and the possession of 'science' by emphasising, for example, the vibrant nature of India's pre-colonial scientific knowledge and practices in fields such as medicine, astronomy, and mathematics, allows for 'science' to be better contextualised upon a world-wide scale.[43] Examinations of such pre-colonial scientific pursuits have also served to develop a recognition of a hybridised Indian-colonial science, in which European scientific knowledge and practice is adapted, or inflected, to specific social, cultural, and political contexts by Indians themselves, including the cause of nationalist modernity.[44] In this respect, Tony Ballantyne has recently argued against conceptualising empire as a centre with numerous peripheries, but rather, has characterised it as a 'web', given that knowledge (as well as personnel and capital) circulated in an 'integrative' fashion.[45]

Nicholas Dirks has expressed uneasiness with such re-characterisations of knowledge processes in empire as 'dialogue', 'exchange', or even 'conversation', and by extension a revision of the 'transactions of imperial power', for the damage these are perceived to do to our need to emphasise the inherent limiting of forms of Indian agency through Western subjugation of the subcontinent.[46] In an acerbic critique of 'Cambridge school' historiography (which, at times, borders on parody), Dirks has argued that the assertion that colonial knowledge was dependent upon Indian sources is tantamount to 'blaming the victim', while also equating a recognition of 'agency' on the part of Indians within the colonial sphere with, in essence, an argument for their complicity in imperialism – as architects of their own oppression.[47] Certainly, analyses of colonial representational systems made by reference to European epistemology and dominant power have served to isolate colonised peoples from participation in colonial knowledge creation, as well as from potential charges of 'collaboration' in colonial exploitation and repression.[48] In this sense, the Subaltern Studies project, while important for its role in qualifying the historical focus upon elites in varieties of 'nationalist' cultural production, also served to equate autonomous subjectivities with historical agency through the overt resistance to, or opting-out of, most elements of elite epistemologies.[49] Yet arguably, the foregrounding of the inequitable nature of Britain's empire through broad invocations of colonial power in itself seems only to reify an ahistorical understanding of the processes of imperialism. The complexity and often hidden nature of colonial apparatuses demand a detailed historical examination of their power dynamics: a close interrogation of the ways in which social, cultural, and political institutions operated to simultaneously oppress some, and empower other people, and to recognise the possibilities for a destabilisation of the colonial state through its very own dynamics. To argue this is not to dismiss the obscenity of imperialism, and it is emphatically not the same as claiming that colonialism 'never happened' as Partha Chatterjee has charged.[50]

Indeed, there is an increasing realisation that historical analysis can encompass a far more complex understanding of the interaction of all actors within the confines of a colonised space, without necessarily sacrificing a notion of the inherently oppressive nature of imperialism. As David Scott has argued, colonialism should not be viewed as a 'singular reiterated instance', but instead, one should insist upon a historicisation of the 'making of *modern* power' in Europe's empires.[51] Equally, empire can also be viewed as a 'shared, but differentiated space', where hierarchies are worked out, universalist notions tested, and, ultimately, understandings of difference to oppose European superiority constructed.[52] Thus Paul Gilroy notes, even in the contexts of the most extreme brutality, the cultures and consciousness of colonisers and the colonised are not 'sealed off hermetically from each other', but rather affected one another in dynamic and surprising ways through 'fractal patterns of cultural and political exchange and transformation'.[53] In other words, the various actors within a colonised space can, and should, be understood as sharing the same historical-analytical space.[54] In this regard, it is imperative to examine the array of relationships forged with colonial intermediaries, and to break down the simplistic binary of 'collaboration' and 'resistance', for these categories have served to predetermine, in a most simplistic fashion, the types of activities which should be understood as oppositional or agentive. Considered engagements by the colonised with the structures and knowledges of Western imperialism are as important as those which consisted in an abjuration of all European forms, though, ultimately, the former may challenge our understandings of the genealogies of anti-colonial nationalism and the processes which underpinned the weaknesses and strengths of the colonial state. The variety of distinct social, cultural, and political projects which impelled different groups to oppose, or work within, the structures of the colonial state are simply unaccounted for within an over-determined reading of 'agency' or 'resistance'.[55]

In intellectual histories of colonial India (or rather, histories of knowledge), we might then ask whether the attempts made to emphasise the complexity of epistemological processes, in the form of 'dialogue' and 'exchange', have been sufficient to invoke the kinds of historical complexities in imperial relationships which seem desirable without inherently sacrificing the broader picture of empire as inimical. For indeed, within South Asian historiography, epistemology has essentially stood-in as a conceptual framework for understanding the power structures of imperialism. First, it would appear that the notion of exchange in itself, while probably a more accurate portrayal of many cultural and epistemological processes within empire, does not invoke any specific dynamic of power, and thereby obscures important enabling and limiting factors, including the roles of institutions, economic conditions, or state censorship. Foucault, for example, in his critique of Habermasian communicative 'utopias', has noted that he could not envision a 'state of communications' in which 'games of truth ... circulate freely, without any constraints or coercive effects'.[56] In this regard, some writers interested in 'dialogue' have explicitly noted at the outset of their studies that power relationships within a colonial context are necessarily uneven, but also dynamic and changeable in significant respects.[57] This acknowledgement is evidently intended to invoke both European epistemic and material oppression, and, at times, moments of colonial agency and 'resistance' without explicitly being able to account for it in purely epistemological terms.

In addition, notions of dialogue and hybrid scientific practices have served, in essence, to set up an interface for two distinct, nearly static bodies of knowledge, one 'Western' and one 'native', and a process of adaptation on their margins. For Bhabha, the hybridisation of colonial discourse is produced by virtue of Indians' standing within a discrete cultural or epistemic space, while the process underlying 'nationalist science' and dialogic 'changed significations' can be understood similarly. Here a narrative of something approaching 'first contact' is evoked, perhaps best illustrated by Mary Louise Pratt's notion of the 'contact zone', which is intended to draw attention to the 'spatial and temporal copresence of subjects previously separated by geographic and historical disjunctures, and whose trajectories now intersect'.[58] Gilroy has noted that the understanding of simplified 'collisions' between mutually exclusive cultural communities lends itself to historiographies which foreground 'illegitimate intrusions' into the imagined authenticities of national life.[59] Less dramatically, the construction of an interface between two distinctive bodies of knowledge inevitably contributes not only to an understanding of singular 'national' knowledge and culture, but also to the stereotyping of historical actors upon the basis of the knowledge which they are purported to possess by virtue of that 'national' standing. Within 'dialogic' analyses of colonial South Asia, *paṇḍits* are most often viewed as the 'traditional' guardians of Sanskrit-based *śāstrik* knowledge, conduits to an intellectual past (Wagoner, for example, has described the Indian interlocutors working with Colin Mackenzie at the beginning of the nineteenth century as 'precolonial intellectuals'),[60] while colonial administrators and educators are often caricatured as evangelical Macaulay-clones.[61] It is obviously important to take into account the influences of intellectual genealogies upon historical actors, through processes such as education and apprenticeship, but it will be profitable to ask whether historical analyses benefit from a reduction of such actors to instances of particular cultural or knowledgeable configurations.

The ability to theorise purely epistemological processes – the construction and reconstruction of knowledge, as well as its transmission – has, I think, in many ways reached the limits of its usefulness for writing the histories of colonialism. Is it possible to further complicate – that is, to make more complex – our understandings of how a discourse, an example of knowledge, or representation, was produced in colonial India? Would such complexity in itself sufficiently account for the various competing interests, the power dynamics at work, and the extent of the circulation of ideas or texts? Tony Ballantyne's 'web' metaphor, for example, which grounds his study of the circulation of the idea of Aryanism, certainly improves upon diffusionist models, by providing a complex of nodes for knowledge production, movement, and reception.[62] But this complexity is still systemic, and by and large is unable to account for why certain concepts or ideas move, why some become popular or influential on a more or less global scale, and why yet others retain only a specific local importance. The metaphor of the 'web' can also tell us relatively little about the complexities of power which operated at local and supra-local contexts, and seemingly cannot account for differences which distinct mediums of knowledge transmission (textual, oral, performative, etc.) possessed for their receptivity. Indeed, one might ask what it is, exactly, which is transmitted through this 'web'. Can knowledge traverse contexts with its intended meaning intact, or is simply 'information' which travels well? How can one account for localised interpretations, or differences in the perception of an idea's authoritativeness? In an important manner, such a 'web' implies a degree of continuity within a system of knowledge circulation, which diminishes the interpretive potentials of local contexts, though Ballantyne works to minimise this in his analysis.

Indeed, in order to begin to forge a distinctive intellectual history, it might ultimately be asked whether knowledge should any longer even be the principal object of analysis. While this is obviously something of a provocation, it seems to me that intellectual histories of imperialism in South Asia might do well to leave behind understandings of knowledge as a 'noun', to incorporate analyses of knowledge as an 'adjective' and an 'adverb' (if you will), in order to write histories of the knowledgeable, and those who act knowingly.

In this book I am interested to examine some of the relationships between knowledge, colonial institutions, and forms of social, cultural, and political authority within colonial north India through an interrogation of knowledge principally as a form of social and cultural capital. Intellectual history has typically concerned itself with ideational genealogies, adaptations, and innovations, and to some extent this book addresses these, though for the most part it attempts to elucidate the valuations made of knowledge and representation in particularised local contexts, and their relationships to the fashioning of forms of power, as part of what Foucault has labelled an 'ascending analysis'.[63] In short, this book ventures to understand why certain knowledges gained social currency locally, and could be converted to forms of power in the contested realms of colonial India, through an analysis of knowledgeable strategies and practices. There are two central, interconnected elements to an intellectual history of this sort.

First, I consider the ways in which particular knowledges become powerful through their value in the furthering of specific socio-cultural projects. How do certain representations or bodies of knowledge become endowed with authority which makes their possession, or utilisation, an asset within the realms of social life? What are the conditions under which a form of knowledge is accepted as authoritative or rejected as illegitimate? To begin with, the role of educational institutions, familial standing, as well as specific forms of pedagogy and knowledge transmission, such as the *guru-śiṣya* (teacher-student) lineage, or the orientalist's relationship with a learned *paṇḍit*, in producing authoritative knowledge are considered. The incorporation of these into intellectual history is approximated in Pierre Bourdieu's development of forms of symbolic power,[64] including 'academic capital' and also 'symbolic capital', the latter being a social resource drawn from a dialectic of knowledge possession and the recognition of others.[65]

More centrally, the book is concerned with an analysis of the ways in which specific instances of knowledge are characterised by the historical actors of a local context, and the rhetorical work which such characterisations perform in the construction of socio-cultural authority. In this regard, I ask how intellectual 'values' such as the 'rational', the 'scientific', or the ' religious' are themselves negotiated within different contexts, and how these values are then made to work in the furtherance of representational power. 'Science', for example, has been characterised as having a substantially unique claim on 'truth' by reference to its use of the 'rational' methodology of hypothesising and testing through experimentation, its explanatory power, and tendency to material benefit, while forms of religion, similarly, were distinguished by reference to their exalted status as 'divine revelation', and being conducive to moral awakening and redemption. Of particular interest is the invocation of universals such as 'reason' and 'rationality' in the production of authority for a body of knowledge. In many cases, culturally significant 'plural or conjoined genealogies',[66] concepts largely shared between Indians and Europeans but with distinctive lineages, allowed for such characterisations to become powerful tools by which specific knowledgeable traditions may be repositioned and recharacterised with respect to one another. That is, historical actors invoked distinctive local characterisations of such 'universals', noting for example that Indian rationality (*tarka*) was far older, and more deeply theorised, than its European counterpart, or alternatively, that Indian philosophical enquiry, while complex and nuanced, was also unconcerned with the truth status of its premises, and thereby divorced from the 'scientific' endeavours which were peculiar to Europe. Moreover, such localised particularisations of universal values should not be traced in intellectual history solely by reference to overly abstract genealogies (the 'Scottish Enlightenment' for example), or highly textualised 'big thinkers' (such as Adam Smith), but when possible to the ways in which these genealogies were understood by local intellectuals, and the uses made of such previous intellectual production – the referencing of intellectual authority (on the premise of Adam Smith, for instance) – in furthering a specific intellectual product.[67]

Second, this book attempts to forge a closer link between intellectual and social history through an interest in tracing how people in the colonial context used their education and institutional standings, and the strategies for producing forms of authority for knowledge, in the furtherance of different social, cultural, and political projects. That is, I enquire how specific characterisations and valuations of instances of knowledge, when endowed with a degree of authority and power, were utilised as a resource. Ultimately, this book views these processes as part of the practice of historical self-fashioning, in which historical actors, drawing from the diversity of resources available to them, are continually constructing an authoritative, because specifically inflected, site of knowledge production. In this way, groups of *paṇḍit*s, for example, can be perceived to be engaging with the presentation of Western knowledge as a part of the process of articulating a specific version of 'Indian knowledge', while constantly redefining their own roles in cultural production, social interaction, education, religious practice, and governance. Indeed, the institutional apparatus within which such actors work, including the government college at Benares, should also be viewed as not only always present in the processes of such self-fashioning, but also as being always remade in these interactions. Thus, groups of individuals (and indeed the institutions from which they draw resources) are not stagnant in historical processes – they are irreducible to broad stereotypes – but instead should be understood as constantly taking some part in their own becoming.

The elements of intellectual history here outlined, both the processes which underlay the authorisations of knowledge, and the socio-cultural uses of the resultant resources, must be viewed as co-implicated – as working in a dynamic. Similarly, the practices of knowledge fashioning in colonial India are ones which must be accounted for by reference to the negotiations and conflicts of Indians and Britons within the same 'analytical space'. This book, taken as a whole, strives to accomplish this as far as available sources allow. Of course, it should not be thought that these processes take place without the imposition of barriers and restrictions by the colonial state, or indeed by Indians themselves. But instead of positing these beforehand, it is an object of this book to examine how these were constructed, and to what extent they were successful in limiting the production of alternative subject positions. In this way, I believe that questions of historical agency in the colonial sphere become rather more open-ended and responsive to account for processes of social and cultural change, rather than necessarily being content with invocations of a 'breaking out' from beyond dominant representational systems. Localised interactions often retain only a local significance, but they are as often a starting point, and so we are compelled to trace their investment, transformation, and extension to the realm of empire.

1
Orientalism and the Writing of World History

Orientalist research was an integral component of the East India Company's conquest and governance of India. This chapter seeks to unambiguously reassert the important connections between a history of eighteenth-century orientalist research, in particular, with the rise of British imperial power in India. At the most basic level, orientalist research served to provide the colonial state with cultural information by which to rule the Company's territories authoritatively, and with a strategy it conceived conducive to a minimum of disruption to existent cultural and social structures. Yet simultaneously, orientalism, as practised, addressed questions fundamental to Europeans' understanding of self and the patterns of world civilisation, by seeking to establish authoritatively the historical relationships between language, religion, culture, and society in imperial contexts. The ancient Sanskrit texts of India became the principal medium through which the nature of the subcontinent's civilisational heritage was understood, while linguistic knowledge became the required mark of orientalist expertise. It is argued that orientalist research in this context was inherently comparative, and was thereby conducive to an evaluation of Indian society by the colonial state within an emerging paradigm of historical progress. In this way, early orientalist research, rather than being necessarily devoted to a humanistic ideal, as is often thought, was in fact an important element within the construction of notions of a degraded Indian civilisation in need of uplift through colonial interventionism. Eighteenth-century orientalist research, in other words, was crucial in the ideological underpinning of the East India Company's nascent state.

The set of orientalist ideas and British understandings about India enumerated here also had considerable ramifications well beyond the eighteenth-century context. Rather than viewing orientalist research produced during the British colonial consolidation in the eighteenth century as epistemologically isolated from the culturally confident liberalism of the nineteenth century, this chapter provides an initial framework for an argument more fully elaborated in subsequent chapters. That is, that there was in fact a considerable transference of ideas across the turn of the century, and a sort of institutionalisation of elements of orientalist research within strains of British liberalism, as well as an evolving set of constructive orientalist practices. This included the focus upon Sanskrit textual sources as the repository of an 'authentic' Hinduism, and, as we shall see in the next chapter, the important role to be played in British endeavours by Sanskrit *paṇḍit*s, viewed as India's culturally authoritative intellectual leadership. This chapter thus also serves to establish the groundwork for later discussions of nineteenth-century educational imperatives and the advent of revived Indian cultural identities.

Early orientalist research and British governance

The expansion of British scholarly enquiry into Indian society and history during the seventeenth and early eighteenth centuries corresponded closely with the East India Company's burgeoning trading interests in Asia. Travelogues published by Company servants such Dr John Fryer and the chaplain John Ovington served to familiarise the British public with the perceived exoticism of India, though these early authors wrote their accounts without a substantial depth of understanding of the subcontinent.[1] Both British religious and civilisational prejudice, as well as a general unfamiliarity with the region's people and history, contributed to the relatively superficial nature of these works. British orientalist research began in earnest, however, in the 1760s, and coincided with the East India Company's piecemeal conquest of Bengal, and its assumption of responsibility for land revenue management (as the *dīvān*).[2] Chris Bayly, for example, has described this event as a decidedly important factor in the enablement of British information collection in Bengal, as it provided the Company with an official legitimacy and sanction within the ascendant Mughal political structure for relatively free European travel and observation within Bengal (and somewhat beyond), as well as access to a wider variety of official information sources.[3]

The Company's need for reliable military intelligence and authoritative information about Indian society and Mughal forms of governance was further highlighted with the Company's early mismanagement of revenue administration, which resulted in the devastating Bengal famine of 1770, as well as with the outbreak of armed conflicts within Europe and India from 1776.[4] The Company's urgent need for authoritative cultural information about India was recognised early on by the Company's first Governor-General, Warren Hastings. Hastings believed that the key to the Company's successful governance of its Indian territories lay in the conciliation of 'native sensibilities'; a goal which, it was thought, would best be served by modelling the Company's rule to take account of Indian societal norms and values. Debates in the early 1770s regarding the administration of law in Bengal are particularly illustrative in this regard, not least because of the close connection perceived between the regular and equitable administration of justice, and the Company's capacity to both efficiently extract taxation revenue and avoid economic and humanitarian disasters such as famine.

In August 1772 Warren Hastings issued a plan for the administration of justice[5] in an attempt to systematise the existent court system in Bengal, which was hampered by overlapping and competing spheres of influence, as well as corruption. This document outlined the arrangements for the dispensation of civil justice in Bengal according to one's religious affiliation within a regularised judicial system, and was conceived by Hastings to be a 'reinstatement' of the 'ancient constitution' of the Indian people, within an improved, 'modern' judiciary modelled upon Mughal institutions.[6] Hastings described this system of governance to the Court of Directors in London, noting, 'we have endeavoured to adapt our Regulations to the Manners and Understandings of the People, and the Exigencies of the Country, adhering as closely as we are able to their ancient uses and Institutions'.[7]

However, in the mid-1770s, a British parliamentary committee and the Supreme Court in Calcutta proposed to administer English law throughout the Company's Indian territories upon the basis of the perception that India had been subject to a despotic regime, and was hence without law.[8] Hastings, who would eventually succeed in implementing his vision of judicial administration in Bengal, argued that Indians were in possession of 'laws, which have continued unchanged, from the remotest antiquity'(i.e. their 'ancient constitution'), and further, that 'it would be a grievance to deprive the people of the protection of their own laws, but it would be a wanton tyranny to require their obedience to others of which they are wholly ignorant'.[9] In essence, Hastings' vision of legal administration in India may be said to be informed by the principles of common, or natural law, systematised by Sir William Blackstone in England in the late 1760s,[10] in which law was considered to be the product of an on-going rational process, and further reflected the values and concerns of the society which it applied to.[11] The judicial plan of 1772 was intended to provide the basis for administering India's 'ancient constitution(s)' within the civil judiciary on this basis, and to provide the Company with a solid foundation upon which to base its governance. As will be argued in the next chapter, however, Hastings' legal vision was also significantly influenced by existent modes of judicial administration within the *navāb* of Bengal's *darbār* and the Company's concern for constructing political legitimacy upon 'native' models.

The implementation of Hastings' policies in the early 1770s had several important consequences within the realm of British scholarship on Indian history and society. The first of these was that the Company's requirement for authoritative cultural information to be used in governance gave rise to an expansion of orientalist scholarship and publication, officially sanctioned through the patronage of the Company's government or from Hastings himself. Hastings often called directly upon individual Company servants to undertake specific research or translation projects, thus both initiating their orientalist careers, and then later sustaining them through patronage.[12] This is most certainly the case when we consider the early careers of Nathaniel Brassey Halhed and Charles Wilkins, the two most important orientalists during the decade before the arrival of William Jones in India.

Nathaniel Halhed had been well educated in England, first at Harrow, and then at Christ Church in Oxford, and enjoyed a scholarly reputation. As such, he was asked by Hastings to undertake the translation of the Sanskrit 'legal' compilation (a *nibandha*), the *Vivādārṇavasetu* ('a bridge over the sea of litigation'), from its Persian rendering into English.[13] This was published in London in 1776 at the Company's expense, as *A Code of Gentoo Laws*.[14] While the Persian version of the *Code* was destined for use in the Company's courts, in accordance with the judicial dictates of 1772, the English translation was intended by Hastings to serve largely as a demonstration to a domestic British audience that Indians were a 'civilised nation', as they were in possession of a civil code governing the right of property.[15] Following the publication of the *Code*, Halhed also published in 1778 a Bengali grammar, and in this regard, Hastings not only helped Halhed to meet the cost of employing a *paṇḍit* to assist him, but also arranged for the Company to underwrite the costs of publication.[16]

Similarly, the orientalist scholarship of Charles Wilkins also benefited from Hastings' patronage. Wilkins, who had come to Bengal as a writer in 1770, first became involved in the publication of orientalist works when Hastings called upon him to construct a set of Indian language type faces for use in the publication of the *Code of Gentoo Laws*.[17] Wilkins later began to learn Sanskrit (he was, in fact, the first Company servant to gain competency in the language), and with the assistance of Hastings, was transferred more permanently to the city of Benares where he completed his original translation from Sanskrit of the *Bhagavad Gītā* in the company of the city's *paṇḍits*.[18] This text was also published at the Company's expense in London in 1785. Wilkins continued to enjoy the benefits of Hastings' friendship and active patronage upon their return to England, as Hastings not only encouraged him in the publication of his translation of the *Hitopadeśa*,[19] but, following the conclusion of his impeachment trial, wrote to the Court of Directors in 1799 to support Wilkins' (ultimately successful) application to become the Company's librarian at India House.[20]

The second consequence of Hastings' policy of governance proceeded from his focus upon recovering and reinstating the 'original', or 'pure', socio-cultural norms (read here as the 'ancient constitution') of the Hindus, thought lost by a long period of despotic Muslim rule, with reference to ancient Sanskrit texts.[21] In essence, this would lend to subsequent orientalist scholarship a largely Sanskrit textual bias, and in time, to a largely unproblematic equation of 'India' with 'Hinduism'. In many ways, this bias towards ancient texts in the investigation of India's past, and the tenets of Hinduism in particular, reflected Hastings' classical education, and the attendant understanding that religious tenets are defined by their appearance in a representative text, such as the *Qur'ān* or the *Bible*. Moreover, this bias was consistent with the notion that India's ancient textual productions contained a remnant of 'ancient wisdom' which might shed light upon the mythology shared by all the civilised nations of antiquity in the time of Noah. The shift in the appearance and character of orientalist research from the mid-1770s is demonstrative of this point.

Prior to Hastings' 1772 juridical declaration, the two celebrated texts of British orientalism were J. Z. Holwell's *Interesting Historical Events, Relative to the Provinces of Bengal and the Empire of Indostan*, published between 1765 and 1771, and Alexander Dow's translation of Firishtah's history of Hindustan, the *Ta'rīkh i Firishtah*, which appeared in print between 1768 and 1772. Holwell's text contains a discussion of 'the religious tenets of the Gentoos, followers of the Shashtah of Brahmah', the content of which has largely confounded scholars ever since.[22] Regardless of the numerous confusions in the text, Holwell's deist beliefs informed his view that the scriptures of Hinduism, given their extraordinary antiquity, contained the remaining 'primitive truth' of the original, universal religion. As such, he regarded these texts as containing the 'missing link' to the full and proper understanding of the Old and New Testaments of the *Bible*.[23] It is unclear exactly which Sanskrit texts Holwell referred to in his analysis, but it is apparent that he did not understand Sanskrit, and that his principal sources of information on Hindu doctrines were members of the *kāyasth*, or scribal caste, who themselves would have had a limited knowledge of the actual content of the sacred Sanskrit texts.

Alexander Dow's translation of the *Ta'rīkh i Firishtah* also contains an original 'dissertation concerning the customs, manners, language, religion and philosophy of the Hindoos', in which he drew on an understanding of the contents of several Sanskrit texts, possibly including the *Bhāgavata Purāṇa*, and something from the *nyāyaśāstra*,[24] in an attempt to demonstrate that the Hindu religion was in fact monotheistic.[25] Yet Dow similarly didn't understand Sanskrit, and had relied instead upon his knowledge of Persian and the 'vulgar tongue of the Hindoos' to 'inform himself as much as possible, concerning the mythology and philosophy of the Brahmins'.[26] Dow described Holwell's text as 'unintelligible' on the basis that he had gained his information by 'convers[ing] upon the subject only with the inferior tribes, or with the unlearned part of the Brahmins'. In distinction, Dow claimed authority for his own text by noting that he himself had consulted a learned *paṇḍit* who 'served to give him a general idea of the doctrine'.[27]

Despite Dow's characterisation of the distinction between his and Holwell's texts, both of these differed markedly from the other early orientalist productions of Halhed and Wilkins produced after 1772, in the fact of the conditions of their production. Both Dow and Holwell relied upon verbal accounts or translated renditions of the content of Sanskrit texts (albeit of assuredly different qualities), rather than upon the Sanskrit texts themselves. Halhed's *Code of Gentoo Laws*, although an English translation of a Persian rendering of the original Sanskrit *Vivādārṇavasetu*, was nevertheless a translation of an authoritative compilation of identifiable extracts from the Sanskrit corpus of the *dharmaśāstra* (normative texts). Moreover, Halhed's 'Preface' on Hindu belief systems included translated extracts from the *Bhagavad Gītā* and the *Bhāgavata Purāṇa*, among other Sanskrit texts.[28] The first orientalist production of Charles Wilkins, as noted earlier, was an English translation of the *Bhagavad Gītā* from the original Sanskrit text. It is worth recalling here, however, that both Dow and Holwell had to rely upon informants or Persian sources due to the simple fact that the *paṇḍits* were reluctant in the 1760s to impart a knowledge of the Sanskrit language, and closely guarded many of their religious texts as well. Yet following Hastings' call to recover India's 'ancient constitution' by reference to the contents of the *śāstra*, changing patterns of socio-cultural patronage in India resulted in both access to Sanskrit textual materials and a knowledge of the Sanskrit language itself to proliferate among Europeans. As such, the conditions under which orientalist scholarship on India could be considered authoritative slowly began to change, contributing to the (re-)construction of Sanskrit as India's principal cultural-textual media.

William Jones and the Biblical history of Asia

It is William Jones, however, who is most certainly the central, paradigmatic figure of early British orientalist research, and an examination of Jones' scholarship touches upon nearly all the principal themes of early British orientalism. As such, he has been the subject of a wide-ranging body of secondary scholarship, which includes near-hagiography as well as more critical discussions of Jones' contributions to comparative philology, law, Asian history, and literature.[29] Jones was educated at Harrow and University College, Oxford, and enjoyed a wide range of scholarly pursuits, from classics to astronomy to Oriental languages.[30] Before he arrived in Calcutta to take up the post of judge of the Supreme Court of Judicature at Fort William, Jones had enjoyed in England a relatively successful career in law, having published the influential tract *Essay on the Law of Bailments* in 1781. This success came approximately ten years after he had abandoned a somewhat less lucrative career as a scholar of Persian and Arabic, and tutor to Lord Althorp (later the second Earl Spencer).[31] Jones professed politically radical views while living in England, which often included elements of Republicanism.[32] For example, Jones wrote a polemical tract calling for parliamentary reform, entitled *The Principles of Government*, and became a member of the similarly minded Society of Constitutional Information in 1782.[33] In this regard, several authors have argued that Jones' political radicalism likely constrained the fulfilment of his ambitions in England, and thus provided the impetus for his eventual move to Calcutta.[34] Javed Majeed, however, has persuasively argued against viewing Jones' orientalist scholarship in India as a product of that political radicalism, but instead as reflecting the newly conservative ethos generated in the wake of the French Revolution. Majeed interprets Jones' orientalist scholarship as an attempt to understand cultures upon their own terms, and argues that this is consistent with Edmund Burke's notion of an inherited constitution, itself grounded in English common, or natural law traditions.[35]

Jones' orientalist scholarship in India might be divided into several distinct, but interrelated strands, including his legal researches in India and the attendant compilation and translation of an authoritative digest of 'Hindu law'; his enquiries into the Sanskrit language and the formulation of the Indo-European language family; as well as his research into Indian history and the formulation of a historiographical methodology. Elements of Jones' legal research in India will be considered in the following chapter (namely his desire to control elements of the *paṇḍit*-orientalist relationship), but here the focus will be upon Jones' linguistic and historical research, with a view to elucidating not only the impact which Jones' work had on later generations of orientalists and linguists, but also the major concepts which informed and underpinned his thought.

Jones first arrived in Calcutta in September of 1783, and by the following January, he had helped to establish a learned society 'for inquiring into the history and antiquities, the natural productions, arts, sciences, and literature of *Asia*'.[36] The Asiatic Society, as it was known, endowed orientalist scholarship in India with an institutional base. Its centralised venue in Calcutta allowed for easier information exchange, and the much wider and formalised dissemination of its findings was eventually effected through the publication of the Society's journal, *Asiatick Researches*.[37] While Jones was already an accomplished orientalist, with knowledge of Arabic and Persian, he professed that he had no plans to learn Sanskrit, as he felt happy to leave its prosecution in the able hands of Charles Wilkins.[38] Yet two years after his arrival in India, by September of 1785, Jones had begun to undertake the study of Sanskrit, largely in an effort to be able to verify the authenticity of the *vyavasthā*s (a 'legal' opinion) of the *paṇḍit*s attached to the court.[39] It was a mere five months later, then, on 2 February 1786, that Jones delivered his influential third anniversary discourse to the Asiatic Society, entitled 'On the Hindu's'. In it, he famously pointed to the affinity between Sanskrit, Greek and Latin, and further, posited a common origin for all three:

> The *Sanscrit* language, whatever be its antiquity, is of a wonderful structure; more perfect than the *Greek*, more copious than the *Latin*,

> and more exquisitely refined than either, yet bearing to both of them a stronger affinity, both in the roots of verbs and in the forms of grammar, than could possibly have been produced by accident; so strong indeed, that no philologer could examine them all three, without believing them to have sprung from some common source, which, perhaps, no longer exists.[40]

Jones' discussion of the relationship between Sanskrit, Greek, and Latin was to support a specific historiographical agenda; namely, the conversion of the study of language into a discipline from which historical 'truth' might be elicited. Of course, in the late eighteenth century, the study of language was already being used within a variety of historical enquiries, and so Jones must be understood as here promoting an innovative, and superior, methodology within the study of language itself, so as to render it a more suitable tool for eliciting historical truth.[41]

The principal object of Jones' criticism was the historical analysis of the relations of languages by reference to an often 'speculative' or conjectural etymological method. In this regard, Jones singled out for criticism Jacob Bryant's use of comparative etymology in his *A New System, or, an Analysis of Antient Mythology*, stating that, while 'etymology has, no doubt, some use in historical researches', it is 'a medium of proof so very fallacious, that, where it elucidates one fact, it obscures a thousand, and more frequently borders on the ridiculous, than leads to any solid conclusion'.[42] Bryant was attempting to construct an etymological genealogy which substantiated the Genesitic account of Creation. In essence, this meant a recovery of the obscure 'traces' of humanity's first civilisation, and its original mythology, through an examination of the languages of the contemporary Asian world. Take, for example, Bryant's etymological analysis of the story of Babel's construction by Nimrod. Nimrod's character, as a 'mighty one', and a 'mighty hunter' were thought to be reproduced under the mythological character of Alorus, or Orion, 'represented by Homer as of a gigantic make; and as being continually in pursuit of wild beasts'. Moreover, the word 'Nimrod' found its counterpart in the Greek word 'Nebrod', and in Greek place names such as 'Nebrodes', 'Nebrissia', and in Sicily, the mountain 'Nebrodes' (incidentally, a famous place for hunting).[43] Interestingly, the term 'Belus', historically associated with the construction of the tower in Babylon, was viewed by Bryant as the same word as 'Babel', and therefore also indicative of the confusion of speech recounted in Genesis XI. As such, the dispersion at Babel was rendered for Bryant simply a 'labial failure ... a prevarication of the lip', which ultimately could give credence to his conjectural etymology, and thereby confirm the historicity of Biblical narrative.[44]

Jones considered pure etymology, however, at least as it had been utilised by Bryant, as principally an *a priori* method of investigation, and therefore insufficient for historical research. Jones illustrated this point by arguing that etymological analysis alone could never prove a historical relationship between languages (one that is already known to exist) based upon a comparison of dissimilar words, such as in the case of the English *uncle*, which comes from the Latin *avus*. Moreover, the comparison of similar words by way of etymology can furnish a false basis for attributing a certain relationship to languages. In this regard, Jones provided the example of the unrelated English *hangar* and the Persian *khanjar*, both of which refer to swords, but of different types.[45] In essence, Jones objected to an etymological method, which, through an 'arbitrary transposition of letters', would allow the postulation of a relationship between almost any two languages.[46] Jones thereby called for the analysis of language to be *a posteriori*, or based in 'extrinsick' evidence. As such, the historical study of language, Jones thought, should be pursued in conjunction with philosophical and religious texts, the remains of sculpture and architecture, and 'written memorials of ... *Sciences* and *Arts*'.[47] One interesting example of 'extrinsick evidence' which Jones pursued in his discussion of the relationship of Sanskrit, Greek, and Latin, is an analysis of the characters in which these languages are written. Mirroring the linguistic relationship, Jones posited an ultimately common origin for the *devanāgarī* script, and the Phoenician, from which Greek and Roman were formed.[48] In this anniversary discourse, as well as in other, later scholarship, however, Jones more commonly invoked correspondences in religious belief or mythology as confirmatory to his thesis, including an apparent commonality among the mythological gods of ancient Greece and Rome, and contemporary India.[49] Pursued *a posteriori* in this manner, Jones believed that etymology may be made a suitable and an important, but not an exclusive, tool for elucidating the historical relationships of languages.

Jones also advocated in his third anniversary discourse that relationships between languages should be attributed upon the basis of a comparison of respective grammatical structures, rather than simply vocabulary. He demonstrated this point most effectively through an examination of Persian in his sixth anniversary discourse, in which he asserted that there exists a close affinity of that language with Sanskrit, and not with Arabic, as is commonly supposed.[50] Persian, Jones noted, contains not only a large number of nouns which 'are pure *Sanscrit*', but also that:

> very many *Persian* imperatives are the roots of *Sanscrit* verbs; and that even the moods and tenses of the Persian verb substantive, which is the model of all the rest, are deducible from the *Sanscrit* by an easy and clear analogy: we may hence conclude, that the *Parsi* was derived, like the various *Indian* dialects, from the language of the *Brahmans*.[51]

Jones, by reference to grammatical structure alone, also provided evidence for discounting any historical relationship between Persian and Arabic. Persian, he stated, like Sanskrit and Greek, allows for the compounding of words, whereas Arabic 'abhor[s] the composition of words, and invariably express very complex ideas by circumlocution'.[52] In addition, Sanskrit, like Persian, is said to contain verbal roots that are largely 'biliteral'(i.e. composed of two 'letters') while those of Arabic are usually 'triliteral'.[53] These features alone were deemed sufficient for Jones to declare that Persian and Arabic 'seem totally distinct'.[54]

The empirical and systematic comparative study of the grammatical structure and vocabulary of language, together with supporting evidence from the comparative study of religious doctrines and mythology, as well as archaeological evidence, formed the basis for Jones' new methodology to discern the historical relationships between languages, and by extension, their speakers. It is in the elaboration of this final point, though, that Jones' larger historical project becomes apparent. Jones' scholarship was, at heart, not linguistic, but to adopt Trautmann's terminology, ethnological,[55] for Jones was essentially interested to use this new methodology of orientalist research into India's ancient past to provide a further, and in this case, a 'scientific' substantiation of the Mosaic account of creation as it appears in the Book of Genesis.

The orientalist discoveries of Holwell, Dow, and Halhed, while generally being favourably received in Europe, also contained elements which could be interpreted as undermining the Biblical account of early human civilisation, and, in particular, the dating of the creation of the world, the universal deluge, and the subsequent dispersal of nations. Certainly during the eighteenth century the tenets of Christianity were consistently exposed to searching critiques based in rationality and scientific discovery, rather than in faith, especially as a part of the Scottish Enlightenment. James Hutton's theories of geological time, for example, were interpreted by more conservative members of the Scottish church as undermining Archbishop James Ussher's accepted chronology of the creation of the Earth (dated to 4004 BC),[56] despite Hutton's own claims to perceive 'design' and 'wisdom' in his findings.[57] Similarly, early orientalist researchers such as Halhed, while maintaining an outward adherence to Mosaic chronology, also asserted that the Hindu scriptures made a convincing claim to an extreme antiquity. In essence, Halhed asserted that Hindu texts were likely authored some 900 years before the Deluge (conventionally dated to 2348/9 BC), as this coincided with the beginning of the *Kali Yuga*, and, additionally, explained their notable omission of any flood narrative.[58] Moreover, Halhed went so far in undermining Mosaic authority as to suggest that the laws contained in his *Code* so closely corresponded to the 'Institutes of Moses' that it was possible that 'the doctrines of Hindostan might have been early transplanted into Egypt, and thus have become familiar to Moses'.[59]

The 'discoveries' of early British orientalism, therefore, provided ammunition to doubters of orthodox Christianity in France, and supported the conclusions of writers on ancient astronomy and mythology working in the sceptical tradition of Voltaire. Jean-Sylvain Bailly, for example, argued that Indians had an advanced knowledge of astronomy some 6,000 years previous, thereby substantiating the claims of their civilisation to an extreme antiquity (and consequently undermining Biblical narrative and authority).[60] Of course, British writers outside the sphere of orientalist research also stepped forward to defend the Mosaic chronology. The Revd George Costard, for example, published a pamphlet criticising Halhed's findings, noting that only the contents of the Bible represented a dependable guide to deciphering ancient history.[61] Bryant's *Analysis of Antient Mythology*, which is Jones' main point of historiographical contact, is also an attempt to defend Biblical accounts of creation, though as we have seen, on the basis of a linguistic analysis centred in conjectural etymology.[62] In this context, therefore, we should view Jones' body of scholarship as, quite simply, an attempt to forge what he considered a more rational and, ultimately, scientific basis for utilising orientalist research in the confirmation of Mosaic ethnography and the attendant Biblical chronology. Jones' faith in Biblical chronology seems to have been steadfast, for although he noted in his essay 'On the Gods of Greece, Italy, and India', with reference to Halhed's suggestions, that:

> it is not the truth of our national religion, as such, that I have at heart: it is truth itself; and, if any cool unbiased reasoner will clearly convince me, that Moses drew his narrative through Egyptian conduits from the primeval fountains of Indian literature I shall esteem him as a friend for having weeded my mind from a capital error, and promise to stand among the foremost in assisting to circulate the truth, which he has ascertained,[63]

Jones nevertheless favoured the dating of the law book of Manu, India's first legislator, to an era significantly subsequent to Moses in his own preface to the translation of that Sanskrit work.[64] Elsewhere, Jones surgically dismantled traditional Hindu chronology, asserting that the first three eras (*yugas*) of extreme antiquity were 'chiefly mythological', while the current, *historical* era (the *kali yuga*) could be carried no further back than about 2000 BC.[65]

The Mosaic account, found in Genesis X and XI, states that following the Deluge, the three sons of Noah, named Shem, Ham, and Japheth, and their respective offspring, began to settle in various parts of the globe. Among the descendants of Ham, for instance, was Nimrod, whose kingdom was located in Babylonia and Assyria (Genesis X: 6–12). Following the Deluge, it is also said that the 'whole earth had a common language and a common vocabulary' (Genesis XI: 1). Yet following the building of the tower of Babel (in Babylonia), which was intended to enable its inhabitants to reach heaven, God is said to have 'confuse[d] their language'(Genesis XI: 7) and spread the people 'across the face of the entire earth' (Genesis XI: 8). Central to this narrative is the notion that before the Tower of Babel, all the inhabitants of the earth spoke one common language, and that after it, the world was composed of a variety of peoples, or 'nations', each descended from one of the three sons of Noah, and unified in its distinct language and geographical location.

During the course of his anniversary discourses, Jones described the five 'nations' of Asia, namely the Hindus, Arabs, Tartars, Persians, and Chinese, and on the basis of conclusions drawn from his new historical methodology, Jones was able to identify three basic groups of people:

> the first race of *Persians* and *Indians,* to whom we may add the *Romans* and *Greeks*, the *Goths*, and the old *Egyptians* or *Ethiops*, originally spoke the same language and professed the same popular faith,

> is capable, in my humble opinion, of incontestable proof; that the *Jews* and *Arabs*, the *Assyrians*, or second *Persian* race, the people who spoke *Syriack*, and a numerous tribe of *Abyssinians*, used one primitive dialect wholly distinct from the idiom just mentioned, is, I believe, undisputed, and, I am sure, indisputable; but that the settlers in *China* and *Japan* had a common origin with the *Hindus*, is no more than highly probable; and, that all the *Tartars*, as they are inaccurately called, were primarily of a third separate branch, totally differing from the two others in language, manners, and features, may indeed be plausibly conjectured ... the whole earth was peopled by a variety of shoots from the *Indian*, *Arabian*, and *Tartarian* branches, or by such intermixtures of them, as, in a course of ages, might naturally have happened.[66]

Here Jones identified these three basic groups of people according to their descent from the sons of Noah. The Indians and Persians, together with the Greeks, Romans, and Egyptians were descendants from Ham, and originally spoke a common language. Similarly, Jews, Arabs, and Assyrians were descendants of Shem, and the Tartars were likely the descendants of Japheth. Moreover, Jones asserted that these three basic groups, which are distinguished by essentially common 'language, religion, manners, and other known characteristicks', migrated outwards from the central, original homeland of Iran (or Chaldea).[67] Jones also confirmed the Biblical chronology of the settlement of the Earth by stating that he found no evidence to support the Indian claims to a great antiquity:

> We find no certain monument, or even probable tradition, or nations planted, empires and states raised, laws enacted, cities built, navigation improved, commerce encouraged, arts invented, or letters contrived, above twelve or at most fifteen or sixteen centuries before the birth of Christ, and from another fact, which cannot be controverted, that seven hundred or a thousand years would have been fully adequate to the supposed propagation, diffusion and establishment of the human race.[68]

It is the descendants of Ham, however, who were thought by Jones, as well as by Bryant, to compose the ancient civilised nations of earth. Jones noted that it is this group of people who:

> founded in *Iran* itself the monarchy of the first *Chaldeans*, invented letters, observed and named the luminaries of the

> firmament, calculated the known *Indian* period of *four hundred and thirty-two thousand years*, or an *hundred and twenty* repetitions of the *saros*, and contrived the old system of Mythology, partly allegorical, and partly grounded on idolatrous veneration for their sages and lawgivers.[69]

Yet Jones also recognised that the descendants of Ham, in time, 'were dispersed at various intervals and in various colonies over land and ocean'. Some were said to have settled in Africa and Asia, some into Egypt, Italy, and Greece, and from there spread as far as northern Europe, China, and Peru.[70] Jones' singularly important, but often overlooked, contribution to subsequent European scholarship on India was, then, the provision of a standard by which comparisons of civilisational progress might be made through the attribution of a common ethnological origin and a common original knowledge to Indians and Europeans as the descendants of Ham.[71] Jones, in essence, was attempting to understand the cultural difference of Europe and India by reference to (what he conceived to be) a set of shared, and therefore neutral criteria.[72]

Jones' wide-ranging essay 'On the Gods of Greece, Italy, and India' is, as such, an attempt to demonstrate, through comparison, the common origins of ancient Greek, Roman, and Indian mythology. Jones noted, for example, that the Roman god Janus shared many attributes with the Indian god Ganesha, as both were considered the fount of wisdom, and the originator of all things religious. Such similarities demonstrated, Jones conceived, 'a general union or affinity between the most distinguished inhabitants of the primitive world, at the time when they deviated … from the rational adoration of the only true God'.[73] Similarly, Jones examined the correspondences between the Greek and Hindu zodiacs, positing that their astronomical systems shared a single, original source, namely, that the 'practice of observing the stars began, with the rudiments of civil society, in the country of those, whom we call *Chaldeans*'.[74]

Yet simultaneously, the comparisons contained inherent reference to differential achievements within a universal time scale: Europe had had thrown off the 'classical' paganism of Italy and Greece, while India clearly had not. Note, for example, Jones' comments in a 1787 letter to the second Earl Spencer, in which he placed himself in Europe's past (but India's present):

> To what shall I compare my literary pursuits in India? Suppose Greek literature to be known in modern Greece only, and there to

> be in the hands of priests and philosophers; and suppose them to be still worshippers of Jupiter and Apollo ... Such am I in this country; substituting Sanscrit for Greek, the *Brahmans*, for the priests of *Jupiter*, and *Vālmic*, *Vyāsa*, *Cālīdāsa*, for Homer, Plato, Pindar. Need I say what exquisite pleasure I receive from conversing easily with that class of men, who conversed with Pythagoras, Theles, and Solon ...[75]

As such, the comparative element of the analysis inevitably could also be directed towards civilisational evaluation, based in a notion of historical progress: a point elided by Jones' hagiographers.[76] While in Jones' work the analogy to classical Europe sometimes lent worth to Indian civilisation, he also noted, for example, in his second anniversary discourse that in the pursuit of scientific knowledge (a prominent measure of respective progress), the '*Asiaticks*, if compared with our western nations, are mere children'. Moreover, the mathematical knowledge contained in a Sanskrit text he inspected was composed of 'only simple elements', and not of a sophistication comparable to that of Newton.[77] In other words, the intrinsic worthiness of a classical civilisation, which Jones so often ascribed to India, was simultaneously tempered by an awareness of the different historical trajectories which had since been followed. Jones ultimately confirmed the comparative nature of orientalist research in his tenth anniversary discourse, given in 1793, the year before his death, in which he declared that the object of the historical investigations of the members of the Asiatic Society must be the 'respective progress in *science* and *art*' which the Asiatic nations had made.[78] In many ways, Jones's scholarship contained an internal stress, which afflicted much of orientalism, between the concern for civilisational progress, evinced especially in Scottish Enlightenment thought, and Biblically inspired antiquarianism. The former conceived knowledge, especially, as a progressive enterprise, while the latter looked backwards to its original completeness. The focus upon civilisational comparison stressed by Jones, however, and his enumeration of an accepted basis for conceptualising historical 'progress', upon which such a comparison could proceed, established the basic norm for later orientalist scholarship, as we shall see in Chapter 3. Moreover, through the introduction of an ultimately evaluative component in that comparison (through analyses of historical 'progress'), Jones also provided a framework which could later be utilised in nineteenth-century British educational initiatives in India.

'Ancient Wisdom' and the valuation of Sanskrit text

Taking the conception of an original unity of Hamian civilisation, in which there existed a knowledge of the antediluvian monotheism of Noah (though obscured under the veil of a popular mythological-paganism) as well as an advanced astronomical knowledge as a basis, and that with the subsequent dispersal of the descendants of Ham, this knowledge was, in time, lost in degrees, Jones' orientalist scholarship into India's ancient texts is rendered an essentially historical enquiry. The ancient knowledge of the Hindus, as descendants of Ham, was therefore thought by Jones to provide not only an independent confirmation of the Biblical account of creation, but was also held to have a measure of value, in and of itself, as a source of information on the knowledge systems of that first civilisation. Knowledge was conceptualised as providential, that is, as originally a unity, which was then later dispersed and degraded. Jones was attempting to add to the storehouse of human knowledge, in essence, through a recovery of lost, ancient knowledge. The Sanskrit texts of the Hindus, being among the oldest existent writings known to humankind, were thought to be closer in time to that original and ancient unity, and as such, valued as a potential source of 'ancient wisdom'.[79] This conception, that the original unity of knowledge might be partially restored from ancient Sanskrit texts, certainly seems to be supported by the remarks of Charles Wilkins, for example, who characterised Jones' research into India's past as an exercise in 'seeking fresh sources of knowledge'.[80]

Many of the orientalists who succeeded Jones, both in India and in Britain, continued the principal historiographical agenda set out in the anniversary discourses by utilising Indian sources as confirmatory of Biblical narrative, and increasingly, as valuable in and of themselves in an exposition of the nature of the ancient world. But it must be stressed that Indian textual and linguistic sources were utilised by these orientalists to serve a uniquely British agenda, whether through the support they were perceived to lend to Biblical chronology, or by reference to their underpinning of an emergent conception of British cultural superiority.

Francis Wilford, for example, who had worked as a surveyor in the Bengal Engineers before marrying an Indian woman and retiring to Benares, devoted himself to exploring the mythological and geographical material contained in the *Purāṇa*s, and over the course of numerous and lengthy essays published in *Asiatick Researches*, drew correspondences between Sanskritic and Judaeo-Christian narratives of ancient history, intended to fortify the Mosaic chronology.[81] For example, Wilford argued in the first of his essays, entitled 'On Egypt', that India was the ultimate source of Egyptian civilisation. Wilford claimed as his source the indistinct '*Padma Purān*', which reportedly also contained an independent (and hence confirmatory) account of the postdiluvian dispersal. In it, the patriarch Satyavrāta's three sons, Jyāpeti, Charma, and Sharma were said to have settled the earth following the building of the *Padmā-mandira* ('lotus-temple'), which Wilford identified with the tower of Babel.[82]

Similarly, in London, the Revd Thomas Maurice, who was assistant keeper of manuscripts in the British Museum from 1798, published a series of prolix 'mythographical' texts between 1793 and 1820, which were based largely upon the contents of *Asiatick Researches*, the work of Bryant, Costard, Hyde, and Kircher, as well as the manuscripts and translations of orientalists returned to England. Maurice's numerous books, all self-published, speak to an intellectual and personal ambitiousness which was never fulfilled. He often complained, for example, in the prefaces to his work that unenlightened critics were proving 'extremely injurious' to his book sales. The main object of Maurice's enquiries was the mythology and religion of India, and like Jones and Wilford, he sought primarily to demonstrate that the content of ancient Sanskrit texts confirmed the Mosaic narrative.[83] Maurice seemingly drew comfort in the parallels which he observed between Hindu and Christian theological concepts, such as the Trinity and the 'divine triad' of Brahmā, Viṣṇu, and Śiva, which he thought confirmed God's 'sublime mysterious truth'.[84] This was deemed especially important in the context of the ideological challenges of the French Revolution, which he characterised as a 'momentous crisis' spurred by 'infidelity', and which imperilled the 'national faith'.[85]

Maurice endeavoured to substantiate his arguments with reference to what he called 'astronomical-mythology'. Rejecting Indian claims to an extreme antiquity, Maurice instead argued, with Jones, that human postdiluvian origins were located in Chaldea, and that ancient Greek, Egyptian and Indian astronomy all had their origins there. The mythologies of the ancient world, in turn, were all based upon this shared ancient astronomy, as astronomical figures were thought to record the most important ancient historical events.[86] The history of the earliest human civilisations, then, was thought to only be recoverable through a reconstruction and comparison of their mythological forms. For example, Maurice believed that the southern constellation of *Argo Navis*, recognised by ancient Greeks, Egyptians, Persians, and

Indians as a ship, and around which distinct mythologies were constructed,[87] represented a shared remembrance of the ark of Noah. In addition, Maurice viewed Noah and the Hindu lawgiver Manu as being in fact the same person (as narrators of the creation of the world), and interpreted the *matsyāvatāra* ('fish incarnation') of Viṣṇu, also a symbol in the Indian zodiac, as evidence of the universal experience of the Deluge.[88]

Ultimately, however, the scholarship of both Wilford and Maurice could still, some 20 years after Halhed, be used to argue the possibility that it was ancient Indian civilisation which was the source for Western knowledge and religious belief, and not the other way around. Indeed, Maurice found himself battling against such alternative, and ultimately subversive, interpretations of the links made between Indian mythology and Christianity. The fifth volume of *Asiatick Researches*, for example, when reprinted in London in 1799, contained an additional unauthorised 'advertisement' which noted the similarity of Hebrew and Hindu scripture, as well as the 'very high antiquity' of the latter. Whether 'the Hindu Brahmens borrowed from Moses, or Moses from the Hindu Brahmens', the editor stated, was a matter for further investigation.[89] Maurice railed against such suggestions. While arguing that Noah was likely the same historical personage as Manu, and that, as such, the Code of Manu and the Mosaic Pentateuch closely corresponded, it still by no means followed for Maurice that Moses borrowed from Hindu scripture. Rather, Maurice argued, Moses was divinely inspired, and the Hindu law codes of Manu dated to some 200 years after Moses' departure from Egypt.[90] Elsewhere Maurice was also forced to explain, for example, why, despite the apparent etymological similarity, it was impossible that 'the history and miracles of Christ were borrowed from those of the Indian Creeshna', as had been suggested by Constantin François de Volney.[91] Such subversions of the uses made of orientalist scholarship may indeed have contributed to more forceful declarations of Europe's superiority which emerged in the nineteenth century, but interestingly, they also foreshadow similar trenchant critiques made by Indians themselves of Christian missionary rhetoric and the 'constructive orientalist' educational project. We will return to these issues in greater depth in later chapters.

Despite Jones' initial call for historiographical strategies which utilised a variety of source material, it was undoubtedly the focus upon utilising Sanskrit texts for their mythological content, as well as the Sanskrit language itself, as source material which predominated much orientalist analysis (including his own) throughout the later part of the eighteenth century. This, in turn, further established the textual bias of orientalist scholarship in India, and attended the consolidation of Sanskrit as the central and authoritative cultural media of India. In essence, Sanskrit came to be viewed as the storehouse of India's authentic ancient history and culture, as opposed to Persian, or popular practice. Jones' own orientalist work, as we have seen, largely proceeded from an examination of Sanskrit textual sources. Two of Jones' major essays, 'On the Gods of Greece, Italy, and India', and 'On the Chronology of the Hindus', are composed almost entirely by analyses of the contents of Sanskrit texts. 'On the Chronology of the Hindus', in particular, undermined Jones' call for constructing Indian history from a variety of sources by purporting to give, as far as possible, 'a concise account of Indian chronology' by reference to 'Sanscrit books'.[92] There was also very little orientalist research on Indian forms of Islam published in the early volumes of *Asiatick Researches*, and alongside the few contemporary ethnographic and archaeological observations, travelogues, and scientific articles which did appear, the journal was largely dominated by the Sanskrit textual analyses of Jones, Wilford, and H. T. Colebrooke, not to mention the 'second level' analyses published in England by the likes of Thomas Maurice. In a significant way, then, authentic or authoritative Indian civilisation was increasingly conceived by Europeans to reside within Sanskrit texts, and therefore also in the ancient past, and contemporary, 'degraded' Indian society, including Indian Islam, was conceived to be of relatively little value to the principal aims of orientalist scholarship.

Among the orientalists who flourished subsequent to Jones' death in 1794, it is Henry Thomas Colebrooke who was often viewed as Jones' most worthy successor, on account of his mastery of Sanskrit, his extensive record of publication on Sanskrit and Hindu belief systems, and his presidency of the Asiatic Society in Calcutta between 1806 and 1815. The handover of orientalist primacy to Colebrooke was effectively illustrated, moreover, in that Colebrooke completed Jones' partial English translation of the Sanskrit legal text, the *Vivādabhaṅgārṇava* ('the ocean of the resolution of litigation'), which was then published to great acclaim in 1798 as *A Digest of Hindu Law*.[93] Colebrooke's scholarship, then, also served to solidify many of the dominant strands of Jones' work, including the attribution to Indian civilisation of an ancient chronology which supported, rather than challenged, Biblical narrative, as well as, most prominently, the tendency to equate the authentic substance of Indian civilisation with the contents of the ancient Sanskrit texts.

H. T. Colebrooke was the son of Sir George Colebrooke, a member of the House of Commons and, from 1769–1772, the Chairman of the East India Company. Following his arrival in Calcutta in 1783, Colebrooke found a position as Assistant Collector in Tirhut, and soon began the study of Sanskrit. Following the publication of *A Digest of Hindu Law* in 1798, Colebrooke advanced to the position of judge of the Calcutta Court of Appeal, and was also appointed as the professor of Sanskrit and Hindu Law at the College of Fort William.[94] In his first orientalist publication, 'On the Duties of a Faithful Hindu Widow', Colebrooke began by invoking Jones in a call to 'reject the authority of every publication preceding the translation of the *Gita*', and moreover, pointed to a series of recent orientalist publications which 'betray great want of judgement in the selection of authorities'.[95] This was only preliminary, however, to Colebrooke's wider historiographical agenda, which was to correct previous orientalist error, and set subsequent research into Indian civilisation upon an authoritative base, by reverting to 'original authorities'. In other words, Colebrooke advocated resorting to Sanskrit texts as the authentic repository of Indian civilisation.[96] In this regard, Colebrooke departed from Jones' call for an essentially interdisciplinary historiographical methodology, though he followed Jones in much of his actual scholastic practice. Colebrooke's 'On the Duties of a Faithful Hindu Widow', for example, sought an explanation for the contemporary rite of *satī*(the burning of widows upon their husband's funeral pyre), through an examination of the scriptural origins of that practice. In this respect, Colebrooke cited the *Ṛg Veda*, the *Bhāgavata* and *Brahma Purāṇa*s, as well as the *Gṛhya Sūtra*s, and not only concluded that *satī* was a sanctioned religious practice, but also explained the manner in which the rite was ideally to take place.

A good deal of Colebrooke's later work followed the same basic pattern. In a series of essays on the 'religious ceremonies of the Hindus, and of the Brahmens especially', Colebrooke provided an essentially ethnographic account of brahmanical funerary, marriage, and bathing rites, but furnished the cultural explanation of these rites by reference to Sanskrit texts, such as the *Parāśarasmṛti*, rather than by reference to any contemporary understanding of the place of those texts in informing religious practice. Colebrooke also noted in the first part of the essay that as 'Hindus are by no means communicative' on the subject of their religious rites, it was necessary to consult the Sanskrit texts for an 'explanation of the ceremonies'.[97] The contemporary cultural meaning of ritual practice was, then, attributed wholly upon the basis of the content of these Sanskrit texts, thereby granting these texts a virtual hegemony over the perceived conduct of religious actions. The pervasiveness of this approach is further demonstrated by W. C. Blaquiere's translation of the 'Rūḍhiradhyāya' ('chapter on custom') of the tenth- or eleventh-century *Kālikā Purāṇa*, which appeared in the fifth volume of *Asiatick Researches*. Blaquiere noted that he conceived his translation primarily as an attempt to explain the contemporary 'sacrifice of human and other victims, and the sacrificial rites celebrated by the *Hindus*'.[98]

To a significant extent, orientalist textual practices such as these served to construct a vision of 'Hindu religious practice' with reference to an idealised, brahmanical vision set out in the ancient Sanskrit *śāstra* (philosophical-religious texts), and which served to further marginalise 'popular', or syncretic religious practices in European understandings of Indian religion. In essence, time was perceived to have stood still in India, at least as regards the social and cultural meaningfulness of religious doctrine. Bayly has also argued that this bias towards seeing ancient Sanskrit text as the repository of authentic 'Hinduism' was closely linked to the veritable transformation of Indian society during the course of the nineteenth century. In particular, Bayly has noted that social rigidification resulted from institutionalising brahmanical concepts of Indian society.[99] While orientalist texts were certainly not written with a view to 'create Hinduism', but rather, as an attempt to present a systematised vision of Hindu religion to a domestic audience,[100] orientalist representations of Hinduism did often become endowed with some measure of power to impact upon the character of Indian society. For example, in the case of Colebrooke's translation of *A Digest of Hindu Laws*, the vision of contemporary Indian societal norms and values as residing in ancient Sanskrit texts found its (at least partial) implementation through the use of the *Digest* in the Company's courts. Although the *Digest* was often regarded as being too complex to be a practical legal guide,[101] its driving spirit aided in the determination of the operative civil law of the Company's Indian territories. Moreover, with regard to the early nineteenth-century debate in Bengal over the legality of *satī*, Colebrooke's essay on Hindu widows was cited by religious conservatives such as Rādhākānt Deb to authoritatively demonstrate the *śāstrik* sanction of the act.[102] Both sides of the debate argued their case solely with reference to the validity of the prescriptions contained within the Sanskrit texts,[103] demonstrating the extent to which orientalist analytical premises had penetrated the discourses of British and Indian elites.

The following chapter now moves on to examine in some detail the enabling contexts for the production of orientalist scholarship in India by reference to the relationship between British scholars and their *brāhmaṇ paṇḍit* assistants. An investigation of the political, social and cultural dynamic between these groups of individuals is crucial to understanding the ways in which the claims to authoritativeness made by orientalism became widely accepted.

2
Sanskrit Erudition and Forms of Legitimacy

Studies of early orientalist research in India have only sporadically considered in any detail the material, social and political contexts in which that body of scholarship was produced. British knowledge about India during the eighteenth and nineteenth centuries, for example, has largely been delineated by reference to European metropolitan intellectual genealogies, reflecting the recent historiographical emphasis upon colonial discourse analysis and the role of the colonial imaginary. In recent historical studies, an explicit consideration of the processes underlying the political and military consolidation of the East India Company has largely been wanting, not to mention analyses of the important ways in which orientalist scholarship was closely linked to patterns of cultural patronage and the production of ruling legitimacy in the (pre-colonial) late Mughal imperial structure. In other words, intellectual histories of orientalism, like Edward Said's famous study, while making the link to the rise of imperialism, have nevertheless neglected detailed analyses of the Asian social and cultural contexts, and enabling conditions, in which this body of scholarship was produced. In this regard, Tom Trautmann has noted in his *Aryans and British India* that the relationship of British orientalist scholars to their Indian teachers and assistants is 'of fundamental importance' in any analysis of orientalism.[1] Even Thomas Metcalf, whose *Ideologies of the Raj* rarely touches upon material contexts, acknowledges that British orientalists may have adopted their informants' peculiarly brahmanical views of Indian society and culture, though they most often inflected these understandings in their own way.[2] Neither of these writers, however, has attempted to historicise the nature of this relationship, and make explicit the particular conditions which underpinned it. Brian Hatcher, however, has in a recent article drawn explicit attention to the need to historicise our understanding of the roles which *paṇḍit*s played in a variety of colonial-era endeavours.[3]

This chapter, therefore, proceeds from the understanding that an examination of the roles which *paṇḍit*s played in government service, and the relationships which were forged with them, can lend itself to an elucidation of elements of the social, political, and cultural context for the production of orientalist scholarship, as well as also highlighting the dynamic nature of knowledge production in eighteenth-century India and beyond. Yet it must simultaneously be stressed that the nature of the historical record makes it difficult to construct anything but a very partial and incomplete assessment of the roles of *paṇḍit*s in eighteenth-century orientalist endeavours.[4] Moreover, the relationship of *paṇḍit*s to the Company and its servants was neither uniform nor static, but rather, shifted in character over the course of time. With these caveats in mind, then, it is argued here that deciphering early orientalist scholarship in India through the lens of the *paṇḍit*-orientalist relationship provides an opportunity to highlight the conditions which allowed and encouraged orientalist knowledge production, as well as the ways in which orientalists utilised this relationship in either the creation of political legitimacy in India, or to construct cultural authority for their body of scholarship among a British readership. In other words, it is my contention that one of the most important features of orientalist scholarly practices in India was that they were grounded in the Indian political and social context (though of course a distinction should be made between such an enabling context and the uses made of that scholarship by the Company). The courting of *paṇḍit*s through patronage in the legal and cultural-scholarly spheres allowed the Company to claim elements of continuity with past practice in their Indian territories, and to thereby situate themselves within the established languages of South Asian sovereignty and cultural authority. At the same time, however, the *paṇḍit*s' involvement in orientalist scholarship rendered it unstable as a colonial project. The reliance upon *paṇḍit*s for their expertise in Sanskrit literature consistently opened up the possibility of subversion, and enabled their articulation of distinct cultural projects from within the heart of colonial governance. This, in turn, also promoted a prolonged British anxiety over the status and truthfulness of their interlocutors, and measures to more fully control them. The variety of uses made by *paṇḍit*s of their valued place in colonial governance, scholarship, and education will be discussed more fully toward the end of the book.

Paṇḍits and the forging of British political and scholarly legitimacy

Early British orientalist works on Hindu belief systems published primarily in the late 1760s, including those of J. Z. Holwell and Alexander Dow, relied heavily upon Persian or vernacular renderings of Sanskrit texts, as well as upon information on religious and cultural practices provided by a variety of non-*brāhmaṇ* informants. Holwell, for example, sought assistance from members of the *kāyasth*, or scribal caste. Yet the administrative and juridical changes brought about by Hastings in the early 1770s, which shifted the focus of governing regulation to the protection, or reinstatement, of the 'ancient constitution' of the Indians (and in particular, the 'Hindus'), brought about an attendant administrative need for authoritative knowledge about that 'ancient constitution'. Hastings' strategy, of course, was to rule through the conciliation of 'native sensibilities'. The perception and construction of Sanskrit texts as the principal source of information regarding the nature of ancient Indian civilisation has already been discussed. Closely connected to this, there occurred a shift in the British perception of what constituted an authoritative *process* of orientalist knowledge construction in India. On the one hand, the search for a textual basis upon which to construct orientalist knowledge rendered a knowledge of Sanskrit, so as to investigate the contents of the *śāstra*, essential to any worthy scholarly endeavour. On the other hand, orientalists also required regular access to a 'learned *paṇḍit*' who could provide instruction in Sanskrit itself, as well as an explanation of the content (and cultural context) of Sanskrit texts.[5]

On the eve of the Company's governance of Bengal, *paṇḍits* played important social, political, and cultural roles in India, as they had for generations, and to a large extent still do today. *Paṇḍits* are *brāhmaṇs*, members of the highest and ritually purest caste,[6] and are distinguished by their education in Sanskrit, their knowledge of the *Vedas*, and erudition in elements of the *śāstra*.[7] *Paṇḍits* traditionally have earned their livelihood through providing Sanskrit education to *brāhmaṇ* youths. Early European travellers often commented upon this. François Bernier, for example, who resided at the court of the Mughal emperor Aurangzeb between 1659 and 1669, described the presence of numerous 'pendets' in the city of Benares, who, in the manner of the 'School of the Antients', taught Sanskrit to between four and 15 students each thanks to the patronage of wealthy merchants.[8] *Paṇḍits* have also served as spiritual guides and 'legal' experts to the Indian populace at large, as well as to ruling elites. Indeed, *paṇḍits* have sometimes pursued government employ, for example as ministers within 'Hindu' kingdoms such as those of the Marathas. The Benares *paṇḍit* Gāgā Bhaṭṭa played an important role in legitimating the high-caste *kṣatriya* status of the founding Maratha ruler Śivajī, thereby allowing him to take the title '*chatrapati*', identifying him as a great king of the Hindus.[9]

Yet most important, perhaps, is the role which the *paṇḍit* has played in the very embodiment of the Sanskritic, and thereby of India's religious and cultural heritage.[10] *Paṇḍits* were duly recognised by the Company's servants as the authoritative 'guardians' and interpreters of Sanskritic knowledge, and their consultation was sought after (though, as we shall see, this dependence upon 'native' interlocutors was also often fraught with a measure of ambivalence and suspicion). Alexander Dow, though his own interaction with the *paṇḍits* was limited, anticipated the larger shift in official attitudes when he criticised Holwell in 1768 for relying upon 'inferior tribes' or the 'unlearned part of the Brahmins' for his cultural information.[11] This sentiment was made rather more explicit by William Jones in his tenth anniversary discourse, delivered to the Asiatic Society in 1793, in which he announced that 'an accurate knowledge of Sanscrit, and a confidential intercourse with learned Brahmens, are the only means of separating truth from fable'.[12] The extent to which the social and cultural valuation in India of the *paṇḍits*' Sanskrit erudition changed through such colonial recognition is a question which will be considered in subsequent chapters.

In the context of the later eighteenth century, however, the importance placed upon access to the *paṇḍits*' expertise in the production of authoritative orientalist knowledge can profitably be viewed, in the first instance, as an extension of the process to establish the Company's politico-ruling authority in Bengal. The Company's rise to political power in Bengal was the result of a complicated mixture of processes, not least of which was the Company's formidable military strength, its desire to protect its trading interests, and its belief that it possessed inalienable rights in Bengal, granted to it in a *farmān* (decree) by the Mughal emperor in 1717. Following the Company's ascension to the elevated status of *dīvān* (allowing it to collect land revenue) in 1765, the processes of state-building for the remainder of the eighteenth century can be seen to have drawn upon a series of distinct ideologies, both European and Indian in origin. This reflected the 'dual' nature of the Company's authority in India, which was derived from both the British Crown and the Mughal granting of the *dīvānī*.[13] For example, the guiding values of access to impartial justice, and the transparency and accountability of government, which informed many of Warren Hastings' reforms of the 1770s (like those of Cornwallis two decades later), undoubtedly found their origin in European Enlightenment thinking,[14] and took as their object Montesquieu-like visions of despotic Asiatic governance.[15] Equally, though, the concern evinced by Hastings in maintaining a measure of continuity with at least the appearance of the late-Mughal imperial order remained a paramount concern, as did the assuagement of entrenched public expectations of government. Of course, complicating the situation in Bengal was the presence (below the increasingly abstract Mughal imperial structure) of competing ideals of kingship and sovereignty at the local level, which though overlapping in some regards, found their origins in quite distinct Islamic and Hindu religious traditions. In any case, consistent with the Company's newfound role as an 'Indian state' of sorts, the patronage of educated elites, including particularly *brāhmaṇ* Sanskrit scholars, within the judicial administration and in the furtherance of 'indigenous' education, played an important role in the process of 'naturalising' the Company's presence and ruling authority in northern India.

A significant part of the Company's governmental responsibilities in Bengal from 1765 was the execution of civil justice, as questions of succession and inheritance constituted an integral element of the regular collection of taxation revenue. Between 1765 and 1772, however, the Company was content to leave many aspects of judicial administration in the hands of Muhammad Rezā Khān, the *naib dīvān*, at the Bengal *navāb*'s *darbār* (the royal court) in Murshidabad. In this form of indirect rule, Khān exercised the criminal jurisdiction of the *navāb* of Bengal (the king), and together with the British Resident at the *darbār* oversaw the administration of civil justice.[16] While it is difficult to know the exact nature of how civil law had operated under the *navāb*'s exclusive sovereignty prior to 1765 with respect to the 'Hindu' inhabitants of Bengal, questions of inheritance and succession among the Muslim population were often settled by reference to the decision of a *qāzī* (Islamic judge) in the *navāb*'s civil court (the Dīvānī Adālat).[17] It would appear, however, that the majority of similar civil disputes between Hindus were settled by means of arbitration, locally by village *pañcāyat*s (councils) or caste tribunals, for example. These processes would have drawn upon a sense of local custom, but also upon the opinions of *brāhmaṇpaṇḍit*s, who were versed in the behavioural-moral dictates of the *dharmaśāstra*.[18] It needs to be stressed, however, that *paṇḍit*s were in no ways 'lawyers' or 'judges' in the Western sense, but rather, advisors in the normative and religious sphere, which had but a tenuous relationship to actual juridical procedure.[19]

The East India Company 'stood forth' in 1772,[20] dispensing with many of the administrative features of indirect rule, and claiming exclusivity over juridical matters as the 'prerogative of sovereignty'.[21] Warren Hastings' 1772 plan for the administration of justice served to place juridical procedure firmly within the control of the Company by the establishment throughout Bengal and Bihar of a series of regional civil courts (the Dīvānī Adālats) as well as a supreme civil court at Calcutta (the Sadar Dīvānī Adālat) for the hearing of appeals. In keeping with the prescription that civil law be administered in accordance with one's religious affiliation, *paṇḍit*s and *maulavī*s were appointed to each court 'to expound the law ... and assist [European judges] in passing the decree'.[22] In cases to be decided according to 'Hindu law', then, *paṇḍit*s were to issue a *vyavasthā* (opinion) summarising the relevant prescriptions from the corpus of the *dharmaśāstra*, while *maulavī*s decreed a *fatvā* from the *Qur'ān*. Despite the near-continual reorganisation of the regional civil court structure between 1772 and the Bengal Regulations of 1793, as well as jurisdictional disputes between the Company's Sadar Dīvānī Adālat and the British Crown's Supreme Court of Judicature at Calcutta,[23] the role of *paṇḍit*s and *maulavī*s in providing legal guidance to British judges remained relatively consistent throughout the late eighteenth century, and into the early nineteenth as well.[24] *Paṇḍit*s attached to the *adālat*s (courts) consistently provided European judges with *vyavasthā*s in order to decide privately disputed cases in which, for example, several individuals claimed the right of inheritance from a deceased relative.[25] The Khālsā (the treasury), which was actively administered by Europeans from 1772,[26] and the Company's Revenue Council at Fort William also requested that *paṇḍit*s be consulted over questions relating to the succession of *zamīndārī* (land holding) rights through inheritance.[27] Moreover, the *paṇḍit*s' decisions on matters such as these were later used by Philip Francis as evidence in his struggle with Warren Hastings to define *zamīndārī* rights in Bengal as the right of land ownership.[28] Indeed, *paṇḍit*s' *vyavasthā*s were even presented as evidence in the early 1820s as the British Parliament enquired into the cultural validity of the rite of *satī*.[29]

It has been argued in the previous chapter that Hastings' decision in the Judicial Plan of 1772 to administer distinct bodies of law according to religious affiliation was informed by the principles of English common law and his vision of 'Hindu' India as an ancient theocracy, as well as his belief that Indian access to a regularised system of justice would facilitate revenue collection and the security of Company rule through a measure of cultural conciliation. Most characterisations of the process of judicial revision and legal codification in late eighteenth-century Bengal have tended to highlight the role of European, rather than Indian, understandings of law and its role in society and government.[30] In other words, legal measures taken by the Company's government in 1772 have most often been viewed as innovatory to the subcontinent. Yet the steps taken by the Company also proceeded from an understanding that while the imposition of regularised justice was a basic responsibility of government, such juridical reform should include important practical elements of continuity, including the use of *paṇḍits* as legal experts, intended to assuage public opinion through conformity to some late-Mughal governing norms.

The Company first began to consider juridical reform in 1771. The Court of Directors eliminated the arbitrary fines imposed upon claimants, and in order to prevent a substantial increase in cases brought to court, also recommended promoting the method of arbitration for settling disputes, at least in the civil realm. The further reformation of juridical practices was also to be undertaken in order to promote the 'free course of Justice', including the aforementioned administration of law by reference to religious affiliation.[31] In a subsequent survey of local legal procedure in Bengal, however, disputes arose over the extent to which the *navāb*'s government had actually consulted *brāhmaṇs* and administered 'Hindu law'. Samuel Middleton and the Council of Revenue at Murshidabad wrote in April of 1772 that while the Company wished to preserve the appearance of 'Mahomedan government', it would also seem that the *navāb* had excluded 'Gentoos' in the public administration of justice, rendering the Company's plans problematic.[32] The *naib dīvān*, Muhammad Rezā Khān, concurred, objecting to the idea that *brāhmaṇs* might have any official status in the judicial administration, and declaring it to be in contravention to the accepted status of Islamic law as the law of Bengal.[33]

Members of the Council at Fort William, however, clearly understood that *brāhmaṇ paṇḍits* played a significant role at the *darbār*, and in a response to Khān, it was noted that the consultation of *brāhmaṇs* in 'all matters respecting inheritance and the particular laws and usages of the casts of Gentoos' was viewed as 'the invariable practice of all

Mahomedan Governments in Indostan'.[34] Robert Travers has suggested that the *naib dīvān*'s vehement denial that *paṇḍit*s played any role in the *navāb*'s judiciary likely reflected his unhappiness with the increasingly active role the Company was beginning to take in governing Bengal and his desire to maintain the integrity of Muslim rule, rather than necessarily the actual judicial practices in question.[35] Certainly later correspondence between Murshidabad and the Council in Calcutta points to the existence of the long-standing practice in Bengal of the *navāb* allowing Hindus to settle property and inheritance disputes privately by reference to *paṇḍit*s and the *dharmaśāstra*.[36] Rosane Rocher has also recently argued that it was accepted practice for the *navāb*'s government to encourage private arbitration by reference to *paṇḍit*s.[37] Moreover, in a land dispute settled by the Council of Revenue in Murshidabad in June of 1772, the written opinion of the *naib dīvān* on this case cited the opinion of the 'learned ... according to the precepts of the sacred scriptures', referring most probably to *paṇḍit*s and the *śāstra*.[38]

Recent research has also suggested that the *navāb* did indeed sponsor *brāhmaṇ* scholars (such as the famed legal scholar Jagannātha Tarkapañcānana)[39] and poets, as well as Vaiṣṇava communities, as a part of his cultural patronage activities. Indeed, in 1836 Rādhākānt Deb recalled that the Muslim government were 'great patrons of learning', and 'bestowed many villages on the Pundits and others, for the promotion of education'.[40] Other Hindu groups, such as *kāyasth*s (scribes) and *vaidya*s (medical scholars), also formed an integral part of the *navāb*'s administration. While this evidence can not yet be deemed definitive, it does at least point to a wider pattern of *navābī* patronage to elite non-Muslim groups as comprising an important element of the *navāb*'s political legitimation. Certainly patronage of this sort would have been especially important given the existence of contesting claims to local sovereignty by large Hindu *zamīndārs* (land holders).[41] Of course, the Company's understanding of the operation of law in pre-colonial Bengal, especially with respect to Hindu communities, was an over-simplication of a complex, fluid, and even overlapping series of institutions and practices. Even so, Hastings' appointment of *paṇḍit*s to advise in civil legal matters with respect to the 'Hindu' population would seem to represent a measure of continuity with established late-Mughal modes of governance, and an effort to produce political and ruling legitimation for the Company by reference to that late-Mughal political structure.

In order to implement the Judicial Plan of 1772, Bengal's court system required substantial expansion. In particular, to fill the demand for *brāhmaṇ* legal advisors, both within the court system itself and in the writing of legal digests from the Sanskrit *dharmaśāstra*, the Company recruited *paṇḍit*s from the courts of prominent local men and minor Hindu *rāja*s. In this respect, the Company's practice of hiring *paṇḍit*s for their legal service also mirrored wider, established indigenous 'Hindu' modes of cultural patronage to *brāhmaṇ* scholars.[42] This was an activity considered to confer upon the patron spiritual merit and social standing, both also being integral elements of the legitimation to rule.[43] For example, the well-known *paṇḍit* Bāṇeśvara Vidyālaṅkara, who was appointed in 1773 to work on the Company's first legal digest, the *Vivādārṇavasetu,* was hired from Mahārājā Nabakṛṣṇa, a prominent Hindu merchant-trader (and former banian to Robert Clive) who maintained in Calcutta a *sabhā* of some of the most celebrated Sanskrit scholars and poets in Bengal, such as the poet-singer Haru Ṭhākur. This prominent member of the city's emerging *bhadralok* (lit. 'respectable') community had also been patron to two of Bengal's most authoritative legal *paṇḍit*s, Rādhākānta Tarkavāgīśa and Jagannātha Tarkapañcānana, both of whom were hired by the Company to author their second legal digest two decades later.[44] Rādhākānta also served as legal advisor to the Sadar Dīvānī Adālat.

In addition, the Company competed with potential political rivals in the countryside through patronage activities. The powerful *zamīndār* of Nadia, *rāja* Kṛṣṇa Candra, was a prominent patron of cultural activity, including the composition and performance of *Mangalkābya*s (vernacular narrative poetry)[45] and Sanskrit scholarship. Nadia was considered the foremost centre of Sanskrit scholarship in Bengal, enjoying a formidable reputation for the production of *nyāya* (logic) scholars. The *rāja* financially supported much of this activity, providing teachers with rent-free lands for their support, and students with monthly stipends. He also conferred titles upon graduates, and funded *yajña*s (sacrificial ceremonies) for *brāhmaṇ*s.[46] In 1773 the Company hired several of the *paṇḍit*s who compiled their first legal digest away from the Nadia court,[47] in effect usurping the role of cultural patron. The Company continued the financial support of Sanskrit studies in Nadia, and in the early 1770s also persisted with the established practice of issuing of tax-free grants from land revenue income for the support of scholarly *brāhmaṇ* communities not associated directly with government service.[48]

Outside the realm of purely legal scholarship and service, similar patterns of wider cultural patronage served to underwrite the Company's rule. In addition to his active patronage of European orientalists such as

Nathaniel Halhed and Charles Wilkins, Hastings privately employed both *paṇḍit*s and Muslim *littérateurs*, in the established style of Bengal's most wealthy and powerful men. These including the poet of Persian, Minnat (Mīr Kamar al-Dīn),[49] as well as *paṇḍit* Rādhākānta Tarkavāgīśa, who composed for Hastings the *Purāṇārthaprākāśa*, a Sanskrit digest of the *Purāṇa*s.[50] This was repeated on a larger, institutional scale within the realm of 'native' education. In Calcutta, the establishment in 1781 of a *madrasā* to educate Muslims for government service was described by Hastings as being a responsibility consistent with the norms of legitimate governance in Persia and India. Calcutta, however, was by the early 1780s already being perceived as 'the seat of a great empire',[51] and the Company's status as *dīvān* in effect reflected its standing as the paramount political and military power of Bengal. Further up the Ganges river, in Benares, there existed a somewhat more confused and ambiguous political and diplomatic situation for the Company which in itself necessitated concerted efforts in the construction of legitimacy. The establishment of the Benares Sanskrit College there in 1791 served as the 'flagship' for the Company's early patronage activities, highlighting their eagerness to preserve and perpetuate Sanskrit tradition.

In the eighteenth century, the city of Benares was not only amongst the most sacred of northern India's 'Hindu' pilgrimage sites, but also possessed a population of some 200,000 people and served as a principal hub of economic activity in the *doab*.[52] Merchants from Nagpur, Pune, Hyderabad, Agra, and the Punjab were attracted to the city and region, while *gosāīṃ*s (mendicant trader-soldiers) used Benares as the hub to an extensive network in the transportation of goods across northern India and into the Maratha territories of the Deccan.[53] A diverse community of merchant bankers provided insurance, money-lending, and credit note facilities for traders and pilgrims to the holy city, as well as facilitating the collection and payment of land taxation.[54] The city also drew, in addition to pilgrims, students from across the subcontinent in search of religious and literary instruction in Sanskrit.[55] As such, Benares was, at the dawn of British imperialism in the region, both an economically and culturally important city.

Yet Benares also represented very much a colonial frontier for the Company, as it was bordered by the powerful late-Mughal successor states of the Marathas. Indeed, Hastings often noted that the Marathas were 'dangerous neighbours' who threatened the integrity of the Company's land holdings and revenue stream.[56] Many prominent Maratha families lived part of the year in Benares, and consistent with their political identity as the 'upholders of Hindu *dharma*',[57] lavishly patronised religious activities, and constructed many of the city's landmarks, including several of the waterfront *ghāṭs*.[58] The region of Benares had been ceded to the Company's sovereignty in 1775 by the *navāb* of Awadh, and as in Bengal, the Company ruled indirectly at first, through the offices of the *rāja* of Benares and his *bhūmihār brāhmaṇ* subordinates.[59] But the nature of that rule was also inherently fragile. At the time of *Rāja* Cet Siṃh's (Chait Singh) rebellion in 1781, which was sparked by increased revenue demands made by Warren Hastings,[60] there was widespread disruption to the Company's authority in Benares, as many commercial and administrative elites supported the *rāja*. The *naupaṭṭī sabhā*, an exclusive organisation of trader-bankers who largely controlled that industry, gave the Company only ambiguous support.[61] In the years that followed, the Company attempted to solidify its rule through locally authoritative figures, including this time through the chief magistrate 'Ali Ibrāhim Khān, a member of the old Persianate service class of the Mughal empire. Similarly, the Company sought to settle property and inheritance disputes in the region with reference to Hindu and Muslim religious law, and appointed both *maulavīs* and *paṇḍits* to the Benares Dīvānī Adālat.[62] The increased political profile of the British Residency within the administration of Benares during the tenure of Jonathan Duncan (1788–1795),[63] however, meant that the Company continued to face a series of local challenges to its sovereignty. Maratha princes and their agents regularly demonstrated the precarious nature of the Company's political and judicial authority, as they broke the laws of the city with relative impunity. For example, 'Nanajee', a prince of Nagpur, abducted and killed a merchant whom he suspected of cheating him in 1792. Jonathan Duncan was only able to write to his superiors in Calcutta to inform them that 'I saw no advantage, but on the contrary, much risk, in adopting any offensive steps either towards them or their agent ...'[64]

The establishment of the Benares Sanskrit College by Duncan in late 1791 was ostensibly intended for 'the preservation and cultivation of the law, literature, and religion' of the Hindus.[65] Yet the Company acknowledged that the patronage of Sanskrit learning in Benares 'must be extremely flattering to their [Hindus'] prejudices, and tend greatly to conciliate their minds towards the British Government'.[66] Founded with the assistance of the *rāja* of Benares, the Sanskrit College was run by its principal, Kāśīnātha Śarmā, who had formerly been an assistant to the orientalist Charles Wilkins as well as Jonathan Duncan. The college employed at least nine *paṇḍits* in various capacities, in addition to subsidising the maintenance costs for their *brāhmaṇ* students. These *paṇḍits* taught only the 'traditional' branches of Sanskrit literature, including *vyākaraṇa*, *vedānta*, *nyāya*, and the *jyotiḥśāstra*.[67] It is apparent that Duncan intended that the patronage of purely 'traditional' Sanskrit learning would not only provide legitimacy to the Company's tenuous government in the region by rendering it as a 'protector' and 'cultivator' of Sanskrit literature, but also through the direct patronage of the city's diverse *brāhmaṇ paṇḍit* community, members of whom were viewed with respect and reverence by a wide cross-section of the city's inhabitants, including the Maratha aristocracy and the merchant-banking community. Such forms of patronage, it was clearly hoped, would serve to further solidify the social basis of the Company's authority in the city, while marginalising other competing patrons.

Institutionalising the cultural authority of the *paṇḍit*

It has been argued by Bernard Cohn that in the late eighteenth century, the European preparation and translation of Sanskrit digests of 'Hindu law', the codification of Indian languages into representative grammars and dictionaries, as well as the partial institutionalisation of Sanskrit-based education, was undertaken by the Company largely in an attempt to break the *paṇḍits*' perceived 'monopoly' on Sanskrit-based knowledge, thereby making it potentially available to all in an uncorrupted form.[68] Kate Teltscher has memorably described this process, with respect to William Jones, as an attempt to 'out-pandit' the *paṇḍits*.[69] Certainly the legal codification project begun under Jones and the subsequent translation of ancient *dharmaśāstra* texts, including the publication of Colebrooke's *Digest*, was intended to gain control of Indian legal knowledge, and had resulted by the 1820s and 1830s in a substantial lessening of British judges' dependence upon *paṇḍits* for access to 'Hindu law'[70] (though *paṇḍits* did still play important roles in the judiciary well into the middle of the nineteenth century, however, not least as judges in *zilā* [district] courts). The establishment of Fort William College in 1800 also served to further lessen the dependence upon *paṇḍits* for language instruction through the formalisation of Indian language learning among Company servants, and the simultaneous publication of Indian language grammars and vocabularies.[71] Indeed, the first Sanskrit-English dictionary, published by H. H. Wilson in 1819 explicitly in order to enable the wider European cultivation of the language, was based upon a compilation of Sanskrit lexicons earlier prepared by *paṇḍits* at Fort William College.[72]

These efforts at codification and institutionalisation have been interpreted as British attempts to turn Indian languages and cultures into 'instruments of colonial rule', but may also be profitably viewed as an attempt to bring under British control the *paṇḍit*-orientalist dynamic: the site of orientalist knowledge production. In this section of this chapter it is argued that while Cohn's vision of the Company wresting control of Sanskrit-based knowledge from Indian elites is in essence valid, it tells only a part of the story. The more important element to be considered here is that both the processes of codification and institutionalisation served to more formally enshrine the cultural authority of these elites within the social and governing contexts of the Company's realm. In other words, these processes, while seeking to undermine the *paṇḍits*' control over matters relating to Sanskrit-based knowledge,[73] simultaneously strengthened their ascendant sociocultural status. The *paṇḍits*' entrance into a more substantial public sphere through government service helped to further consolidate their authority within both the realms of governance and wider Indian society. Understanding something of this process will allow us to enquire further about the ways in which Indian elites utilised their positions and the authority thus enshrined, especially within the realm of educational and cultural projects, in Chapter 6.

In the early years of the Company's rule, *paṇḍits* were initially reluctant to expand their disclosure of the principles of Sanskrit and the *śāstra* beyond that which was involved in the execution of their legal duties. Nathaniel Halhed, for example, noted in the introduction to his 1776 *Code of Gentoo Laws*, that 'the Pundits who compiled the Code were to a man resolute in rejecting all his solicitations for instruction in this dialect, and that the persuasion and influence of the Governor-General were in vain exerted to the same purpose'.[74] Following the compilation of the *Code*, however, Halhed did manage to study Sanskrit with a *paṇḍit* for several years,[75] though he also described the prevalence of a religious conviction among the *paṇḍits* which prohibited them from disclosing the content of the *śāstra* to Europeans: 'the Pundit who imparted a small portion of his language to me, has by no means escaped the censure of his countrymen ... [and] he has invariably refused to develop a single article of his religion'.[76] William Jones also found it difficult to procure the services of a *paṇḍit* in 1785, and as such, originally learned Sanskrit from an elderly non-*brāhmaṇ vaidya* (medical) scholar at Nadia, and even then, the man placed strict conditions upon his pedagogic relationship with Jones, such that he also would only disclose elements of Sanskrit grammar.[77]

The 1780s and 1790s, however, proved to be a time of significant transformation for the relationship between *paṇḍits* and the Company's servants, as increasingly, *paṇḍits* became involved in a host of occupations outside the strictly legal sphere. For example, *paṇḍits* employed privately by European orientalists began to facilitate access to most areas of Sanskrit scholarship to further their pursuit of Indian cultural-textual history, and several *paṇḍits* were employed by the Company within educational institutions such as Benares Sanskrit College. Whether this shift in the relationship between *paṇḍits* and the Company and its servants was due to the gradual erosion of the *paṇḍits*' traditional sources of patronage within Indian society, as has often been suggested,[78] or was due to the *paṇḍits*' gradual acceptance of the Company as the legitimate government, and hence an unproblematic employer, is difficult to establish definitively.[79] What is clear, though, is that this relationship soon became an important one for the legitimation of all forms of orientalist research, as well as a source of intense British unease.

It has already been noted that the *paṇḍits*' high social standing and their status as the 'guardians' of Sanskrit-based religious knowledge were highly valued by the Company in their attempts to create political legitimacy in the late eighteenth century, as well as for the construction of social legitimacy for the legal codification project. Similarly, within the realm of orientalist research, the acknowledgement of a working relationship with a *paṇḍit* became within the pages of *Asiatick Researches* a mark of professional legitimacy. It was, in other words, common practice for orientalists to invoke within their published scholarship the assistance which a *paṇḍit* had given them as a means to produce authority for their particular interpretation of Indian cultural history. It was the *paṇḍits*, after all, who possessed the knowledge of Sanskrit grammar and vocabulary, of the content of Sanskrit texts, as well as relatively unfettered access to Sanskrit manuscripts which Europeans often found difficult to acquire. Samuel Davis, for example, noted on the first page of his 1790 article 'On the Astronomy of the Hindus', which spoke to the contentious debates which surrounded the status of Indian astronomy, that the Sanskrit *jyotiḥśāstra* texts were easily understandable with 'the help of a *Paṇḍit*'.[80] William Jones had in 1793 praised the 'confidential intercourse' which orientalists enjoyed with *paṇḍits* as essential to the discovery of truth. This sentiment was echoed by Colebrooke the following year, when he called for a rejection of all orientalist work prior to Wilkins' 1785 translation of the *Bhagavad Gītā*, which had been produced with the help of several *paṇḍit*s in Benares, as essentially unauthoritative.[81] Here Colebrooke was undoubtedly thinking of the fact that Wilkins had translated a significant Sanskrit text, but no less important to the perception of authoritativeness was the manner in which he effected it.[82]

The city of Benares also played a prominent role in the process of validating orientalist scholarship. Described as the 'seat of the Hindoo Religion' by Warren Hastings,[83] Charles Wilkins requested that he be transferred to the city, the 'grand seminary of India', in order to have access to Sanskrit texts of 'indubitable authority'. Benares' reputation as a city of antiquity, Hindu religious importance, and Sanskrit erudition was well known to Europeans, and Wilkins considered Benares as the most suitable place to gain access to 'able Brahmans' for an authoritative elucidation of these works, so that he might present to the English literary world a 'true idea' of Indian history and mythology.[84] Even in the nineteenth century, the standing of Benares as the home of 'authentic' Hinduism continued to underscore orientalist claims, as in 1831, when H. H. Wilson cited the time which he spent at Benares Sanskrit College studying Sanskrit literature with the city's *paṇḍit*s as a professional asset in his letter of application for the Boden Professorship of Sanskrit in Oxford.[85] Similarly, Warren Hastings, on the eve of his impeachment trial in 1787, had collected on his behalf testimonials from Benares *paṇḍit*s which lauded his enlightened governing policies and protection of the holy city.[86]

As *paṇḍit*s were drawn into the realm of the Company and its servants, these relationships initially maintained a highly personalised character, even within the judicial service. Late eighteenth-century orientalists tended to employ privately a *paṇḍit* who was known to them through their work in the legal system, or by virtue of having worked for another Company servant. In this respect, the Asiatic Society in Calcutta may be viewed as serving as an informal network which eased British orientalists' procurement of the services of a *paṇḍit*. Rādhākānta Tarkavāgīśa, after working for Warren Hastings, was employed by John Shore and then, somewhat later, by William Jones, finally accepting an appointment to the Sadar Dīvānī Adālat in 1794.[87] Similarly, appointments to the judiciary were often conducted through personal channels, as in the case of *paṇḍit* Govardhana Kaula, who was employed by Sir Robert Chambers and had applied to an official position within the Supreme Court at Calcutta on the recommendation of Charles Wilkins' *paṇḍit*, Kāśīnātha Śarmā.[88] In addition, Kāśīnātha then went on to be the first principal of the Benares Sanskrit College in 1791, after having served as Jonathan Duncan's own personal *paṇḍit* for a time, as well as having previously compiled a Sanskrit-English lexicon for William Jones.[89]

Yet given the importance which the Company and its orientalists placed upon their relationship with *paṇḍits*, both in the legitimation of their government and individual scholastic endeavours, it is little wonder that they also sought its more aggressive regulation and control. At the heart of the *paṇḍit*-orientalist relationship was a deep-seated ambivalence, and apparently little in the way of trust. This most often manifested itself as suspicion and doubt, on the part of Europeans, with respect to the intentions and truthfulness of their Indian interlocutors. William Jones (in)famously decided to learn Sanskrit as he felt that his 'native' assistants were largely without integrity,[90] and he could 'no longer bear to be at the mercy of our pundits, who deal out Hindu law as they please, and make it at reasonable rates, when they cannot find it ready made'.[91] Jones in particular seemed obsessed with discovering ways in which to guarantee the truthfulness of *paṇḍits*' statements in the judicial setting, enquiring at length, for example, into 'traditional' oaths which the *paṇḍits* might be persuaded to take.[92]

This ambivalence can also be found in European concerns over the way in which their assistants were perceived by the Indian populace, as well as by their own peers. After all, the unblemished reputation of *paṇḍits* appointed to the Company's legal service was a paramount concern by the 1780s if, as Jones noted, 'the Hindus may be convinced, that we decide on their law from the best information we can procure'.[93] In other words, the legitimacy of the Company's legal apparatus depended upon the acceptance of the *paṇḍits* working therein by the Indian populace. In this respect, Jones had drafted the most well-respected *paṇḍit* he could find in Bengal to lend his name to the second legal digest: the aged and venerable Jagannātha Tarkapañcānana.[94] Governor-General Cornwallis remarked that the compilation would 'derive infinite credit and authority both, from the annexation of his name as a compiler, and from his assistance'.[95] Consistent with this sentiment, Governor-General John Shore removed two *paṇḍits* from the Company's Supreme Court in 1794, remarking that they were 'not held in repute', and replaced them with two *paṇḍits* who had worked with Jones on his legal digest.[96] Oaths were once again introduced into the legal system for *paṇḍits* in the Regulations of 1793, to ensure they conducted their duties with 'uprightness',[97] though most *paṇḍits* evidently objected to taking them on 'religious grounds'.[98]

But by the 1790s, certainly, the Company attempted itself to determine a *paṇḍit's* cultural standing, and to bring his reputation within the purview of British oversight, by taking more formal control over the *paṇḍits'* scholarly training and activity. When Jones' 'confidential intercourse with Brahmens' was located within the context of the facilities of institutionalised education by the early nineteenth century, rather than being informally affiliated with one British individual, an accessible and Company-governed resource with which to authorise orientalist scholarship was thought to have been created. This authority might then have been used in the policing of 'authentic' views of Indian civilisation, by emphasising a particular knowledge-making process.

In the Sanskrit College of Benares, the Company had found the fortunate confluence of nominal Company control over the pedagogical process[99] with the city's sacred character and scholarly reputation. Certainly, the college soon provided an institutional base for the education of 'native assistants' to the courts in a regularised and ultimately controllable fashion.[100] By 1794 the Company was undertaking a wide-ranging review of the *paṇḍits* appointed to its lesser courts, renewing only those it deemed qualified by training.[101] Then, in 1795, the Governor-General ordered that the informal, patronage-based appointment of *paṇḍits* to law offices be abolished in favour of graduates from the programme administered under the auspices of Benares Sanskrit College.[102] In time, the college also served to centralise and coordinate the systematic collection and copying of Sanskrit manuscripts, so that they could be made widely available to European orientalists.[103]

Yet early events at Benares Sanskrit College demonstrated that the processes of institutionalisation, and even codification, served neither to regulate and control the *paṇḍit*-orientalist dynamic, nor produce the kind of freedom from anxiety about their interlocutors which the Company desired. In the first years of its operation, the college's principal, Kāśīnātha Śarmā as well as other *paṇḍits* employed at the college were dismissed for 'corruption', having apparently thought that the stipends paid by the Company to attract students were in fact a part of their own personal salaries.[104] The College seemingly also failed as a substantial source of legal specialists, providing just three or four graduates to the Company's courts by 1810.[105] Potentially most damaging to orientalist claims, however, was a 1799 revelation from the very heart of the Company's Sanskrit enterprise. Francis Wilford, who had retired to Benares to pursue mythographical history, complained that the Benares Sanskrit College's professor *paṇḍit* Vidyānanda had 'imposed on him forged extracts' of *Purāṇik* text, and brought the 'authenticity' of his orientalist scholarship into some doubt.[106] This realisation was made public in a revealing foreward to Wilford's 1805 *Asiatick Researches* essay 'On the Sacred Isles in the West'.[107] Wilford explained that he had directed his *paṇḍit* to 'make extracts' from the *Purāṇas*, as he perceived in these texts the 'most interesting legends bearing an astonishing affinity with those of the western mythologists'. But 'in order to avoid the trouble of consulting books', Wilford explained, Vidyānanda had 'conceived the idea of framing legends from what he recollected from the *Purāṇas*, and from what he picked up in conversation with me'. Wilford claimed, however, that the forgeries had done little to undermine his principal conclusions regarding the historical links between India and Britain, as Vidyānanda had 'studied to introduce as much truth as he could, to obviate the danger of immediate detection'.[108] Similarly, H. T. Colebrooke, in an essay in the same volume of the journal, dismissed the ability of *paṇḍits* to perpetrate fraud at any great length, claiming that such 'interpolations' had always been discovered, and assumedly always would be.[109] Such caveats, however, must have provided but little comfort to European orientalists, whose scholarship relied so heavily upon Sanskrit textual sources.

In this regard, doubts about the character of the *brāhmaṇ* informant and the veridicality of textual sources continued well into the nineteenth century, and served to undermine notions of independent or veridical Indian intellectual achievement. The fear of forgery remained a topic for extensive debate among orientalists.[110] Other historians, such as James Mill, for example, in his 1817 *The History of British India*, repeated Jones' attack on the 'monopoly' of sacred knowledge which the *brāhmaṇs* held with respect to legislation and the administration of justice,[111] and invoked established arguments that Indian claims to an advanced knowledge of science in antiquity might be founded upon textual forgery.[112] Earlier, the renowned Scottish historian William Roberston argued that the monopoly which *brāhmaṇs* held over sacred knowledge, and their propensity to 'conceal truth' when discovered, prevented the downfall of 'false religion',[113] while philosopher Dugald Stewart came to believe that Sanskrit itself was an imposition and a fraud, constructed by the *paṇḍits* from a knowledge of ancient Greek, and intended to keep their sacred knowledge a secret from India's masses.[114] In addition, missionary William Ward denounced at length the Catholic-like avarice of *brāhmaṇ* priests.[115] Most notably, the Revd Thomas Maurice, shaken by the revelation that Wilford's scholarship was based upon forged Sanskrit texts, and the sceptical uses of orientalist and mythographical research to undermine Biblical narrative, claimed that India's *paṇḍits* were not only wholly unreliable, but had also exaggerated their chronology and stolen elements of Christian scripture for their own mythology.[116]

Yet despite allegations of fraud and untrustworthiness, the role of *paṇḍits* as authoritative intermediaries, tutors, and sources of legitimacy remained important to the Company's governing and scholarly activities, though the tension and ambiguity remained. In particular, the high social status of the *paṇḍits* was coveted by the Company, as was their perceived 'intellectual leadership' amongst the Indian populace. While within the legal sphere, *paṇḍits*' authority may have become subject to orientalist expertise and government regulation, as a group, their cultural authority amongst the greater Indian population remained an important resource to attempt to harness. As we will see in later chapters, the 'constructive orientalist' educator James Ballantyne relied heavily upon the *paṇḍits* both to help explain and translate difficult philosophical texts in Sanskrit, as well as for their role in 'naturalising' his pedagogical programme amongst the students of Benares College. The continuing dilemma for nineteenth-century European educators and missionaries in India was, therefore, that the cultural authority of *brāhmaṇs* represented the key to the greater success of their respective projects, while they also posed a principal impediment by virtue of the perception of their moral and civilisational shortcomings. As such, this elite group had to be courted and simultaneously disavowed.

Though the Company increasingly attempted to bring the *paṇḍit*'s status, as well as the dynamic of orientalist knowledge production, under its own determining control by the turn of the nineteenth century, orientalist practices revealed themselves to be inherently unstable and uncontrollable as a colonial enterprise. Subsequent chapters will explore how *paṇḍits* utilised their role as intermediaries of a sort, between the colonial government and northern India's community of Sanskrit scholars, to unambiguously assert distinct cultural projects from within the heart of colonial education. For although *paṇḍits* ensconced within institutions such as Benares College would become the symbolic key to authorising within wider Indian society the improving educational projects of nineteenth-century 'high imperialism', the vision of brahmanical intellectual leadership within Indian society so forcefully articulated by the colonial state also became a relatively unbounded and potentially subversive cultural resource, which could be redirected by *paṇḍit*s to the forging of renewed cultural identities. The next chapter begins to substantiate these arguments by demonstrating that while nineteenth-century British liberalism appeared to distinguish itself from the orientalist scholarship of earlier decades, there were important continuities and cross-influences, including that many Company officials understood that winning over their *brāhmaṇ* intermediaries was crucial to realising the success of the emerging imperial-liberal project of 'improvement'.

3
An Empire of the Understanding

While an integral element of the East India Company's governance of India in the eighteenth century was its policies of cultural conciliation and the courting of indigenous elites for the influence they wielded, historiographies of the nineteenth century have tended to highlight the relative power and aloofness of the British imperial state. Certainly, the attitudes of cultural superiority and self-confidence which were a part of British strategies of rule after 1800 have frequently been interpreted as integral to the 'imperial century', and contrasted with the apparently 'friendlier' cosmopolitanism of the early empire. Of course, few would care to argue that British rule of India in 1772 closely resembled that of 1835, nor would many deny that the personal qualities and governing policies of Warren Hastings and William Bentinck were significantly distinct. But there are important reasons for questioning the viability of drawing broad chronologically-based distinctions about the 'character' of Britain's empire in India, and the usefulness of such distinctions for a historiography which recognises complex metamorphoses in the broad variety of personal and institutional relationships which composed and underpinned the imperial state. Ascribing to the Company's eighteenth-century state a character of cultural 'tolerance' based upon selected cross-cultural marriages, for example, obscures the inherent violence of the Company's expansion, in much the same way as overemphasising the importance of T. B. Macaulay's intemperate rhetoric in his (in)famous minute of 1835, which promoted the virtues of English, has served to elide the greater significance of its critiques in determining educational policy in the 1840s and 1850s.

This chapter, therefore, questions the attribution of a fundamental disjuncture between the late eighteenth and early nineteenth century based upon perceptions of a drastic change in cultural policy within colonial governance, by tracing elements of the genealogy of liberal thought, and examining the reemergence of orientalism as a strategy for improving Indian society in the first decades of the nineteenth century. On the one hand, liberal thought, with its emphasis upon a comparative national hierarchy and 'progress' through education and rational legislation, nevertheless drew substantially from early orientalist research, and reproduced many of its principal concerns. On the other hand, orientalism was similarly transformed by liberal thought in the early nineteenth century, and emerged less as an unabashed 'appreciation' for Indian society, than a shifting set of localised strategies to produce forms of cultural authority intended first and foremost to secure British rule and bring about Indian 'improvement'.

Most importantly, for our purposes here, was the continued focus of orientalists upon utilising forms of Indian authority in the furtherance of colonial projects. While the *paṇḍits*' authority in the legal sphere may have been compromised by British oversight, it emerged once again as a crucial element of 'constructive orientalist' educational initiatives, simultaneous to British attempts to increase control over their Indian interlocutors. Thus, people who identified themselves as 'orientalists' in the early nineteenth century emphasised the imposition of Indian 'progress' through Indian languages, textual traditions, and a recognition of the intellectual leadership role of the *paṇḍit* in Indian society. The characterisations of orientalism and anglicism as wholly oppositional has, in fact, obscured important elements of continuity between them. For nineteenth-century orientalists, Indian 'tradition' was valued not necessarily for its intrinsic value, (though this was certainly a part of their strategy), but principally for its conciliatory value amongst the Indian *paṇḍits*, and as a precursor to the introduction of Western knowledge. This sense of the entangledness of two seemingly distinct genealogies of British thought serves principally in this chapter, therefore, to emphasise the transformations in orientalism during the early nineteenth century, and to recognise its continued importance in strategies of British governance.

Orientalism and liberalism

British thinking about history, the nature of knowledge, and the relations of human civilisation underwent a series of transformations as Britain's eighteenth-century empire was expanded and consolidated. Indeed, the essentially contradictory elements which combined in the scholarship of William Jones became distinguished, as people increasingly turned away from the intellectual hegemony of the Bible and the conception of knowledge as 'providential'[1] and unfragmented at the commencement of human civilisation, towards an understanding of knowledge as the gradual accumulation of truth, or rather, as a progressive enterprise governed by scientific and rational modes of enquiry.[2] Historical scholarship became much more a part of a forward-looking project of societal improvement, rather than a retrospective enquiry into the wholeness of mankind's first knowledge. Moreover, the Biblical conception of the original relation of nations was neglected in the new focus upon a hierarchy of nations, graded from savage to refined, based largely upon their relative progress in material and mental pursuits. For most Britons in the early nineteenth century, knowledge was expected to effect 'progress', and as such, the original orientalist project of the eighteenth century to recover the 'ancient knowledge' of India came to be regarded by many as a largely trivial pursuit.

The text which has most often been used to illustrate the transformation in thinking about the nature of India's relationship to Britain, in historical and civilisational terms, is James Mill's *The History of British India* (1817),[3] which gained influence both through Mill's own employment with the Company, and the *History*'s status as required reading for the Company's civil service.[4] The *History* offered up what Mill considered to be a wide-ranging critique of almost all aspects of eighteenth-century orientalist scholarship: appreciative appraisals of Sanskrit, for example, were rejected with the pointed phrase: 'it is remarkable ... to find that which is a defect and a deformity of language, celebrated as a perfection by European literati'.[5] At its core, this critique of early orientalism represented an attempt to replace previous analyses of the state of Indian civilisation with a distinctive methodology, and thereby to reassess India's relative status in the worldwide scale of nations, as an inherent critique of the British administration of India.

The History of British India took as its basis the notion of civilisational hierarchy, and that the nations of the world undertook a gradual, and uneven, progress through that hierarchy: from rude to cultivated, ignorance to knowledge, simplicity to complexity, and from the concrete to the abstract.[6] This was an idea central to eighteenth-century Scottish Enlightenment scholarship, having been elaborated by Adam Smith, Adam Ferguson, John Millar, and Dugald Stewart.[7] Adam Smith, for example, was initially interested to explain historically the generation of property rights in law, and did so by reference to a framework in which these rights necessarily developed along with the gradual political and economic refinement of society. Smith posited four basic 'stages' of civilisation in this framework, which advanced from that of hunters, to shepherds, to agriculturists, and finally, to a commercial civilisation. With each step, the economic, social, and political structures of civilisation become more complex as well as potentially inegalitarian, and as such, an increasingly elaborate set of laws would be required to define and protect land ownership. In his most famous work, *The Wealth of Nations*, Smith utilised this framework to argue that civilisational progress was closely linked to economic development, which in itself was based in free trade, the division of labour, and the protection of rights of property.[8]

Dugald Stewart described Smith's work as 'conjectural history', a term which could equally be applied to much of Scottish Enlightenment scholarship. In short, conjectural history encompassed scholarship which took as its object the origins and development of 'cultivated language', the origins of science and the arts, the development of government, and the improvement of the human mind. Stewart noted, however, that the discipline of history itself could provide few insights into these processes, and as such, conjecture based in a knowledge of 'human nature' and 'the circumstances of society' must supplement the analysis.[9] In this regard, John Millar elaborated the progress of human society from a rudimentary organisation to a complex commercial society which protects its citizens through law and government with reference to the notion that all people share a common human nature, defined as a 'disposition and capacity for improving his condition, by the exertion of which, he is carried on from one degree of advancement to another'.[10] Of course, most writers of the time agreed that civilisations could degenerate, following the fall of the Roman Empire, for example, as well as become 'stuck' in a certain stage of advancement, such as in the case of native Americans.

In many ways, James Mill was writing within a paradigm substantiated by William Robertson, a prominent and highly regarded Scottish historian of the late eighteenth century. Robertson utilised information on distant civilisations gathered as a part of Britain's imperial expansion to verify and elaborate upon the theorisations of earlier stages of civilisational development and test the notion of a universal human nature, though ultimately he was interested in the conditions for the expansion of Christianity. (Mill drew explicit parallels, for example, between his own writing of a history of India without knowledge of Indian languages, or direct experience of India, by reference to

Robertson's important work, *The History of America*, which had been produced by an author who had 'never beheld America'.)[11] In his *Historical Disquisition*, Robertson drew upon early orientalist findings that ancient India was 'more early civilized', and that Indians had 'made extraordinary progress in science and arts'.[12] He used orientalist publications to elaborate his definition of what constituted high 'civilisation' in the ancient world by reference to the 'advanced' division of labour to be found in caste, for example, as well as India's longstanding system of justice, the presence of large ancient public structures, and literary achievements in Sanskrit, such as the *Mahābhārata*.[13] Importantly, Robertson also reflected upon Indians' early attainments in philosophy and science. In this regard, he argued explicitly within a universal ('conjectural') frame of development:

> ... as soon as men arrive at that stage in social life, when they can turn their attention to speculative inquiries, the human mind will, in every region of the earth, display nearly the same powers, and proceed in its investigations and discoveries by nearly similar steps.[14]

Drawing upon Wilkins' 1785 translation of the *Bhagavad Gītā*, Robertson argued that Indians were interested in the 'same speculations which occupied the philosophers of Greece', and that in the realm of ethics, Indians anticipated the teachings of the Stoics.[15] It was Indian knowledge of astronomy, however, which most clearly distinguished their early civilisation from that of the Greeks. The Indian method of predicting eclipses, for example, 'founded on principles and on an analysis of the motion of the sun and moon', was superior to that of ancient Greece and Chaldea, based as that was upon 'the observation of a certain period or cycle'.[16] Moreover, Robertson argued on the basis of Jean-Sylvain Bailly's findings that ancient Indian astronomical tables demonstrated their advanced scientific knowledge in humanity's infancy, and that such knowledge was surely based on observation, together with an understanding of trigonometry, rather than retrospective calculation as had sometimes been charged.[17]

Robertson's high appraisal of ancient Indian civilisation was ostensibly also a mild critique of the Company's governing policies, as he hoped that his elucidation of ancient Indian 'progress' should 'have some influence upon the behaviour of Europeans towards that people'. In this regard, Robertson praised the rule of Akbar as a model for Britain, given that Akbar's knowledge of Indian civilisation led him 'to consider the Hindoos as no less entitled to protection and favour than his other subjects, and to govern them with such equity and mildness'.[18] James Mill, by contrast, explicitly rejected the notion that ancient societies in general, and ancient Indian society in particular, possessed any semblance of 'advanced' civilisation. Mill invoked Adam Smith's own early scepticism over reports of high scientific achievement in ancient Chaldea and Egypt in his 'History of Astronomy'[19] to buttress his claim, noting that Smith was prescient in his explanation that '"despotism is more destructive of leisure and security, and more adverse to the progress of the human mind, than anarchy itself."'[20] Indeed, Mill's *History* was distinct from earlier Scottish historical writing in that he defined the different states of civilisation in a global context not according to the wide-ranging criteria utilised by Robertson, nor even according to economic and juridical criteria, as in Adam Smith's *Wealth of Nations*, but by reference to a society's degree of adherence to the principle of 'utility', as formulated by Jeremy Bentham:

> In looking at the pursuits of any nation, with a view to draw from them indications of the state of civilization, no mark is so important, as the nature of the *End* to which they are directed.
> Exactly in proportion as *Utility* is the object of every pursuit, may we regard a nation as civilized. Exactly in proportion as its ingenuity is wasted on contemptible or mischievous objects, though it may be, in itself, an ingenuity of no ordinary kind, the nation may safely be denominated barbarous.[21]

Mill explicitly distinguished his methodology from Robertson only occasionally, however, noting, for example, that Robertson had 'sadly mistaken' Hindu 'litigious subtletly' for a 'sign of high civilization'.[22] But Mill spared no occasion to critique William Jones, and in the *History* charged him with having no definite idea of what characteristics should distinguish the 'relative position' of nations on 'a scale of civilization', given that he had described the Arabs as 'eminently civilized' due to their 'love of poetry and eloquence', but also as devoid of philosophy and prone to ferocity.[23]

The elaboration and clear delineation of the Indians' 'state of civilisation' was of the greatest importance to Mill in order that the policies of government be formulated accordingly. Government could only be successful, Mill claimed, when 'adapted to the state of the people for whose use it is intended'.[24] In this respect, Mill also believed that civilisations in less advanced stages of progress did not necessarily deserve representative government, or indeed, would even benefit from it, but instead, required the guiding hand of 'improvement' provided by British imperial rule.[25] Indian society could thus be entirely remade into an advanced, modern civilisation by means of rational educational policies and sound governance. Mill followed, for example, Bentham's attack on the notion of the common law and an 'inherited constitution', as delineated by William Blackstone and Edmund Burke, arguing that law should be constructed upon rational, utilitarian principles. As such, the methodology of the *History* represented a critique of Hastings' rule according to Indian norms, and moreover, the construction of 'Hindu law' according to established usages.[26] In particular, the common law (as well as rule by 'inherited constitution') did not correspond to the principle of utility, given that it was necessarily overly complex and thereby inaccessible to all but specialists (in the form of lawyers, or *paṇḍits*), but also because it was based on the principles of the past, rather than being forward-looking and conducive to social and economic progress. Mill was also a firm believer in the centrality of education in effecting civilisational improvement, arguing that 'education wholly ... constitutes the remarkable difference between the Turk and the Englishman', and that 'the business of education, then, is to work upon the mental succession'.[27] In Uday Mehta's words, education was thought to be the 'engine' which drives improvement,[28] but this, as with legislation, must be based in rational and utilitarian principles.

Mill's discussion of Sanskrit, as well as Indian grammatical analysis, *vyākaraṇa*, is illustrative of the way in which he made use of the concept of 'utility' to determine India's civilisational worthiness. Mill argued, from a reading of Colebrooke's essay 'On the Sanscrit and Pracrit Languages', that Pāṇini's ancient grammatical treatise, the *Aṣṭādhyāyī*, rendered *vyākaraṇa* 'obscure', 'difficult', 'ambiguous', and ultimately 'frivolous'. It's 3,996 aphorisms, Mill thought, were formulated to correspond with the number three, 'rather than the number with the rules'. The rules themselves, moreover, were 'dispersed in apparent confusion through different portions' of the treatise, making it difficult to comprehend. The tradition of *vyākaraṇa* was thus not thought by Mill to be conducive to 'rendering language a more commodious and accurate instrument of communication', but was rather 'a remarkable specimen of the fooleries of a rude and ignorant age'.[29] Moreover, Mill felt that Sanskrit itself was overly complicated and contained too many synonyms, when 'the perfection of language would consist in having one name for every thing which required a name, and no more than one'.[30]

Similarly, literature was conceived by Mill to be one of the surest means by which to determine a people's civilisational status, given that literary production was intimately connected with the knowledge conducive to 'improvement in the condition of human life'.[31] As such, Mill reflected upon a well-established progression, elaborated by L'Abbé Etienne Bonnot de Condillac, in which the 'first literature' of poetry, as the language of feeling, through which men give expression to their 'passions', inevitably precedes the more advanced prose literature of 'speculation', or philosophy, science, and history.[32] Mill argued that the literature of the Hindus had remained in this initial, poetic stage, and denied the possibility that Indians had written historical works, characterising the *Mahābhārata* and *Rāmāyaṇa* as principally 'allegorical'. Historical literature, in particular, was considered a crucial determining component of an advanced state of civilisation by Mill, as an analysis of the past was thought to provide 'guidance for the future', and as such, was an instrument to be wielded for progress.[33]

Javed Majeed has persuasively argued that despite his claiming a 'break' with past histories of India, one can perceive in Mill's work important elements of continuity with early orientalist scholarship. Both William Jones and James Mill utilised elements of cultural comparison in their analyses, and ultimately, this comparison was directed to evaluate the status of Indian civilisation with respect to Europe.[34] Mill's *History* also reflected concerns with historical progress, and adopted the orientalist historiographical mode of analysing Indian society through a reading of Sanskrit texts, thereby reproducing a textualised, brahmanical vision of Hindu social and religious practice. In addition, it would appear that in places Mill drew upon an emerging polyvocality within the shifting world of historical research based on orientalist findings. That is, the *History* also articulated a series of wider critical methodologies and findings in the evaluation of India's society and history, relative to Britain, many of which would not trace their genealogy directly to utilitarian thought.

This is nowhere clearer than in his discussion of the state of Hindu scientific achievement. Mill wished to debunk notions of an advanced knowledge of mathematics and astronomy among ancient Indians, first popularised by Jean-Sylvain Bailly, and repeated by William Robertson. In particular, Mill objected to the notion that Hindu astronomical knowledge could be deemed as advanced, given that it was primarily directed not to the furtherance of knowledge, but to the pursuit of astrology, which Adam Smith had noted to be '"the very first of the sciences which is cultivated by a rude people."'[35] Mill's analysis was inspired by the arguments of John Bentley, a member of the Asiatic Society in Calcutta, which had been published in *Asiatick Researches* at the very end of the eighteenth century.

Bentley had sought, in the first instance, to overturn the claims to an extreme antiquity of Indian astronomical science and establish the European investigation into Indian chronology on 'true principles', through a scientific examination of Sanskrit astronomical treatises. In addition, rather than impute to Sanskrit astronomy a genealogy which tended to confirm (rather than undermine) Biblical accounts, as Jones and others had done, Bentley sought to demonstrate that Indian astronomical science was in fact of a much more recent origin than that of Europe. Solely by examining the degrees of error in the astronomical calculations of the celebrated *Sūrya Siddhānta*, Bentley pronounced that this Sanskrit text, rather than being of an ancient origin, was most likely dated to the eleventh century (1068 AD). In a similar manner, the astronomical tables of 'Trivalore' which Bailly had dated to some 3,000 years before Christ, were in fact datable to approximately 1283 AD by this method. Bentley thus concluded that many Sanskrit texts, including the bulk of the *Purāṇas*, could safely be dismissed as of a relatively recent origin.[36] While Bentley's arguments were later disputed by Alexander Hamilton[37] and H. T. Colebrooke,[38] Mill nevertheless invoked them in a wider critique that characterised Indian astronomy as being 'in the very same state of infancy among the Hindus with all the other branches of knowledge'.[39]

Other authors argued, in a similar vein, that while elements of sophisticated astronomical knowledge were present in Sanskrit texts, this knowledge was now all but forgotten. John Playfair, Professor of Mathematics at Edinburgh University, in a short article published in *Asiatick Researches* in 1795, commented that research into the *Sūrya Siddhānta*, and its commentaries, revealed a 'retrograde order in the progress of eastern science'. Playfair believed that the *Sūrya Siddhānta* was the representative text of Indian astronomy, and that this science, as practised in India, 'must have had its origin in a very remote age'.[40] Yet he also disputed Samuel Davis' earlier claim that 'the Hindu science of astronomy will be found as well known now as it ever was among [Indians]'[41] by explaining that the relatively recent commentator on the *Sūrya Siddhānta* which Davis had quoted in his article seemed not to understand a difficult theorem contained in that text.[42] By utilising British orientalist research, therefore, Playfair sought to confirm the belief, which he first expressed before the Royal Society of Edinburgh in 1789 on the basis of French astronomical scholarship, (and which had been also been articulated by William Robertson),[43] that despite the sophisticated nature of ancient Indian astronomical science, contemporary *brāhmaṇs* now understood only its basic rules, and not the principles upon which it was originally constructed.[44] Of course, Mill had explicitly rejected claims that contemporary India represented a degeneration of an ancient advanced civilisation as an orientalist artifice.[45] In any case, he also made use of Playfair's observations to argue (in a somewhat confused fashion) that, if anything, Indian astronomy represented 'mere observation and empiricism', rather than 'the commencement of science'.[46] Such notions retained an efficacy: in an 1844 edition of the *Calcutta Review*, for example, T. Smith made the argument that ancient Indians had an accurate astronomical science, but that they had since 'retrograded in their knowledge of the principles of science'.[47]

While Mill's *History* has often been highlighted as somehow representative of the impatience and intolerant imperialism of the nineteenth century, it in fact sits in a rather more ambiguous relationship to much of nineteenth-century educational policy. Many of the basic concepts which underpinned Mill's thought continued to be important. The notion of civilisational hierarchy, based in Scottish Enlightenment conjectural history and popularised in the Indian historical context by Mill, and the perception of a need for British interventionism in the forms of education and legislation, are lasting legacies of the *History* which even the most ardent advocates of orientalism accepted in some form. As well, the superior 'utility' of imposing improvement through Indian languages, rather than English, was a point of convergence for Mill and orientalist educators. Yet the assignation of civilisational status on strictly utilitarian terms was more muted than the celebrity which Mill's *History* enjoyed might suggest. Disagreements on Indian astronomy are representative of the wider debates on the nature of Indian society, its place in world historical narrative, and role in confirming (or not) European narratives, which were enabled by the increased availability of orientalist research in Europe by the beginning of the nineteenth century. Many of these voices retained influence in forming Company policy, including those who advocated a vision of Indian civilisational degeneration and, quite simply, the inherent 'glory'[48] of purely antiquarian research. Moreover, anglicism, which is so similar in tone to the *History*'s rhetoric, was criticised by important liberals in the 1830s as contrary to the doctrine of utility, making reluctant allies of Mill's son John Stuart and the orientalists on Calcutta's General Committee of Public Instruction. The remainder of this chapter now turns to examine changes in educational policy in India, and in particular the evolution of 'orientalist' views on the role of Indian language, literature, and social structures in the advancement of educational policy. It is argued that orientalist-inspired strategies were in fact favoured by the Company overall, not least because the extreme anglicism of 1835, rather than the utilitarianism of Mill, tempered many of the heirs to *The History of British India*.

Orientalism and educational policy

Education had played an important role in the East India Company's strategy of governance from late in the eighteenth century. The Company established educational institutions in Calcutta and Benares as a way to promote political legitimacy through cultural patronage and a perception of continuity with late Mughal practice, as well as to regulate elements of the education of the Company's future interlocutors within the judiciary. With British political paramountcy, however, it was education's redemptive power, both for the colonised subjects of India and the colonisers themselves, which was most highly prized: a 'liberal justification of the empire'.[49] An 1854 despatch from the Company's directors, for example, noted that the support of education in India was 'one of our most sacred duties', and that the impartation of 'useful knowledge' was a 'moral and material blessing' for Indians.[50] The 1835–1836 examination script of an Indian student from Benares similarly noted that education 'brings mankind into civilization, cultivates their minds with good and virtuous principles', and that it had enabled the English to 'put a stop to their savageness' while making them 'learned, wealthy, and polite'.[51] Forwarded to government for reproduction in the Company's official reports, this examination paper of course represents less an Indian voice, than a reminder of an apparent desire among Britons to perceive an acceptance of their virtuous motives in India.

The East India Company Charter Act of 1813 effectively transformed the nature of the Company's presence in India, as it set aside at least one *lākh* (100,000) rupees for the promotion of education, while also abolishing the Company's monopoly on trade and permitting the proselytisation of Christianity within India. In this respect, the Charter Act represented an official recognition that the Company, given its relatively stable military position, as well as its role as the effective government of large tracts of the subcontinent, now also possessed responsibilities towards its subject population to promote their 'interests and happiness'.[52] Yet the Charter Act's education provision also embodied a fundamental clash of ideas about the type of education to be pursued, for it stipulated that funds should be 'applied to the revival and improvement of literature, and the encouragement of the learned natives of India', as well as 'for the introduction and promotion of a knowledge of the sciences among the inhabitants of the British territories in India ...'[53]

On the one hand, this policy reflected the emerging preoccupation with civilisational and moral progress through the rational promotion of Western science and knowledge. Its advocacy in this Act was almost certainly the result of the substantial influence of Charles Grant, a noted evangelical and associate of William Wilberforce, at the Court of Directors in London.[54] Grant had argued in a contemporary polemical tract that India's relatively low state of civilisation could be attributed to the moral depravity encapsulated within Hinduism, and as such, progress could only be brought about by moral means, and specifically, by the introduction of Christianity. Yet Grant also recognised the importance of proceeding slowly and methodically in reform, and so recommended as a first step the promulgation in India of a knowledge of Western science and literature through the medium of the English language.[55] This, then, represented the first influential articulation of a reformist agenda which specifically targeted Hastings' conservative policy of rule by Indian norms and institutions, though unlike James Mill's trenchant critique of several years later, Grant was specifically concerned with the promulgation of Christianity.

On the other hand, the Charter Act also promoted specifically Indian forms of learning, registering an apparent persistency of older orientalist ideas regarding the preservation of Indian knowledge and culture which had been based in notions of political legitimacy and the inherent value of 'ancient knowledge'. This policy had received a renewed endorsement by Governor-General Lord Minto (1807–1813) in his minute of 6 March 1811,[56] which emphasised the importance of revitalising the institutions of traditional 'native' education, including Sanskrit education in the 'principal seats of Hindu learning', given that the Company's territorial expansion had resulted in the diminishing patronage of *zamīndār*s and 'native princes'. Minto's planned reforms included establishing a new series of government-sponsored schools in the traditional centres of education, including Nadia and Tirhut. These were expressions of a desire to improve Indian society upon its own terms, however, rather than a need for political legitimacy, as in Hastings' era. Minto argued from within a paradigm of Indian civilisational degeneration, stating that the 'ignorance' of the 'natives', born from a 'want of due instruction in the moral and religious tenets of their respective faiths', resulted in crimes such as perjury and forgery, as well as crimes 'against the peace and happiness of society'. In this respect, Minto articulated an educational strategy which emphasised the importance of more effectively imparting Indian languages and Indian knowledge, and the beneficial effect which such a strategy would have upon Indian moral 'progress'.[57]

Yet new educational initiatives in northern India were largely suspended under the Governor-Generalship of Earl Moira, later the Marquess of Hastings (1813–1823), as the Company directed itself to conflict with Nepal and the Maratha states. Governmental measures were restricted largely to the 'reinvigoration' of traditional curricula in established colleges, and heightened oversight by Europeans. In Benares, for example, *paṇḍit*s at the Sanskrit College continued to oversee the impartation of a wholly traditional Sanskrit curriculum, though under the nominal superintendence of a European committee. In 1820, this committee reported on the 'utility and credit' of the college, stating that while it had undoubtedly served to endear the city's residents to the Company's government, they were generally pessimistic regarding the college's future prospects, given the students' 'want of acquirement' under the current administrative arrangement. It recommended, therefore, the introduction of a 'regularity of method, and incitement or enforcement of attention', so that 'the College may conduce very powerfully to preserve and diffuse the knowledge of Hindu literature, language, and law amongst the class of men whose duty and business it is particularly to possess it'.[58] The measures suggested included, most importantly, increased European superintendence, as well as the reintroduction of yearly examinations, disputations (*śāstrārtha*), and the issuance of certificates of proficiency. No specific recommendations were made for the introduction of Western knowledge into the curriculum. In 1821 the students were asked to debate, for example, whether 'immortality is obtained from divine knowledge only', as a part of the *vedānta* examination, while *mīmāṃsā* students were asked about 'the benefits resulting from performance of holy rites'.[59]

The principal authors of this report were the celebrated orientalist H. H. Wilson and his protégé Edward Fell, who held the position of Secretary to the Benares Sanskrit College.[60] Wilson, a prodigious

Sanskrit scholar, had published in 1813 a translation of Kālidāsa's *Megha Dūta*, as well as the first Sanskrit-English dictionary in 1819.[61] Although he had arrived in India on the Company's medical service, later becoming Assay Master of the Mint in Calcutta, he held a place of influence as the Secretary of the Asiatic Society from 1811.[62] In this regard, Wilson was active in an attempt to resurrect Lord Minto's 1811 plans for the extension of 'Hindu learning'. Specifically invoking the notion of 'decay' in India's scientific and literary scholarship, Wilson reported to government in 1821 that very little had been accomplished in the attempt to establish further 'oriental' colleges in the 'once celebrated places' of Nadia and Tirhut.[63] As such, he suggested instead that the funds be transferred for the maintenance of a 'Hindu College in Calcutta', which would be of 'much more advantage to the people'. Nadia's 'character as a Seminary', Wilson claimed, was due to it former political importance, and 'little more than the shadow of its reputation now remains'. Tirhut, as well, was no longer 'a place of any reputation or resort'. The principal point which informed Wilson's recommendation, however, was the ease with which a Sanskrit college could be superintended by Europeans in Calcutta, as compared with remote, upcountry sites. This superintendence, Wilson noted, was both acceptable to Indians, and a necessity if such an institution was to achieve its purpose: the improved cultivation of Hindu learning.[64] The Marquess of Hastings accepted Wilson's recommendations, and resolved to establish a 'Hindoo College' in Calcutta (which opened in 1824 as the Calcutta Sanskrit College).

Yet the nature of the curriculum at 'traditional' Sanskrit institutions continued to be contested along the lines first defined by the Charter Act of 1813. Shortly after the formation in July 1823 of the General Committee of Public Instruction (GCPI) to regulate educational policy on behalf of government,[65] the Committee was directed to undertake measures to introduce into the Calcutta Sanskrit College's curriculum 'European science as far as practicable'.[66] This directive reflected both the sentiments of the Marquess of Hastings, who had expressed the view that it was 'a purpose of much deeper interest to seek every practicable means to effecting the gradual diffusion of European knowledge',[67] and the GCPI's general mandate to promote the 'better instruction of the people', 'the introduction among them of useful knowledge', and 'the improvement of their moral character'.[68]

In a series of letters to government, the members of the GCPI agreed that 'the diffusion of sound practice knowledge' among the *brāhmaṇ* elite of Bengal was desirable for its 'beneficial effects', but emphasised that it was of the utmost concern to conciliate this class of men, and not 'give any alarm to the prejudices of the Brahmanical members of the college'.[69] *Paṇḍits* were thought to be 'satisfied with [their] own learning', and so had to be courted, and gradually convinced of the desirability of improving upon their 'traditional' knowledge with reference to that of Europe.[70] The GCPI also argued that some Sanskrit literature was worthy of being studied in its own right, and that the arithmetic and algebra of the Hindus, in particular, were 'grounded on the same principles as those of Europe'.[71] Wilson, who was Secretary of the GCPI from its founding, had originally advocated government support for Sanskrit education in Calcutta because it was the 'classical language' of India, its literature 'offers much that is really valuable', and because it would prevent Indians from falling into error due to an 'imperfect acquaintance with their own sacred literature'. In this regard, Wilson reiterated Lord Minto's desire to improve Indian society through a renewal of its own cultural heritage.[72]

The basic educational methodology followed at the Calcutta Sanskrit College was distinct from Minto's vision, however, and came to be known as 'engraftment': a term which finds its origin with J. H. Harington, a founding member of the GCPI, who had suggested a decade earlier that neither the exclusive promotion of Indian languages and literature, nor that of Western science, was sufficient in and of itself. Instead, he argued that 'to allure the learned natives of India to the study of European science and literature, we must, I think, engraft this study upon their own established methods of scientific and literary instruction'.[73] 'Engraftment' was an inherently conciliatory policy therefore, which nevertheless proceeded upon an understanding that a 'rational' comparison of the contents of Indian and European science would always favour the latter. Charles Lushington elaborated on this notion in 1824, with respect to the Calcutta Sanskrit College, stating that although 'it may be the immediate object of the institution to cherish Hindu literature', it was also reasonable to hope that the teaching of Western science 'may awaken curiosity to more enlightened studies, and tend, by the gradual diffusion of European information, to the promotion of useful learning and sound morals'.[74]

In an 1824 despatch drafted for the Court of Directors, James Mill expressed the Company's 'zeal for the progress and improvement of education among the natives of India', but noted that the GCPI's 'slight reforms' to gradually introduce Western knowledge into the 'traditional' Sanskrit-based curriculum at the Calcutta Sanskrit College were thought insufficient to bring about much in the way of improvement. Importantly, Mill did emphasise the utility of imparting European knowledge to Indians through 'Hindoo *media* or Mahomedan *media*', for its conciliation of Indian prejudices, and the opportunity to retain anything found 'useful' in oriental texts.[75] The use of Indian languages to promote Western knowledge had been advocated sporadically by the GCPI, including by Harington in 1814, who wished to produce 'good translations of the most useful European compositions',[76] while in 1821 Wilson had envisioned Calcutta as a centre for the translation of European books into Sanskrit.[77] Yet in years following, educational institutions in northern India increasingly adopted the study of the English language for the study of European knowledge, without any necessary reference to Indian languages or texts. At the Calcutta Sanskrit College, for example, the study of English and European science was steadily increased,[78] while in Delhi a yearly grant was offered to the government's college in 1827 for the separate study of English as well as astronomy and mathematics 'on European principles'.[79] In Benares, Edward Fell wrote to H. H. Wilson in 1823 that 'at Benares the Sanskrita College should remain inviolate', and that the teaching of Western knowledge would 'subvert the basis on which the College was originally formed'.[80] By 1830, however, a new English seminary had been established in the city, 'the object being to stock the minds of a certain portion of the rising generation with true and useful knowledge'.[81] Though it was initially hoped that the seminary would attract the children of the 'native gentry',[82] it was instead filled by those of a generally lower social standing, and so came to be perceived as less influential in terms of the authoritative spread of Western 'useful knowledge' to the city's general population.[83]

Outside the realm of government, educational initiatives were also made by missionaries, especially, concerned not with 'traditional' learning *per se*, but rather with the impartation of Western knowledge as preparatory to the reception of Christian doctrine. In 1818, both the Serampore College for 'higher education in arts, science, and [Christian] theology'[84] and the Bishop's College in Calcutta were founded. Bishop's College, in particular, was intended to provide a broad education to Indians through instruction in mathematics, the various physical sciences, and philosophy, in an attempt to 'emancipate the Hindu mind from its bondage to error and superstition', and prepare students for employment 'in diffusing the truths of Christianity in the East'.[85] Missionaries were also actively involved in the establishment of school and school book societies which sought to encourage the increased writing and publication of textbooks for use in Indian schools. Of particular note, the Calcutta School Book Society

(CSBS) was established in 1817, and included among its members prominent missionaries such as Thomas Thomason and William Carey, members of the emerging Bengali intelligentsia such as Rādhākānt Deb and Rāmkamal Sen, as well as prominent servants of the Company, including W. B. Bayley and J. H. Harington. Indeed, the CSBS received from 1821 a government grant to further its publication activities. This organisation concentrated in the first instance upon the publication of books in Bengali, but also published several works written in Sanskrit, English, Persian, Arabic, and Urdu, on topics such as grammar, arithmetic, geography, English and world history, natural history, and 'moral tales'.[86] School book societies were subsequently established at Agra and Benares, among other north Indian cities, and in many ways, reflected (or anticipated) the wide-ranging publishing activities undertaken by Britain's own Society for the Diffusion of Useful Knowledge (SDUK), instituted by Lord Brougham in 1823.[87]

Consider, for example, the Baptist missionary Revd William Yates's *Elements of Natural Philosophy and Natural History*, or, in Sanskrit, *Padārthavidyāsāra*, ('a compendium of knowledge of material objects'), which was published by the Calcutta School Book Society in 1828. Yates' text is a treatise on natural philosophy and natural history, published in a dialogue format in Sanskrit, as well as in a dual-language English and Bengali version.[88] The text draws upon a variety of natural religion and useful knowledge tracts, including J. F. Martinet's oft-reprinted 1777 *Catechism of Nature*, a Dutch schoolbook which promoted a 'commercially focused piety', moral instruction, and the rationalisation of science with theology,[89] and William Bingley's encyclopaedic 1816 *Useful Knowledge*, which sought to enumerate the animal, mineral, and vegetable products of nature 'for the use of man'. The *Padārthavidyāsāra* itself encompassed an enquiry into the firmament and heavenly bodies, man, animals, plants and flowers, and minerals, among other topics, while simultaneously following the argument for the existence of God from the evidence presented in the design of the universe, popularised by Paley and Butler, and which Yates hoped would 'excite [a student's] mind to higher attainments'.[90] Moreover, by virtue of its dialogue format, which although 'traditional' within much pedagogical Sanskrit literature, as well as in English schoolbooks, Europe was rendered in the role of the *guru*, and India in the role of *śiṣya* (student).

The focus in the school book societies upon publishing elements of Western scientific knowledge was driven not simply by the desire to effect 'progress' through the diffusion of veridical information and the banishment of superstition and irrational belief, but also in many cases as a necessary preparation for receiving God's 'special revelation' in the form of the *Bible*. Importantly, Indian languages were viewed by these missionaries and educationalists as a valuable medium for instruction, for the role they played in both accessibility and conciliation. Early missionary experience of the need for *Bible* translation and vernacular-language preaching in Bengal undoubtedly would have been significant in this regard, including the Bengali and Sanskrit translations of the Bible, known as the *Dharmapustaka*, begun by William Carey.[91] Indeed, following early discussions with both H. T. Colebrooke and Francis Wilford, Carey came to believe that Sanskrit in particular was not necessarily affiliated with any particular branch of religious knowledge, but could be utilised to effectively and authoritatively convey Western science, and in time, Christianity to Indians.[92] In this use of Sanskrit, as well as the format of a dialogue between *guru* and *śiṣya*, missionary contributions to school book societies and educational institutions such as *Padārthavidyāsāra* anticipated, and served in some cases as a source of inspiration for, the educational methodologies of 'constructive orientalism' practised in government institutions, which followed the short-lived ascendancy of anglicist educational policy in the 1830s.

Anglicism, 1835, and the rise of 'constructive orientalism'

Following the departure of H. H. Wilson for Oxford in 1833, Charles Trevelyan, a member of the Church Missionary Society,[93] was appointed in his place to the GCPI. Together with other like-minded anglicists, Trevelyan promoted a radical agenda of educational reform which targeted the 'traditional' curricula at the Company's Sanskrit and Islamic colleges, as well as the funding for various orientalist translation and publication projects undertaken jointly with the Asiatic Society. Trevelyan was immediately said to be 'extremely anxious to change the language of Hindostan ... into English'.[94] In March of 1834, John Tytler wrote to Wilson to complain of the 'great changes' taking place in Calcutta, explaining that it seemed to have become the policy of government that 'Oriental literature is useless, that Oriental books are utterly unworthy of study, and the Oriental languages, particularly Sanscrit, Arabic and Persian are barbarous dialects which it is worse than useless to attempt to learn'. Moreover, he reported that the government planned to teach only the English language, and seemed 'determined on the destruction of Orientalism'. Tytler's own translations of English literature into Arabic, he noted, had been stopped at Trevelyan's request.[95]

Tytler's fears were fully realised in the February 1835 minute on education of Thomas B. Macaulay, legal member on the Governor-General's council and Trevelyan's brother-in-law.[96] Macaulay sought to dismiss Indian language and learning as inconsequential, and establish the basis of the Company's educational policy solely in a curriculum of European science and literature, taught through the medium of the English language. His minute is the clearest statement of the way in which anglicists believed that Indian society would be uplifted, and eventually brought into the light of Christianity, through not only education, but a wholesale cultural assimilation. Macaulay characterised the contents of Sanskrit and Arabic literature as 'worthless', or more famously, as less worth than 'a single shelf of a good European library'. Moreover, he argued that the simple fact that the 'superior' scientific knowledge of the British was contained wholly in the English language was sufficient reason to promote education in that language alone. Macaulay also rejected the orientalist argument for a policy of conciliation in education, stating that the majority of the Bengali elite desired an English education for the material benefits which it incurred. As such, he summed up the aim of the anglicist education policy in the desire to create a new intellectual leadership in India, one which would form 'a class of persons Indian in blood and colour, but English in tastes, in opinions, in morals, and in intellect'.[97]

Macaulay's views were adopted in Governor-General Bentinck's Resolution of 7 March 1835,[98] though the government was ultimately limited in its ability to completely curtail the study of Indian languages and 'oriental learning' by virtue of the separate measures of funding which supported many of the oriental institutions.[99] Bentinck did, however, impose several measures which he believed would further the government's new policy, including the abolition of the stipendiary system for new students in 'traditional' subjects, arguing that such a system would 'give artificial encouragement to branches of learning which, in the natural course of things, would be superseded by more useful studies'.[100] This policy resulted in a drastic drop in enrolment at Benares Sanskrit College, for example, where student numbers more than halved between 1836 and 1840.[101] In addition, conditions placed by government upon new appointments in 'native' seminaries left both the Benares and Calcutta Sanskrit Colleges without Secretaries, until the GCPI could determine whether the service was 'indispensably necessary', or whether it might be otherwise rendered 'at a small expense'.[102] Yet there were still limits to anglicism, as the GCPI refused to consider any direct promulgation of Christianity in its colleges. When in 1838, for example, the Religious Tract Society in London sent a box of books to the Benares English Seminary, with titles such as *Divine Origin of Christianity* and *Christian Biography*, the GCPI did 'not approve of [their] reception', and directed they be returned to the Society's agents in Calcutta.[103]

The sole promotion of English was looked upon with scepticism by many. Frederick Shore, son of Lord Teignmouth, wrote to Trevelyan in 1834 that he doubted the viability of education in English, and advocated instead 'the vernacular character as well as language'.[104] Rādhākānt Deb, a member of the GCPI, complained also that the effective abolition of the study of oriental languages compared unfavourably with Mughal government, who though 'tyrannical in the extreme', were also 'great patrons of learning'.[105] John Tytler wrote to Macaulay directly outlining numerous objections, including that anglicist policy denied Indians the opportunity to compare 'their falsehoods with our truth'.[106] Indeed, the real, but most often overlooked, importance of the adoption of anglicist educational policy in 1835 was that it served in the months following to elicit a series of heated responses which consolidated and brought to full articulation a set of ideas which would coalesce into a 'constructive orientalist' educational practice. Prior to 1835 there was little consensus, even among orientalists, how best to amalgamate traditional curricula with Western knowledge in the promotion of the latter. Constructive orientalism, however, which built upon the policy of 'engraftment', emphasised the importance of explicitly adapting Indian languages and knowledge, as well as social structures, within a universal developmental framework. This strategy would, in time, prove to be far more long-lasting and influential in determining the future course of educational policy in India, and certainly, the future course of meaningful intellectual contestation at the heart of the Indian empire, than is typically suggested by analyses of Macaulay's rhetoric. It is the purpose of the remainder of this chapter, therefore, to suggest that the significance of the year of 1835 within historical analyses of 'British India' might be significantly reevaluated.

The first point elaborated by critics of anglicism was that the conciliation of 'native sensibilities' was crucial to the success of the educational project in order to secure the cooperation and consent of India's learned elites. This was noted in one of the earliest critiques of anglicism published in 1835, a series of letters which appeared in the *Friend of India*, authored by Brian Houghton Hodgson, the British resident in Nepal, under the pseudonym 'Junius'.[107] Hodgson argued principally for a 'vernacularised' educational system which would enable the effective diffusion of Western 'useful knowledge' within India, but also stressed that the peculiar socio-cultural conditions of India itself must be accounted for within the Company's educational policy. These included, most importantly, the caste system, which allowed for the influence of 'priestly sages' who utilised their ascendant social position, and attendant virtual monopoly in learning, to perpetuate 'the enthralment of the popular mind'.[108] Hodgson argued that despite the Company's 'paramount' political and military position in the subcontinent, the *paṇḍits*' 'empire over the hearts and understandings of the people has been and is almost entirely unaffected by it'.[109] Hodgson cleverly invoked in this passage the language and sentiments of John Malcolm, a leading adherent of the Munro school of administrators (whose long Indian career culminated with his appointment as Governor of Bombay 1827–1830). Hodgson agreed with Malcolm and the 'Munro school' that the British empire in India was an 'empire of opinion', and that British rule depended to a large extent upon the cultivation of Indian loyalty through administrative policies which took into account, wherever possible, the history and peculiar circumstances of Indian society.[110] Yet Hodgson also drew attention here to Malcolm's ancillary belief that Indian awe of, and reverence for, 'superior' British knowledge and institutions played a part in securing Indian opinion in support of the Company's rule. Malcolm wrote in his 1826 *The Political History of India*, for instance, that:

> there can be no doubt that empire is held solely by opinion; or, in other words, by that respect and awe with which the comparative superiority of our knowledge, justice, and system of rule, have inspired the inhabitants of our own territories; and that confidence in our truth, reliance on our faith, and dread of our arms, which is impressed on every nation in India.[111]

In essence, Hodgson's reference to the *paṇḍits*' 'empire over the hearts and understandings of the people' was intended to remind his readers that the Indian 'respect and awe' invoked by Malcolm must also be consciously cultivated, through a displacement, or perhaps an appropriation, of the *paṇḍits*' social status and cultural legitimacy, and that popular 'opinion' is not so easily won as Malcolm might suggest, especially given what was considered to be India's religiously sanctioned social structure. It is this empire, then – the *paṇḍits*' 'empire of the understanding' – Hodgson argued, which the Company must target through a carefully formulated educational policy in order that the British empire in India, and its attendant mission to bring 'civilisation' to its inhabitants, may ultimately be successful.

This sentiment was repeated by H. H. Wilson in a December 1835 letter to *The Asiatic Journal*.[112] Of course, the conciliation of Indian elites had been a prominent feature of Warren Hastings' administration, as well as the educational policies of the GCPI during the 1820s. Yet Wilson elaborated upon Hodgson's argument by noting that it was the 'traditional' elite who would be most effective in disseminating 'useful knowledge', rather than the emerging English-educated middle class. Wilson noted, for example, that there were a number of 'able English scholars' among the Bengalis who labour for 'the enlightening of their fellows', but that 'because they are not masters also of the learning of their people ... [their] efforts are of little avail'.[113] This point was also picked up by John Stuart Mill (James Mill's son), who in a draft despatch of 1836 (which was based on Wilson's article)[114] noted that the emerging class of English-speaking Bengalis was of little use in diffusing 'useful knowledge' to the mass of Indians, and that the Company's educational policies should take a special consideration of 'the learned class: men of letters by birth and profession'. It was this 'traditional' intelligentsia, Mill warned, that the anglicist educational policy risked alienating.[115]

Prior to 1835 a variety of languages had been enlisted in the promotion of useful knowledge in India, including English, Indian vernaculars, and the 'classical' languages of Sanskrit, Arabic, and Persian. In this regard, the critique of anglicism emphasised the importance of specifically Indian languages as the principal medium of instruction. Wilson had argued that the study of English, in and of itself, was of little use to 'work a beneficial change in the principles of the people', noting that a 'command of the English language' was 'quite compatible with gross ignorance and inveterate superstition'.[116] Mill concurred, claiming that 'the mental cultivation of a people' could never take place 'through the medium of a foreign language'.[117] The vernacular languages of India, in particular, were recommended, for as Mill noted, they were the only suitable vehicles for the diffusion of useful knowledge given that they were so widely understood.[118] Yet simultaneously, it was argued by Wilson that India's vernaculars were 'utterly incapable of representing European ideas', and needed to be improved accordingly. In essence, Wilson argued that Sanskrit and Arabic required government sponsorship as the vernaculars were 'dependent' upon their classical parent languages for their ability to express difficult concepts. If English were to replace these classical languages as the 'parent', the result would inevitably be a 'grotesque patchwork'.[119] Hodgson also promoted the vernacular languages as the principal medium of instruction, noting that by virtue of their historical relationship to Sanskrit they in fact enjoyed an advantage over the English language, which was unable 'without extreme periphrasis' to express the 'recently elaborated truths of all departments of the philosophy of life'.[120]

Orientalists had also consistently defended what they perceived to be the intrinsic value of the study of Hindu philosophy and mathematics.[121] Following the anglicist dismissal of the value of 'oriental learning' this point was often reiterated. Wilson, for example, again following Lord Minto, argued that the study of Indian languages and literature was of some value to Europeans, but most assuredly, was of a great value to Indians, 'in maintaining a respect for science, a veneration for wisdom, a sense of morality, a feeling of beauty, a regard for social ties and domestic affections, an admiration of excellence and a love of country'.[122] John Tytler, similarly, attacked anglicist policy on the basis that it would destroy 'the inestimable and irretrievable remains of antiquity', entailing 'the curse of the Muses'.[123] Yet importantly, the notion of 'intrinsic value' was elaborated to include the assertion that there existed a measure of developmental continuity between Western and Indian scientific knowledge. This point had been debated from the eighteenth century onwards, and had first been touched upon by the GCPI in their policy letter of 1824, when it was noted that Hindu arithmetic and algebra, for example, were 'grounded on the same principles as those of Europe'.[124] As well, Tytler admitted that while there was much falsehood contained within the 'Eastern sciences', he asserted that there is also 'some truth', and that the admittance of that 'truth' would only be of benefit to educational initiatives.[125] Most critics of anglicism, however, made explicit reference to the recently publicised 'educational experiment' being undertaken in Sehore by Lancelot Wilkinson, to prove that elements of Indian scientific literature could be utilised as a starting point for the impartation of veridical Western scientific knowledge.[126] Wilson, for example, noted that Wilkinson had demonstrated how the Sanskrit astronomical texts, the *Siddhānta*s, 'might be made introductory and subservient to accurate information'.[127] Hodgson similarly argued by reference to Wilkinson's work that the accepted authority of the Sanskrit *śāstra* made it a formidable weapon in the spread of 'useful knowledge' and even the doctrines of Christianity, as the *paṇḍits* '*dare not* deny the authority of [them], *however used*; and [they are] assuredly capable of being used for *the diffusion of Truth!*'[128]

Lancelot Wilkinson's 'educational experimentation' at Sehore in fact served to redefine the standard for 'experimental' educational initiatives of the mid-nineteenth century.[129] Wilkinson was the political agent at the native state of Bhopal,[130] and had come to be involved with the *pāthśālā* at Sehore where he undertook to utilise the 'most rational' Sanskrit astronomical texts, the *Siddhāntas*, and specifically the *Sūrya Siddhānta*, to overthrow the much more popular *Purāṇik* conceptions of the earth and solar system, which were dominated by 'seas of sugar cane juice' and planets 'supported by the great serpent Shesha'.[131] In particular, Wilkinson thought that Bhāskarācārya's twelfth-century commentary on the *Sūrya Siddhānta*, the *Siddhānta Śiromaṇi*, was of value in the spread of veridical astronomical knowledge, as this author had not only ridiculed *Purāṇik* astronomy, but had also 'always professed ... the greatest admiration for the learned men of the West'.[132] Moreover, these texts were considered as authoritative, being held in 'profound veneration' by the *paṇḍits*.[133] As such, Wilkinson believed that the *Siddhānta*s 'afford us beyond all comparison the best means of promoting the cause of education, civilization, and truth, amongst our Hindu subjects'.[134]

In essence, Wilkinson argued that the *Siddhānta*s contained a system of astronomy approximately equivalent to the Ptolemaic, and therefore they could be utilised not only to incur the abandonment of *Purāṇik* astronomy, but might serve as a foundation from which the *paṇḍits* could 'also readily receive the additions made during the last few hundred years in science'.[135] As such, Wilkinson envisioned a unilinear, and universal, developmental scheme in the progress of astronomical science, in which the *Siddhānta*s represented a level of attainment in scientific knowledge (and civilisation) which Europeans had already surpassed. All that was necessary, therefore, was to demonstrate to the *paṇḍits* the further steps which had not yet been undertaken in India. Wilkinson also remarked, however, that the knowledge contained in these texts had been largely forgotten by the learned men of India, thereby reiterating the orientalist trope of degeneration which was commonly articulated in debates over Indian astronomy in the late eighteenth century.[136] As such, it fell to Europeans to revive and recommunicate the 'lost' knowledge of India, and make it serve the higher purpose of improvement. Wilkinson's project encapsulated the core of nascent constructive orientalist practice, and a development over the process of 'engraftment': Indian learning and language, together with the cultural authority gleaned from the *śāstra* and the *paṇḍits*, were to be used to elaborate a developmental and hierarchical scheme of civilisations, and enshrine Britain's role as the *guru* to India's *śiṣya*.

Bentinck left India shortly after confirming the terms of Macaulay's minute, to be replaced by George Eden, the Earl of Auckland (1835–1842). Orientalists could not have been more pleased. James Prinsep, for example, wrote to H. H. Wilson in 1836 to say that members of the Asiatic Society had been invited *en masse* by Auckland to his 'monthly *soirées à la* Duke of Sussex',[137] in essence symbolising their return to official favour. Yet changes to educational policy were slow to develop. William Adam, who had been appointed by Bentinck to investigate the state of education in Bengal, issued a series of reports between 1835 and 1838, and in the last of these outlined a series of recommendations which confirmed much in the critiques first voiced by Wilson, Mill, and Hodgson. In particular, Adam recommended the extension of Sanskrit education for its conciliatory value, cultural authority, and as a resource for the improvement of the vernacular languages.[138] Importantly, Adam also collected numerous signatures from *paṇḍits* associated with the Calcutta Sanskrit College, as well as numerous private seminaries, to confirm a *vyavasthā* ('opinion') that Western knowledge translated into Sanskrit would be 'of great use in the conduct of worldly affairs', and that there would be 'not the least objection' to this practice amongst India's traditional intelligentsia.[139] Similarly, in Benares, Rājendra Mittra, a member of the Local Committee of Public Instruction (LCPI), called for the 'improvement' of Sanskrit and a Sanskrit-based curriculum, by reference to Western knowledge, given that Sanskrit 'embraces most of those sciences that are now in English'.[140]

In a minute of 24 November 1839, Auckland finally sought a 'compromise' settlement of the education question, by reinstating the level of funding which the 'oriental institutions' had enjoyed before 1835, and emphasising the need to hire the 'most eminent professors for the colleges', as well as the preparation 'of the most useful books of instruction, such as of the Siddhants and Sanscrit version of Euclid which Mr. Wilkinson urged upon us'.[141] Indeed, Auckland looked to Wilkinson's educational experiments as the source of his 'chief instruments in the propagation of a new knowledge and more enlarged ideas'.[142] In so doing, Auckland gave both his sanction and encouragement to the nascent constructive orientalist educational strategy. The Company's Court of Directors then reaffirmed the prioritisation of the diffusion of 'useful knowledge', primarily through vernacular languages and what they called its 'engraftment' upon the studies of the 'existing learned classes'. Funds for orientalist publishing through the Asiatic Society, and scholarships for 'oriental colleges' were also reinstated.[143]

Over the next two decades the constructive orientalist educational project would find its ultimate expression as the 'Anglo-Sanskrit' programme in Benares College under the superintendency of James Ballantyne. In anticipation, a writer to the *Asiatic Journal* in 1841 recommended 'grappling with the learned Brahmans on their own ground, ... acquiring skill in their language, and penetrating into the arcana of their philosophy', in order to facilitate the 'progress of truth'. Yet while this writer envisioned that such an undertaking would result in a decline in the 'veneration for the privileged caste',[144] the next generation of educators instead counted upon exactly the opposite: an enlistment of Sanskrit *paṇḍits*, with their socio-cultural authority intact, to the cause of Indian improvement. The next chapter now turns to examine this project in detail.

4

Enlisting Sanskrit on the Side of Progress

Benares has long been characterised as a paramount city within the religious landscape of Hinduism. It is perhaps best known as a place of pilgrimage for Hindus, as well as a centre of Sanskrit-based learning. Benares is mentioned as a *tīrtha* in the *Mahābhārata*, and figures prominently in several *Purāṇa*s, where its sacred geography and connection to Śiva, as the source of all sacred knowledge, is described.[1] In early European travelogues, the city's religious and learned character was often presented as its most important aspect. François Bernier described Benares as the 'Athens of the Gentry of the Indies where the *Brachmans* and the *Religious* ... come together', and where religious education resembled 'the way of the School of the Antients'.[2] It has been argued in Chapter 2 that during the eighteenth and early nineteenth century, the strengthening of characterisations of Benares as a sacred Hindu city, and as central to an understanding of Indian civilisation, was intimately connected with both the authorisation of early orientalist scholarship, and the establishment of cultural and political legitimacy for the Company's government. In essence, Benares' reputation for cultural authenticity could be turned to the substantiation of cultural-religious production of varying sorts. Later in the nineteenth century, this reputation was further solidified, as representations of the city as both highly brahmanical and containing a population representative of the entire subcontinent became prevalent.[3] During the 1860s, for example, Matthew Sherring, a leading member of the London Missionary Society, argued that Benares 'represents India, religiously and intellectually, just as Paris represents the political sentiments of France', as a part of his history of the city, which was at least partially intended to fortify missionary efforts there.[4] Similarly, Bholanauth Chunder described Benares as 'the city of Shiva, the great stronghold of Hindooism, the holiest shrine for pilgrimage in India, and the nucleus of the wealth, grandeur, and fashion of Hindoostan',[5] in a travelogue which sought largely to enumerate the contemporary degeneracy of popular Hinduism in the cause of the reformist Brahmo Samāj.

Matthew Sherring's belief that Benares would hold a 'foremost position' in the 'new era of enlightenment'[6] wrought by Christianity corresponds closely with the rhetoric which upheld the centrality of Benares College to the colonial state's educational experimentation during the 1850s. The 'constructive orientalist' pedagogical programme developed at Benares College under the superintendence of James R. Ballantyne to bring 'useful knowledge' and 'improvement' to the traditional intelligentsia of the city represented the culmination of decades of British debate surrounding the status and relative importance of Indian languages, philosophical and religious literature, and 'traditional' Indian scholarly elites in the self-justificatory project of colonial education. In essence, Ballantyne sought to turn 'traditional' Sanskrit education into an instrument of 'civilisational progress'. By utilising Indian languages, textual forms, and the cultural authority of the *brāhmaṇ paṇḍits*, Ballantyne hoped to characterise Western scientific knowledge and Christianity to his students at Benares College as the natural 'development' of the knowledge contained in the Sanskrit *śāstra*. The central standing afforded to Benares within the Hindu-Indian intellectual landscape, therefore, was crucial to rendering the college, in the words of Lieutenant-Governor James Thomason, a beacon in the midst of a waning brahmanical system, from which enlightenment would spread forth: 'one instrument in the mighty change'.[7]

This chapter examines the ways in which early orientalist knowledge, preconceptions, and methodologies, constructed largely during the late eighteenth century, were partially utilised by constructive orientalists within a specific project of colonial education underwritten largely by liberal conceptions of civilisational hierarchy, the attendant concerns for 'improvement' and 'progress', as well as for the justification of empire. In particular, while the early orientalist defence of the Mosaic chronology was abandoned, constructive orientalist educational practices drew inspiration from the Burkean analysis of a culture upon its own terms, while also proceeding upon an ultimately comparative understanding of Indian society through the medium of Sanskrit texts. In this regard, James Ballantyne was something of a 'synthesising intellectual', working within a broadly defined conjectural hierarchy much in the manner of William Robertson or James

Mill. Yet the constructive orientalism of Benares College was also crucially dependent upon *paṇḍit*s, both for their expertise in Sanskrit-based knowledge, and most particularly for their social standing in naturalising Western knowledge in the Indian setting, analogous with early orientalist strategies for the authorisation of their scholarship to European audiences.

Constructive orientalism, moreover, represented a far more important and influential mode of British engagement with Indian society and culture than the 'crude disparagement' that was typical of anglicist and evangelical-inspired authors and educators such as Macaulay and Trevelyan. The type of educational practices pursued at Benares College contributed to a further consolidation of a Sanskritised and textualised vision of Indian society, and importantly, a resituating of brahmanical authority to speak to issues of nationality and identity within the burgeoning north Indian public sphere. In later chapters it is argued that the capacity of many Indian Sanskrit scholars to emerge as broadly influential cultural commentators, or perhaps cultural critics, was related closely to the engagements made by 'traditional' *paṇḍit*s with the arguments presented within constructive orientalist discourse in educational institutions such as Benares College.

John Muir and educational reform in Benares

Perhaps inspired by the apparent successes of Lancelot Wilkinson's educational experiments in Sehore, George Nicholls, the Headmaster of the Benares English Seminary, attempted in 1838 to informally introduce a selection of useful knowledge – the geometry of Euclid – to the Benares Sanskrit College. This work, which Nicholls had optimistically hoped to use to divert the *jyotiṣa paṇḍit*s' attention from the pursuit of astrology, proved unpopular, however. The book was said, in fact, to have remained 'neglected [upon the shelf] except by the orthodox dust floating in the college atmosphere'.[8] Yet following the abandonment of extreme anglicist policies in 1839, suggestions to incorporate Western knowledge into the Sanskrit College's curriculum, in conformity with Auckland's directive,[9] were pressed more officially. An 1841 investigation into the college by Captain Marshall, Secretary to the College of Fort William, for example, concluded that the *paṇḍit*s teaching at the college were 'well qualified', but it was thought 'desirable that the knowledge and science of Europe ... be brought within the reach of the students of this institution'. As such, Marshall recommended instituting a Professorship of Arithmetic and Natural Philosophy[10] – a position which was filled the following year with one of the first graduates of Lancelot Wilkinson's educational experimentation in Sehore, a young *paṇḍit* from Nagpur by the name of Bāpūdeva Śāstrī.[11] At this time, Bāpūdeva was celebrated as an example of what could be accomplished in the cause of 'improvement' through 'native education' on Wilkinson's nascent constructive orientalist model. Indeed, it was argued by Wilkinson himself that Bāpūdeva's appointment at Benares, the so-called 'seat of brahmanical learning', would 'serve to impress the rising generation ... at Benares with very proper notions of the vast superiority of European over Native science'.[12]

In 1844, responsibility for education in the North-Western Provinces shifted from the General Committee of Public Instruction (GCPI) in Calcutta, to the provincial government, with its seat at Agra.[13] This shift in responsibility was especially significant because the Lieutenant-Governor of the province between 1843 and 1853, James Thomason, was a moderate evangelical Christian affiliated with the Clapham Sect of the Church of England, (whose membership included Charles Grant and William Wilberforce, among others), which had agitated from early in the nineteenth century for the abolition of slavery and the opening of India to missionaries.[14] Thomason championed an essentially paternalist approach to his administration, and advocated a conciliatory governmental programme of social and intellectual improvement through the diffusion of a secular education which, nevertheless, had as its aim the eventual spread of Christianity in India. In this respect, Thomason would come to give substantial support to the elaboration of the constructive orientalist educational programme under James Ballantyne, but also to attempts to promote the most basic level of education in the villages of the North-Western Provinces.[15]

Among the first educational reform measures undertaken by Thomason was his appointment of John Muir to the position of Superintendent of Benares Sanskrit College. Muir was initially charged with delineating the current state of the Sanskrit College, and extending the very tentative reform measures suggested by Captain Marshall in 1841. Muir, however, was perhaps a risky choice for the job, for although he was a committed Christian with evangelical leanings, he was also a Christian polemicist, who had authored a Sanskrit tract entitled *Mataparīkṣā* ('an examination of views [on religion]') which sought to overthrow the principal tenets of Hinduism in favour of those of Christianity.[16] Unofficially, Muir had also become involved with Benares Sanskrit College in 1838, when he had offered a sizeable

Rs 50 prize for the best essay in Sanskrit verse on the 'evidences of design and of the power, wisdom, and goodness of God, displayed in Creation' which was 'free from any reference to the peculiar dogmas of Hinduism'.[17] As such, Thomason's government, working within the guidelines set out by Lord Auckland, was also careful to point out in its letter of appointment that Muir should act in a conciliatory manner towards the *paṇḍit*s of the Sanskrit College, and attempt to actively involve them in proposed reforms.[18]

Muir's preliminary report on the Benares Sanskrit College highlighted many of the preconceptions which he brought in this early stage of his career to the analysis of Hinduism and Indian civilisation. Indeed, the report reads largely like a wholesale condemnation of Hinduism and its attendant philosophical and scientific literature in Sanskrit. The fundamental problem with the college, Muir stated, was that, with the exception of teachings delivered by Wilkinson's protégé, *paṇḍit* Bāpūdeva, it was otherwise wholly devoted to imparting knowledge based in ancient Sanskrit literature, which, he thought, was riddled with error:

> ... the religion, ritual and social institutions, the Mythological legends, and the Astrological superstitions as well as the philosophical and scientific systems of the Hindoos with all their errors, form a considerable part of the subjects of the college course. The Metaphysical systems are notoriously characterized by grave errors, the Vedanta being decidedly pantheistic, the Nyaya maintaining the eternity of matter, and the Samkhya in one of its branches being of an atheistic tendency; and even the Astronomy which the scientific books of the Hindoos teach, is the exploded Ptolemaic. It may therefore not unnaturally be asked by a person not acquainted with the history of the various educational schemes which have been current in India, how such a system as this, (which would appear to have a directly opposite tendency to that of the English and Vernacular schools established by Government for the enlightenment of the people, and the removal of their ancient errors), how such a system as this ever came to receive the patronage of the state.[19]

Yet the recommendations which Muir made to the NWP Government for the reform of Benares Sanskrit College were far less radical than one might expect, given his severe indictment of the college's curriculum.

Muir was convinced of the important role of the *paṇḍit*s in effecting the diffusion of useful knowledge and Christianity in India, 'on account of the influence which they exert on the population around them'. Indeed, it was apparent to Muir that in Benares, unlike in Calcutta, there was little prospect of quickly creating an English-speaking middle class, perhaps because Benares represented a centre of Hindu 'tradition'. The 1840s in Benares was a period of economic growth and consequently of religious patronage, such that the Company found itself increasingly outpaced by the local patronage of *paṇḍits* by aspirant Hindu merchants and *rājas*.[20] But Muir was equally convinced of the intransigence of these 'traditional' *paṇḍits*, noting that 'the pride and prejudices of the class in question are indeed serious obstacles in the way of their adopting sound principles in religion and philosophy'.[21] Muir therefore advocated a policy of conciliation in education and proselytisation, suggesting, for example, that Sanskrit be used as a medium for the communication of Western knowledge. In many ways, Muir's *Mataparīkṣā* can be viewed in this manner also, for it attempted to utilise Sanskrit and the concepts elaborated in its attendant philosophical literature to argue for the truth of Christian scripture.[22]

Muir recommended, therefore, that the government continue to 'indulge the natural predilections of the Hindoos by affording them facilities for the study of a literature of which they might well continue to be proud', while simultaneously introducing several useful knowledge tracts which he had written in Sanskrit, including a description and history of England, 'which would tend to open their minds', and a history of India, *Itihāsadīpikā*, 'with reference to that of the Greeks and Romans'. Muir thus recommended that the Sanskrit version of the *Padārthavidyāsāra*, William Yates' tract on natural philosophy and history, be introduced into the curriculum.[23] He also delivered a series of lectures in Sanskrit based on the Scottish doctor John Abercrombie's popular works on mental and moral philosophy (in the tradition of Thomas Reid and Dugald Stewart),[24] which he later published as *Vyavahāraloka* ('a work on general conduct').[25] In an address given in Sanskrit to the college's *paṇḍits* and students in April of 1844, Muir emphasised these points by praising Sanskrit-based grammar, poetry, and philosophy, noting that 2,000 years previous, the 'reputation of the knowledge' (*jñāna-kīrtti*) of India was 'echoed' (*pratinādita*) by the distant Greeks and Romans, and that even now, the learned (*paṇḍita*) of Europe desired a familiarity with Sanskrit literature. He also concluded that the pursuit by Indian students of the knowledge of their homeland (*svadeśīya-vidyābhyāsa*) was desirable for the 'increase in the power of the mind' (*buddheḥ śakteredhanārthaṃ*) it effected.[26] Simultaneously, Muir also warned that 'foreign knowledge' (*videśīyavidyā*) should not be neglected, but rather investigated for the benefit, or rather, 'development', it could bring to India's scholarly traditions and the Indian intellect itself (*buddherapi puṣṭiḥ sambhavati*).[27] The 'form' (*rūpa*) and 'substance' (*dravya*) of this foreign knowledge was then enumerated in the main body of the *Vyavahāraloka*, and in particular, Western mental philosophy, which Muir hoped to use to demonstrate 'the instruments we have to work with in seeking after truth'.[28]

Yet Muir was clearly impressed with the 'dialectic subtleties' of 'Hindu philosophy', and the 'acuteness' with which the *paṇḍit*s and students of the Sanskrit College were trained.[29] He argued, for example, that the study of the various divergent schools of Indian philosophy may be converted 'from being sources of error ... into tolerable instruments for strengthening the reasoning powers', by examining students so as to compare each system with the other, and 'bring them to the test of reason'.[30] This, Muir hoped, might 'lead to the formation of precise and accurate habits of thought, and train the pupils not only to subtlety which the existing system gives, but also to soundness of reflection which it fails to impart'.[31] In addition, Muir also suggested that the Benares English Seminary and the Sanskrit College be amalgamated into one college (to be referred to simply as 'Benares College'), so that the physical proximity of students studying English and Western learning to the Sanskrit students might enable a further, critical comparison of these bodies of knowledge. Muir here clearly conceived that the *paṇḍit*s' acceptance of Hindu philosophy was necessarily based upon 'the ground of authority',[32] and that the 'dialectic subtlety' of their philosophical systems was nevertheless directed towards pure speculation, producing 'no tangible advantage'.[33]

The programme of reform which Muir undertook at Benares College was largely one of 'engraftment', directed towards the gradual impartation of 'truth' in the sciences through a process of familiarisation through Sanskrit. Muir clearly hoped that the measures he outlined, which he envisioned would develop the faculty of reason in his students, would in time also enable them to accept the claims of Western civilisation and Christianity upon the basis that these alone were consistent with the dictates of reason and historical evidence, as well as being more generally conducive to spiritual and material betterment.[34] This sentiment can be perceived in Muir's parting address to the students of Benares College, in which he recommended as role models both the Sanskrit grammarian Pāṇini and the philosopher Gautama, noting them to be 'enquirers after truth'. Muir did add a caveat, though: 'rather than men who had actually found it'. In addition, Muir lauded Bāpūdeva as a 'real lover of truth ... an enlightened young pandit ... [who] is in no instance content to receive any truth on the authority of the ancients, but invariably requires demonstration'.[35] But in many respects, Muir should also be regarded as an important forerunner to the constructive orientalist educational project at Benares, for he shared many of the concerns, and preconceptions, which drove Ballantyne. Indeed, Muir used his short experience in Benares to speak authoritatively to issues of educational reform, while also implicitly reassociating himself in an article in the *Benares Magazine* with the success, and praise, which the new curriculum at Benares enjoyed in the 1850s.[36]

Constructive orientalism at Benares College

James Robert Ballantyne began his 15-year tenure as the Superintendent of Benares College in January of 1846, at the age of 32. Before this appointment, he had taught 'oriental languages' in the Scottish Naval and Military Academy in Edinburgh, as well as having published several works for use in that institution, including Hindustani, Persian, and Marathi grammars, *Principles of Persian Caligraphy*, and *The Practical Oriental Interpreter*.[37] Born the son of a printer in December of 1813 in Kelso, in the Borders region of Scotland, he was educated in classics, logic, geology, natural history and moral philosophy at the Edinburgh Academy, as well as the University of Edinburgh.[38] Ballantyne, like his predecessor John Muir, was educated in the latest stages of the Scottish Enlightenment, and many of his ideas about civilisational hierarchy and advancement were clearly derived directly from the institutional context of early nineteenth-century Scotland. Ballantyne had also attended the East India College in Haileybury beginning in 1829 to study oriental languages, and upon graduation was able to boast of a certificate of competency to instruct in Persian, Arabic, Hindustani, Bengali, Marathi, and 'the elements of Sanskrit'.[39] After failing to secure a cadetship with the East India Company, however, Ballantyne took charge of the Oriental Department of the Scottish Military and Naval Academy in 1832. He soon became dissatisfied with the meagre income associated with his position, and so nearly six years after first lobbying for the support of H. H. Wilson (then Boden Professor of Sanskrit at Oxford), he received a recommendation to the post in Benares early in 1845, the same year he received his doctorate from Glasgow University.[40] Ballantyne, however, might at first glance have seemed an unusual choice for the superintendent of a government college which boasted the most prestigious and symbolically important Sanskrit department in the Company's Indian territories. His publications were confined to Persian, Hindustani, and Marathi, and he possessed no official qualifications in Sanskrit, save that which he received from Haileybury. His accomplishments in Indian languages and general linguistic aptitude were well proven, however, and he was able to demonstrate a breadth and depth of knowledge in Western science, philosophy, religion, and literature.

Ballantyne was also a committed Christian, whose stated purpose in the educational service of India was the conversion of educated Hindus to Christianity.[41] The constructive orientalist project, which reached its apogee under Ballantyne's superintendence, then, aimed to incorporate the use of Indian languages and texts, and the cultural authority of the *paṇḍits*, in order to bring about this preconceived purpose. In this respect, there are two distinct, but intertwined, components to Ballantyne's approach as it evolved over the 15 years he was superintendent, which need to be emphasised separately at the outset. The first of these is his belief that Christianity was an inherently rational religion, and that its tenets and scriptures were supported and reinforced by the scientific and philosophical endeavour. Ballantyne was clearly working within a framework elaborated and popularised by William Paley's natural theology, and the distinction between God's 'general revelation', which provided evidence for the existence and character of God in His Creation, and the 'special revelation', constituted by the Christian scriptures, and which provided the basis for salvation. In essence Paley's work had served to authorise a 'productive harmony' for lay British scientists and writers between the discoveries of European scientific enquiry and the claims of Christianity for much of the nineteenth century.[42] In this regard, the motives and preconceptions which drove Ballantyne's pedagogy do not differ significantly from many of the earlier educational strategies already discussed.

But secondly, Ballantyne also began to explicitly characterise the Indian knowledge contained in the Sanskrit corpus, the *śāstra*, and Western science and religion, as distinct levels of intellectual accomplishment on a single developmental, and perhaps 'conjectural', scheme. Ballantyne perceived Indian society to be 'stuck' at a lower level of civilisational development than had been achieved by Britain, and as such, he set out to utilise the 'common intellectual ground' found in Sanskrit and English scholarly texts as a way to both demonstrate Britain's civilisational advancement, and the path to be taken in improving India intellectually, socially, and materially. In this regard, Ballantyne also identified 'Hinduism' and in particular the privileges enjoyed by *brāhmaṇs* as key factors in the stultification of Indian 'progress'. The constructive orientalism of Ballantyne, therefore, shared significant elements of Lancelot Wilkinson's educational experiments in Sehore, but also aimed at a comprehensiveness which Wilkinson's predominant focus on astronomical knowledge lacked.

Ballantyne arrived at Benares College in January of 1846, and seems to have devoted much of his attention at this early juncture to the English classes of the college, reading with them, for example, *Hamlet* and Whatley's *Logic*.[43] This focus was likely to have been largely a function of Ballantyne's limited capacity in Sanskrit upon his arrival.[44] However, Ballantyne also began in these early years to publish a series of introductory Sanskrit grammatical treatises and synopses of Hindu philosophy. These were ostensibly to enable the students of the college's English Department to enter into a dialogue with the students of the Sanskrit Department, and thereby further enable a critical comparison of Indian and European learning, as Muir had suggested in his 1844 report on the college. Yet perhaps these publications also reflected Ballantyne's own programme of learning in these fields, and as such, the progression of his own ability to engage with the *paṇḍits* in their own areas of expertise. In this way, Ballantyne was fulfilling what John Muir had outlined in 1845 as a 'primary qualification' for one who wished to reason with 'the votaries of false religion': namely, 'an accurate knowledge and a candid estimate of our opponent's tenets'.[45] Among the first translations published by Ballantyne was a Sanskrit and English version of the *Laghu Kaumudi*, a simplified version of Pāṇini's grammatical aphorisms, which Ballantyne characterised as 'one of a series of attempts to encourage and facilitate the interchange of ideas between the *paṇḍits* and the senior English students of the Government Colleges'.[46] Ballantyne noted, however, that the *paṇḍits* of the Sanskrit Department disapproved of his publication plan, arguing that 'it will promote indolence by encouraging the student to rely upon his marginal references instead of upon his memory'.[47] Ballantyne also published a series of short works which, modelled upon his lectures to the English Department, outlined the basic contents of the various Hindu philosophical systems. The first of these was the lectures on the principal tenets of the *nyāya*, delivered in 1848, and which was then followed in subsequent years by lectures on the *sāṅkhya* and *vedānta*.[48] Ballantyne was drawn, in particular, to the *nyāya*, which would in time serve as the basis for his elaboration of a developmental scheme of logical reasoning and metaphysical speculation.[49] Ballantyne also began in the early years of his superintendency to focus upon the teaching of vernacular languages within the English Department of the college, a measure which had been introduced in the early 1840s.[50] In particular he was concerned with what he viewed as the 'bad style of written Hindi', which proved an impediment to the diffusion of useful knowledge in that language.[51]

By 1847–1848, Ballantyne began to turn his attention to the Sanskrit Department of the college, as he often characterised the *paṇḍit*s who taught there, and the *brāhmaṇ* students which constituted this department, as the intellectual and religious leadership of the Hindu 'masses'. They were, therefore, to be considered as the key to the moral and intellectual development of India. In this respect, Ballantyne quoted in one of his early articles for the *Benares Magazine* both John Malcolm and Brian Hodgson's views on this point,[52] adding that 'the unlearned Hindu takes the Brahman at his own valuation; and neither our power, nor our scientific superiority, has as yet much lowered this'.[53] Ballantyne simultaneously realised that even the *brāhmaṇ* students being educated in 'useful knowledge', English, and the vernacular languages within the English Department of the college would be of little practical use in effecting India's civilisational improvement in this regard. In Ballantyne's words, these students would be without 'moral influence' in Indian society, as they lacked the 'amount of Sanscrit erudition which is indispensable for securing any degree of respectful attention to his words'.[54] In this regard, Ballantyne noted:

> The great influence which the Europeanized ideas of the learned Brahmin, Ram Mohun Roy, exerted upon the native mind of Bengal, when contrasted with the comparatively slender influence exerted by well educated and intelligent men of a different class, has always struck me as pointing to the combination of conditions which we must strive to bring about if we would aim successfully at raising the native character.[55]

Ballantyne wished to capitalise upon the cultural authority which derived from the *paṇḍit*s' social status combined with the respect given to their erudition, and in so doing, aimed to transform the Sanskrit Department into a vehicle for the diffusion of Western knowledge, and hence turn the department to the cause of India's civilisational improvement.[56] Ballantyne therefore outlined in his 1846–1847 yearly report to the NWP Government what he considered to be a 'new constitution' for the Sanskrit Department of Benares College. He desired to make the 'primary object' of the department the means of studying 'the most valuable branches of Sanscrit learning', without expense to the student. The 'secondary, [but] not subordinate object' was to be to provide the department's most senior and accomplished Sanskrit scholars with an opportunity to learn English, as well as the knowledge 'which constitute[s] the glory of the nation which founded this College'. This was to be accomplished by holding out the prospect of lucrative scholarships to eligible students, and to allow them to hold these scholarships past the normal cut-off age of 23. Of course, that arrangement, in essence, amounted to bribery, which Ballantyne recognised, but he also justified it with regard to its noble end.[57] This programme would, in time, evolve into what became known as the Anglo-Sanskrit Department.

Ballantyne's first attempt to convey Western useful knowledge to the *paṇḍit*s of the Sanskrit Department was undertaken from 1848, when he began to publish, in both Sanskrit and English, several parts of a treatise entitled *Lectures on the Sub-Divisions of Knowledge*. Ballantyne conceived this text to be a preliminary outline of the totality of Western knowledge, which would then serve to 'pave the way for the easier preparation of a systematic set of works'.[58] He also prefaced the first part of the book with an illustrative 'moral tale' in order to demonstrate the text's usefulness to the *paṇḍit*s. In it, Ballantyne related the story of a group of South Seas islanders who believed that there was nothing beyond their own island, and that the ocean was created just for them to fish in. A person 'whose attention is confined to a single act', Ballantyne noted, was 'apt to fall into the analogous error'. As such, the *Sub-Divisions of Knowledge* was presented to acquaint the students of the Sanskrit Department 'with the mutual relations of all the sciences', so that they will not 'be in danger of incurring the ridicule of the intelligent, by mistaking the twig for the tree'.[59]

In the book, Ballantyne characterised all human knowledge as being divisible into two general categories: knowledge of spirit, or 'relating to man as the possessor of mind' (*ātmīya jñāna*), and knowledge of matter (*anātmīya jñāna*). These were then further broken down and summarised. Knowledge of spirit was divided into knowledge obtained by an inquiry into man's mental nature (*manuṣya ātma*): metaphysics, morals, grammar, logic, and rhetoric, as well as knowledge of spirit obtained through an inquiry into man's history (*manuṣya itihāsa*): political, religious, philosophical, and scientific history, as well as the critical analysis of history's claims. Ballantyne next divided knowledge of matter into that obtained through observation (*pratyakṣa*), and that obtained through reflection (*anumāna*). The former branch included astronomy, geography, zoology, botany, mineralogy, geology, and chemistry, while the latter branch included arithmetic, algebra, calculus, geometry, and the physical sciences.[60] Presented in its Sanskrit version, this outline of the division of human knowledge (*jñānaviśeṣapradarśana*) was termed the '*vidyācakra*', or 'circle of the sciences'. All branches of knowledge rested upon and simultaneously confirmed the other branches, and at the epicentre of the circle lay the Special Revelation, evidenced by a History (*itihāsa*) which began with the sentence 'the world was created by God' (*īśvareṇa sṛṣṭo 'yaṃ saṃsāraḥ*).[61]

The organisation of the *Lectures on the Sub-Division of Knowledge* was based on Ballantyne's belief that the knowledge conveyed by the Christian Revelation could be imparted to the Hindu learned elite only by first providing them with a rational and scientific basis for its acceptance. Christianity, he supposed, 'bases its claims on historical evidence', and as such, 'presupposes not merely an acquaintance with historical assertions, but a cultivation of the critical faculty, so as that the force of the historical evidence may be intelligently felt'.[62] In order for a Hindu to embrace Christianity 'on principle and conviction', Ballantyne felt (as John Muir did) that it was necessary for him to both present the evidence, and to ensure that the Hindu 'critical faculty' was sufficient to perceive it in its 'proper' light. While such an approach would have been at least partly a practical consideration, for direct proselytisation of Christianity within Company-sponsored educational establishments was prohibited, it also reflected Ballantyne's background in the study of natural philosophy and history. Near the end of his educational career, Ballantyne fondly quoted the views of Revd John Penrose, whose 1808 Bampton Lectures were inspired by William Paley's *Natural Theology*, and as such, sought to establish evidence for Christianity outside the realm of miracles, in the arena of rationality. Ballantyne's educational labours were undoubtedly inspired by the same sentiment which motivated Penrose to downplay the efficacy of missionary activity in Britain's colonies for the propagation of Christianity: the missionary's want of 'an enlarged and comprehensive intellect' was thought to have rendered them unfit for the task of enabling 'those persons to whom our religion is offered ... to determine for themselves, concerning its records and evidences ... [so] to admit its truth on rational principles'.[63] Ballantyne considered all knowledge, empirical and trans-empirical, to be a self-supporting unity, and so he referred to his own approach to the propagation of Christianity in India, which emphasised the empirical, as an appeal to the head, rather than the heart. It was an approach which he felt to be in accordance with what he considered God's greatest gift to humanity: the faculty of reason.[64]

What the *paṇḍits* lacked in Ballantyne's view, however, was an understanding of 'History' (with a capital 'H') and the methods by which to judge the veridicality of historical evidence:

> To put the case upon even the lowest ground, we think that the conversion of the learned Hindus (whose conversion would involve the conversion of India) would, humanly speaking, be greatly facilitated, if the assent of their understandings were gained to the historical proofs which we can give them of the truth of what we allege. But, as we have said, amid the learning of India, history holds no place. A proof drawn from history has no weight with a Hindu; nor can it ever have much until he shall have learned well to estimate the force of historical evidence.[65]

Ballantyne's educational project was aimed, therefore, at providing the necessary basis for the rational acceptance of that historical evidence upon which Christianity based its claims.[66] In order for such an educational project to be effective, Ballantyne thought that it would have to be comprehensive and systematic, for while he considered all knowledge to be a unity, the sciences in particular were seen to be mutually supportive and reinforcing. That is, 'the immediate preparation for a critically intelligent study of history is the study of physical geography', for without a proper understanding of physical geography, history is liable to descend into that expressed in the *Purāṇas*, with its stories of 'oceans of treacle, cane-juice, and butter-milk'. Further, the study of physical geography was thought to be dependent upon zoology, botany, and geology, and these in turn depended upon chemistry, physics, and also logic.[67] Ballantyne also realised that any attempt to impart Western knowledge to the *paṇḍits* would have to present that knowledge as a systematic whole, in accordance with their own conception of the *śāstra* as a singular and consistent body of knowledge. In essence, Ballantyne's *Lectures on the Sub-Divisions of Knowledge* was his preliminary attempt to construct for the *paṇḍits* a 'complete sastra of [his] own', which he could then 'oppose to the Naiyayiks'.[68] Ballantyne's proof that any course of Western knowledge presented to the Hindu elite should necessarily encompass such a totality was evident in what he considered to be the failure of similar previous educational efforts. Wilkinson's attempt to overthrow 'Hindu prejudice' by way of Western astronomy was, he thought, admirable, though it fell short of what was required because it lacked the comprehensiveness required to place the historical basis of Christianity in its supportive context. This was amply demonstrated to Ballantyne by an episode which occurred in 1847, in which several *paṇḍit*s who had calculated an eclipse with a high degree of accuracy on the basis of Western methods, reportedly utilised their new-found expertise to 'enable them to ascertain with greater precision the moment beyond which they must not delay plunging into the Ganges'.[69]

Increasingly, however, Ballantyne also came to realise that the *paṇḍit*s of the Sanskrit Department were not an easy audience to convince, for their 'prejudices' were apparently deep-seated, and furthermore, they seemed to be convinced of their own 'inherent sanctity', as well as considering themselves to possess an 'infinite superiority to us in philosophical speculation'.[70] Ballantyne reported in 1847, for example, that the study of John Muir's *Vyavahārāloka* was 'performed grudgingly', and that he often had to answer the question 'what is the use of such studies as these?' noting the 'mournful tone of the question' and the 'unsatisfied look of the querist'.[71] In this regard, shortly after undertaking the publication of the *Lectures on the Sub-Divisions of Knowledge,* Ballantyne came to realise that his attempt to impart Western useful knowledge to the *paṇḍit*s could be much more easily facilitated by presenting it in an attractive manner: as the development of the 'old truth' contained in the Hindu *śāstra*. This realisation is noted in his 9 December 1847 report on the college:

> During the past year the Sanscrit Department of the College has engrossingly occupied my thoughts, and I have become more and more convinced that, for the sake of India and its living languages, the study of Sanscrit ought to be encouraged: that the study if conducted merely according to the old routine, will do less good than it might be made to do: and that we shall find ourselves struggling against a needlessly created current of prejudice whenever we attempt to direct the attention of the pundits or pupils to entirely new subjects of enquiry, without taking care to conciliate both their judgement and their taste, by moulding what we present to them as nearly

> as possible into accordance with what is sound in their own systems, and thus claiming for it their attention, less as a contradiction of what is false in those systems, than as the legitimate development of what is true.[72]

This realisation must have been based at least partially in Ballantyne's increasing familiarity with Hindu philosophy and the contents of Sanskrit texts. Moreover, it seems also to have been expressed initially in the language of the conciliation of the *brāhmaṇs* to Western learning. In this regard, Ballantyne once quoted a sentiment which both he and John Muir admired, expressed by Pascal in this manner:

> When one wishes profitably to stop another, and show him that he deceives himself, it is necessary to observe from what side it is that he views things, for from that side it is ordinarily true, and to avow to him this truth, but to discover to him the side from which it is false. He is pleased thereby for he sees that he was not altogether deceived, and that he only failed to see all the sides. Now one does not distress one self about not seeing all, but one does not like to have been altogether deceived.[73]

Certainly the importance of conciliation is evident in Ballantyne's later reworking of the *Lectures of the Sub-Divisions of Knowledge*, which he republished as *A Synopsis of Science*, and which appeared in two editions between 1852 and 1856. This text deviated from Ballantyne's previous attempt at a systematic treatise in the physical manner of its presentation, for while the *Sub-Divisions of Knowledge* was presented in English and Sanskrit prose, the *Synopsis of Science* adopted an 'oriental guise' to facilitate its acceptance by the *paṇḍits*, as it is framed into aphorisms and commentary, in accordance with the general style of *śāstrik* literature. Ballantyne commented that the English prose of the *Synopsis of Science* might seem 'stiff and ungainly', but that he had 'intentionally imitated the established style of exposition'. Moreover, he noted that his 'object was, not to introduce a new style, but to convey truth in the style which, as being the established style, was the least likely to provoke cavil'.[74] In this respect, an undated lithographed pamphlet found amongst Ballantyne's unsorted papers, (in Ballantyne's hand), which presents a dialogue between a *paṇḍit* and a *śiṣya* (student) on the subject of European knowledge, does so in the perfect past tense, which is normally reserved for relating events in the remote past. Its style, however, does correspond closely with that found in the *Bhagavad Gītā*: *paṇḍita uvāca* ('the *paṇḍit* said').[75]

The most significant development in Ballantyne's thought, however, was the conception that Western scientific and philosophical knowledge ('new truth') could be presented to the *paṇḍit*s as the development of those basic elements which were already contained within *śāstrik* knowledge ('ancient truth'). Ballantyne thus both emulated the methodology of Lancelot Wilkinson, and constructed a hierarchy of intellects and civilisations based upon a singular developmental scheme. In an article for the *Benares Magazine*, 'On the Nyaya System of Philosophy, and the Correspondence of its Divisions with those of Modern Science', Ballantyne set out to demonstrate the 'scientific character' of the *nyāya*, and to show that it contained the 'starting points' for the learned of India to enter into a programme of learning the sciences of the West.[76] By so doing, he conceived that he was showing the *paṇḍit*s a shared frame of reference – shared truths, in essence – and simultaneously that the knowledge which they possessed 'halted at a stage short of that which [the British had] reached'. The 'superior' knowledge of the West was thereby presented as 'the legitimate development of what is true in their [the *paṇḍit*s'] views, and not in the shape of a contradiction to anything that is erroneous'.[77] For example, Ballantyne noted that the *nyāya* enumerates within its first category (*padārtha*) for exposition, 'substance' (*dravya*), the sub-category of 'earth' (*pṛthivī*), which itself includes that which is 'eternal in the forms of atoms', and that which is 'transient in the form of products'. Ballantyne stated that here 'we note ... the first point in the system at which we can distinctly and intelligibly acquaint the learned Hindu with one of our own marked scientific divisions'. In essence, Ballantyne believed that the division of earth into 'atoms' and 'mass' may then be used to analogously demonstrate to the *paṇḍit*s the 'modern division of physical science into the chemical and the non-chemical'.[78] Moreover, Ballantyne reported that even in his initial experiments with this methodology, the *paṇḍit*s were 'gratified by the admission that their own view' was 'correct so far as it goes', and that they 'laid aside their jealous hostility' to Western knowledge, and exhibited a 'lively curiosity to know how the thing could be carried further'.[79]

With his realisation that the *nyāya* philosophical system could provide the basis upon which a knowledge of Western science, and its methodology, could be imparted to the *paṇḍit*s, Ballantyne used it in particular to facilitate a comparison of 'Eastern' and 'Western' views on the constituents of knowledge as well as the methodology for obtaining it within his new systematic treatise on knowledge, the *Synopsis of Science*. This text begins by following the outline of the *Nyāya Sūtra* of

Gautama, a foundational philosophical text on logical argumentation as a means to liberation through the removal of ignorance and erroneous knowledge. The text itself begins with a benedictory verse, and then moves on to assert a commonality in scholastic purpose between the learned of India and those of Europe:

> It is agreed alike by the learned of India and by the learned of other countries that the Chief End of Man, (*parama-purushartha*), is not to be attained without a knowledge of the truth in regard to our souls and other things which it is desirable should be rightly known. Therefore those who desire to attain the Chief End of Man ought certainly to strive to obtain a knowledge of the truth in regard to the soul, and in regard to things other than the soul.[80]

The pursuit of 'correct knowledge', or 'truth' (*tattva-jñāna*) is agreed to be conducive to the 'chief end of man', though Ballantyne declared that Indians and Europeans disagree as to the exact nature of that 'chief end'. Gautama, on the one hand, defined it as the annihilation of pain, i.e. liberation from rebirth, (*tad [duḥkha] atyantavimokṣo 'pavargaḥ*) while Ballantyne, on the other, asserted it to be that which 'is to be attained through the grace of God' (*parameśvara-prasādāt paramaḥ puruṣārthaḥ*), adding his view that any pursuit of simple liberation was ultimately 'empty'.[81] Nevertheless, the *Synopsis of Science* is an attempt to enumerate the points of agreement, and disagreement, as to the instruments and methodology for attaining correct knowledge, as well as the objects of such an inquiry, i.e. the things 'which it is desirable should be rightly known' (*prameya*). In essence, the *Synopsis of Science* is a comparative text on scientific method and its results. For example, Ballantyne listed the instruments for obtaining knowledge, or the varieties of evidence (*pramāṇa*), upon which the determination of right knowledge is dependent, to be the senses (*pratyakṣa*) and inference (a 'knowledge of signs', *anumāna*). These, he argued, corresponded with two of the four listed by Gautama, adding that the latter's additions of 'knowledge of likeness' (*upamāna*) and 'verbal testimony' (*śabda*) might be subsumed under the category of 'inference', and as such, should not be considered as independent.[82] A substantial portion of the *Synopsis of Science* is dedicated to an examination of the topic of inference, and includes detailed considerations of induction, deduction, rhetoric, logic, and so forth. The remainder of the text then goes on to detail what were considered by Ballantyne to be the objects of correct knowledge (*prameya*). These included the constituents of the

Sub-Divisions of Knowledge, represented, however, in an order that catered to a follower of the *nyāya*: the 'independent' sciences of mathematics, formal astronomy, and mechanics were presented at the outset, so as to provide a frame of reference to the subjects of chemistry, mineralogy, botany, physiology, geology, geography, history, ethics, law, and natural theology.[83]

The *Synopsis of Science* ends by considering the argument from design, taken in this instance from a version found in the *Siddhānta Muktāvalī*, which is a sixteenth- or seventeenth-century gloss on the *Bhāṣā-Pariccheda*, an important text of the 'new' *nyāya* scholarship centred at Nadia:

> Such productions as a water-jar are produced by a maker, and so also are the earth and the trees; and to make these is not possible for such as we are; hence the existence of the Deity, as the Maker of these, is established.
> *yathā ghaṭādi kāryaṃ kartṛjanyaṃ tathā kṣityaṃ kurādikamapi na ca tatkartṛtvamasmadādīnāṃ sambhavatītyatastatkartṛtveneśvarasiddhiḥ*[84]

Ballantyne asserted that if one accepts that the evidence of design in the natural world proves the existence of a designer – and indeed one should, having studied the entire book – then the natural consequence is to ask after the intentions of that designer. Ballantyne asked the reader 'has the God of Nature anywhere directly revealed himself to man?'[85] The answer, he believed, was in the scriptures of Christianity, and so he therefore directed the enquirer to continue his pursuit of the 'chief end of man' through an examination of those scriptures which did not 'encourage the worshipping of idols' or promoted 'many cruel vicious and frivolous practices', in which God's will was most certainly set forth.[86]

The *Synopsis of Science* was undoubtedly Ballantyne's attempt to construct a *śāstra* of his own: Western knowledge of logic, science, history, and natural theology, presented in a manner which was thought to suit the tastes of the Sanskrit *paṇḍits*, and which took the *nyāya*, a philosophical system accepted as authoritative, as its starting point of reference. This 'digest' of knowledge, which was in reality little more than an outline of principal tenets of these subjects, was then supplemented between 1850 and 1855 by a series of reprints – the 'Reprints for the Pandits' – which presented voluminous extracts from the works of major Western thinkers on the topics of physical science, logic, metaphysics, rhetoric, political economy, and physical geography.[87]

These texts were all printed in the original English (with the occasional addition of Sanskrit terminology) and so were intended to be read primarily by the few senior *paṇḍit*s who spoke English, such as Bāpūdeva Śāstrī and Viṭṭhala Śāstrī,[88] as well as to constitute the textbooks for Ballantyne's special English-language seminar within the Sanskrit Department – the '*paṇḍit* class' – composed, at least initially, of the senior Sanskrit students whom Ballantyne had allowed to continue their studies, on the condition that they learn English.[89]

The foundational text of the 'reprint' series was an explanatory version of Francis Bacon's *Novum Organum*.[90] Although this text was considered 'out of date in Europe as the actual guide in scientific investigation',[91] the *Novum Organum* represented to Ballantyne and his contemporaries a seminal text in Western philosophy. Its focus on a rational scientific methodology directed philosophical inquiry away from the 'unfruitful' speculation, or syllogising, of ancient Aristotelians to the discovery of 'new' and 'useful' truth which would materially improve the condition of mankind. Baconian induction was deemed conducive to ascertaining scientific truth, whereas Aristotelian syllogising neglected the truth status of its premises, and so the *Novum Organum* was thereby characterised as the text which best represented Europe's transition into modernity through the presentation of an enabling scientific methodology. Indeed, T. B. Macaulay's anonymous review in the *Edinburgh Review* of the collected works of Francis Bacon noted that the *Novum Organum* was held to be significant not because of the methodology it advocated (induction), but because it turned philosophy to a new object: the 'accumulation of truth' for the purpose of 'increasing the power and ameliorating the condition of man'.[92]

Ballantyne felt that the *Novum Organum*'s detailed treatment of the scientific methodology of induction correlated closely with the discussion of the method for apprehending invariable concomitance (*vyāpti-grahopāya*) found in the *nyāya*, and particularly in Gangeśopādhyāya's *Tattva-Cintāmaṇi*, and as such represented a measure of intellectual 'common ground' between Indians and Britons. Yet Ballantyne also believed that the methodologies and habits of thought of the contemporary *paṇḍit*s held much in common with that of the ancient Aristotelians. In the first instance, Ballantyne thought that the 'Hindu mind' currently resided in what William Whewell had termed the 'commentorial stage', in which 'originality is forbidden and shunned'.[93] Further, Ballantyne considered that the established practice of attempting to reconcile three inconsistent philosophical systems (the *nyāya*, *sāṅkhya*, and *vedānta*), such that 'the same assertion [is viewed] as true at one moment and false the next', had led to 'the existing remarkable indifference as to what is truth in itself'. Truth, he believed, had become 'a matter of taste' for the *paṇḍit*.[94] This was amply demonstrated to Ballantyne when he witnessed a *paṇḍit* passionately defend the most indefensible of positions, namely that Aristotle's claim that a thing cannot at once both 'be' and 'not be' was incorrect:

> Our visitor was disposed as little to grant this as anything else, – and he had made some way towards demonstrating the perfect compatibility of 'being' and 'non-being' under certain circumstances, when fortunately another pandit came in – and to him we resigned the conduct of the argument. Quotations from all the most profound authorities on the subject of Non-existence were soon flying about our ears – each disputant screaming at the highest pitch of his voice – and, some other pandits having come in and seated themselves as spectators and judges, the contest raged so 'fast and furious' that our little boy slunk out of the room in a state of alarm in which we ourself began rather to participate. At length the arguments on the side of Artistotle were found to be in accordance with the dicta of authorities – whereupon the stranger gracefully gave in and was complimented on the vigour with which he had fought a losing battle.[95]

By equating the 'fruitless' speculation and disputation of the Hindus with the 'fruitless' speculation of pre-Baconian, i.e. Aristotelian, syllogistic philosophy, Ballantyne thereby also equated contemporary Hindu civilisation with Europe before the Enlightenment, and obviously intended the *Novum Organum* to bring about an evolution in Hindu philosophy similar to that which had occurred in Europe several centuries previously. In this way, Ballantyne further confirmed the developmental hierarchy which simultaneously underpinned, and provided justification to, his constructive orientalist educational project.

In this regard, it should be noted that John Muir had also recognised the importance of Bacon's text in a very similar manner, writing in an 1838 article in the *Calcutta Christian Observer*:

> The truth and common sense of Bacon's philosophy has commended it to the learned of Europe; and with what splendid results everyone knows. The command of nature, and the material benefits resulting to men, are there sought after with adequate zeal and

> energy. The application to India is obvious. The followers of Plato ... and of Seneca, are paralleled or out-heroded in Hindustan, by the disciples of Vyasa, Kupila, Patanjali, and Gotama, the adherents of the Vedanta, the Mimamsa, the Samkhya, and the Nyaya schools of philosophy. ... Their spirit coincides with that of the Grecian and Roman philosophy, or is even more exclusively speculative. ... Those systems whose aim and boast it is to train up ascetic gymnosophists, are obviously most eminently adverse to the scientific cultivation of the arts which civilize and adorn human life.[96]

Ballantyne's 'reprint' series also included more advanced and up-to-date works on the methodology of induction to supplement the *Novum Organum*, which included voluminous extracts from John Stuart Mill's *System of Logic, Ratiocinative and Inductive*, as well as portions of Whewell's *Philosophy of the Inductive Sciences*, and which took care to include further comparisons with *vyāptigrahopāya*, the 'strategy for the recognition of invariable concomitance'.[97] These detailed considerations of the processes of Western scientific method and reasoning were then supplemented in the 'reprint' series with several works on physical science, chemistry,[98] and physical geography. Further, Ballantyne also arranged for the practical demonstration of Western science in the college – rendering science a 'spectacle' – by purchasing, for example, a telescope,[99] as well as the apparatus for conducting experiments in photography.[100] Indeed, together with Viṭṭhala Śāstrī, Ballantyne published a treatise in 1857 which claimed to be the 'first manual of photography in any oriental language'. *Heliographic Rules and Reasons*, or *Ravikiraṇkūrcikayā citralekhana, prakriyopapattivarṇanaṃ* ('a description of the rules and reasons, [for] painting with the brush of the rays of the sun') presented technical directions in English, Sanskrit, and Hindi, for calotype photography (salt prints), and drew heavily upon the outline of chemistry presented in the *Synopsis of Science*, not least for its Sanskrit terminology.[101]

Considered together, Ballantyne intended that the 'reprint' series and scientific experimentation would display to the *paṇḍits* what he considered the 'deficiencies or errors which in their systems branch away, fruitlessly, opposite the richly fructiferous scientific branches, which European culture has elicited from truths that have here remained barren or run wild'.[102] That is, he intended to contrast the results of a Western scientific method which shared its foundations with that found in Hindu philosophy. The object of philosophical inquiry in India was thereby to be turned away from 'speculation' to the pursuit of 'useful truth' and the consequence was intended to be the material, social, intellectual, and of course, moral 'progress' of India upon the developmental-historical model of Europe.

A fundamental component of both the *Lectures on the Sub-Divisions of Knowledge*, and the *Synopsis of Science*, as well as the 'reprint' series, was the aim to construct a suitable vocabulary in Sanskrit for the diffusion of Western science and philosophy in that language, either by reference to existent word usage in the *nyāya* or some other branch of Hindu philosophy, or alternatively, through the devising of altogether new terms. Indeed, Ballantyne noted at the start of the dual-language *Lectures on the Sub-Divisions of Knowledge* that one of the text's main purposes was to 'ascertain experimentally what technical terms were already available in the Sanskrit, and what terms were best fitted to convey the meaning in cases where the novelty of the subjects, as regards the language and the notions of the pandits, necessitated the devising of new terms'.[103] Yet Ballantyne did not intend for that terminology to remain 'locked up' in the Sanskrit, but rather intended to use Sanskrit terminology to 'enrich' the vernacular languages, which, in turn, were conceived to be the primary vehicles for the diffusion of useful knowledge to the masses.[104] Ballantyne published Hindi versions of *A Synopsis of Science*,[105] as well as some of the 'reprints' series[106] in addition to Hindi versions of Sanskrit texts, such as the *Hitopadeśa*.[107] While language and translation is the subject of the next chapter, it should be noted here that the process of translation into the vernaculars at Benares College was conceived as being a necessary requirement of the 'improvement' project, given the socio-cultural status of the *paṇḍits* in India. On the one hand, Ballantyne depended upon the *paṇḍits* to lend cultural authority and legitimation to his system of pedagogy, but on the other hand, he also recognised that they constituted the principal obstacle to its success. It has already been noted, for example, that Ballantyne had commented upon the *paṇḍits*' deep-seated 'prejudices' and belief in their own intellectual superiority. Ballantyne also identified the *paṇḍits*' insistence upon limiting scholarly discourse to a Sanskrit medium, and thereby, to a small, exclusive segment of the Indian population as a key problem which limited the diffusion of Western knowledge.[108] As such, the translation of European texts from English into Sanskrit, through the *paṇḍits*, and thereafter into Hindi, was conceived by Ballantyne as a way to invoke the *paṇḍits*' authority, as well as that of Sanskrit itself, while releasing knowledge in India from the control and misdirection of the *paṇḍits*. In effect, Ballantyne was attempting, on yet another level, to reproduce the intellectual history of Europe in India, by consciously attempting to recreate the processes by which scientific knowledge in Europe was released from Latin and Greek, as well as from the clutches of the clerical elite, during the Scientific Revolution. This process in Europe both improved the capacity of the vernaculars, such as English and German, and simultaneously allowed for the wider proliferation of scientific knowledge through society, thereby enabling its material as well as moral 'improvement'.[109]

Ballantyne's system of pedagogy received enthusiastic support from NWP's Lieutenant-Governor, James Thomason, who, for example, praised Ballantyne and his publications in a speech commemorating the opening of the new Benares College building in 1853.[110] Monier Williams, then Professor at the East India College at Haileybury, remarked in 1851 that Ballantyne's 'energetic' labours made him 'eminently fitted' for his position.[111] Early drafts of the 1854 despatch from the Company's Court of Directors outlining their views on the subject of 'general education' explicitly invoked Ballantyne's project in Benares as illustrative of the way in which their 'oriental colleges' could be made great use of. The cultivation of vernacular languages and literature amongst the 'learned classes' was endorsed, as well as the diffusion of a knowledge of Hindu and Islamic law, together with European science and philosophy.[112] In addition, a writer to the *Calcutta Review* argued that Ballantyne's pedagogy, if successfully carried out, would serve to make Britain 'God's own messenger to civilise and Christianise the land' of India.[113] Other Christian commentators, such as Revd William Kay of Bishop's College in Calcutta, praised Ballantyne's publications as a '*Preparatio Evangelica*, from which abundant fruits of solid Christianity shall have dated their commencement'.[114]

Yet not all commentators were so enthusiastic, though the influence of critiques in determining educational policy seems to have been minimal. In the introduction to his *Synopsis of Science*, Ballantyne had felt it necessary to publicly defend the East India Company's continued sponsorship of institutionalised Sanskrit education in Benares against its more outspoken critics, by claiming that his endeavours in this regard were not driven by 'a fond admiration of Sanskrit scholarship and an injudicious undervaluing of everything else in comparison', but rather by his desire to 'enlist ... Sanskrit on the side of progress'.[115] Indeed, many British writers remained opposed to the use of Indian texts and Sanskrit as a medium to impart Western knowledge, and especially to impart the doctrines of Christianity. One writer to *The Record* thought that utilising Hindu philosophy in this regard was to utilise the 'delusions of Satan'.[116]

Some Indian educators in the Company's service also overtly resisted the drive to emulate Ballantyne's work and the curriculum at Benares College. In 1853, Ballantyne had been asked by the government's Council of Education to travel to the Calcutta Sanskrit College, and compare its pedagogy with that pursued in Benares. Ballantyne warned that the separation of English- and Sanskrit-based curriculum in Calcutta posed the danger of persuading students that 'truth is double'. He therefore recommended the promotion of an 'Anglo-Sanskrit education', on the model of Benares College, which would 'tend to facilitate the reception, by the less advanced nation, of the science and philosophy of the more advanced one'.[117] Īśvaracandra Vidyāsāgar, the principal of Calcutta Sanskrit College, objected to Ballantyne's comparative approach, and what he considered the confirmation of the 'false systems' of *vedānta* and *sāṅkhya* by presenting them with reference to Western philosophical thinkers. Instead, he insisted upon being able to 'counteract [the] influence' of necessarily having to teach Hindu philosophy in the Calcutta Sanskrit College with the simultaneous presentation of 'sound philosophy in the English class'.[118] The Revd K. M. Banerjea apparently also wrote to complain to Thomason about the pedagogy being undertaken at Benares College, going so far as to characterise Ballantyne as a 'Sanskrit bookworm'.[119]

Most deliberately vindictive, however, was a series of critiques published by Arthur Wallis, who had briefly taken over as superintendent of Benares College following John Muir, before being unceremoniously replaced by Ballantyne.[120] Wallis lampooned the scientific nomenclature created for Sanskrit for Ballantyne's publications, characterised his books as plagued by 'unscholarlike inaccuracy', and accused him of plagiarising the English of his *Novum Organum* from a faulty translation published by Thomas Smith in Calcutta in 1843. Wallis also characterised the *nyāya* as 'gravely and radically vicious', so that it could never be rendered 'a congruous and harmonious frame-work for an encyclopaedic body of doctrine', as Ballantyne hoped. Wallis discountenanced the treatment of 'essential errors' as 'matter of opinion', and advocated retaining Īśvaracandra Vidyāsāgar's educational programme in Calcutta, on the basis that Ballantyne was 'so very far his inferior'.[121]

God, *vedānta* and Bishop Berkeley

In nineteenth-century Benares, the missionary endeavour to proselytise the tenets of Christianity was confined largely to the practice of 'bazaar preaching', which most often invoked the Christian doctrine of salvation. In other words, Christian missionaries often proceeded from the assumption that a person could not be 'saved' on account of their works, but rather, required the divine grace of God. In this respect, the noted Benares missionary William Smith once remarked that the 'incarnations' of Hinduism 'destroyed sinners' while the God of Christianity 'destroyed sin'.[122] Ballantyne referred to this methodology as an 'appeal to the heart', and he had little patience for it, or its principal practitioners, the missionaries whom he once described as 'those who arrogate to themselves the exclusive stewardship of God's word [and] are often touchily sensitive as a bear with a sore head'.[123]

Ballantyne sincerely believed that knowledge of the Christian God was available to all people of the earth, regardless of whether they happen to be a 'pandit' or 'the pope'.[124] Moreover, he believed that a meaningful conversion to Christianity from some other faith needed to be based in a rational acceptance of Christianity's tenets. In this regard, Ballantyne conceived that his educational programme in Western science and philosophy at Benares College constituted the initial part of an 'appeal to the head', in which the 'critical faculties' of the Hindus were cultivated for the reception of Christianity's historical claims. This method of approaching the impartation of Christianity, Ballantyne believed, was consistent with both the methodology undertaken by William Paley,[125] and the absolute interconnectedness of science, reason, and the Christian religion.[126]

At the end of the *Synopsis of Science*, following his discussion of natural theology and the argument from design, Ballantyne asked his readers: 'has the God of Nature anywhere directly revealed His will to man?'[127] This, in effect, was an injunction to his Indian audience to compare the claims of Christianity and Hinduism, and come to a conclusion as to which constituted a more reasonable body of doctrine, rather than rely simply upon received 'authority'. Ballantyne's next major publication, *Christianity Contrasted with Hindu Philosophy* (1859) sought to do just this – though it was never a part of the college curriculum – and set out the argument in Sanskrit and English for Christianity's higher claim to truth. The first section of the text begins with an explanatory exposition of Christian doctrine, including the 'chief end of man' (*paramapuruṣārtha*) according to the Bible, the nature of God, and God's role as the creator of the universe. On each subject, dissenting views in 'Hindu' philosophy were noted and disposed of. For example, when considering the unity, or oneness, of God, as opposed to the multiplicity of India's 'gods', Ballantyne asserted that the truth of the former conception is proven by the 'unity of design [which] runs through all created things'.[128]

Christianity Contrasted with Hindu Philosophy also considered the 'evidences of Christianity'. Ballantyne here asserted that a true religion is one which is necessarily of divine origin, and as such, is attested by miracles. Ballantyne outlined the miracles performed by Christ, and argued that these miracles were to be reasonably believed. For example, Christ's miracles were performed in front of many witnesses, all of whom attested to their truth. Moreover, these witnesses included Christ's enemies, as well as those who suffered persecution for their beliefs. Therefore, the miracles of Christ, as recounted in the Bible, fulfil the criteria for establishing the veracity of witnesses. Ballantyne then applied these criteria to the 'Hindu scriptures'. He argued, for example, that the suffering of Indian ascetics cannot be considered as of value in establishing truth, as these sufferings are 'self-inflicted'. Moreover, the miracles recounted of Kṛṣṇa, including his lifting of the mountain of Govardhana, cannot be properly considered as miracles, for there were no 'reliable' witnesses to these acts who had undergone suffering for their belief in them.[129]

Ballantyne went on to discuss at length the reasonable nature of the argument from design, as well as outlining some of the 'mysteries' of the Christian religion, such as the trinity and the problem of evil. It was clearly noted, however, that such 'mysteries' were not unique to Christianity.[130] This point, perhaps, was intended by Ballantyne to ward off potential criticisms directed at the perceived inconsistencies in Christian doctrine, such as those which were elaborated in the responses to John Muir's *Mataparīkṣā* earlier in the century.[131] Ballantyne concluded his exposition of Christianity by stating that there is a high probability that its scriptures are true, and that if they are indeed true, then there will be 'tremendous consequences' for rejecting them.[132] He therefore enjoined his readers to 'search the scriptures', and to facilitate this task, he published in 1861 a Sanskrit and English version of the first three chapters of the Book of Genesis, entitled *The Bible for Pandits*.

While the publication of *Christianity Contrasted with Hindu Philosophy* and *The Bible for Pandits* represented the pinnacle of Ballantyne's attempt to construct a *śāstra* of his own, complete with rational methodologies for discovering truth, and the findings of truth in science and religion, he had also perceived points of connection between Indian theistic philosophy and the metaphysics of Europe. In this regard, Ballantyne simultaneously attempted to elaborate the continuities and differences in the theistic philosophical system of *vedānta* with the sentiments of Bishop Berkeley's *Treatise Concerning the Principles of Human Knowledge*, in which God was conceived to play a central role in ordering men's perceptions of the outside world. This comparison exactly mirrored his earlier comparison of the *nyāya* with Bacon, Mill, and Whately. Indeed, Ballantyne remarked that while the *nyāya* represented in India an accepted and authoritative methodology for investigation and reasoning, it was not generally as revered as the *vedānta*, which dealt exclusively with matters of theology, including the nature of reality, the Deity, and its relationship to the human soul and its creation. It was, therefore, all the more important to exploit the *vedānta* in a similar way as had been already attempted with the *nyāya*. Ballantyne remarked that:

> whatever, therefore of truth and soundness may belong to Indian speculation in its ulterior and more recondite forms [speaking of the *vedānta*], it is expedient that we should claim also as our own. The points at which any system of truth begins to branch out into error, are the actual points which it is of all things important to determine and to deal with.[133]

As such, Ballantyne remarked that by utilising the concepts developed in *vedānta*, and their points of connection to Berkeley's metaphysics, he might promote each of the *paṇḍit*s to become 'as good a Christian as Bishop Berkeley'[134] by changing the follower of the *vedānta*'s 'pantheistic formula that "God is all," into the Christian doctrine, that, "in Him we live and move and have our being."'[135]

Ballantyne understood the *vedānta* in its *advaita* (non-differentiated) form, as delineated in the *Vedānta-Sāra*: that 'nothing really exists besides *one*', God, and that 'the soul *is* God', but does not recognise itself as such 'because it is obstructed by ignorance (*ajñāna*)'. This 'evil' can only be removed through a 'right understanding' of the formula 'that art thou' (*tat-tvam-asi*), which results in a transcendence of subject-object distinctions.[136] While a detailed analysis of Ballantyne's comparison of the *vedānta* and the writings of Bishop Berkeley must be beyond the scope of this book, a few examples will adequately illustrate Ballantyne's basic argument. Ballantyne first asserted that the conclusion drawn from the *vedānta* philosophy was incorrect, in that it allowed for a conception of man to overcome the power of God, expressed as man's *ajñāna* (ignorance) of the true nature of the world, through the acquisition of knowledge of the world. In essence, Ballantyne thought that man remained dependent upon God and His omnipotence, rather than transgressing God's power through the realisation of the true nature of reality. In this regard, he remarked that 'a man bound is not released by having light thrown upon his fetters'.[137] But having establishing this point, Ballantyne then went on to argue that the spread of Christianity could be furthered not by arguing against the *vedānta*, but by pointing out its departure into error by reference to the philosophy of Bishop Berkeley, and indeed, his followers in the Scottish Enlightenment.[138]

The first point of comparison to be established related to the respective views on 'existence', or 'being'. The *vedānta*, Ballantyne stated, includes the notion of being, 'in its highest sense' (*pāramārthika sattva*), and being, 'such as has to be dealt with' (*vyāvahārika sattva*). These two types of 'being' refer to the 'being' of God, which is substantial and independent existence, and the 'being' of the world, which is phenomenal or dependent existence. These relate closely to Berkeley's idea that 'there is no other substance than *spirit*, or that which perceives', and that the things perceived lack an independent existence of their own.[139] In other words, Berkeley and the *vedānta* agree upon a basically sceptical view of the nature of existence and its perception, which in the European philosophical tradition, at least, was immediately traced to the ruminations of René Descartes. In this regard, Ballantyne noted that 'the Vedāntīs, in allowing the rank of Substantial Existence to Spirit alone, hold the opinion which one of the most pious and thoughtful of Christian bishops advocated, not as merely harmless, but, as a grand bulwark of the truth against the assaults of a debasing Materialism'.[140] The second point of comparison made by Ballantyne related to the conception of the Supreme Deity in the *vedānta* (known as *brahman*) as *nirguṇa*, or 'devoid of qualities'. This, Ballantyne argued, is simply a denial of the attribution of phenomenal characteristics to the Deity, and as such, corresponded very closely to Berkeley's views, in which God is thought to be immaterial. Ballantyne further remarked that this seems the correct view to be taken of God, although it stands in opposition to the 'semiconscious Anthropomorphism' popularly elaborated by Milton.[141]

If the doctrines expounded in the *vedānta* might furnish Ballantyne with a measure of 'common ground' with which to promote the tenets of Christianity within India, he was nevertheless constrained by the practical considerations of non-proselytisation within the Company's educational establishments. While Ballantyne did publish two 'reprints' containing elements of the works of Locke, Berkeley, and Dugald Stewart,[142] as well as addressing elements of the *vedānta* in his *Christianity Contrasted with Hindu Philosophy*,[143] his explicitly religious arguments seem to have elicited responses principally from Christian theologians and European orientalists. Without question, the doctrines of the *vedānta* had interested British orientalists for several decades previous to Ballantyne's exposition, and had also proven contentious in regard to the exact manner of their interpretation. Vans Kennedy, for example, attacked in 1831 H. T. Colebrooke's interpretation of *vedānta* as tending towards materialism, instead arguing that the *vedānta* condoned a notion of 'spirit' anathema to materialism.[144] The *vedānta* had also furnished an indigenous Indian conception of monotheism which could be utilised to counter the claims of Christian missionaries, as, for example, in the case of Rām Mohun Roy's works, or the *Tattva Bodhinī Patrikā*, a periodical published in Calcutta by the Brahmo Samāj.[145] In contrast, Nīlakaṇṭha Goreh, a Benaresi *paṇḍit* who converted to Christianity, argued that the *vedānta* was a false doctrine, without relevance to the promotion of Christian beliefs in India, and that the 'hypothetical Brahma of the Vedantins' ultimately 'comes out to be a nonentity'.[146]

Not unexpectedly, then, a writer to the *British and Foreign Evangelical Review* wrote in 1860, in response to Ballantyne's *Christianity Contrasted with Hindu Philosophy*, arguing that Ballantyne had presented 'too favourable' a characterisation of the *vedānta*: this doctrine represented an unsuitable means to promote Christianity in India, as it, in essence, asserted that God was nothing at all by virtue of its characterisation of God as *nirguṇa* ('devoid of qualities'). This term, the writer argued, meant not simply being devoid of material, or phenomenal, qualities, as Ballantyne believed, but also intellectual and moral characteristics. To say that God is *nirguṇa*, therefore, is to say that God is 'destitute ... of all qualities whatsoever'.[147]

In order to substantiate his own interpretation of the concept of *nirguṇa*, and its applicability to the promotion of a Berkleyian Christianity in the subcontinent, Ballantyne referred the matter to Viṭṭhala Śāstrī, the *sāṅkhya* professor at Benares College, and published his *vyavasthā* ('opinion') within the pages of *The Bible for Pandits*. Signed by no less than 16 *paṇḍit*s, including Bāpūdeva Śāstrī, and several of the *paṇḍits* who attended the court of the *mahārāja* of Benares, the *vyavasthā* stated that:

> The author of the Review, though of an inquisitive mind, yet unacquainted with any of the Hindu systems of philosophy speaks of your [referring to Ballantyne] having made a too favourable representation of the Vedanta Philosophy. I myself, however, with the other Pandits in the College and in the city, look upon your representation of the Vedanta theory not as your own, but merely as a discovery of an already established fact, for the European learned audience. ... We admit that there is not an impossibility in conceiving wrongness in the Vedanta, and so do not refuse to listen to the arguments intended to show its wrongness. But if our opponents will not accept the terms which occur in Vedanta books, in the same sense in which we use them when explaining the theory, he is not an opponent to us but a man of straw framed by himself.[148]

As such, Ballantyne drew upon the cultural authority, and the intellectual expertise, of the *paṇḍits* attached to the college to not only authorise and substantiate his pedagogy of improvement within Benares, but also to position himself authoritatively to speak to principally European debates over the methodology to be pursued to further the impartation of Christianity to Indians.

The following chapter now proceeds with a more in-depth examination of the practices of translation in Benares College under Ballantyne's superintendence, and how these practices were constructed upon notions of the relationship between language and civilisation to produce authoritative representations of European ascendancy. In addition, some wider connections are drawn between the pedagogy taking place in Benares and other institutional contexts in northern India. This leads, then, in Chapter 6 to a closer analysis of the roles which the *paṇḍits* played in facilitating constructive orientalism, and how they utilised and developed their institutionally-consolidated role as India's cultural and intellectual guardians to promote a specific, and often competitive, interpretation of Sanskrit-based knowledge systems.

5
On Language and Translation

Translation has often been characterised as a 'central act' of European imperialism.[1] It has been argued that translation was utilised to make available legal-cultural information for the administration and rule of the non-West, but perhaps more importantly, translation has also been identified as important for the resources it provided in the construction of representations of the colonised as Europe's 'civilisational other'. On the former point, Cohn has argued that the codification of South Asian languages in the late eighteenth and early nineteenth centuries served to convert 'indigenous' forms of textualised knowledge into 'instruments of colonial rule'.[2] Most recent discussions of translation in this context, however, have focused rather more upon the act of translation as a strategic means for representing 'otherness' to primarily domestic British reading audiences. In this case, the act of linguistic translation is more clearly being enumerated as a practice of cultural translation. English translations of the 'ancient' Sanskrit texts of India, for example, have been analysed for the rhetorical work that the text performed in certain contexts.[3] On the one hand, European-produced translations of these texts might serve to reinforce the dominance of a European aesthetic sensibility through a process of 'naturalisation', in which the culturally specific is 'sanitised', subordinated to a European norm, thereby inherently limiting the 'artistic achievement' of the colonised. William Jones' erasure of the motif of sweat as an indication of sexual interest and arousal in his translation of Kālidāsa's fourth- or fifth-century Sanskrit play *Śakuntalā* is a case in point.[4] On the other hand, literary translations from Sanskrit might also foreground the 'otherness' of Indian texts and cultural norms through a strategy of 'foreignisation';[5] that is, by registering for the European reader differences in language and cultural content. For example, European translations from

Sanskrit might include anthropological notations which explain the cultural relevance of the text, or might instead adopt an overly literal rendering of prose, thereby foregrounding differences in syntax, vocabulary, symbol, or motif.[6] Both such rhetorical devices, it can be argued, leave the reader tripping over the text, giving him pause to consider the very strangeness of its appearance and contents.

In each of these cases, the work of translation into English operates to construct European authority, whether that authority be of an eminently practical kind for the extension of the structures of rule, or as a cultural authority for the effective representation of the colonised as 'other'. The focus of this chapter, however, rather than examining translation into English, will instead be upon the strategies and practices of rendering European texts into Indian languages, principally within the context of Ballantyne's constructive orientalism in Benares College during the mid-nineteenth century. It is argued that such translation evolved principally from European ideas about the status of language within the imperial project of imposing 'civilisational advancement' upon the non-West through education. In particular, the connections perceived by Europeans between the features of a particular language and the collective mind of its speakers, or indeed their state of civilisation, were fundamental in driving the translation of Western English-language educational textbooks into Indian languages.

In essence, this chapter develops the recognition that, in a study of translational strategies within the colonial context, it is important to not only look at the rhetorical impact of translated texts, but also to attempt to historicise the range of factors which influenced colonial educationalists' own perceptions of the 'fidelity' of the translations they were making, and the 'work' which they were intended to accomplish in the colonial sphere. In the context of constructive orientalism, translation, together with language itself, was perceived fundamentally as instrumental by colonial educators such as Ballantyne. The European ideational genealogy which linked a language's character with the speakers' civilisational status, in other words, brought with it an understanding that the colonial state needed to adopt an interventionist role in order to improve Indian languages first, so as to bring about the civilisational progress of their speakers.

Language, Sanskrit, and civilisation

The story of Babel, as it appears in the Book of Genesis, tells us that God dispersed the unitary population of the globe by confusing the single, common, or 'natural' language. For many eighteenth- and nineteenth-century European thinkers, this narrative lay at the very center of an intellectual tradition that viewed language as a principal marker for cultural and national difference. This difference, however, had always been a productive one for European intellectuals. Indeed, language was a key component of orientalist research. In the late eighteenth century, for example, William Jones advocated the comparative study of grammatical features in order to convert language into a more reliable source for historical research. Yet orientalist research in India also served to characterise different languages, and by extension, the speakers of those languages, in generalised, but nevertheless influential, ways. This was largely a direct result not of historical research, *per se*, but rather, was a part of the process of codifying Indian languages through the production of grammars, dictionaries, and representative dialogues. In essence, orientalists such as William Jones, H. T. Colebrooke, Charles Wilkins, and William Carey, through the construction of a particularised vocabulary and imagery, significantly institutionalised a particular way of writing about Indian languages and the 'culture' or 'civilisation' of those languages' speakers.

In the course of their linguistic researches, these orientalists were inheritors of a body of thought developed by European philosophers who were attempting to explain the origins of human language and linguistic diversity, and understand the relationship between thought and speech, outside the realm of purely Biblical narrative and epistemology, during the seventeenth and eighteenth centuries. The cornerstone text for these discussions was John Locke's 1690 *Essay Concerning Human Understanding*, the central thesis of which had been formulated to reject the prevalent philosophical notion of innate ideas. In essence, Locke argued that language had a human origin, and that its creation and continued use were 'primal expressions of our humanity'.[7] Hans Aarsleff explains that in Locke's view, languages 'have a history that reflects the experience and thought of their speakers', and that the study of a language's features may reveal 'the trains of thought that had been in the minds of speakers in the course of the progress of the mind'.[8] The notion that the structures of language were representative of its speakers' minds was further elaborated during the course of the eighteenth century by writers such as L'Abbé Etienne Bonnot de Condillac in his 1746 *Essai sur l'origine des connaissances humaines*,[9] and, later, by John Horne Tooke in *The Diversions of Purley*, culminating in Wilhelm von Humboldt's authoritative 1836 explication of language as a (ceaseless) activity (*energeia*).[10] In sum, language became conceptualised as being closely linked to the minds of the people who give rise to that language, and the historicity of language itself was borne in changes introduced by the mental or civilisational development of its common speakers. The characteristics of language, as such, could be made to demarcate 'national' distinctions.

Condillac's treatise, in particular, was a most influential expansion upon the conceptual apparatus developed by Locke, though ultimately the two men disagreed upon the exact nature of the relationship between sense perception, human reason, and language.[11] Condillac's interests lay in the origin and development of human language, and he described in detail the apparent process of language acquisition 'according to the ordinary course of nature', initially through the figure of two children in the desert, at a time after the deluge (thereby sidestepping questions of the language facility granted to Adam and Eve).[12] For Condillac, the development of verbal language, from an initial gestural form of communication, and its increasing complexity, was quite clearly a process concomitant with cognitive development:

> The use of those signs insensibly enlarged and improved the operations of the mind, and on the other hand these having acquired such improvement, perfected the signs, and rendered the use of them more familiar. Experience shews that these two things assist each other.[13]

The development of language, in other words, was a phenomenon which both assisted, and reflected, the advancement of human civilisation from its origins.

Amongst the first forms language took, Condillac argued, was the poetical, as early language was devoted to 'depicting the most sensible images of our ideas', and in this form was, moreover, most easily recalled.[14] These early languages were figurative and metaphorical, rife with pleonasms, due to the need to supplement the relative paucity of vocabulary with appropriate imagery. As well, ancient languages often required the addition of key words by the hearer. In other words, such languages lacked 'accuracy and precision'.[15] Vocabulary, however, developed in complexity over time, from the base and sensual, to terms for the expression of abstract ideas, such as 'essence', 'substance', and 'being'.[16] Similarly, grammatical structures evolved to the purpose of such 'precision'. Taking Latin as his model of a language which 'retains something of the nature' of ancient languages, Condillac argued that Latin's extensive systems of declension and conjugation, for example, gradually became necessary as the ideas which the language was used to express became more complex. These features were introduced, in essence, so that the meaningfulness of the relationship between the parts of the sentence might be retained.[17] Similarly, Condillac argued that the particles of speech, (such as *in*, *over*, and *on*), developed very late in language evolution, as these 'express the manner in which the objects affect us', which, Condillac noted, is a substantial cognitive development from the early time when 'mankind ... were very ill qualified to reflect on themselves'.[18] Pronouns were the last part of speech to be invented, 'because the want of them was felt the last', and even then, Condillac argued, people would have found it 'difficult', for some time, 'to use ... a word which stood for another, and sometimes for a whole sentence'.[19] With such 'revolutions of languages', including the advances made in both vocabulary and grammatical complexity, Condillac noted that poetry, with its figures and metaphors, became a medium for amusement, or simply 'an ornament to discourse', and was replaced in everyday communication by what might be called modern language.[20]

Condillac also perceived contemporary differences in the world's languages to be the result of processes which paralleled the initial development of language. The character of a language, he noted, ultimately 'expresses the character of the people that speak it'.[21] Indeed, on several occasions Condillac utilised the example of 'oriental languages' to substantiate his arguments regarding the features and developments seen in ancient languages. Asian languages, in other words, retained much of the character of ancient language, as they (and their speakers) had not significantly evolved. Chinese was thus characterised as retaining the prosodic character of early language due to its continued emphasis upon tonal changes to mark distinctions in meaning.[22] Southern Asian languages were characterised as continuing to be pleonastic, while ancient Asiatic authors, together with the contemporary Chinese, were said to be devoted to figurative speech, due most likely to the influence of hieroglyphics.[23] In contrast, the 'northern nations', in Condillac's view, had been the first to develop 'precision' in language. This he attributed to a variety of factors, including the effects of climate, and also the form of government. Northern nations, due to their possession of 'cold and flegmatic constitutions', were thought to be 'readier to part with any thing that resembled the mode of speaking by action', for example.[24] Yet equally, neither climate alone, nor the form of a nation's government, could be held principally accountable for distinctions amongst nations in scientific and artistic progress. Rather, these factors contributed in a variety of ways to the structures of language, and thus to the complex interconnections between language and thought. This was considered by Condillac to be the vital point. Scientific and civilisational advancement, in other words, depended rather more upon 'the progress of the language' than it did upon individual genius, for a language 'defective in words' or inefficiently constructed, could ultimately pose an insurmountable obstacle to advancements in thought: 'Consequently, it is demonstrable that there can be no such thing as a superior genius, till the language of a nation has been considerably improved.'[25]

But in Condillac's assessment there also arose something of a paradox. The classical languages such as Latin, he noted, with their elaborate systems of declension and conjugation, maintained a certain precision over current European vernaculars. Indeed, it took many years until French was an equal, let alone superior, medium for the expression of advanced ideas. Even so, Condillac maintained that contemporary French was now able to avoid some forms of indistinctness which inevitably arose in Latin by the former's possession of a variety of past tenses, for example, as well as the use of definite articles. Ultimately, it was the progress of the modern vernacular, the French language, which Condillac argued had accompanied significant progress in Europe, as men were liable to the limitations imposed upon them by their mother tongue, rather than a second 'learned language'. The classical Latin, in an important sense, represented both the basis for European intellectual tradition, but also an impediment to be surpassed (though perhaps never entirely). Interestingly, Condillac noted in this regard that 'we did not begin to write good Latin, till we had learnt to write good French'.[26] Orientalist views of language, as we shall see, embraced a very similar dichotomy. Sanskrit, as a classical language, was esteemed for its complexity and power of expression, as well as its classical status as the foundation of Indian civilisation. But simultaneously, on the one hand, Sanskrit was contrasted with the 'degraded' Indian vernaculars, and on the other, subordinated to the world's ultimate vernacular language, and scientific culture, English.

Elements of the arguments of Condillac can be glimpsed as informing, in a quite general manner, William Jones' analysis of the 'poetry of the Eastern nations'. Jones explained the 'genius' of Asian nations, and hence the character of their poetic expression, by reference to Asian nations' climates and forms of government, though in this instance he was concerned principally with Arabic and Persian literature, and not Sanskrit. For example, he argued that in the East, 'the immoderate heat disposes ... people to a life of indolence, which gives them full leisure to cultivate their talents', and that '*Asiaticks* excel the inhabitants of our colder regions in the liveliness of their fancy, and the richness of their invention'.[27] The pinnacle of pastoral poetry, he argued, was to be found in Yemen, as 'no nation at this day can vie with the *Arabians* in the delightfulness of their climate, and the simplicity of their manners'. Indeed, Aden, a city 'surrounded with pleasant gardens and woods' was equated by Jones with Eden, the 'garden of paradise', and as such was placed in what arguably amounts, once again, to a differential time-frame.[28] Equally important to the character of poetic expression was, of course, a nation's government. Kashmir, Jones noted, with its picturesque valleys, had once been a contender as the home of exemplary poetic expression, but 'when its inhabitants were subdued by ... a *Mogul* prince, they lost their happiness with their liberty'.[29] Under Mughal despotism, in other words, Kashmiris lost their ability to produce prosody.

It has been argued that Jones' interest in Eastern poetry was principally derived from his belief that it would reinvigorate the artistic expression of Europeans.[30] Certainly this would seem to be the case, though of course he also cautioned that his 'zeal' for Asian literature was not meant to 'place it in competition with the beautiful productions of the *Greeks* and *Romans* ... the standard of true taste'.[31] Yet equally, in the context of Jones' wider orientalist project, which we have seen in Chapter 1 was both comparative and committed to an ideal of historical progress, such characterisations of the language and literature of Asians also served to construct a civilisational dichotomy. In an important sense, Jones' valorisation of Asian poetry as instrumental in the reinvigoration of European imaginative production was founded upon the idea that Europeans had moved beyond poetic expression, and the realm of the 'passions', into the advanced state of 'modern' scientific rationality (an understanding put to considerable polemical effect in Mill's *History*). Very similarly, in the case of Sanskrit, British orientalists in the late eighteenth and early nineteenth centuries adopted a general set of characteristics for that language which invested it with a specific place in a hierarchical scheme of 'national' entities. These characteristics were essentially evaluative, so that the status of a language and its speakers may be judged to be 'religious' or 'scientific', 'weak' and 'degraded', or perhaps 'copious' and 'powerful'. In this manner, these representations also came to have a powerful influence over the particular strategies employed in later colonial educational institutions, and their programmes of translation, for the 'improvement' of Indians.

Sanskrit was understood by orientalists, first and foremost, as the language most intimately associated with the Hindu religion by virtue of it being the medium for various religious texts, as well as being the language of learned (i.e., religious) intercourse and religious ritual. Indians were understood to believe Sanskrit to be *deva-bhāṣā*, the eternal and uncreated 'speech' or 'language of the gods'. As such, Sanskrit was India's 'national language', and the Hindu religion was equated with India's 'national character'. William Carey recorded in the early nineteenth century, for example, that 'many of the Pundits assert that it is the language of the gods, and was never used as a common medium of communication among men, but revealed from heaven as a vehicle for the divine will, all the books esteemed of divine authority being written therein'.[32] H. T. Colebrooke argued that Sanskrit 'is cultivated by learned Hindus throughout India, as the language of science and of literature, and as the repository of their law, civil and religious'.[33] Orientalists therefore understood Sanskrit to be a key component to India's civilisation given its intimate connection with Indian cultural norms. H. H. Wilson commented in 1819 'it is an assertion that scarcely requires proof, that the *Hindu* population of these extensive realms can be understood only through the medium of the *Sanscrit* language: it alone furnishes us with the master spring of all the actions and passions, their prejudices and errors, and enables us to appreciate their vices or their worth'.[34]

In addition to the recognition of Sanskrit's 'sacred status', orientalists had little doubt that Sanskrit was a language of great antiquity. In 1778, Nathaniel Halhed described Sanskrit as 'of the most venerable and unfathomable antiquity'.[35] While later debates would rage over the exact extent of Sanskrit's antiquity, as well as over the nature of the interrelationships between Sanskrit, Greek, and Latin, it was clear to most that significant parallels existed between these ancient languages (and their civilisations). In other words, it was apparent to European orientalists that Sanskrit was the medium for a body of ancient literature, science, and religious and philosophical thought which corresponded, in some degree, with that which could be found in the European classical world of ancient Greece and Rome. This pedigree of a shared place in the ancient world, then, led to attributions to Sanskrit of a 'classical' status, due to its correspondence with a European historical chronology, rather than from any particular Indian characterisation. In this way, Sanskrit became associated, along with Greek and Latin, with the 'classical' as a valued source of civilisational attributes.

As European linguistic expertise in Sanskrit spread in the early nineteenth century, characterisations of the language also became based in Indian and European philological research. Following the discoveries of Nathaniel Halhed and William Jones on the affinity of Sanskrit to Greek and Latin, a large number of Sanskrit dictionaries and grammars were published, first in India and then increasingly in Europe. These represented an effort to not only enable the wider study of India's textual records, but to further philological research into the historical relationships of languages, given Sanskrit's centrality in this regard.[36] Charles Wilkins' 1808 Sanskrit grammar, for example, was hailed upon its publication as the best of the Sanskrit grammars published to that point, not only because of its ready availability in Europe, but because it made accessible to a European audience both a knowledge of Sanskrit grammar upon a largely European model, as well as the rudiments of Indian grammatical science, *vyākaraṇa*.[37] Wilkins noted in the grammar's opening pages that the term *Saṃskṛta*, when analysed according to the dictates of *vyākaraṇa*, 'denotes a thing to have been composed, or formed by art, adorned, embellished, purified, highly cultivated or polished, and regularly inflected, as a language'.[38] Sanskrit was considered, then, in the famous words of William Jones, to be 'of a wonderful structure ... copious ... exquisitely refined'.[39] Sanskrit's complex grammatical structure, its ability to express a range and a depth of meaning through compounding, its extensive vocabulary, and its ability to allow the coining of words from verbal roots together with a variety of prefixes and suffixes, rendered the language, according to William Carey, both 'copious' and 'expressive'.[40] Sanskrit was considered by European orientalists, then, to be a 'powerful' language in terms of its expressive capabilities and flexibility. The subsequent publication of several Sanskrit lexicons and dictionaries further impressed upon Europeans the sheer extent of the range of Sanskrit literature.[41]

While Sanskrit's copiousness and grammatical 'perfection' could be viewed as a reflection of the relatively advanced status of ancient Indian civilisation, in addition to its standing as a marker of India's antiquity and inherent religiosity, the increased interest in Indian vernacular languages manifest in the early nineteenth century resulted in the subjection of these, as well, to philological analysis and a searching critique of their character. During the course of his researches, William Jones had recognised that although Hindi and Sanskrit differed markedly in their grammatical structures, they shared a significant percentage of their vocabularies. He erroneously believed that 'the pure *Hindi*, whether of *Tartarian* or *Chaldean* origin, was primeval in Upper *India*, into which the *Sanscrit* was introduced by conquerors from other kingdoms in some very remote age'.[42] This notion was soon overturned, however, as Colebrooke's early nineteenth-century studies of Sanskrit established that it was the 'fountainhead' from which all of India's vernacular languages had been derived.[43] Colebrooke analysed the large shared vocabulary of Sanskrit and Hindi, and persuasively argued in 1801 that, 'where similar words are found in both languages, the *Hindi* has borrowed from the *Sanscrit*, rather than the *Sanscrit* from *Hindi*'. The historical relation between Sanskrit and Hindi was further solidified by its correspondence to the accepted general rule that, over time, 'the progress has been from languages rich in inflections, to dialects simple in their structure'. This change in language structure, in which 'auxillary verbs and appendant particles supply the place of numerous inflections of the root' was clearly in evidence with respect to Hindi and Sanskrit.[44] The notion that Hindi was a 'derivative language' of Sanskrit, in the same way that Italian was of Latin,[45] soon became a generally accepted maxim.

By the second decade of the nineteenth century, a series of new vernacular dictionaries and grammars were being published in India which were able to take full account of the established historical relationship between them and Sanskrit. William Carey's 1815 dictionary of Bengali, for instance, noted that the majority of Bengali's vocabulary was derived directly from Sanskrit. His dictionary purported to provide an etymology for all its words, and included an appendix that listed all the Sanskrit roots (*dhātu*) from which much of the Bengali vocabulary was thought to have been derived.[46] Yet Carey also noted the irregularity in the way Bengali was spoken, and even in how it was written (or spelled). He expressed the hope that with the increased study of Bengali, and eventually the translation of a variety of literary and scientific texts into that language, Bengali would soon 'be enriched by many words borrowed from other tongues'.[47] The comparison of the vernacular languages with Sanskrit, in particular, led many orientalists to claim that the vernaculars possessed very little in either expressive capability or refinement which could not be traced directly to Sanskrit. Wilkins noted, for example, that 'the several dialects confounded under the common terms *Hindi*, *Hindavi*, *Hindostani*, and *Bhasha*, deprived of *Sanskrit*, would not only lose all their beauty and energy, but, with respect to the power of expressing abstract ideas, or terms in science, would be absolutely reduced to a state of barbarism'.[48]

While the comparison of the vocabulary and grammatical structure of the Indian vernaculars and Sanskrit contributed to the perception of the former's 'degraded' status, the increasing publication during the course of the early nineteenth century of bilingual dictionaries, and several multilingual technical vocabularies, served to further highlight and systematise either the dependence of the vernaculars upon Sanskrit for their expressive capability, or those subject areas in which the vernaculars lacked any sort of vocabulary at all in comparison with English. The ideological work that comparative dictionaries do has been discussed in a quite different context by Lydia Liu. She argues that bilingual or multilingual dictionaries proceed upon the inherent assumption that 'languages are commensurate and equivalents exist naturally between them'.[49] But when these equivalences are not forthcoming, that is, when there is no word in language B for a particular word in language A, this can be interpreted as one language possessing a 'lack', which, in turn, lays the foundation for comparative constructions of the collective mind of other civilisations, as well as one's own identity.[50]

Comparisons of the respective vocabularies and grammatical structures of Sanskrit and the Indian vernaculars tended to highlight, then, a process of degeneration and reliance upon the intellectual achievements of an ancient age, while dictionaries that included English could be made to highlight India's relative lack of scientific and civilisational progress in relation to Europe. Peter Breton's 1825 medical vocabulary is an illustrative example of this latter process. Breton, a surgeon in the service of the East India Company, surveyed a series of medical texts, dictionaries, and vocabularies in Arabic, Persian, Sanskrit, Hindi, and English in an attempt to highlight possible sources of cross-lingual misunderstanding among medical practitioners.[51] The vocabulary lists, which cover everything from basic anatomy to surgical instruments and diseases, begin with the English terms, thereby setting the standard against which all others are compared, and then present in adjacent columns the corresponding words (if any) in the other languages. Apart from the purely visual aspect of this arrangement, which would highlight the 'lack' of a particular language with a blank space, Breton noted that many 'Oriental languages' either utilised the same terminology to describe quite different anatomical entities, or had a variety of terms (or a vagueness of terms) to refer to the very same thing. Breton attributed the perceived inadequacies of the technical vocabularies that could be found in Indian languages solely to the speakers' ignorance of modern, Western medical science. For example, he noted that:

> they [i.e., the 'Asiatics'] have no distinct words for nerve and therefore call it Nus, Asub, Shirra, etc. in common with Ligaments and Tendons. ... they do not know the distinction between an Artery and a Vein and consequently the appellation of Rug and Shirra are indiscriminately applied to both. The Hindee word Rug and Shirra according to the Soosrut, a Sanskrit work on Anatomy and Pathology, means blood vessels or tubular vessels of any kind.[52]

These early European characterisations of language, and the potential extension of these characterisations to the collective mental or civilisational state of India, can now be further analysed with reference to ways in which they found renewed influence in the educational programmes of the government colleges at Delhi and Benares during the middle of the nineteenth century. Both of these colleges undertook the large-scale translation and publishing of Western scientific texts with a view to the 'intellectual and moral improvement' of north Indian society. While the European superintendents of these colleges agreed that the vernacular languages of India also required 'improvement' in order to make them suitable vehicles for the transmission of Western knowledge, they took radically different views of the translational strategies which were to effect this improvement. While this difference reflected their distinct views on how best to produce cultural authority for their translations of Western knowledge, both men agreed that European intervention was required in the first instance to effect this linguistic enhancement, and, further, that it was an essential prerequisite to India's civilisational progress.

The power of English: translating science into Urdu at Delhi College

In 1834, during the education controversy in Calcutta, John Tytler wrote in an article published in the *Calcutta Literary Gazette* that plans to introduce exclusive English education were doomed to failure. Basing his argument in Locke's *Essay on Human Understanding,* Tytler stated that the base 'ideas of sensation' were practically the same throughout the world, but that the abstract 'ideas of reflection', being constructed, were thus also culturally determined:

> ...where nations like those of Europe have similar manners and frequent intercourse, the ideas [of reflection] thus formed will, like those of sensation, be nearly the same, and expressed by parallel words; among nations, on the other hand, whose manners are different, and between whom intercourse is comparatively rare, as those of Europe and Asia, it will in almost all cases happen that the ideas of reflection are quite different, and that there are few or no parallel words by which those of the one language can be expressed in the other.[53]

The difficulties of translating abstract terms such as 'instinct', 'reason' and 'natural affection', and the lack of scholars who possessed an advanced knowledge of both linguistic-cultural systems, for Tytler, served as definitive evidence that the continued promotion of parallel educational systems in India, the English, and the Sanskrit, was most preferable.

Yet as educational policy in northern India came to reflect the 'compromise' of Lord Auckland, in which the liberal concern to impart Western learning and science was combined with the orientalist emphasis upon the use of Indian languages and cultural forms, the translation of key texts was to play a larger role in educational initiatives than ever before. And while a variety of Indian-language textbooks in Western learning already existed, European educators realised in the late 1830s that these initial attempts were inconsistently translated, largely unreadable, or insufficiently tailored to suit 'native' taste and sensibility. For example, Revd J. J. Moore, Secretary of the Agra School Book Society, noted in 1839 that 'bald and unadapted translations of English works' did not hold the attention of the 'native reader', nor command his respect.[54] Lancelot Wilkinson also remarked that George Jervis's translations of mathematical works in Bombay suffered from his substitution of terms 'of his own coining, which must be wholly unknown' to Indians.[55] Lord Auckland thus called for an investigation into the best means for constructing a comprehensive corpus of textbooks 'under one general scheme of control and superintendence', which resulted in the formation of a GCPI sub-committee.[56] Yet while this sub-committee pondered at length how best to initiate a systematic programme of translation and textbook composition which would ensure their unproblematic reception, without coming to any substantive recommendations, Felix Boutros, the Superintendent of Delhi College, had already undertaken the initial steps in constructing a corpus of elementary school textbooks in Urdu.[57]

By the mid-nineteenth century, it was generally agreed by British educators in India that the 'vernacular' dialects of the subcontinent were not (to use the words of Macaulay) to be considered 'fit vehicles' for the conveyance of Western knowledge in their current state.[58] Indeed, nearly a decade after Macaulay's minute was issued, it was stated in an annual *General Report on Public Instruction* for the North-Western Provinces (NWP) that 'the Hindostanee language [i.e., Urdu] is at present exceedingly deficient in compass, in precision, and generally in its power of expression for what we propose to teach by its means'.[59] Yet at Delhi College Felix Boutros also felt that Urdu was clearly the most appropriate language to use for educational translations in NWP, given that it was widely spoken throughout northern India, and that it was now the official language of the courts.[60] Moreover, Boutros argued that the very character, and indeed history, of Urdu recommended it as the most suitable language for the transmission of European scientific knowledge, especially given the translational strategy which he had in mind. Urdu simply required improvement.

The programme for vernacular textbook production at Delhi College was first outlined in an educational minute written by Boutros in 1842. After describing his plan for publications, which included an edition of Dr John Abercrombie's general works, William O'Shaughnessy's chemistry text, elements of Dugald Stewart's moral philosophy, and William Robertson's *History of America*, Boutros then suggested guidelines for the maintenance of consistency across the translational scheme. These included the direct transfer of transliterated English-language scientific terms into the text in cases where no direct equivalent in Urdu could be found, such as for 'sodium' or 'chlorine'. As well, he recommended the maintenance of attested 'scientific' terms in Urdu, such as *loha* for 'iron', wherever an equivalent could be found; and similar guidelines for the composition of compound terms. Interestingly, Boutros also sanctioned the inclusion of Greek prefixes such as 'mono', 'di', 'proto', 'hypo', or 'peri', in the composition of compound Urdu words, though he gave no examples of how this might be effected.[61]

In essence, Boutros felt that it was the English language which should be considered as the most suitable 'feeder language' for the introduction of scientific terminology into Urdu. This was a policy that reflected views of English as a 'powerful' vehicle for the expression of scientific truths, but also, and more importantly, the desire to reaffirm within the colonial educational context the civilisational ascendancy of Britain through its historical connection with scientific discovery and progress. Indeed, it was this history that authorised the entire colonial translational project. Moreover, Urdu recommended itself as the most appropriate Indian vernacular language for the spread of Western 'useful knowledge' due to its peculiar ability to easily absorb foreign nomenclatures. Urdu's already-syncretic historical character, and its status as the product of cultural interaction (between the former ruling elite, the Mughals, and the 'mass' of Hindus) together were thought by Boutros to render Urdu all the more easily amenable to the engraftment of English scientific nomenclatures into its vocabulary.[62] It was thought that, in time, this engraftment of scientific terms direct from English would result in Urdu being rehabilitated for the task of conveying Western knowledge.

Yet the perceived 'lack' in Urdu – the absence of equivalent terms for the expression of Western scientific knowledge – was in Delhi College interpreted as indicative not only of the degraded status of the language but, by extension, the degraded status of its speakers, and the civilisation which it somehow represented. Linguistic comparison inevitably invited in this context an attendant civilisational comparison. For instance, it was argued in contemporary official accounts that the responsibility for the translation of English scientific works into Urdu, and the attendant improvement of the language, must, in the first instance, be carried out by Europeans in the employ of government. The actual task of 'drawing out' the linguistic resources of the vernaculars, by a careful selection of English terms for engraftment during translation, was thought to require a 'correct knowledge' of scientific and other 'useful' topics, but also the possession of a 'critical taste' that was thought to be 'more readily ... found among European minds than among those of Natives'.[63] This claim was strengthened by assertions that there existed a great paucity of qualified 'native' teachers, and that the lack of appropriate vernacular textbooks only exacerbated this shortage.[64] The situation thus described created a vicious cycle of sorts, which, it was thought, could only be broken by European interventionism.

As noted above, Boutros' scheme for translating English textbooks into Urdu soon found official government sanction with its wide-ranging publication in the NWP Government's reports on public instruction during the first half of the 1840s. By 1844, the year before Boutros left Delhi College, it would seem that his activities largely determined, or perhaps constituted, governmental views on vernacular publishing. There was a veritable explosion of Urdu-language textbooks prepared at Delhi, which were then published by either the college itself or the Agra School Book Society.[65] Publication lists for this period show that the majority of vernacular textbooks of European knowledge published in NWP were composed in Urdu.[66] This expansion of publication, in itself, led the NWP Government to establish a centralised clearinghouse at Agra to provide a 'general office of reference' for educational officers.[67] Further, at both Delhi and Agra, several Urdu journals were published in the mid-1840s from the government's colleges, including the *Qiran al-Sa'ādain*,[68] which were reported to 'discuss in Oordoo scientific and other subjects, and endeavour to make known all kinds of practical European inventions'.[69] By the mid-1840s, then, Urdu had become the principal vernacular medium for the publication of European 'useful' knowledge, and Delhi and Agra, with their large Muslim and Urdu-speaking populations, had become important locations of textbook translation, publication, and distribution.

The power of Sanskrit: translational strategy at Benares College

In 1845, Felix Boutros left the position of Superintendent of Delhi College, and with his departure the impetus behind the Urdu translational project waned. As unsold 'improved-Urdu' textbooks began to pile up in the NWP Government's book depository during the later 1840s,[70] the focus of both textbook production and translational activity shifted eastward, to Benares College under the superintendency of James Ballantyne.[71] The translation of key Western scientific and philosophical texts formed a cornerstone of Ballantyne's project, and he believed that the 'proper' translation of these English works was fundamental to extracting their maximum educational value for his Indian students. In this regard, he disagreed with the earlier translational strategy outlined by Felix Boutros, particularly the transliteration, or 'engraftment', of English technical terminology directly into Indian languages. Ballantyne thought this would bring about a 'barbarisation' of language. For example, he once commented that the use of English-language terminology in Indian-language textbooks would inevitably 'degenerate into a gibberish', such as had already happened in the case of 'the *digarī* of our law-courts, for a "decree," the *tārpīn-kā-tel* of our laboratories, for "turpentine," or the *māmlet* of our kitchens, for an "omelette."'[72]

Drawing upon Brian Hodgson's characterisation of the Indian vernacular languages as possessing 'great resources' on account of their historical connections with the more powerful classical languages, such as Persian, Arabic, and Sanskrit,[73] Ballantyne believed that the translation of Western science and 'useful knowledge' into the vernacular (in particular, Hindi) for use in mass education required that it first be rendered into Sanskrit. At the most fundamental level, it was thought necessary to initially present Western knowledge in Sanskrit so that it would be readily available, and attractive, for the traditional intellectual leadership of India, the *paṇḍits*, 'none of whom seem to like to read any thing but Sanscrit'. In other words, the use of Sanskrit was considered to be an 'indispensable condition' to conciliate the 'class of men' whose cooperation in constructive orientalist educational practices Ballantyne very much needed to gain those practices intellectual and social legitimacy among India's masses.[74] Moreover, the predominant orientalist characterisations of Sanskrit – as *deva-bhāṣā*, the 'language of the gods', revered by the *paṇḍits* and the medium for their religious and scholarly discourse – were thought to invoke a further measure of cultural authority for the presentation of Western 'useful knowledge' to these men. In this regard, Ballantyne argued that Sanskrit represented the 'key' to the 'hearts' of Indians.[75]

Nevertheless, Ballantyne believed that Sanskrit itself also had to be 'developed', or rather, improved, to make it adequate for the 'reproduction of European thought'.[76] This 'development' was to be effected, quite simply, through the processes of translation from English. This process would result in what Ballantyne described, rather colourfully, as Sanskrit 'paying tribute instead of scowling defiance'.[77] From this perspective, Sanskrit may be said to have possessed a 'lack' when compared to English, for although it was an ancient language of refinement and representative of a 'classical' civilisation, its speakers were thought to have impressed upon it very little in the way of a significant progression, for it still possessed a limited vocabulary to express the advanced scientific knowledge of Europe.

However, the translation of knowledge expressed through the English language into the Sanskrit presented Ballantyne with several fundamental methodological difficulties. On the one hand, it was thought that the use of already-existing Sanskrit terms to express Western notions, such as technical terms from the *jyotiḥśāstra* for treatises of Western algebra and mathematics, would further demonstrate to the *paṇḍits* the points of connection between their own philosophical 'traditions' and Western 'science' and scientific methodology, and also facilitate the introduction of that knowledge.[78] In this way, the use of a common terminology allowed for a common ground of dialogue and comparison between adherents of 'Western' and 'Indian' learning, while simultaneously highlighting the point of departure of European knowledge. On the other hand, the use of extant Sanskrit terms could confuse readers rather than lead them to the conclusion desired in a comparative exercise, since these terms often retained their 'Hindu' philosophical or religious connotations. In other words, while Sanskrit's 'depth of meaning' was considered a virtue for the expression of Western knowledge, the fact that this meaning was often already determined within self-referential philosophical systems presented a potential hurdle to the realisation of 'progress'.

Ballantyne was well aware of this problem, and discussed it in the 'Preface' to his *Christianity Contrasted with Hindu Philosophy*. Here he warned that in producing a translation into an Indian language, one must ensure that one's words are 'rightly comprehended' by the target audience, and he gave as a cautionary example the first Bible translation into Sanskrit (the *dharmapustaka*) of the Serampore Baptist missionaries, executed under the leadership of William Carey. The first verse of Genesis in the *dharmapustaka*, Ballantyne noted, states that God created heaven and earth, but by reference to the terms *ākāśa* and *pṛthivī*. This was problematic because in most Indian philosophical systems, including the *nyāya* and *sāṅkhya*, these terms refer to just two of the five elements ('ether' and 'earth', respectively) and so when the 'learned Hindu reader' comes to the next verse and reads about God's spirit moving upon the face of the 'waters', (which is considered to be a third element), he 'is staggered by the doubt whether it is to be understood that the waters were *uncreated*, or whether the sacred penman had made an oversight'.[79] Indeed, Ballantyne related how one *paṇḍit*, thinking within 'the categories of the *nyāya*', had told him upon reading these verses that the Bible contained a 'palpable contradiction'.[80] Therefore, he argued that this translation could in no measure be considered as conducive to the spread of veridical knowledge about Christianity in India. Indeed, just the opposite.

Ballantyne thus recommended that already-existing Sanskrit terminology only be used in translations from English with a full understanding of the established nuances those terms had in 'Hindu thought':

> only by tracing the development of Hindoo thought, and of the terminology in which it clothed itself, can we hope to avoid

completely all such misappropriation of terms, as that which has, to a certain extent, baffled all European attempts at translation into the Hindoo dialects whenever the subject of discussion transcended the palpable.[81]

Ballantyne's strategy for the use of already-existing Sanskrit terminology in his translations was probably derived directly from William Carey's successor in the Baptist Bible translational project, William Hodge Mill. In 1828, Mill published his *Proposed Version of Theological Terms*, with the help of H. H. Wilson, in order to explicitly consider the established nuances of meaning for all Sanskrit terms proposed to render Christian concepts, and to suggest ways to harness and employ those meanings in the propagation of Christianity. For example, Mill suggested that the term *deva* be used for 'God', for although it was sometimes used in a polytheistic sense in Sanskrit literature, in many instances it also implied 'the supreme all-pervading Mind'.[82] However, Mill also suggested that the phrase 'son of God' should not be rendered as *deva-putra*, since *putra* implied, etymologically, 'one who redeems his father from that hell to which the childless are condemned'.[83] Ballantyne's own translation of the first verse of Genesis reflected this etymologically and contextually nuanced translational methodology:

In the beginning God created the heavens and the earth.
āditaḥ sasarjeśvaro divaṃ bhūmiṃ ca[84]

Here Ballantyne used the terms *diva* for 'heaven', derived from the verbal root *div*, which is also the basis for *deva* (a deity), as well as *bhūmi* for 'earth', which carries the dominant meaning of 'place' or 'territory'. Through these usages, Ballantyne managed to avoid confusion with the latter term, since it has no distinct philosophical associations, and with the former term he invoked a connection with the divine through an implicit etymological association.[85]

That said, Ballantyne also believed that there were significant portions of European science which could find no exact correspondent within the corpus of Sanskrit literature, the *śāstra*, and that therefore the translation of this knowledge into Sanskrit would require the 'devising of new terms'.[86] Translation here served to highlight the differences, or deficiencies, of Sanskrit-based knowledge systems through the perceived need for 'supplementation' and the improvement of Sanskrit's vocabulary. These fields of knowledge were thought to include formal logic, described as 'a subject neglected or overlooked by the Hindus',[87] physics, and chemistry, which in the *śāstra* was thought by Ballantyne to amount to little more than 'purified alchemy'.[88] The question that needed to be addressed in the production of translations was how exactly to devise these new terms, and thereby 'supplement' Sanskrit with the requisite terminology.

It has already been noted that Ballantyne had explicitly rejected the direct imposition of English scientific terms into Sanskrit, because he worried that the language would degenerate into 'gibberish'. However, several other, more fundamental, considerations drove this translational strategy. On one basic level, Ballantyne clearly considered such a transliteration of English to be simply unnecessary, for he thought Sanskrit to be a powerful language by its very subtlety and complexity, able to express a wide range and a depth of meaning; that is, he adopted the orientalists' (and *paṇḍits*') characterisations of Sanskrit as *saṃskṛta*, 'that which is perfected'. In particular, Sanskrit's organisation into a large number of verbal roots (*dhātu*) meant that nearly endless new vocabularies could be easily coined.[89] In this regard, Sanskrit's very structure was thought to be particularly suited for the expression of scientific knowledge, and Ballantyne often compared it to Latin and Greek, languages that still supplied English with many of its technical terms.

A further rationale behind Ballantyne's innovative translational methodology is best glimpsed through an examination of his attempt to construct a Sanskrit vocabulary for the Western science of chemistry. Western knowledge of chemistry had already been treated, to some extent, in William Yates' 1828 *Padārthavidyāsāra*,[90] as well as in John Mack's 1834 English and Bengali text *Principles of Chemistry*[91] and in a simple primary school textbook in Hindi published by the Agra School Book Society in 1847.[92] Yet these texts all followed the translational methodology first systematised by Boutros in Delhi, utilising transliterated English technical terms. For example, *aksijān* or *āksajin* were used for 'oxygen', *haidrajān* or *hāiḍrojin* for 'hydrogen', and *phosphoras* or *phāspharas* for 'phosphorous'. Ballantyne discussed this methodology in his writings, with particular reference to John Mack's text, and while he questioned the notion that English terminology could ever become fully naturalised in an Indian language, the principal concern that drove him to reject this strategy was that it diminished educational value.[93] That is, Ballantyne believed that the memorisation of English technical terms served not to educate India's youths, but rather to 'make a convenience' of them through a mere technical training. He noted that the study of chemistry in German, the speakers of which language had 'indigenated for themselves the language of chemistry', was far more profitable as a 'mental exercise', than it was for the 'English villager who does not know Greek and Latin'.[94] An appropriately coined Sanskrit terminology in scientific textbooks, therefore, would serve to maximise the potential within education for India's intellectual and civilisational progress.

On this basis, Ballantyne outlined a comprehensive chemical nomenclature in Sanskrit. Several words for metals and other common substances already appeared in Sanskrit, and Ballantyne suggested maintaining the use of those. For example, *gandhaka* and *loha* for 'sulfur' and 'iron' both appeared in the *Amarakośa*, a revered Sanskrit lexicon, while terms such as *suvarṇa* for 'gold' and *aṅgāra* for 'carbon' were also well known. Otherwise, the nomenclature created anew was entirely descriptive, and 'self-interpreting'. For example, 'hydrogen' was rendered *jalakara*, 'the maker of water'; 'nitrogen' became *jīvāntaka*, 'that which puts an end to life'; while 'chlorine' was translated as *harita*, 'greenish-coloured'. Reflecting the evolving nature of his endeavour, Ballantyne had originally translated 'oxygen' as *aṃlakara*, 'one which forms an acid', but later changed this to *prāṇaprada*, 'that which gives breath', lest the former term 'preserve the exploded theory that there is no generator of acids besides oxygen'. This quite extraordinary translational strategy was further applied to the construction of compound words. Here, Ballantyne noted, the similarity of terminations such as '-ic', '-ate' and '-ous' in Latin and Greek to those in Sanskrit (*-ika*, *-āyita* and *-ya*) was sufficient to provide the basic model. 'Sulphuric acid', therefore, became *gandhakikāmla* (where *amla* denotes 'acid'), while 'sulfate' was rendered as *gandhakāyita*. Moreover, the use of the Sanskrit suffix *ja*, indicative of the use of the verbal root *jan*, 'to be born', in an *upapāda tatpuruṣa* compound, resulted in the coining of such terms as *prāṇapradaja*, 'that which is born from oxygen', or an 'oxide'.[95]

While Ballantyne's translational scheme was relatively straightforward, it could also produce rather lengthy compounds that, in effect, served to express the process by which a material was produced rather than simply the material itself. A good example of this is Ballantyne's translation of the word 'magnesia', which in Sanskrit became the rather cumbersome *adāhyapaṭamūlajanakasya prāṇapradaja*, or, 'that which is born from oxygen, i.e. an oxide, of that which produces the basis of cloth, i.e. fibre, which cannot be burned', referring to the magnesium component of asbestos.[96]

Once the translation of key English scientific and philosophical texts into Sanskrit was underway at Benares College, Ballantyne undertook to superintend the further translation of these texts into Hindi and other Indian vernaculars. In particular, he advocated the direct engraftment into the vernaculars of the newly coined and heavily Sanskritised technical scientific vocabulary, which would render these languages sufficient for the task of expressing Western 'useful' and scientific knowledge. A substantial number of Hindi textbooks were published under the auspices of Benares College during the 1850s which incorporated highly Sanskritised vocabularies, including Hindi versions of Ballantyne's *A Synopsis of Science*,[97] and a number of the translations of the 'reprints for the pandits' series.[98] Several of the *paṇḍit*s employed at Benares College also published vernacular textbooks on Ballantyne's model. Bāpūdeva Śāstrī, for example, wrote books on algebra[99] and world geography in Hindi,[100] while his Sanskrit *Elements of Plane Trigonometry* was translated into Hindi in 1859 by Venī Śaṅkara Vyāsa.[101] Another of the college's *paṇḍit*s, Mathurāprasāda Miśra, translated Mann's *Lessons in General Knowledge* into Hindi, as well as Ballantyne's edition of the Sanskrit grammatical text *Laghu Kaumudi*.[102] The highly Sanskritised vocabulary utilised in all of these texts was further consolidated by the publication of a series of Hindi dictionaries prepared by *paṇḍit*s employed in Benares College during the 1860s, including the 1865 English-Urdu-Hindi dictionary of Mathurāprasāda Miśra, and an 1870 Hindi translation of H. H. Wilson's Sanskrit dictionary by *paṇḍit* Rām Jasan.[103] Miśra's trilingual dictionary, in particular, served to highlight the importance of the Sanskritic components of Hindi by a comparison to, and lexical separation from, Urdu's Arabic or Persian influence.[104] Miśra listed almost all of Ballantyne's constructed Sanskrit chemical nomenclature as Hindi vocabulary, including *amlakar* and *prāṇaprad* for 'oxygen', as well as attested terms such as *gandhak* for 'sulfur'. In this regard, Miśra noted that 'Sanskrit words are given rather profusely ... both by choice and necessity: by choice, in order to make it generally useful, ... by necessity, because the Hindi vocabulary is rather poor'. Here Miśra reiterated Ballantyne's basic argument, noting that 'the expression of the nobler sentiments and finer sensibilities of a busy mind, and of philosophic and scientific truths, is far beyond its [Hindi's] genius and capability'. It was then noted that Hindi, 'like a child', must resort to its parent, the Sanskrit, rather than to some 'foreign aid'.[105]

This final stage of Ballantyne's translational strategy represented its most fundamental and important aspect, for it was realised that the vast majority of the Indian population would never have access to Western knowledge in Sanskrit. In official parlance, translation into the vernaculars was thought to demonstrate that 'the Government of Great Britain in India recognises no hereditary distinction in the realm of intellect, but wishes that all knowledge that is valuable should be placed within the reach of every man in the country who has a mind capable of appreciating its value'.[106] India's civilisational 'improvement' could only be effected when the vernacular languages used in the education of the mass of the people were first rendered capable of expressing scientific 'truth'. It was thought that the European-sponsored translation of Western knowledge into the vernaculars, through a process of naturalisation and authorisation through Sanskrit and the offices of the *paṇḍit*s, would therefore serve to 'democratise' knowledge throughout Indian society. The translational scheme undertaken at Benares College, therefore, represented an attempt to recreate the European Enlightenment in India by imposing essentially the same process (in which the release of scientific knowledge in Europe from Latin and Greek, as well as from the clerical elite, enabled Europe's material and moral advancement).

But as in Delhi College, it was thought that European initiative was necessary to effect this revolution in language, and subsequently, in thought within India. This is clearly demonstrated by the official appointment of Fitz-Edward Hall to the position of Anglo-Sanskrit Professor of Benares College in 1853, charged with overall responsibility for the rendering of European knowledge into 'pure and classical Hindi'.[107] It was noted that Hall possessed sufficient knowledge of Sanskrit and Hindi 'for enriching the latter with the accurate mode of expression as well as the deep train of thought which are to be found in the former'. This, the government thought, would result in the 'moulding upon an approved classical model the Vernacular language which more and more is daily becoming [the] medium through which the intelligent Natives of the Country acquire useful knowledge themselves and communicate it to others'.[108]

In a subsequent 'Memo on Hindee' to the Lieutenant-Governor, dated 1854, Hall duly reiterated Ballantyne's principal ideas: first, that the *paṇḍit*s represented the principal impediment to improving Hindi, and thereby wider Indian civilisation, by their obstinacy and love of Sanskrit alone, but at the same time they were the principal means by which Sanskrit vocabulary could be 'naturalised' into Hindi to improve its expressive capability. Second, Hindi, rather than Urdu, was singularly well suited to expressing 'useful knowledge' given its close relationship with Sanskrit, the principal language of Indian civilisation. Third, and most importantly, Hall argued that the task of improving Hindi to render it capable of expressing Western science must fall to Europeans, since 'the natives ... unaided will never unfold or discover the powers of their language to the satisfaction of just views of exactness and propriety'.[109]

There can be little doubt that many Hindi texts, as well as the Hindi dictionaries produced throughout the 1850s, 1860s, and 1870s, forged a close link with the vocabulary of Sanskrit. However, there was inevitably some measure of opposition to the wholesale importation of Sanskritic terms into the vernacular. For example, in March of 1853 the government distributed a Hindi version of *A Synopsis of Science* throughout NWP in order that its suitability as a textbook might be assessed.[110] The response received from British educators and their Indian assistants clearly indicated that, for many of the vernacular speakers of NWP, it represented an example of 'harsh and unidiomatic language', and that it was not within the comprehension of those who could not already read Sanskrit.[111]

Moreover, Ballantyne's advocacy of a highly Sanskritised vocabulary for Western science was largely ignored by the emerging class of Indian educators in their publication of Hindi school books in subsequent decades in north India, as these writers reverted instead to a transliterated English vocabulary. These men were often employed by government educational institutions, but in time, many of them would also come to form a culturally significant group of agitators for the promotion of Hindi and a strengthened form of Hinduism in northern India. For example, *paṇḍit* Sevaka Rāma's 1873 *Śabda Prabandāvalī* utilised terms such as *arsenik* for 'arsenic',[112] while *paṇḍit* Śivdayāl Upādhyāy, employed by the Mayo College at Ajmere, wrote a basic scientific reader which incorporated terms such as *megniśiyā* for 'magnesia' and *phāsphorik esiḍ* for 'phosphoric acid'.[113] In 1877, Rājendralāl Mitra, a prominent Bengali orientalist and antiquarian, outlined in an English-language pamphlet his own translational scheme for the rendering of European scientific terms into Indian vernacular languages. Mitra agreed partially with Ballantyne's methodology in that he advocated the retention of attested Indian terminology for common substances such as sulfur and gold, and the translation into Indian languages of chemical processes, such as precipitation or crystallisation. Yet he also recommended the direct transliteration of 'scientific crude names', such as 'oxygen'. Here Mitra referred back to Ballantyne's attempt to translate this term, noting that 'no good' could possibly come of it.[114]

Even the official *śuddh* (pure) Hindi scientific lexicon published in 1906 by the Benares-based Nāgarī Pracāriṇī Sabhā ('Society for the promotion of the Nāgarī script') effectively advocated the use of English terminology in the absence of attested Hindi equivalents, and even the adoption of suffixes based upon an English, rather than a Sanskrit, model. For example, while *amlajan* was recommended as the equivalent of 'oxygen' (a still-current term), 'carbon' became *karban*, and 'nitrogen' was rendered *natrajan*. Moreover, the suffixes '-ate' and '-ous' were to be written '*-it*' and '*-as*', so that 'carbonate' became *karbanit* and 'ferrous' *lohas*.[115] Indeed, it would have been much to Ballantyne's consternation to discover that in a single 1878 issue of the *Hindī Pradīp*, a monthly Hindi journal published in Allahabad by Bālkṛṣṇa Bhaṭṭ, a prominent promoter of the Hindi language, that the term *jalkar*, ('hydrogen') which had been coined for Ballantyne's *The Sub-Divisions of Knowledge*, was used alongside that of *tārhpīn kā tel* for 'turpentine'.[116]

Yet it would be a mistake to dismiss Ballantyne, and constructive orientalism more generally, as ultimately unimportant on the basis that many of these initiatives were criticised, or indeed, not adopted into general usage in the manner which had been foreseen. At the very least, the fact that translational strategies employed in institutions such as Benares College were grounded within notions of a 'classical' Sanskrit, and its 'mothering' relationship to the vernaculars, should raise important questions about the genealogy which lay behind the construction of 'modern' languages in India, and in particular, their functioning to somehow represent national or communal identities. Thus, the 'Sanskritisation' of Hindi pursued at Benares College by the *paṇḍits*, and not just Ballantyne and Hall, may very well represent an important contributing factor in the evolution and politicisation of Hindi during the later nineteenth century, as Hindi increasingly was being used as a mode of self-description evocative of specific, Sanskritic civilisational associations.[117] This realisation would complicate the understandings of Bhāratendu Hariścandra's formulation of Hindi as India's 'national language' (*deś-bhāṣā*), as indeed his notion that the linguistic improvement of Hindi must necessarily precede north Indian social evolution.[118] Equally, even figures such as Rājā Śivaprasād, an administrator in the education service in Benares who consciously attempted to forge a revised Hindi vernacular without solely relying upon Sanskrit as a feeder language, implicitly adopted the exclusive equivalences forged of language and civilisation, even if he battled against them. Thus, Śivaprasād advocated the adoption of words such as *madrasā* (from the Persian for 'school'), rather than the Sanskrit *pāṭhśālā*, or the Arabic *maktab*, in order that it might be viewed as an inclusive medium of communication for both Hindus and Muslims.[119]

Lastly, it might be charged that by focusing upon the European intellectual genealogies that underpinned translation, this chapter has effectively marginalised the impacts that the colonised had upon the development of European knowledge and educational strategy. As we have already seen, European writers and translators working in India derived much of their linguistic skill, as well as their knowledge of the cultural meaningfulness of Indian languages, from interaction with their tutors and assistants, the *paṇḍits*. Thus it can be argued that the ideas Indian *paṇḍits* held about Sanskrit had important impacts upon British thinking about their translational project, and indeed, I don't doubt this. The rather more important historical question, I think, relates to what particular uses Indians themselves made of these ideas, or rather, how Indians drew upon, altered, or contested these ideas in the furtherance of their own distinct educational, cultural, or nationalist projects. This contestation is the subject of the next chapter.

6
Paṇḍits, Sanskrit Learning, and Europe's 'New Knowledge'

The trope of Sanskrit scholarship's decline is well established. British orientalists and educationalists from the mid-eighteenth century onwards argued that Sanskrit, as an intellectual enterprise, was in a state of terminal decay, and required European intervention in order to resurrect it and turn it to the cause of improvement. Similarly, contemporary Hindu extremists, in their promotion of Hindutva at the expense of Indian minorities, have characterised Hindu cultural decline (and ongoing Hindu civilisational 'imperilment') partly by reference to the historical abuse Sanskritic traditions are thought to have suffered at the hands of Muslims and Europeans. The apparent demise of Sanskrit was also made to answer an inherently anti-colonial nationalist cause by P. V. Kane in his multi-volume *History of Dharmaśāstra* (published between 1930 and 1962), which reconstructed an encyclopaedic understanding of Hindu *dharma* while claiming that this sort of Sanskrit scholarship came to an end at the close of the eighteenth century.[1] More recently, Sheldon Pollock has diagnosed Sanskrit's death in the modern world, and sought to explain historically what he perceives as the 'precipitous decline' in the quality of Sanskrit scholarship from about the fourteenth century onward. Pollock notes that the rise of European power in South Asia was a factor in the diminishing dynamism within the language's scholarly traditions, and that as a medium of thought, Sanskrit's 'creative vitality' and its ability 'to make history' had disappeared by 1800. In essence, Sanskrit literary activity is thought by Pollock to have become by that time a 'practice of repetition and not renewal', and that Sanskrit itself was no longer a language for engagement with the evolving nature of Indians' lived experiences.[2]

The claim of Sanskrit's decline, viewed as a part of Hindu cultural deterioration during foreign rule, is understood as ideologically driven when presented as a part of the caricatured self-understandings of Hindutva. The detailed, substantiated claim made by Pollock, however, has potentially important implications for the way historians understand the cultural significance within colonial India of Sanskrit intellectuals, the *paṇḍits*, and the variety of institutions and the social contexts which sustained them. The upshot of Pollock's diagnosis is that it declares Sanskrit, as a medium of thought, a medium of communication, and as an intellectual 'tradition', unable to speak to the changed circumstances of the colonial era.[3] Pollock has rightly identified a series of transformations in the social and political conditions which had contributed to the support of Sanskrit scholarship. As Brian Hatcher has noted, the era of British rule in India was witness to an array of changed circumstances for *paṇḍits*, as traditional Sanskrit pedagogy declined in favour of colonial-sponsored educational institutions, and critiques of Hindu philosophy and theology flourished.[4] Yet the pronouncement of Sanskrit's death seems injudicious if we accept as its corollary that Europe's modernity ran roughshod over India's Sanskrit scholars. Certainly the media through which Indians produced textual scholarship, including critiques of British civilisation (especially Christianity), expanded to include not only Sanskrit, but also the vernaculars and English. Sanskrit, however, retained an important cultural resonance, and *paṇḍits* utilised the language itself as a medium of expression (though not necessarily exclusively), and as a cultural-textual resource, to produce critical cultural understandings of Indian history and European claims to superiority which did, in fact, 'make history'. Pollock's critique, however, can also be read to infer that if the 'traditional' forms of Sanskrit scholarship were indeed being surpassed by 1800, then, in a peculiar way, it may well be because *paṇḍits* were engaging with many of the dramatic changes taking place in colonial India, and themselves adapting to these new circumstances.[5] I choose to read Pollock's thesis in this manner, and thus highlight the need for an essentially open-minded approach to writing a history of the *paṇḍits*' scholarship during the colonial era.[6]

Recent studies, however, of the production of Sanskrit-related scholarship by Indians during the colonial period have tended for the most part to fall into two rather disparate categories.[7] On the one hand, some histories of *paṇḍits* have been produced nearly as an invocation of nostalgia for lost scholarly traditions, or as an enumeration of scholars and their *guru-śiṣya* (teacher-student) lineages. These amount essentially to a form of hagiography, or, at least, have presented uncritical surveys of lives lived and scholarship, replicating in essence the treatment meted out to William Jones as scholar extraordinaire.[8] On the other hand, the concern with interrogating India's 'traditional' colonial intermediaries, rather than English-educated nationalist elites, in the construction of essentially hybrid forms of colonial knowledge, has similarly tended to carve out for these scholars a wholly 'traditional' space of agency. In such studies *paṇḍits* are represented as guardians of age-old Sanskrit-based ways of knowing, in a binary interface between East and West. It has been argued by Nita Kumar, for example, that those *paṇḍits* who cooperated with British educational initiatives in cities such as Benares in essence went over to the 'other side', becoming part of a government 'plot' to anglicise and Christianise the Indian populace. Those who turned their back on government-sponsored education, in contrast, to continue in wholly 'traditional' forms of pedagogy outside the realm of government superintendence, are conceived to have expressed some form of 'resistance' and 'agency' in so doing, even if it rendered them obsolete 'wise fools'.[9] Less derivatively, the intrepid act of *Purāṇik* 'forgery' committed by Francis Wilford's *paṇḍit* Vidyānand, which was recounted in Chapter 2, has been interpreted by Nigel Leask and C. A. Bayly as an instance of 'resistance' to colonial representational authority through the articulation of what is considered, in essence, an 'indigenous' intellectual space for the *paṇḍits*. Leask, for example, has argued that the *paṇḍits*' complicated notions of 'authenticity' within the Sanskrit 'scriptural tradition' would have been at odds with Wilford's vision of the *paṇḍits* as a 'pure' conduit of Indian knowledge.[10] Bayly has substantiated this point by arguing that the practice of rewriting and 'adjusting' the *Purāṇas* was a perfectly acceptable and justifiable one, given *paṇḍits*' earlier relationships to Maratha chieftains who wished to gain dynastic legitimation through acts of 'creative' genealogy, and the traditional Sanskritic doctrine that, at any rate, all knowledge was contained within the *śāstra*.[11]

Earlier chapters of this book have repeatedly emphasised the importance of *paṇḍits*' social and cultural authority to the East India Company's government, from the legal codification project of the eighteenth century to constructive orientalist education in the mid-nineteenth. This chapter moves on to examine the 'other side' of this relationship, initially through an exploration of some of the possible factors which lay behind *paṇḍits*' entry into forms of government employment. It then analyses how some Indian Sanskrit scholars in the city of Benares, especially, engaged with the changed circumstances of colonialism, including forceful characterisations of the *nayā vidyā* ('new knowledge') of the West, as well as the attendant representations of 'traditional' Sanskrit-based knowledge within British orientalist scholarship and educational initiatives. This chapter is an enquiry, in essence, into some of the transformations observable in the social and cultural roles of this elite group of Indian scholars during the nineteenth century by virtue of their involvement in government-sponsored educational programmes and the institutions of governance.

Thankfully, there exists a significant, though certainly not abundant, amount of source material to attempt to address these issues. In addition to official education reports and the correspondence of government functionaries, one can find within the colonial archive occasional examples of *paṇḍit*s' petitions, class reports, and *vyavasthā*s ('opinions'), most often in Sanskrit, though sometimes in Hindi and English, as well as published copies of their original scholarship in a variety of forms and languages. It is possible, therefore, to write elements of the history of *paṇḍit*s' scholarly activities which takes into account the engagements, adaptations, and critiques of the political and intellectual worlds of the coloniser: a history which details forms of interaction between Britons and Indians, highlighting the agency of the latter, and testifying to their distinct set of priorities.[12] Crude stereotypes of *paṇḍit*s as 'collaborators' or 'unworldly' and naïve are simply insufficient to account for the range of activities and engagements which an examination of the available source material demonstrates *paṇḍit*s undertook in the nineteenth century, including particularly the ability of *paṇḍit*s in government employ to express distinct and diverse points of view about the Indian past in the course of a reconstruction of a 'modern' Hindu identity.

Indeed, a principal aim of this last chapter, together with the 'afterword' which follows it, is to substantiate the argument that many of the *paṇḍit*s of northern India, by virtue of their connections to government educational institutions, their expertise in Sanskrit and the *śāstra*, as well as elements of Western knowledge, made significant and influential contributions to the characterisation of the Hindu cultural-textual past. These highlighted the Sanskrit intellectual tradition as one which represented elements of India's own distinctive modernity, rationality, and scientific achievement, and which could then be made to form the basis for an alternative claim to Indian nationhood. This is not to argue that 'nationalism', *per se*, was the only viable oppositional voice to European colonialism, or for that matter the natural culmination of orientalist educational initiatives.[13] But this chapter does argue that *paṇḍit*s, by contesting Europeans' characterisations of their own special status, contributed in significant ways to the reinterpretation and 'remaking', if you will, of the cultural meaningfulness of Sanskrit and the *śāstra* within the changed intellectual and political context of nineteenth-century north India, and that this meaningfulness could be enumerated amongst the resources mobilised in a variety of overtly nationalist projects later in the century.

Lastly, it needs to be emphasised that rather than thinking of the social category of the '*paṇḍit*' as historically stagnant, this chapter throughout also endeavours to historicise the scholarly activities of these men, as well as their interactions with religious reformers and the colonial state, as a part of their own ongoing process of self-fashioning. Sanskrit scholars of nineteenth-century northern India were an admittedly diverse lot, incorporating not only specialists in *nyāya* and *vedānta*, but also temple and lineage *paṇḍās*, *jyotiṣīs* (astrologers), and others, who in no way acted with a unified voice or a unified purpose. The scholars who populate the pages of this chapter, however, were constantly instantiating the social and cultural value of what it meant to be '*paṇḍita*' (i.e. 'learned') by adapting and revising the roles they might play in cultural production, social interaction, education, religious practice, and governance. In so doing, they emerged to become prominent cultural commentators, and critics, in the colonial north Indian public sphere.

Government service and the *paṇḍits*' self-fashioning

In his 1821 report to the government on the progress made in establishing 'traditional' colleges in Bengal and Bihar, H. H. Wilson remarked that the prejudices which the *paṇḍits* of Benares once held towards Europeans had now disappeared, following 'the conciliatory effects of a longer intimacy'. The *paṇḍits*, he reported, considered it an 'honour' that the Company took an interest in promoting Sanskrit learning, and, moreover, that they appreciated that their 'contact' with the Company's government through the establishment of Sanskrit colleges tended to 'elevate them in the consideration of their countrymen'.[14] Wilson's remarks were made in the hopes of convincing the government that it was acceptable, given this experience in Benares, to initiate even greater control over *paṇḍits* in the promulgation of Sanskrit learning in Calcutta, and needs to be understood in this context. Wilson's report does raise a series of important issues, however, which deserve further consideration. Namely, it prompts us to ask, how did those *paṇḍits* employed by the Company perceive their connection to government? Did this perception evolve, and did they continue to hold reservations about entering into the service of *mlecchas* (foreigners) as the nineteenth century progressed? Or was contributing to good governance by accepting such employment perceived as tantamount to a duty, which conferred benefits not only for the healthy promotion of Sanskrit literature and Hindu religious practice, but also for the advancement of their own reputations? Did *paṇḍits*, moreover, offer critiques of the colonial governance of Sanskrit education, and if so, how?

In fact, it first needs to be emphasised that during the nineteenth century, most *paṇḍits* in northern India relied not principally on the colonial state for their livelihood, but instead continued to teach Sanskrit literature outside of direct government service, either in their homes for donations, or in small *pāṭhśālās* endowed by generous patrons. Indeed, Charles Wilkins remarked in 1813, as part of an unrealised plan for the 'forming [of] a collegiate establishment at Benares', that it would be most expedient if *paṇḍits* were encouraged to continue giving instruction at their homes, 'in their own way', as he understood that to be the long-established practice.[15] William Adam's wide-ranging surveys of education in Bengal during the 1830s provide us with a partial snapshot of the extent of private Sanskrit education there at that time. In Nadia, for example, the celebrated centre in Bengal of *nyāya* scholarship, some 25 'traditional' Sanskrit schools were thought to be in operation, though that number apparently represented a decline from former years. *Paṇḍits* instructed some 500 to 600 students without charge, drawing their income from grants made formerly by the *rāja* of Nadia, and presents made by local *zamīndārs* (land holders).[16] Similarly, in Nattore, Rajshahi district, Adam described 39 *paṇḍits* teaching at 'unendowed Hindu schools of learning' who ranged in age from 25 to 82.[17] In a later survey of schools in the city and district of Benares made in 1849, 193 'indigenous' Sanskrit schools in the city were enumerated, with a total of 1,939 students, compared, for example, with ten missionary institutions and the one government college. In all, it was estimated that there was one student in the city of Benares for every 43 people, more than 3/4 of whom attended privately run schools. Again, in those schools devoted to Sanskrit learning, the literature was taught gratis, 'more from religious than secular motives'.[18] Up-and-coming urban mercantile communities in Benares increasingly sponsored such institutions, as well as independent Sanskrit scholars, for the social prestige this conferred. Rājā Kālī Śaṅkar Ghoṣāl, (the son of Jay Nārāyaṇ Ghoṣāl), for example, a prominent *zamīndār* who, most famously, opened an asylum for the blind in the city in 1826, is known to have employed a circle of *paṇḍits* who were often consulted by the Company's servants.[19]

Several well-known *paṇḍits* were also employed at the court of the *rāja* (*mahārāja* after 1859) of Benares, across the river at his Ramnagar palace. The patronage of Mahārājā Īśvarī Prasād Nārāyaṇ Siṃh (r. 1835–1889) is now perhaps best known as being linked with the production of an alternative, 'explicitly Hindu symbol of royal legitimacy' through patronage of the *Rāmlīlā* festival, and scholarship associated with the practice of *Rāmkathā* (recitation of stories relating to Rām). This included extensive manuscript copying and the production of *ṭīkās* (commentaries) on the *Rāmcaritmānas* of Tulsīdās (1532–1623).[20] Gaṅgā Dhā, for example, produced a commentary on the *Rāmāyaṇa* in Sanskrit, as well as an exposition of the *Vinaya-patrikā* ('petition' to Rām) of Tulsīdās, while Kāṣṭhajihvā Svāmī (also known as Devtīrtha Svāmī) produced commentaries in Sanskrit on the *Rāmāyaṇa*, *Bhāgavata Purāṇa*, and *Yoga Sūtra*. Other *paṇḍits* known to have been patronised at the Ramnagar court around this time included Devadatta Miśra, Tulsīdatta Jhā, Mahādev Śāstrī (also known as Mahādev Āśram), and Kṛṣṇapant Dharmādhikāri, whose *Kāśīśa vinoda* was a description of Ramnagar and its court.[21] Outside the realm of Rām scholarship, the *mahārāja* funded several *jyotiṣīs* to prepare the publication of a yearly almanac for Sanskrit astrologers, the *Kāśī Rāj Pañcāṅga*. Importantly, Ramnagar also became something of a centre for *nyāya* scholarship (wholly outside of Ballantyne's adaptation of the *nyāya* at Benares College), due to the sponsoring of *paṇḍits* such as Tārācaraṇa Tarkaratna, whose expertise in *nyāya* and *mīmāṃsā* was well-known in the city.[22] Tārācaraṇa wrote the *Tarkaratnākara*, characterised as an exposition of the 'essence' of the *nyāya* (*nyāya śāstra kā sār*), at the behest of the *mahārāja*,[23] and was a prominent participant in the Kāśī Dharma Sabhā's enumeration of Sanskritic philosophical knowledge, as well as the 1869 *śāstrārtha* (debate) with the Hindu reformer Dayānanda Sarasvatī.[24]

Sanskrit scholarship and education, therefore, continued outside governmental control despite the Company's efforts at institutionalisation. What considerations, therefore, led some *paṇḍits* to enter into government employment, or to work with British orientalists? It has been argued, with good reason, that many *paṇḍits* undoubtedly would have entered into these types of relationships due principally to financial hardship, rather than through an unproblematic acceptance of the governing legitimacy of the British. This would have been especially so in the wake of the disruption brought on by the decline in fortunes of their 'traditional' patrons in the immediate aftermath of the Company's ascension to formal political power in the late eighteenth century.[25] It is also well-known that for some time, especially from the 1760s to 1780s, British orientalists had trouble procuring the services of *paṇḍits*, who were naturally reluctant to break their sacred monopoly, and impart their knowledge of Sanskrit texts, though this reluctance was gradually overcome. Rosane Rocher has noted that Rādhākānta Tarkavāgīśa, who worked for both Warren Hastings and William Jones, approached Jones for financial assistance in 1787 when the proceeds from his land grant became severely diminished. The following year, Rādhākānta took a leading role in the compilation of the Company's second legal digest, the *Vivādabhaṅgārṇava*, at a salary of Rs 200 per month.[26] Similarly, the aged Jagannātha Tarkapañcānana, who lent his considerable authority as a scholar to that project, in 1793 requested that Governor-General Cornwallis provide him a continuance of his salary following the digest's completion, citing considerable ongoing financial hardship.[27] In later decades, William Adam's survey of education in Bengal described what he characterised as the extreme poverty which *paṇḍits* lived in, noting the contrast between the 'humbleness ... of their dwellings' and 'the extent of their acquirements and the refinements of their feelings'.[28] Adam, moreover, recognised that the Company's government had played a role in eroding the *paṇḍits*' sources of income, through its displacement of established landed elites.[29]

To be certain, service in the Company's government evolved into a career for many *paṇḍits* from the late eighteenth century, whether in its courts or educational institutions. In a significant respect, however, financial hardship in and of itself seems unsatisfactory as a leading explanation for this phenomenon. Yet it is difficult to determine, in an authoritative manner, the range of other factors which might have been important in this regard. This is not least because of the heterogeneity of *paṇḍits* themselves, the circumstances they may have found themselves in, and the opportunities which may have presented themselves, as well as the patchy nature of the historical record. It has been argued in Chapter 2 that *paṇḍits*, and *brāhmaṇs* more generally, were patronised by most political competitors in eighteenth-century Bengal, including the *navāb*. With the rise of the Company's government, then, the acceptance of British patronage may simply have been consistent with practices already observed under *navābī* rule. Moreover, that *paṇḍits* conceived of government service not necessarily in exclusionary terms, but as one component of a range of sources of patronage, is illustrated by the fact that several of the *paṇḍit*s originally appointed to the Sanskrit College at Benares also accepted further patrons who kept them from their pedagogical duties, much to the frustration of the first principal, Kāśīnātha Śarmā.[30] Most, if not all, of the *paṇḍit*s employed at Benares College later in the nineteenth century, moreover, also continued to teach students independently at their homes, outside the purview of European superintendence.[31]

Perhaps one of the more important arguments to consider in this regard is that British patronage, especially in the eighteenth century, may also have signalled a renewed opportunity for *paṇḍit*s to influence the regulation of matters relating to the promotion and maintenance of *dharma*, through a renewal, or reimagining, of the idealised governing codependency of *brāhmaṇ* and *kṣatriya*. This is most easily substantiated with respect to *paṇḍit*s who entered the Company's legal service, and is certainly the impression given by the prefatory matter to the *Vivādārṇavasetu* ('a bridge over the sea of litigation'), composed between 1773 and 1775 by 11 *paṇḍit*s of Bengal. As noted in Chapter 1, this Sanskrit *dharmaśāstra nibandha* (compilation) was commissioned to act as a legal guide in the Company's courts (in its Persian rendering) following Hastings' 1772 judicial plan, and was published later in a further English translation as *A Code of Gentoo Laws*. Far from simply enumerating normative prescriptions culled from the *dharmaśāstra*, however, the *paṇḍit*s involved in this project also took pains to point out to the Company's government the 'traditional' responsibilities of Indian monarchs.[32] The *paṇḍit*s began the *Code*, for example, with a reiteration and validation of Hastings' own vision of the Company's government in India as providing a 'reinstatement' of India's 'ancient constitution' after a period of relative despotism. The period of Islamic rule in India, they noted, was attended by the application of 'the Laws of Mahomed' as the 'Standard of Judgment for the Hindoos', such that justice was no longer 'impartially administered' and the people suffered 'Terror and Confusion'. Yet Hastings' design to 'investigate the principles of the Gentoo religion', it was stated, would lead to 'a proper Attention to each Religion' so that 'Justice might take place impartially, according to the Tenets of every Sect'.[33]

The *paṇḍit*s next confirmed their own place at the top of the social hierarchy, their intrinsic worthiness of respect from others, as well as their role as primary advisors to 'the Magistrate' (i.e. the king) in the religious and socio-legal principles of the *śāstra*. Indeed, the proper cultivation of the Magistrate's relationship with *brāhmaṇs* was stated to be the most significant factor in promoting the kingdom's prosperity. If *brāhmaṇs* were unable to procure food and clothing, for example, it was warned that such a kingdom would surely become 'desolate'. In this regard, the paramount duty of the Magistrate was to ensure that his infliction of legal sanction, as well as his performance of governmental administration, was, first and foremost, 'in conformity to the *Shaster*'. The Magistrate's employment of ideally ten *paṇḍits* to advise him was said to ensure such conformity. The *paṇḍits* also outlined their own ideal personal qualities, including being men of compassion and clemency, and being born of 'an exalted Family', as well as listing their own duties for 'the Advantage of the Magistrate', such as the performance of particular rites.[34] In a similar manner, several *paṇḍits* from Benares, in their 1784 'ode' to Warren Hastings, characterised the Company as the 'Eye of the Code of Justice, the Defender of Religion,' and Hastings himself as 'an Example of Justice, ... from thy favor the people dwell in the exercise of the Religion'.[35] Of course this is not to suggest that the *paṇḍits* straightforwardly viewed the Company as a harbinger of egalitarianism and justice. But such characterisations on the *paṇḍits*' part, at least, might have been used as part of a wider strategy to influence the Company's support of Sanskrit learning, and the upholding of the tenets of the *śāstra* in their governance of India, given the Company's relative dependence upon *paṇḍits* for legitimacy in the new judicial context.[36] Whether the Company's servants could understand, or would care to observe, such governing traditions in a substantial manner is another issue.

Correspondingly, the *paṇḍits*' association with educational institutions such as Benares College also allowed them to voice their opinions in elements of governance, especially within the realm of socio-cultural policy. Consistent with *paṇḍits*' expressions of governmental responsibility surrounding the Company's judicial reorganisation, it was observed by William Adam that many of the *paṇḍits* he spoke to believed that the Company possessed 'a duty' to promote Sanskrit education; a duty, moreover, which was 'in their minds constantly associated with the obligations attaching to the rulers of the country'.[37] The form and functioning of the collegiate institutions introduced by the Company were undoubtedly innovatory in the South Asian context, in the strictly observed hours, examinations, the taking of attendance, and so forth.[38] Nevertheless, *paṇḍits* would have recognised such institutions as a form of patronage which not only brought desired financial support to young *brāhmaṇ* students for their education and to Sanskrit scholarship more widely, but also, however problematically, as a form of patronage consistent with elements of their expectations for government and their own selves.

In contentious legal cases, for example, the *paṇḍits* of Benares Sanskrit College, as well as those of the Sanskrit College in Calcutta, were often called upon by the Company to issue a further *vyavasthā*, in order to confirm or remedy the opinion of the *adālat* (court) *paṇḍits*.[39] The Benaresi *paṇḍits*' opinions held considerable weight in this regard, by virtue of their authoritative scholarly reputation as a group.[40] Thus, in the mid-1850s the Company's courts asked the *paṇḍits* of Benares College whether it was permissible to raise up and move a temple or an image of Śiva to another place, in order to clear the way for the construction of a new major road. The resulting *vyavasthā*, signed by 13 *paṇḍits* of the college,[41] challenged the propriety of such plans, and the very principles which underwrote the Company's modernising efforts in north India's cities, with a most emphatic reply:

> A Śiva *liṅga* or image is not to be raised up from its previous [original] location, and if it has been lifted up, it should not be placed down somewhere else. One should not move a Śiva *liṅga* that is properly situated or improperly situated. One should not cause it to take another form, nor should one cause it to be established in another place – this is most important. This is based on the statements of the *Agni Purāṇa* [which are] supported by the elucidation of honouring the *liṅga*.
>
> *na śivaliṅgaṃ pratimādikaṃ vā pūrvasthānād uddharaṇīyaṃ na voddhatyānyatra sthāpanīyaṃ. duḥsthitaṃ susthitaṃvāpi śivaliṅgaṃ na cālayet iti nānyākāraṃ na cānyatra sthāpayet tad gurūttamam iti ca liṅgārcanacandrikādhṛtāgnipurāṇavacanāt.*[42]

The outcome of this case, and the role which the *paṇḍits*' objections played in it, are unfortunately not known. Once again, it is not suggested here that the *paṇḍits* freely influenced government in the manner of the idealised *brāhmaṇ-kṣatriya* relationship in Sanskrit literature. The nature, however, of the co-relationship between the Company and its *paṇḍits*, in which the Company relied upon their expertise for a wide variety of forms of legitimacy, did at least enable the articulation of such forceful assertions of Indian cultural autonomy within the Company's realm of governance.

Cultural contestation in an institutional setting

In attempting to understand elements of *paṇḍits'* motivations for accepting patronage and employment from the Company, it also becomes apparent that institutions such as Benares College, rather than being viewed as an unproblematic site of the invocation of colonial authority, are better understood as a shared space: a space of contestation and mutual engagement, in which the identity of the institution itself was always being made and remade in a series of confrontations and subversions. To be certain, the *paṇḍits* who worked in Benares College did so with an understanding not only of their own responsibilities to the state and their students, but also their entitlements as Sanskrit scholars. In this respect, the *paṇḍits'* range of scholarly activities rendered Benares College into an institution that surely bore their very marks, though these marks may no longer be so readily perceptible.

In one important sense, Benares College, while being the Company's flagship Sanskrit enterprise, was also always compromised as a colonial institution by the very terms of its establishment. Indeed, the essential ambiguity which underwrote the college is reflected in its Sanskrit name: *Kāśīstharājakīyapāṭhaśālā*, which can be translated either as the 'government college at Kāśī', or more literally, 'the college belonging to the *rāja* at Kāśī'. Beginning with early forms of indirect rule in Benares, to the college's founding in 1791, and beyond, the Company had always taken care to involve the Benares *rāja* in their administrative and cultural operations, so as to enhance their own political legitimacy through their association with him. The college was financially dependent upon donations from the *rāja* of land and money for its initial establishment, and in return, the Company had, through a treaty signed in 1794, become 'morally bound' to continue to support the Sanskrit College.[43] This symbiotic relationship continued, as the *rāja* of Benares maintained financial contributions to the college well into the nineteenth century, offering, together with other 'native gentlemen', monetary prizes for outstanding students, while also often being present at ceremonial occasions, including presiding over students' public disputations and yearly examinations.[44] Some of these 'native gentlemen', such as Rājā Kālī Śaṅkar Ghoṣāl and Bābū Rājendra Mittra, became honorary members of the Benares Local Committee of Public Instruction (LCPI), charged with oversight of the college during the 1830s.[45] Rājā Kālī Śaṅkar Ghoṣāl took a relatively active part in the college's governance, recommending, for example, that the LCPI fill the senior *vyākaraṇa* position on the death of Viṭṭhala Śāstrī in 1836 with Kāśīnātha Śāstrī, the current *sāṅkhya paṇḍit*.[46] As well, the *rāja* of Benares, together with a few other prominent Indian residents of the city, were appointed as members of the local committee which governed the college following the transfer of direct control over education to NWP in 1844.[47]

Importantly, the *paṇḍit*s retained considerable autonomy in the prescription of their Sanskrit curriculum from the time of the college's first establishment.[48] In early decades of the college's operation Europeans were even barred from examinations in the *Veda*, for example.[49] And while later decades brought some measure of European control over the college, only a few branches of knowledge – those deemed of 'marginal' importance, such as astrology and the recitation of the *Veda* – were explicitly circumscribed.[50] Even by the mid-nineteenth century, outside of Ballantyne's Anglo-Sanskrit class, at least, the *paṇḍit*s largely retained control over the Sanskrit texts they taught. When the Company did attempt to impose pedagogical restrictions on the Sanskrit College, as it inevitably did every decade or so when it produced reports into the college's inevitable 'decline', the *paṇḍit*s invariably objected to such changes. Following the imposition of several cost-saving measures in the mid-1830s, including a reduction in the period of study to just ten years, rather than the standard twelve, and a decrease in the number of stipends paid to students, for example, the *paṇḍit*s petitioned the government to reinstate the original period of study, while also bemoaning the relative lack of financial support given to students, many of whom travelled some distance from home to attend.[51]

Indeed, the college's Sanskrit *paṇḍit*s soon voiced a sense of cultural and social entitlement within their relationships with the government. In essence, it can be argued that, certainly by the early decades of the nineteenth century, *paṇḍit*s understood that if the Company was duty-bound to provide financial support for Sanskrit education and the production of Sanskrit scholarship, then such responsibility also conferred certain rights upon the guardians of Sanskrit; rights, moreover, which the *paṇḍit*s were loathe to allow infringements upon. Jānakīprasād Paṇḍit, for example, in 1841 first petitioned the Sanskrit College's managing committee (in Persian and English) to be appointed to a proposed professorship of *āyurveda* on the basis of his 20 years experience teaching *vyākaraṇa* there. Following his dismissal several months later, however, which had been prompted not by any impropriety on his part, but by a reorganisation of the grammar classes, Jānakīprasād again petitioned, this time to the GCPI in Calcutta, to state that after 20 years of service to the Company's government, he simply did not consider his office to be 'abolishable'. His length of government service, in other words, was thought to have conferred upon him the right to continue in that service.[52]

In addition, *paṇḍit*s articulated this sense of entitlement not simply by reference to 'traditional' forms of authority, such as the extent of their learning in the *śāstra*, but also according to the standards set out by the Company to measure 'progress' in its educational institutions. Thus, Devadatta, a junior *vyākaraṇa paṇḍit* in Benares, petitioned in 1837 for a vacant senior *vyākaraṇa* position at Benares Sanskrit College by noting not only his experience as a teacher there, and his apprenticeship under the well-respected Viṭṭhala Śāstrī, but also by reference to his passing of several examinations in the college, and by his experience in giving answers to legal questions to the government.[53] Hīrānanda Tarkapañcānana similarly applied for a vacancy in the *dharmaśāstra* professorship by citing his possession of a government qualification for the office of 'Hindoo Law Officer'.[54]

Interestingly, in a sort of reversal of typical pedagogical relationships, *paṇḍit*s expressed a sense that their teaching of Sanskritic knowledge to British orientalists was not simply one-way relationship, but conferred benefits and privileges upon them also. In this regard, *paṇḍit*s such as Madhusūdana Tarkālaṅkāra, a graduate of the Calcutta Sanskrit College, actively enlisted the goodwill of men like H. H. Wilson, to whom he wrote in 1839 to offer a copy of the English grammar which he had just published in a Sanskrit translation.[55] That such relationships could be of value to *paṇḍit*s in their dealings with the Company is evident in the correspondence of Rājīvalocana Paṇḍit, for example, who had been released from teaching *vedānta* at Benares Sanskrit College in 1827 as a part of yet another college reorganisation. In his petition to the GCPI for reinstatement, Rājīvalocana included an enumeration not only of his qualifications, but also of his long history of working for Europeans, including ten years' service with Francis Gladwin and six with Francis Wilford, before being appointed to Benares Sanskrit College in 1822.[56]

All of these elements in the evolution of *paṇḍit*s' own sense of their roles in accepting employment with the Company, as well as the rights and privileges this was thought to have conferred upon them, can be perceived in one of the most high-profile and interesting disputes which took place between the Company and its *paṇḍit*s over an apparently dishonest legal opinion issued in 1836. In August of that year, the Sadar Dīvāṇī Adālat (the Company's supreme civil court in Calcutta) referred a series of questions, regarding a complex dispute over the inheritance of a *jāgīr* (land grant) of several villages in the district of Benares, to the *paṇḍit*s of the Calcutta and Benares Sanskrit Colleges.[57] Rāmcandra Śarmā, the *dharmaśāstra paṇḍit* at the Calcutta Sanskrit College, presented his *vyavasthā*, signed jointly with several other *paṇḍit*s of the college, as his counterpart in Benares, Īśvaradatta Śarmā, did also. Yet both *paṇḍit*s were summarily dismissed from their posts early in 1837, on the basis that their *vyavasthā*s had proven to be 'grossly erroneous'.[58]

Rāmcandra Śarmā immediately petitioned the Governor-General, Lord Auckland. He first argued that 'Hindoo Law' was inherently ambiguous, and, moreover, that much of the law of an 'ancient nation' is 'proverbial'. More substantially, Rāmcandra also produced a number of other *vyavasthā*s on the very same issue, which corresponded exactly with the opinion he, and others, had just given. The first of these was written by a number of well-respected *paṇḍit*s (including the present head *paṇḍit* of the Calcutta supreme court, Rāmjay Śarmā), and had been reviewed and approved by the *paṇḍit*s of Benares Sanskrit College before being accepted by the Company in 1832.[59] In Benares, *dharmaśāstra paṇḍit* Īśvaradatta Śarmā referred to the same *vyavasthā* in his petition to the LCPI, stating that 'it is impracticable to give different opinions on a single question put in several times'. The consistency of the *paṇḍit*s' legal opinions, therefore, should be not held against them, especially when the Company could not seem to keep track of an authoritative body of legal precedent.[60] The second *vyavasthā* referred to by Rāmcandra, in his petition to Lord Auckland, was written by H. H. Wilson as a confirmation of yet another legal decision in 1811, and which also corroborated Rāmcandra's original legal opinion. Īśvaradatta, apparently unaware of this document, suggested instead that the dispute be referred to H. T. Colebrooke and H. H. Wilson, the 'two distinguished gentlemen fully conversant with the Hindoo Law', so that they might similarly confirm the validity of his judgement.

The two *paṇḍit*s' petitions were rejected by the Company. Lord Auckland, in fact, felt that there was 'strong preponderating evidence, amounting to presumptive proof, that the pundits were actuated by corrupt motives in the exposition of the law'.[61] The allegation of corruption was deemed 'ruinous' by Rāmcandra especially, who stated that his character, both private and professional, was 'as dear and valuable to him in his own sphere of life and of professional duty' as the reputations of Europeans were to them.[62] Of even greater import was that Rāmcandra, having failed to secure his former position in Calcutta, then wrote a most remarkable petition to the Company's Court of Directors in London, printed in English, in which he alleged that the Company's government in India had had an interest in the outcome of the disputed *jāgīr*, and that this reason alone might have accounted for his dismissal. In essence, he charged that if the *paṇḍit*s of Benares and Calcutta had not confirmed that the land grant could be inherited through a sister of the original *jāgīrdār* (the holder of the *jāgīr*), to a grandson, then it would have inevitably lapsed, and been liable to be claimed 'by the right of sovereignty' by the Company itself.[63] Thus, Rāmcandra reasserted his own unimpugnable character by attaching to his petition a certificate signed by H. H. Wilson in 1827, attributing to the *paṇḍit* 'diligence and zeal', 'amiable qualities and mild and equable temper', as well as a knowledge of the *dharmaśāstra* 'unequally by any pundit'.[64] Rāmcandra then asked the Court of Directors, given the fact that he was a conscientious servant of the government, and essentially correct in his legal opinion, to ensure that in India, not only justice was done, but that justice appear to be done by the inhabitants of India, lest they come to believe that the Company was not the impartial arbiter of justice it claimed to be.[65]

As it turned out, H. H. Wilson, then Boden Professor at Oxford, had intervened in the dispute, and confirmed to the Court of Directors that the *paṇḍit*s' legal opinions were indeed perfectly correct. One Indian correspondent to Wilson later remarked in this regard that the *paṇḍit*s 'cannot express how high your wisdom, eloquence, and ability to the Sastra; and we always wish your prosperity and enjoyment of the health of you and your family'.[66] While Lord Auckland later passed an order proclaiming both Rāmcandra Śarmā and Īśvaradatta Śarmā innocent of the charge of corruption, neither were reinstated to their former professorships, but instead were to be given priority should any new vacancy appear.[67] Rāmcandra, in the meantime, had been reduced to a state of poverty and 'degradation', and again petitioned Lord Auckland in August 1840 to ask for his 'indulgence and commiseration'. Auckland's response was in the negative.[68]

Despite the unhappy ending to these events, *paṇḍit*s in the Company's educational service were evidently quite capable of exploiting the hybrid ruling ideology advocated by the Company, which included both an adherence to Indian ruling norms and British ideals of governance, when aspects of such values were impugned in practice. Through their relationships with British orientalists, but perhaps more importantly, through their entry into a contract, of sorts, with the Company's government, in which *paṇḍits* had a particular understanding of their rights and responsibilities, *paṇḍits* could make their own expectations and desires known, if not always heeded. In so doing, they also exposed the dissimulation which the Company's governance of India often embraced. As a last illustration of this argument, it is worth considering for a moment the way in which the *paṇḍits*' relationship to the government could also be drawn upon by others who wished to pursue goals antithetical to the Company's interests.

In a telling episode of (partial) colonial reversal, Kheda Siṃha, a claimant to the throne of Charkhari, a small state in Bundelkhand, submitted to the Company an 1833 *vyavasthā* arguing that he was the rightful inheritor of the state, as he was the senior-most male of the extended family, and that the grandson born out of wedlock who had been nominated, and duly confirmed by the Company, had no claim because of his illegitimacy. The *vyavasthā* had been issued by nine Benaresi *paṇḍits*, all of whom were employed either at the Company's court in Benares, or at the Benares Sanskrit College. The signatories included Īśvaradatta, the unfortunate law *paṇḍit* of our previous example, who had nevertheless enjoyed a solid legal reputation and had often been consulted by government on contentious issues, as well as Kāśīnātha Śāstrī, the *sāṅkhya paṇḍit,* and Hīrānanda, professor of *sāhitya*. The *vyavasthā* drew on the usual established *śāstrik* authorities, but in this particular context, it must have been considered as most authoritative by the petitioner Kheda Siṃha by virtue of the fact that the signatories were the government's own *paṇḍits*, relied upon and trusted by the Company in its legal disputes. The case had been brought before Lord Bentinck, who admitted that 'Khet Singh has good ground for being dissatisfied with the determination of Government', but ultimately, the Company was unwilling to reverse the decision on principle, though Kheda Siṃha collected a sizable stipend, and eventually was granted the rule of Jaitpur.[69] The *paṇḍits*' *vyavasthā*, therefore, while not serving to overturn the endorsement of an illegitimate heir, did at least serve to illuminate the Company's own fundamental disregard for the Indian laws it had first pledged to uncover and restore, and then to uphold.

This chapter now turns to a discussion of those *paṇḍits* most closely associated with the modernising project of constructive orientalism: the scholars of Benares College during Ballantyne's superintendency. In the face of claims for the rational and scientific character of Christianity, these *paṇḍits* articulated a view of the *śāstra* as a body of knowledge consistent with scientific norms and practices, and therefore, an equally valid and viable, if not superior, 'modern' belief system.

Engaging Europe's 'new knowledge'

It has been argued in Chapter 4 that the constructive orientalist project initiated by James Ballantyne in Benares was highly dependent upon his *paṇḍit*-assistants for their expertise in the Sanskrit language and knowledge of the *śāstra*. As well, it has been noted that the 'developmental' paradigm of Ballantyne's pedagogy had first been formulated only after he had secured recourse to the *paṇḍits*' expertise in order to attain a sufficient understanding of the doctrines of 'Hindu' philosophy. Indeed, Ballantyne's unsorted papers are a testament to the extent to which he relied upon these scholars, as his modest archive is replete with short notes and longer essays by a number of *paṇḍits* which provide, for example: translations of particularly difficult Sanskrit phrases; explanations of important concepts, such as 'being pervaded', taken from Gaṅgeśa's *Tattvacintāmaṇi*, a key text within the *nyāya* corpus; and mathematical calculations, such as the speed at which the sun would have to travel if it were circling the earth (18 miles/second, by the way, is the answer given).[70] Moreover, a close examination of the available sources also seems to indicate that significantly more of Ballantyne's constructive orientalist educational project was a product of the *paṇḍits*' labours than has been acknowledged. The scientific nomenclature in Sanskrit, for example, seems to have been almost wholly their creation, as were the Sanskrit and Hindi translations of key English texts, and so forth.

The issue of Ballantyne's 'reliance' upon the *paṇḍits*, therefore, should be understood not simply in the terms of an enabling relationship, but instead developed further into a series of questions relating to the very authorship of the constructive orientalist educational project, and, moreover, the way in which the *paṇḍits* themselves might have understood the range of scholarly activities they undertook. These points are developed in this section by reference to the published writings of two of Ballantyne's key interlocutors at Benares College, Bāpūdeva Śāstrī and Viṭṭhala Śāstrī.[71] These men shared important characteristics: they were both *brāhmaṇs* from Maharashtra who had been exposed to European science and philosophy during their childhood educations, and both had been, on different occasions, presented to European and Indian audiences as emblematic of the 'success' which could be achieved through the introduction of Western knowledge to the subcontinent's 'traditional' intelligentsia. It is argued here, however, that rather than emblems of an imposed civilisational 'progress', these two men in particular represent the complexities and ambiguities of the colonial encounter, as it was expressed through Sanskrit scholarship. By virtue of their creative and very often subversive interpretations of the relationship between India's cultural-textual heritage and the 'civilisation' represented by European scientific and religious thought, they were able to turn constructive orientalism to distinct, and unimagined, ends, from within the very heart of the British Sanskrit enterprise.

The first *paṇḍit* to be discussed is Bāpūdeva Śāstrī, who was educated at the Sehore *pāṭhśālā* by Lancelot Wilkinson and Subājī Bāpū (author of the *Siddhāntaśiromaṇiprakāśa*, a text which combined elements of Copernican heliocentrism with Bhāskarācārya's astronomical text the *Siddhānta Śiromaṇi*).[72] At Sehore, Bāpūdeva was of course introduced to the nascent constructive orientalist pedagogy pioneered by Wilkinson, which, through a comparative methodology, stressed the shared components, but relative advancement, of European over Indian astronomy.[73] Bāpūdeva's achievements in the curriculum offered at Sehore were significant enough to encourage Wilkinson to recommend him alone to the newly instituted professorship of natural philosophy at Benares Sanskrit College in 1841.[74] Once in Benares College, Bāpūdeva taught *Siddhāntik* and Western astronomy as well as arithmetic, calculus and physics. He was seemingly the first of the college's *paṇḍit*s to provide Ballantyne with a significant amount of assistance in translation and the creation of Sanskrit terminology. Indeed, in 1848 Ballantyne remarked in the preface to his first major work, the *Lectures on the Sub-Divisions of Knowledge*, that 'whatever neatness of Sanskrit expression may be discernible in any portion of these lectures, is due to my valued friend and coadjutor, Bapu Deva Sastri'.[75] The acknowledgement of Bāpūdeva's responsibility for rendering many of the English scientific terms into their Sanskrit versions for use in the college's publications is repeated once more in the later *Synopsis of Science*, in which Ballantyne remarked that the mathematical terminology, in particular, wholly developed by Bāpūdeva, was 'either adopted from established and long accepted Sanskrit treatises, or else (where such terms were not available) has been constructed with the advantage of a complete knowledge of, and with symmetrical reference to, established and accepted terms'.[76] Ballantyne therefore also noted in his *Discourse on Translation* that he had complete confidence in

Bāpūdeva to prepare the entire course of mathematics in the vernacular, and moreover, that he had 'not the presumption to fancy that [he] could offer any needful suggestion' to Bāpūdeva on the topic of mathematical nomenclature.[77]

Bāpūdeva was also a prolific writer within the institutional and pedagogic confines of the college, and from the early 1850s received financial support from the government in order to expedite the preparation of his mathematical publications.[78] In addition to rendering several of Ballantyne's texts into their vernacular versions, he composed his own educational textbooks in both Hindi and Sanskrit, adding to the growing stockpile of treatises initiated under Ballantyne's superintendence in Benares. These texts included Sanskrit and Hindi versions of a tract on the 'calculation of eclipses by the European method',[79] a Sanskrit version of Isaac Newton's *Philosophiae Naturalis Principia Mathematica*, as well as a geographical tract in Hindi, *Bhūgola Varṇana*.[80] Moreover, Bāpūdeva edited, translated into English, and commented in Sanskrit upon several key tracts to be found in the astronomical literature of the *Siddhānta*s, including most prominently the *Sūrya Siddhānta* and the *Siddhānta Śiromaṇi* of Bhāskarācārya.[81]

It has already been noted that Bāpūdeva was esteemed early in his career by Lancelot Wilkinson and John Muir as both a mathematical prodigy and a 'real lover of truth', respectively.[82] He also became in later years something of a *cause célèbre* in Europe for his apparent overcoming of Hindu 'superstition' and adoption of Western scientific rationality. Major Samuel Owen, who had formerly been stationed in Benares, recounted to the Anthropological Society of London in the mid-1860s that Bāpūdeva represented a new class of Hindu scholars, whose exposure to the 'truths' of Western science had forced them to reconsider their scriptures in its light, resulting in the 'first steps' of a civilisational advancement.[83] The American Sanskritist, William Dwight Whitney, however, remained unimpressed with Bāpūdeva's scholarship, characterising his translation of the *Sūrya Siddhānta* as a display of his 'utter subserviency' to H. T. Colebrooke on the issue of asterisms (star groupings).[84] In any case, Bāpūdeva's several publications in English-language European journals, including the *Proceedings* and the *Journal of the Asiatic Society of Bengal*, brought him a measure of notoriety amongst European observers. He was made a Companion of the Order of the Indian Empire (CIE) in recognition of his scholarship in 1878, was an honourary member of the Royal Asiatic Society, and was even fêted within the pages of *The Theosophist*.

Bāpūdeva was clearly an active intellectual in a variety of forums within the city. A useful entry point to discuss his scholarship (outside the realm of his textbooks) is a series of lectures which he presented in the early 1860s on astronomy and astrology. These lectures were given to the Benares Debating Club, (one of several gentlemen's cultural organisations which emerged in the city for the discussion of intellectual and cultural concerns),[85] and were also in later years published in a variety of contexts, as well as in several languages. The first of these was 'The Practice of Astrology by Hindus and Mohammedans and the Influence which it exerts upon them', (in Hindi, '*Phalit kā Vicār*').[86] Bāpūdeva began the lecture by distinguishing the principal branches of astrology in India, including *saṃhitā* (natural astrology), by which auspicious timings are calculated, and *jātaka* (judicial astrology), by which one's fortunes are predicted according to the time and place of birth. He described the prevalence of astrological practices in India, the general belief that 'Astrology is a true science', and, indeed, noted that so closely linked were a knowledge of the movement of the stars with astrological practices that most Indians were 'astonished' to discover that the English, with their expertise in astronomy, 'do not believe in Astrology'. Yet Bāpūdeva also pointed to the essential irrationality of believing in the predictions of astrology, as he admitted that few people wait for an auspicious moment when fetching water to put out a house fire, for example, or in any other urgent matter.[87] The unscientific nature of astrology was further elaborated by reference to the fact that its predictions and causal mechanism could not be corroborated nor disproved. Thus, when predictions turn out to be false, the astrologer was most often faulted, rather than astrology itself; and when coincidences of illness and particular movements of the moon were frequently seen, the coincidence itself was usually deemed sufficient to prove a causal relationship. Moreover, astrology, as currently practiced, contained many contradictions in its methodologies for calculating future destinies.[88] Bāpūdeva concluded his argument, however, not on such methodological points, but by impugning the usefulness of astrology, and its potential for damaging men's characters:

> ... if the Astrologer says that [someone] will lose [in a business transaction], he on hearing this will at once become sad and relax in his endeavours and in consequence of his relation he will be a loser in [that transaction] ... [The] foretelling of future destinies slackens the energies of industrious men, and hence the disbelievers in this science publicly say, leaving yourself in the hands of god do your

work industriously, and so not have recourse to the science of Astrology, then you will be successful and prosperous.[89]

On first sight, then, Bāpūdeva's argument would certainly appear to mimic elements of the colonial rhetoric of improvement, with its imputation of irrationality to much of 'Hinduism'. Although it is clearly couched within the language of moral debasement, this lecture, when seen in the wider context of Bāpūdeva's Sanskrit scholarship, would instead appear to be principally directed at establishing a formal boundary between the astrological and astronomical uses of the *jyotiḥśāstra*, on the basis of relative methodology, utility, and cultural value. Indeed, the overlap between astronomy and astrology in the *śāstra* had often been commented upon by Europeans at Benares College, not to mention the apparent popularity of students utilising the mathematical and astronomical learning they gained at the college to begin lucrative careers as astrologers. Thus Bāpūdeva's dismantling of the astrological uses of *jyotiḥśāstra* literature reflected instead a desire to distinguish the two, and was to serve as an important starting point to authorise *Siddhāntik* (read as 'scientific') over *Purāṇik* (read as 'mythological') conceptions and methodologies, rather than necessarily being an attribution of a superiority to European norms or knowledge.[90]

Bāpūdeva's valorisation of the *Siddhānta*s as a rational and scientific body of literature is further corroborated in another lecture delivered to the Benares Debating Club in 1862, entitled 'On the Sidereal and Tropical Systems'. Once more, Bāpūdeva on first sight appears to use this opportunity to advocate the superiority of European knowledge, by arguing for the correction of Hindu astronomy by reference to Western scientific methodologies. Indeed, it was this lecture which was utilised as evidence by Major Samuel Owen, before a meeting of the Anthropological Society of London, to argue that the 'Hindus are diligently looking into what is written in their Sastras, and comparing that ... with the facts now established by science'. As a race, Owen noted, the Hindus were 'advancing'.[91] Yet while Bāpūdeva certainly did argue that the more correct astronomical knowledge of Europeans had enabled them to travel the world, bringing enlightenment to the 'savages of distant islands' and simultaneously improving their own material wealth, he denied that the enabling rationality of such astronomy was solely the province of Europe.

Bāpūdeva began this lecture by establishing the usefulness of astronomy (as opposed to astrology), noting that a knowledge of the dimensions of the earth, and the relative distances between countries, was an aid to navigation, to commerce, and ultimately, to friendship between nations. One ignorant of the world, and hence ignorant of the knowledge produced by the practice of astronomy, was, moreover, implicitly rebuked in the *śāstra* as being equivalent to a tortoise in a well, and thus condemned both to poverty and being despised by his wife.[92] Bāpūdeva next enumerated some of the points of divergence between the *Siddhāntik* texts of the *jyotiḥśāstra* and the findings of modern Western astronomy. The principal problem, Bāpūdeva noted, was that Sanskrit-based astronomy was dependent upon observation, but as such observations had lapsed in recent times, numerous errors had inevitably entered the texts. On the fundamental, conceptual matters of astronomy, however, such as the relative movement of the sun and earth, or the stars' source of light, on which Western and *śāstrik* texts seemed at odds, Bāpūdeva argued that the ancient astronomers of India did in fact possess correct knowledge of these phenomena. Accordingly, he stated that 'I can prove this, that they conceived the idea of the earth's motion when they composed their works', but that the incorporation of such a conception was unnecessary for the purposes which the *jyotiḥśāstra* had been written:

> Our old astronomers said that the sun revolves round the earth only for this reason that it appears to do so, no palpable error occurs by this assumption, and the student feels no difficulty in knowing the doctrine of the sphere. Therefore, if such facts be not granted, no loss whatever is felt by the people.[93]

Bāpūdeva's attribution of an advanced scientific knowledge to ancient Indian astronomers was a key element of his thought, as he had also written in 1858 a letter to the *Journal of the Asiatic Society of Bengal* on a similar issue. There he purported to show that, despite the general (European) belief that ancient Hindu mathematicians were ignorant of the principles of differential calculus, Bhāskarācārya, the twelfth-century astronomer, had possessed a thorough knowledge of it centuries before it was known in Europe.[94]

On the acknowledged point that errors had crept into the *jyotiḥśāstra*, however, Bāpūdeva next argued in his Benares Debating Club lecture that astronomical calculations should be made in such a way as to agree with the phenomena observed. As proof of precedent, he referred to the sixteenth-century scholar Gaṇeśa Daivajña, who, in his *Grahalāghavam*, had 'corrected the motions of the planets, which he found wrong in the old works, with the aid of observations'. Such corrections, Bāpūdeva noted, had the beneficial effect of ensuring the correct performance of Hindu rites and ceremonies.[95] However, Bāpūdeva also advocated what seemed to be a far more radical method of correction: the abandonment of sidereal astronomy altogether, which was then the prevalent system in use in India, and the adoption in its place of tropical astronomy, which was used in Europe. Sidereal calculations are based upon fixed points of reference in the ecliptic, whereas the tropical system utilises the vernal equinox, and thus takes into account the precession of the equinoxes. Sidereal astronomy, for example, calculates the length of the year as several minutes longer than the actual, tropical year, because of precession.

Bāpūdeva did not advocate tropical astronomy because of its use in Europe, however, but likely did so as a part of his efforts to rehabilitate the *Siddhāntik*, astronomical *jyotiḥśāstra* from astrological pursuits, given that sidereal calculations were considered as key to astrological prediction. But once again, it is important to point out that Bāpūdeva based his argument for the abandonment of the sidereal by reference to the precedence of Sanskritic authorities, and by the substantial religious benefits to be had from being able to provide more accurate astronomical calculation and observation. This, then, served to establish an authoritative link between the astronomy of the *Siddhāntas*, Hindu religiosity, and 'modern' scientific norms and practices. In this regard, the *Vāsiṣṭha, Pulastya, Romaśa*, and *Sūrya Siddhānta* were all described as favouring the tropical system over the sidereal. For example:

> ... in the ROMASA-SIDDHÁNTA:– 'The length of day and night are not determined according to the sun's stellar entrances (but they are settled according to the sun's tropical entrances), and as all religious rites, offerings, etc., depend upon the lengths of day and night, the sun's tropical entrance is virtue-giving.'[96]

Lastly, Bāpūdeva advocated using tropical astronomy because, although it may not have always been advocated by the 'saints', but rather by modest astronomers, it was still, quite simply, a more precise methodology. The acceptance of that precision, moreover, as a part of a scientific practice, was conceived by Bāpūdeva to be a more reasonable position to adopt, rather than the 'obstinate' adherence to the practices of one's forefathers. Again, he quoted a *śāstrik* authority to ground this argument:

> ... the great saint VASISHTHA says in the YOGAVASISHTHA, ... 'That science, which is reasonable, ought to be accepted, although it be the production of a man, and not the unreasonable, though it be composed by a saint ...' Again, he says ... 'The well-founded statement ought to be adopted, though it be given by a boy; and that which is not so, we should abandon, considering it like a straw, though it be uttered by the god BRAHMA.'[97]

The application of reason, and the pursuit of an evolving scientific practice, was thus characterised by Bāpūdeva as a part of India's intellectual heritage. This also pointedly undermined the prevalent constructive orientalist argument, well traded upon by Ballantyne, that so much of Sanskritic knowledge and academic practice was founded solely upon the basis of received authority, rather than the application of an essentially scientific mode of enquiry. It will be recalled that John Muir had characterised Bāpūdeva in his 1845 parting address to Benares College as a 'real lover of truth' unwilling to accept anything upon authority.[98] To be certain, Bāpūdeva required the 'demonstration' of 'truth', though such demonstration was inevitably directed by him towards an end neither anticipated, nor endorsed, by colonial pedagogy.

The second important *paṇḍit*-assistant of Ballantyne to be considered here, Viṭṭhala Śāstrī, was also a Maharashtrian *brāhmaṇ*, though considerably less is known about him. Viṭṭhala Śāstrī appears to have settled in Benares early in his childhood, and after studying the *Vedas*, *kāvya* (poetic literature), and *nyāya* in the city's private *pāṭhśālās*, he entered Ballantyne's '*paṇḍit* class' in Benares College sometime before 1850.[99] Here, Ballantyne tells us, Viṭṭhala Śāstrī made steady progress in learning English, began the study of European literature through the 'Reprints for the Pandits' series, and undertook the translation of English works into Sanskrit as early as 1852, beginning with James Harris' *A Dialogue Concerning Art.*[100] Importantly, Viṭṭhala Śāstrī also rendered 'that great *paṇḍit*' Francis Bacon's *Novum Organum* into Sanskrit, along with a 'traditional' explanatory commentary, which was then published by the college along with an English version.[101] Viṭṭhala Śāstrī was rewarded for these labours in 1853, when he was in his early 20s, with an appointment to the Assistant Professorship of *nyāya* at the college, which he held jointly with another of Ballantyne's 'promising' young students, Veṅkaṭa Rāma Śāstrī.[102] In an 1855 report, Ballantyne described the functioning of the class which they jointly conducted, noting that of the 40 students taught by Viṭṭhala Śāstrī and Veṅkaṭa Rāma Śāstrī under his guidance, 17 were engaged in the study of English, and 23 were 'imbued [in some degree] with European doctrines' through the study of the Sanskrit versions of *A Synopsis of Science* and the *Novum Organum.*[103] The students' text-books included the 'Reprints for the Pandits' series, most notably the *Novum Organum,* as well as Mill's *Logic, Ratiocinative and Inductive.*[104] Then in 1856, Viṭṭhala Śāstrī was promoted to Professor of *sāṅkhya,* a position which he held until his early death in 1867.

During the course of the 1850's, Viṭṭhala Śāstrī also provided Ballantyne with invaluable assistance in his educational endeavours, translating the *sāṅkhya* aphorisms of Kapila and the 'very hard' *nyāya* aphorisms into English, for example, which were then used in Ballantyne's publications.[105] He similarly helped Fitz-Edward Hall with the preparation of an index into extant Sanskrit philosophical manuscripts in the Benares region.[106] Indeed, the range and scale of his involvement with the college's European professors is demonstrated by the fact that, perhaps more than any other single *paṇḍit,* it is Viṭṭhala Śāstrī's notes and letters which compose the bulk of Ballantyne's remaining papers.[107] In addition to his responsibility for constructing the Sanskrit chemical nomenclature used in *A Synopsis of Science,*[108] Viṭṭhala Śāstrī also composed his own Sanskrit textbooks on the telegraph, hydrostatics, the mechanical properties of air, and 'a controversy for the establishment of the weight of the atmosphere by experiments'.[109] He became an early member of the Benares Debating Club, and served as the secretary to the philosophical and literary section of its successor, the Benares Institute, though there is no remaining record of his ever having given a paper. Lastly, he was the co-author, with Ballantyne, of what must have been the first of its kind, a trilingual 'how-to' manual on calotype photography, published in 1857 in Sanskrit, Hindi, and English.[110]

Like Bāpūdeva, Viṭṭhala Śāstrī was also heralded by Europeans as representative of the 'progress' which the 'traditional' Sanskrit intelligentsia might achieve through an education in Western knowledge. In testimony to the House of Lords on educational policy in India, Boden Professor of Sanskrit H. H. Wilson held up a copy of Viṭṭhala Śāstrī's Sanskrit commentary and translation of Bacon's *Novum Organum,* and declared that as a piece of scholarship, its worth 'will bear scrutiny'.[111] Yet like Bāpūdeva, Viṭṭhala Śāstrī's scholarship reveals a more complex engagement with Europe than simply the parroting of the superiority of Western intellectual endeavours within a universalising developmental paradigm. To be certain, Viṭṭhala Śāstrī could be critical of European orientalists, and overtly asserted the superiority of the *paṇḍits*' Sanskrit scholarship. He complained to Ballantyne in 1860, for example, that Edward Roer's translation of the term '*bhāṣā*' as 'category' in his 1850 edition of the *Bhāṣā-Pariccheda*, (which Roer translated as a 'division of the categories' of the *nyāya*) was incorrect.[112] '*Bhāṣā*', he argued, according to the system of the *nyāya* was '*pada*', a 'term', or a 'word', while 'category' was properly '*padārtha*' (and so, a better translation of the text's title, therefore, would be a 'clarification of the terms' of the *nyāya*).[113] Such a rudimentary confusion in terminology, Viṭṭhala Śāstrī noted, between a *pada* and *padārtha*, which in the *vyākaraṇa* mean, at their simplest, a 'word' and the 'referent of a word', would also commit one to syllogistic reasoning,[114] and the absurd conclusions which could result: 'Such confusion as that of *pada* and *padārtha* may satisfy Europeans who are devoted to business but is not satisfactory to *paṇḍits* who love truth and precision of statement.'[115]

Of the few extant materials written by Viṭṭhala Śāstrī, his scholarship is perhaps best encapsulated by reference to his 1859 text, entitled *Pañcabhūtavādārtha, or, Lectures on the Chemistry of the Five Hindu Elements*,[116] especially when read in conjunction with his 1852 commentary upon the *Novum Organum*.[117] The *Pañcabhūtavādārtha* claims on the frontispiece to have as its purpose: 'to make known the view of the European philosophers on the five [Hindu] elements to the students and *pandits* of India.'[118] In fact, however, it presents several finely argued reasons for adopting the European classification of physical matter as consisting of 'simple' (*amiśradravya*) and 'mixed' elements (*miśradravya*), over the division of matter found, for example, in the *sāṅkhya* philosophical system, as well as in the *nyāya*. This classificatory system enumerated five elements which correspond to the five senses: i.e., earth (*pṛthvī*), water (*jala*), fire (*tejas*), air (*vāyu*), and 'ether' (*ākāśa*).[119]

Viṭṭhala Śāstrī began his argument by noting that there were many different ways to classify things; indeed, as many ways to classify things as there are things to classify. Yet classification must serve a purpose, and the foundation upon which classification is based should meet certain criteria, which are quite clearly universally accepted. These criteria include the principle of exclusivity, and that divisions be based upon a 'common nature'. In the case of the division of material substances as pursued in India, he noted, the Indian system was a good one when considered according to these criteria. It does not admit of omission nor confusion, for example, for the categories of the *sāṅkhya* and *nyāya* are both exclusive of one another ('air' does not include 'water') and leave nothing from the material world out, for everything is perceptible by at least one of the senses. Indeed, it is also based in cognisable phenomena, or 'self-evidence', (rather than being arbitrary). Viṭṭhala Śāstrī's implication here is that the Indian system, along with the European system of classification, have evolved according to important shared criteria. Neither systems would admit, for example, that the division of men into 'intelligent and white' or into 'Indians and Europeans' were valid or useful divisions, for there is overlap in the former, and an abandonment of a common nature in the latter.[120]

Having established a universality of norms for the classification of matter, Viṭṭhala Śāstrī then argued that the European system was distinct from the Indian in its usefulness. The *sāṅkhya* and *nyāya* classification, he noted, had served the philosophers of India 'only for debate and wrangling, but not for eliciting hitherto unknown results', whereas the European system was more conducive to producing such 'new knowledge'.[121] This difference, however, was not based in a fundamental disjuncture between the norms of the *sāṅkhya* and *nyāya* and European science, but rather in a difference between what had been considered by their adherents to be an 'important' common nature upon which to base these respective classificatory systems. This, in Viṭṭhala Śāstrī's thinking, was largely the result of Indian philosophy valuing the consultation of the senses alone, rather than the senses aided by experimentation.

In his edition of the *Novum Organum*, Viṭṭhala Śāstrī had already noted that the material world was far too subtle to be perceived solely by the senses, and that the actual constituents of water, for example, were not readily apprehendable by the sense of taste. In this regard, he drew attention to the need for chemical experimentation.[122] Indeed, he had also discussed this perceived difference between the *sāṅkhya* or *nyāya* and European science in that commentary by reference to the distinction between the 'anticipation of nature' and the 'interpretation of nature', though solely in abstract terms. The former was understood as a form of reasoning which explained causality by the appearance of things, while the latter utilised extensive labour and investigation. Importantly, Viṭṭhala Śāstrī here broke the connection often implied by constructive orientalists, such as Ballantyne, by drawing upon Bacon's own distinction between the learned and unlearned in Europe. Thus, he undermined the notion that the 'anticipation' of nature was an

Indian pastime, and its 'investigation' a European, with the example of the majority of Londoners who, despite being based in the 'chief of cities' (as far as the scientific endeavour was concerned), were nevertheless 'marvellously ignorant of the truth in regard to [the production of] dew [during clear nights]'.[123]

In the remainder of the *Pañcabhūtavādārtha* Viṭṭhala Śāstrī explained the nature of the 'five Hindu elements' according to the European classification with reference to a variety of chemical experiments as proof. The decomposition of water into its two constituent elements was discussed, as was the non-elemental nature of fire. At this text's heart is an understanding of scientific practice which encompassed a regime of observation and experimentation. This practice, however, which had strictly speaking not formed a part of India's intellectual heritage, was nevertheless characterised by Viṭṭhala Śāstrī as being consistent with the values and methodologies for classification within the *sāṅkhya* and *nyāya*, and thus within the *śāstra* more broadly. These *śāstrik* norms validated a specifically Indian, rational-scientific methodology, in other words. It is on this basis that Viṭṭhala Śāstrī recommended the adoption of the classification of matter into 'mixed' and 'simple', rather than by any necessary reference to Christianity or European enlightenment.

It should clear from this discussion of the scholarship of Viṭṭhala Śāstrī and Bāpūdeva Śāstrī that they did not accept the 'new knowledge' of Europe wholly within the ideological/cultural superstructure with which it was presented. These *paṇḍits* instead used the opportunities presented by their links to government-sponsored education, and projects such as constructive orientalism (with its furtive Christian agenda), to critique the claims made on behalf of Europe's knowledge and religion, including their inherent rationality and consistency, as well as to unravel the colonial assumption that the 'modern' scientific endeavour was tied solely to a specific European intellectual genealogy. Consequently, they drew upon their valued intermediary positions to push forward their own cultural-intellectual projects for a newly inflected valorisation of the *śāstra*, typically by reference to the authority of shared intellectual values, such as 'rationality' and the use of a 'scientific' methodology. In other words, from the 'common intellectual ground' so valued as a starting-point in Ballantyne's enlightenment pedagogy, as well as the 'common ground' of the colonial educational institution, *paṇḍits* could undermine the claims of exclusivity which underpinned such education, shearing it of its cultural bias. In so doing, *paṇḍits* made use of a wide variety of epistemic resources available to them to actively remake the connections presented between 'science', 'religion', and 'rationality'.

It is recognised, of course, that Viṭṭhala Śāstrī and Bāpūdeva Śāstrī were both extraordinary, in a variety of important senses, and were likely not representative of many of their peers. Yet their activities also represented an important element of Sanskrit scholarship in Benares as it evolved in the mid-nineteenth century, and contributed to the emergence of many *paṇḍits* affiliated with the college as authoritative cultural commentators in the later decades of the nineteenth century. Indeed, in the years following, they were joined by some of Benares' most well-known *paṇḍits*, including Bāla Śāstrī, Rājārāma Śāstrī, Keśava Śāstrī, Govindadeva Śāstrī, and Sudhākara Dvivedī, in a veritable explosion of newly inflected, Sanskritic cultural-intellectual activity. The institutional site which these men occupied was one which brought them a measure of distinction and a host of opportunities, and their entry into the north Indian public sphere, through their involvement with colonial education, enabled them to speak to a range of debates over cultural identity in northern India. While *paṇḍits* were not the only such commentators, of course, their scholarship should, nevertheless, be reckoned amongst the important components of emerging national culture. These last points are substantiated in the final section of this chapter, as well as in the Afterword which follows it.

Sanskrit *paṇḍits*, Hindu religious authority, and the public sphere

In the 1867 obituary of *paṇḍit* Premacandra Tarkabāgīśa, late professor of rhetoric in the Calcutta Sanskrit College, it was noted that until recently, at least, the fame of a *paṇḍit* rarely travelled 'beyond his neighbourhood', and that a *paṇḍit*'s scholarship only became known to his students, or perhaps slightly more widely, through a public contestation or the issuance of a *vyavasthā*.[124] By the middle of the nineteenth century, the 'fame' of certain *paṇḍits*, to be certain, travelled well beyond the local, especially those affiliated with government employment, as *paṇḍits* increasingly published their work in periodicals, books, and participated in debates and literary organisations which received wide coverage in the vernacular- and English-language press.

While print flourished in Calcutta from very early in the nineteenth century, it was not until the 1830s or 1840s that it made its presence substantially felt in northern India. In Benares, a substantial number of

English- and Indian-language periodicals were published, many of which covered matters of religious, literary, and political controversy.[125] In addition to the English *Benares Magazine* and *Benares Recorder*, which flourished in the 1850s,[126] Hindi newspapers such as the *Benares Akhbār* of Bābū Śivaprasād appeared from 1845, *Sudhākar* from 1850, as well as Hariścandra's *Kavivacansudhā* from 1868, and the *Benares Gazette*. Significantly, the late-1860s was witness to an explosion of periodical printing in Sanskrit. The first such periodical to appear was the Sanskrit- and English-language *Kāśīvidyāsudhānidhi* ('the receptacle of the nectar of the learning of Kāśī'), better known simply as *The Pandit*, which was published from Benares College in 1866. The following year there also appeared in the city the dual-language Sanskrit and Bengali *Pratnakamranandinī*, or *The Hindu Commentator*.[127] *Pratnakamranandinī* was published privately by Durgāśaṅkara Mukharjī, and edited by *paṇḍit* Satyavrata Sāmaśramī, who later left Benares for Calcutta, and most famously published an edition of the *Sāma Veda* in the Bibliotheca Indica series.[128] This journal devoted itself principally to the reproduction of classical Sanskrit texts, including extracts from *Kulayānanda*, a work on rhetoric, and *Ṣaḍviṃśabrāhamaṇa*, from the *Sāma Veda*, as well as occasional original articles.[129] The journal was clearly directed to the sizable Bengali community in Benares.

It is worth pausing to consider in greater detail some of the contents of the early volumes of *The Pandit*, which was initially edited by Ralph T. H. Griffith.[130] A former Sanskrit student of H. H. Wilson at Oxford, Griffith had succeeded Ballantyne as the principal of Benares College in 1861. Griffith seemed to have understood the unique, necessarily 'dual' nature of government-sponsored education in Benares, as he wrote to government early in his tenure to advocate the increased study of English and European knowledge combined with a fidelity to the college's founding mandate: the 'preservation of the language, literature and religion of the Hindus'. Griffith had high hopes for the college, without question, given that he perceived that the 'old Pandits are dying out or being pensioned', while 'a younger and more enlightened generation [is] rising in their place'. This 'enlightened generation', of course, was represented by the several *paṇḍits* who had successfully passed through Ballantyne's Anglo-Sanskrit course, such as Viṭṭhala Śāstrī and Veṅkaṭa Rāma Śāstrī, as well as Bāpūdeva Śāstrī and his nephew Govindadeva Śāstrī, all of whom now taught English learning, together with Sanskrit, to their pupils.[131] Moreover, Griffith realised that Benares College had come to be well respected throughout

India. Students reportedly walked from as far away as Madras, Pune, Bengal, and the Punjab to attend, some to perfect their knowledge of the *nyāya* or *sāṅkhya*, others to finish their grammatical or mathematical studies. The reputation of the college for excellence in Sanskrit scholarship, (or, more properly, that of the college's *paṇḍits*), in other words, was perceived by Griffith as providing the British government of India with a renewed opportunity for the extension of a useful education to Indians on the model expounded by Ballantyne.[132]

The publication of *The Pandit*, which began in July of 1866, was intended not principally as a tool for the spread of useful knowledge, however, but, rather, as a medium for bringing the expertise and authority of the college's *paṇḍits* to bear upon the field of Sanskrit scholarship. The journal's mandate was described thus:

> to publish rare Sanskrit works which appear worthy of careful editing hereafter; to offer a field of discussion of controverted points in old Indian philosophy, philology, history, and literature; to communicate ideas between the Aryan scholars of the East and the West; between the Pandits of Benares and Calcutta and the Sanskritists of the Universities of Europe.[133]

The bulk of the journal was composed by printed editions of 'classical' Sanskrit texts, including, for example, Kālidāsa's *Kumārasambhava*, the *Bāla-Rāmāyaṇa*, and the *Kāśikā*, an important treatise on *vyākaraṇa* (grammar). These were supplemented by short works of original Sanskrit scholarship, known as *bhūmikā*s ('introductions'), in which the *paṇḍits* of the college explained the text's contents and its intellectual context. Indeed, outside the pages of *The Pandit*, as well, numerous Sanskrit texts were edited and published by the *paṇḍits* of Benares College, most often with fairly lengthy *bhūmikā*s. These included, for example, professor of *sāṅkhya* Bāla Śāstrī's edition of *Bhāmatī*, a gloss on Śaṅkara's commentary on the *Brahma Sūtra*s, published in Benares in 1880.[134] In addition, *The Pandit* also contained indexes to important works,[135] reprints of Europeans' English-language essays from a variety of orientalist journals, Sanskrit synopses of the different philosophical systems, as well as a variety of reviews, notices, and *paṇḍit* obituaries. Some longer works of original scholarship were published, such as Keśava Śāstrī's consideration of the *vedānta*, which, its European editors remarked, furnished 'an interesting proof of the Vedanta continuing to be a living philosophy and to stimulate the minds of the Pandits to independent exertions'.[136]

The Pandit had a fairly small printing run (250 copies, initially), was relatively expensive, and was also partially exported to Europe.[137] Nevertheless, the pages of *The Pandit* soon became an important medium for the disputation of ideas regarding the status of Sanskrit literature, and indeed, the best methodology for carrying on research in Sanskrit, with letters to the editor being received from not only Benares, but also Pune and Calcutta. Although the multilingual presentation was clearly intended to facilitate the interaction of 'European and Native scholars' of Sanskrit,[138] it was principally the *paṇḍits* of India who invested its pages with a sense of engagement in the practice of Sanskrit scholarship. While it has often been remarked that *paṇḍits* of the late nineteenth century were reduced to the status of so-called '*bhūmikā-paṇḍits*', the pages of *The Pandit* also demonstrate the potentially disputative uses which expertise in Sanskrit literature could be put to at this time.

One important point of contention often touched upon in *The Pandit* was whether commentators were misrepresenting the meaning of the *śāstra* through erroneous, or plainly incompetent, translations from Sanskrit. The practice of translation was, in other words, a site where contestations over the characterisations of Hinduism became particularly visible. We have already seen that Viṭṭhala Śāstrī complained privately to Ballantyne about European editions of Sanskrit works. But in 1873, for example, *paṇḍit* Keśava Śāstrī, who worked closely with the Anglo-Sanskrit Department of Benares College,[139] wrote to the editor of *The Pandit* to 'correct' an error which he had perceived in the Bengali Christian convert Revd K. M. Banerjea's *Dialogues on Hindu Philosophy*, an apologetic tract which purported to overthrow the tenets of Hindu philosophy in favour of Christianity.[140] Keśava Śāstrī was the translator of Bishop Berkeley's *Principles of Human Knowledge* into Sanskrit (entitled *Jñānasiddhāntacandrikā*),[141] and, in addition to his original work on *vedānta*, was also an editor of the *Nyāya Sūtras* and the *Yoga Sūtras*.[142] Keśava Śāstrī argued, in English, that Banerjea had incorrectly interpreted several passages from Śaṅkarācārya's commentary on the *Vedānta Sūtras* through a particularly poor translation of them, and that as such, he had wrongly accused Śaṅkarācārya of perpetuating a 'contradiction' with respect to his views on the doctrine of the soul's preexistence. In essence, Keśava Śāstrī argued that Banerjea had, through a 'cursory' reading of the text, thought that the inclusion by Śaṅkarācārya of an opposing point of view (in this case of the *vaiśeṣika*) was his own instead. In other words, Banerjea had committed an error no one familiar with commentary literature would conceivably commit. While Keśava Śāstrī pointed out that he didn't wish to 'say anything against [Banerjea's] doctrines', he nevertheless significantly undermined Banerjea's ability to authoritatively critique *śāstrik* philosophy. Banerjea had been foolish, he concluded, to not suspect his own misreading and instead accuse the 'so great and ever-esteemed' Śaṅkarācārya of a 'heedless contradiction'.[143]

A similar sentiment was also expressed by an anonymous author, who, while perhaps not a *paṇḍit* himself, would certainly have studied Sanskrit. Identifying himself only as 'A Hindu', he wrote to the editor in 1871 to complain of the terminology being used in A. E. Gough's translation of a commentary by Śaṅkara Miśra on the *vaiśeṣika* aphorisms of Kaṇāda. The term *'ātatāyin'*, he noted, had been rendered as 'felon', which would have been fine had Gough been thinking of 'the English criminal jurisprudence'. The correct translation, based on the etymology of the word, was, instead, 'one who comes with an uplifted weapon', or an 'imminent foe'. Equally 'A Hindu' was indignant at an example of 'European Sanskrit' published by Bābū Śivaprasād[144] in an earlier volume of *The Pandit*.[145] Śivaprasād had reproduced a Sanskrit letter from a German soldier as a model for Indian emulation. 'A Hindu' was unimpressed. He pointed out several errors, and plainly set out a sentiment with which both Viṭṭhala Śāstrī and Keśava Śāstrī likely would have agreed:

> Though it will not be palatable to the Europeans, it had better be set down as an inevitable fact that, unless a long residence among the Pandits of this country should unwontedly ripen their knowledge of Sanskrit, the Europeans pretty often fall into egregious mistakes that would excite the smile of a simple-minded indigenous Pandit. The Anglo-maniacs of our country are welcome to applaud the zeal and perseverance of the European Sanskrit scholars ... but to hold up such achievements as the German soldier's letter as an example is a proceeding that we might fairly ask them to spare.[146]

Though Keśava Śāstrī and 'A Hindu' both drew here upon a sense of the deep expertise in Sanskrit literature which *paṇḍit*s had long possessed, occasional articles in *The Pandit* also positioned the *paṇḍit*s of Benares College in an overtly liminal cultural space. For example, in 1868 there appeared a short exposition in Sanskrit of a reputed cure for leprosy, signed by such knowledgeable and esteemed men as Bāpūdeva Śāstrī, Rājārāma Śāstrī, Bāla Śāstrī, and Govindadeva Śāstrī. In the article the *paṇḍit*s applauded the work of the 'jewel among doctors' (*bhiṣag-ratna*), Bhāū Dājī from Bombay. Noting the doctor's expertise in English medical science as well as his 'great exertions' in the medical *śāstra* of India, the *paṇḍit*s reported that he has been able to cure the most terrible of diseases, including 'acute gout' (*vāta-rakta*), through his 'modern' (*abhinava*) herbal-medicinal prescriptions.[147] Bhāū Dājī was a founding member of the Bombay Association, and an advocate of scientific education. Yet as a member of the Royal Asiatic Society in Bombay, he was also an avid orientalist and collector of Sanskrit manuscripts.[148] The *paṇḍit*s' enthusiastic endorsement of him seems to have been due to his representative status as a hybrid of sorts, a man who had engaged in both Hindu and European science, and combined them to great effect: a particularly 'modern' medical breakthrough. David Arnold has recently written of Bhāū Dājī that he 'straddled two worlds' in his combination of Western medical science with *āyurveda*. Yet Arnold also notes that his experimentation with *āyurvedik* remedies left little doubt that 'India still had a wealth of traditional knowledge to contribute to modern pharmacology'.[149] Indeed, on their part, the *paṇḍit*s of Benares College were unambiguous about the civilisational claim they laid on Bhāū Dājī and his form of modernity, as they also drew a direct parallel between the doctor's medical breakthrough with the revealing to the world of the thousand-fold *Veda* (*śruti*) by the ancient sage Yājñavalkya.[150]

During the 1860s and 1870s a series of literary, scholarly, and religious associations were formed which provided the *paṇḍit*s of Benares College further opportunities outside the realm of print to promote their understandings of Sanskrit literature and its continuing social and cultural relevance. Prominent among these was the Benares Debating Club, later known as the Benares Institute, which was founded in 1861 by a small group of English-speaking 'native gentlemen' for the purpose of furthering the knowledge which each member had gained in his formal education. In 1862 the club was expanded, as the *mahārāja* of Benares joined as patron, along with the 'gentry and respectable men' of the city. Two years later, Europeans were admitted as members, and the topics of discussion ranged from comparative philosophy to educational practices and the history of Benares. Indeed, the membership of the Institute in 1864 reached more than 120 people, and included European government servants, missionaries, a sizable number of *paṇḍit*s, *maulavī*s, the city's rather sizable population of principally Maratha *rāja*s and *mahārāja*s, as well as members of the emerging 'middle class' merchant intelligentsia, including Hariścandra, Śivaprasād, and others.[151]

While the Revd Matthew Sherring, for example, took the opportunity of presenting a paper at a meeting of the Institute to deliver a condemnation of 'Hindu literature', which he thought lacked any concept of history, and to welcome the workings of the 'principles of progress' upon India,[152] Bāpūdeva, as noted above, used his time to valorise *Siddhāntik* astronomy as rational and scientific. Several more of the city's *paṇḍits* discussed at the Benares Institute in the early 1860s the contents and meaning of Sanskrit literature. Paṇḍit Ṭhākur Dāss, for example, presented a paper in Sanskrit entitled 'On the Commentaries of Ramanuja Acharya and Sankara Acharya', in which he compared the merits of these commentators on the *vedānta*.[153] Rājārāma Śāstrī, who was professor of *dharmaśāstra* at Benares College, gave a presentation, also in Sanskrit, on the *Prabodha-Candrodaya*, a celebrated philosophical drama, in which adherents of different Indian philosophical systems outlined the relative virtues of their dogma (and in which the *vedānta* generally comes out on top).[154] Moreover, Hīrānanda Caube, who had been a professor of *kāvya* (poetry) at the college since 1827, argued in his paper entitled 'On the Study of Sanskrit' that it was necessary for students to first obtain a knowledge of Sanskrit before they could undertake the study of English, or any other language, for that matter.[155]

There were several further literary societies established by *paṇḍits* associated with Benares College during this time. The Literary Society of Benares Paṇḍits (also known as the *Brahmāmṛtā Varṣiṇī Sabhā*) counted amongst its membership Bāpūdeva Śāstrī, Bāla Śāstrī, as well as Rāma Miśra Śāstrī (also a professor of *sāṅkhya*). The Society had plans around 1879 to publish a bi-weekly magazine devoted to Sanskrit literature, entitled *Pīyūṣa-Śīkara* ('a drop of nectar'), and held meetings where speeches on a variety of topics were presented in several languages.[156] It also funded the publication of, for example, the 1887 *Vrtāya-saṃskāra-mīmāṃsā* (an investigation as to the person who has lost his caste through the non-observation of the *saṃskāra*, or enjoined rituals).[157] Interestingly, there is an account of the 21 December 1879 meeting of the Literary Society by Colonel Henry Olcott, president of the Theosophical Society. Of note, Olcott reported that he pointed out to the *paṇḍits* the significant role they could play in demonstrating to Indian students 'how much the Aryan thought was in harmony with modern scientific discovery, how his [the student's] ancestors had traversed the whole field of knowledge, and how proud and glad he ought to be that he was of their blood, the heir of their wisdom'.[158] Olcott was made an honourary member of the Society, and once the *paṇḍit*s came to realise that Theosophy was not necessarily aligned with the reformism of the Ārya Samāj, they formalised a relationship with them. The journal, *The Theosophist*, in particular, was thought by these *paṇḍit*s to represent 'the exact measures which should be taken for the revival and perfect development of our Philosophy for the good of our country'.[159] In this regard, an English translation of an exposition of the *vedānta* by Rāma Miśra Śāstrī, written originally in Sanskrit specifically for the Theosophical Society, was published in *The Theosophist* from March 1880 onwards.[160] Similarly, a further 'Sanskrit *Sabhā*', the *saṃskṛta samāj*, presided over by Bāpūdeva Śāstrī, and which included some ten members, most, if not all, of whom were *paṇḍit*s affiliated with the college,[161] entered into a cooperative agreement with the Theosophical Society in 1881 in order to jointly promote 'the interests of Sanskrit Literature and Vedic Philosophy and Science'.[162]

The interests of the Theosophical Society were clearly served by forging such relationships with *paṇḍit*s. The Theosophist understanding of Indian religious 'spirituality' and 'mysticism' as a source of insight into the identity of human and divine was likely founded largely upon European orientalist research, especially on *vedānta*.[163] Yet the concurrence of Benaresi *paṇḍit*s, as the acknowledged preeminent (and, importantly, Indian) specialists in the *śāstra*, clearly would have substantiated the doctrine and goals of the movement to both its Indian and European audiences. The rationale for the *paṇḍit*s of the Literary Society, or the Sanskrit Sabhā, is less clear, though one could speculate that the popularisation and valorisation of specific characterisations of *śāstrik* doctrine to European audiences coincided with the agendas of the *paṇḍit*s' societies, especially if these were anathema to radical reforming movements.

In any case, the somewhat surprising link between the *paṇḍit*s of Benares College and the Theosophical Society also points to the importance of considering the wider relationships forged between *paṇḍit*s and an increasing number of groups actively contesting the meanings of Hindu religious practice in India. The relationship of the most cultural significance, in Benares at least, was that formed between the college's *paṇḍit*s and the rising gentry classes, including not only the *mahārāja* and the largely Maratha *rāja*s, but also the city's mercantile elites. The importance of this relationship is nowhere better demonstrated than in the establishment of the Kāśī Dharma Sabhā ('the Benares society for the promotion of religion'), in which, arguably, the college's *paṇḍit*s came to wield substantial influence in determining a 'Hindu revivalist' understanding of the relevance of Sanskrit literature to 'being a Hindu'.[164]

The Kāśī Dharma Sabhā was formed in late 1869 or early 1870 by the *mahārāja* of Benares, Īśvarī Prasād Nārāyaṇ Siṃh, most likely in response to the challenges presented by Hindu 'reformers' such as Dayānanda Sarasvatī, who had visited Benares in the fall of 1869 to debate the city's *paṇḍits* on the topic of *mūrti-pūja* (image-worship). While elite gentlemen such as Bhāratendu Hariścandra were clearly involved in the Dharma Sabhā, it was primarily the *paṇḍits* of city, both those attached to the court of the *mahārāja* and those who taught at Benares College, who composed the central element.[165] Indeed, one of the principal functions of the Dharma Sabhā, in addition to encouraging and promoting an education in Sanskrit, was to issue *vyavasthā*s on particular elements of what was thought to properly constitute 'Hindu' *dharma*. In this regard, the membership of the Dharma Sabhā in 1871 initiated an investigation into various elements of the *śāstra*, in order to come to decisions on certain points of contention with respect to *dharma*.[166] The head *paṇḍit* at the Ramnagar court, Tārācaraṇa Tarkaratna, led investigations into *mīmāṃsā* and *nyāya*, while college *paṇḍits*, including Bāpūdeva Śāstrī, Rājārāma Śāstrī, and Vāmanācārya, were actively involved in making 'determinations' in other subjects. These *vyavasthā*s would likely have had supra-regional importance, given the symbolic authority of Kāśī *paṇḍits*, both historically and within the late-Company's strategies of governance. In practice, the issuance of *vyavasthā*s by *paṇḍits* affiliated with the Dharma Sabhā most often referred to social customs disputed by religious 'reformers'.[167]

To conclude, it will be advantageous to refer back to the event which precipitated the formation of the Kāśī Dharma Sabhā, namely, the visit to Benares of reformer Dayānanda Sarasvatī[168] in 1869 to debate the city's *paṇḍits* on the validity of *mūrti-pūja* (image-worship) in 'Hindu' practice. By all accounts, the debate, or *śāstrārtha*, was a significant event: dozens of the city's prominent *paṇḍits* turned up, including Tārācaraṇa Tarkaratna and Bāla Śāstrī, as did several thousand spectators. Accounts of the debate, however, are inconsistent and largely partisan. The principal issue at the heart of most centres on whether Dayānanda was fairly, or unfairly, beaten by the *paṇḍits*.[169]

During the course of the *śāstrārtha*, contention tended to focus upon whether the *Purāṇa*s, and other post-Vedic literature, could be considered as authoritative; that is, whether or not they were *veda-viruddha* (i.e. contrary to the *Veda*s). In essence, the *paṇḍits*' strategy seems to have been to persuade Dayānanda to admit that there was nothing in the *Veda*s themselves which expressly disproved or undermined the authority and validity of later literary accretions. At one point during these proceedings, then, one of the *paṇḍit*s quoted an unreferenced verse which purported to settle the matter in their favour. Dayānanda was forced to read and interpret the passage for himself, and this is where the principal difficulty in the divergent accounts lies. On the one hand, the supporters of Dayānanda have claimed that the verse was a forgery, and that he was forced to concede defeat when the *paṇḍit*s grew impatient and noisily walked out of the debate. In essence, the *paṇḍit*s are here accused of having used dirty tricks, and to have been intellectually disingenuous, or even intellectually incompetent. On the other hand, the supporters of 'Hindu orthodoxy' claim that Dayānanda was a lack-lustre Sanskrit scholar, that he didn't have a sufficient knowledge of Sanskrit literature to authoritatively pronounce upon its contents, and that, as such, he had been beaten soundly and fairly.

This *śāstrārtha* was just one of a countless number which had taken place in the city over the centuries, and indeed, is but one example of the increasingly common debates which took place in northern India during the nineteenth century on the relative statuses of religious doctrine, 'science', and rationality. It is significant, however, for while many of the city's *paṇḍit*s might have advocated essentially conservative interpretations of *śāstrik* knowledge, it is also evident that they were innovatory and responsive to the changing criteria of the Benaresi intellectual landscape, not least in the remobilisation of disputative practices to the authorisation of their own views. The practice of *śāstrārtha,* in which *paṇḍit*s tended to engage for the purpose of honing their dialectical skills, as much as for determining meaning within the *śāstra,* was typically conducted between adherents of several of the six *darśana*s (philosophical systems), in attempts to reconcile, or at least to understand the relationship between, their divergent claims. In the context of nineteenth-century Benares, then, *śāstrārtha* became a technique by which *paṇḍit*s were able to authorise a particular understanding of 'Hindu' religious knowledge, by reference to specific textual strategies, and the application of a reasonable methodology (*śāstrārtha* was, after all, considered an inherently rational process). The *paṇḍit*s of Benares College, as well as many of the city's other *paṇḍit*s, were therefore able to transform this ritualised argumentation into a new language – through the use of a specific kind of textuality – in order to produce an authoritative space from which to speak to a new series of cultural debates.

Given the range of *paṇḍits*' engagements with European new knowledge; the demands they placed upon government sponsorship of Sanskrit pedagogy; their characterisations of the *śāstra* as 'rational' and 'scientific' by reference to Indian criteria; and their entry into the public sphere through publishing, literary societies, and public debate, it is clear that the vitality of the enterprise of Sanskrit scholarship in Benares, at least, had not yet perished, nor had it lost its ability to 'make history'. Characterisations of *paṇḍit*s as 'traditional', 'conservative', and 'disingenuous', as well as the comfortable stereotypes of 'orthodoxy' and 'reform', 'tradition' and 'modernity', and indeed, 'defensiveness' and 'innovation', with which we delineate so much of the intellectual encounters of nineteenth-century India, are clearly insufficient to account for the range of these Sanskrit scholars' activities. The challenge for historians will be to substantiate further the ways in which the diverse elements of the 'new', late nineteenth-century Sanskrit enterprise of *paṇḍit*s was meaningful in the production and promulgation of Indian national identities.

Afterword
Sanskrit, Authority, National Culture

In 1881 an author who counted himself amongst the 'intelligent portion' of Benares' agricultural community, anonymously published a tract entitled *Thoughts on India, by a Brahman*.[1] The book was characterised as a true representation of India's depressed, suffering, and discontented population, and went on to identify the cause of that discontent to be the British government's 'more or less disguised policy of selfishness'. The purpose of the book, he noted, was thus to point out to the government the steps it should take to ensure 'peaceful contentment amongst the inhabitants of Hindustan'.[2] In this way, *Thoughts on India* was an early example of a genre of Indian nationalist writing which would soon become commonplace: a critique of British colonial rule presented under the guise of overall loyalty and the proffering of constructive criticism.

As an agriculturalist, the author of *Thoughts on India* was naturally concerned with the extension of practical and scientific education, so as to improve yields from the land and decrease the instances of famine. Indeed, the provision of education, he argued, was a principal duty of any government. Yet given India's historical heritage he also thought that education should communicate to students an apprehension of India's former civilisational glory. To this end, specific suggestions were offered, including the teaching of Sanskrit as a second language in every district school and college, the teaching of 'native medicine' through the medium of Sanskrit, as well as an emphasis upon English and a scientific education. The model he thought best to be emulated was none other than that which had been pursued by James Ballantyne in Benares College more than two decades earlier:

> That eminent man was always for practical and scientific education ... Alas! his scientific instruments, his gallery for giving

> lectures on practical science are all eaten up by rust and white ants. ... The magnificent hall of the Benares College, which was once the pleasure of scientific men and was filled with scientific instruments is now adorned with something else. The magnificent library of the Benares College, where annually metaphysics, logics and scientific books increased in numbers, is now filled with novels and poetry ...
>
> The electric telegraph and the railway, which were never known in India, were first shown in the Benares College by Dr Ballantyne practically and theoretically. The name of that great man will ever live in the memory of the Pandits, who will read his aphorisms of Sankhya philosophy; whose sole happiness was science and Sanskrit philosophy.[3]

The author also valorised the former students of Ballantyne's constructive orientalism, noting that 'it is they who have done something for their country'. Indeed, perhaps our author was amongst them. In contrast, he lamented the current generation of students, or '*Degree wallas*' as he called them, whom he thought possessed only superficial acquirements. Benares' rising generation were thus characterised as lacking an education in their own intellectual and cultural heritage, leaving them 'irreligious' and 'immoral', as well as unable to accomplish much for the cause of Indian 'social progress'.[4]

There are many points of interest raised by the writer of *Thoughts on India*. He continually moved back and forth, for example, between discussions of Sanskrit, the *śāstra*, religious practice, and scientific knowledge, intimating that he perceived an important measure of consistency between them, or, at least, no contradiction in studying them together as part of an education specifically tailored to Indian needs. The invocation of James Ballantyne, as well, indicates that he, and his 'Anglo-Sanskrit' Department, had by then entered the realm of Benaresi popular memory. On the one hand, Ballantyne had seemingly become something of a mythological orientalist figure, for it was thought that he had been H. H. Wilson's successor as Boden Professor of Sanskrit at Oxford, for example, rather than simply as India Office librarian. His relationship with the *paṇḍits*, as well, is apparently understood in an idealised manner reminiscent of that attributed to William Jones. On the other hand, there is clearly a sense in these remarks that Ballantyne's legacy had been largely lost – like his scientific instruments – just 20 years after he had departed from India.

Having spent a fair bit of time in Varanasi and spoken with many of the city's current *paṇḍit*s, both young and old, it has always been somewhat surprising to me that Ballantyne's superintendency at Benares College should still, even now, be recounted so prominently in the city's history of Sanskrit scholarship. Though, of course, the *paṇḍit*s also disagree over how best Ballantyne's pedagogy, and his relationships with *paṇḍit*s such as Viṭṭhala Śāstrī and Bāpūdeva Śāstrī, should be understood. In any case, this feeling of surprise, for me at least, is further substantiated by that same sense of a legacy lost, for certainly in the longer term, outside of the college itself, so many of Ballantyne's initiatives seemed to have foundered. It has been argued in previous chapters that, for example, many people opposed his attempts to use Sanskrit and the *śāstra* for the promotion of Western science and religion, principally on moral grounds. Similarly, his attempts to construct a comprehensively Indian, and thus highly Sanskritised, scientific nomenclature were met with a measure of contempt, the nomenclature being condemned as being largely unreadable by all but *paṇḍit*s.

Yet perhaps it is less Ballantyne's legacy, *per se,* that we should be principally concerned about as historians, than the legacy of the ideas, the institutionalised relationships, and, importantly, socio-cultural structures which were deemed so important to his ambitious civilisational project in Benares. Very possibly Ballantyne is now remembered in the city not because of his scientific demonstrations of the telegraph or his edition of *sāṅkhya* aphorisms, but because his superintendency accompanied a transformation in the role of Sanskrit-based knowledge, and those who possessed it, in the realm of an increasingly contested 'national' public culture. As we have seen, the emphasis placed by constructive orientalism upon *paṇḍit*s' socio-cultural authority, as well as the continuities and 'common ground' of European and Indian knowledge, enabled not only Europeans to make bold claims about respective civilisational statuses, but also the *paṇḍit*s, who quite clearly articulated newly inflected characterisations of *śāstrik* knowledge as rational, scientific, methodologically sound, and above all, Indian. In so doing, *paṇḍit*s, it can be argued, also began to redefine their understandings of the roles they might play in broader, 'public' cultural processes outside the institutional boundaries of colonial education. In important ways, *paṇḍit*s used the experiences and resources of the educational institutions of colonial governance to adapt what it meant to be *paṇḍita* ('learned') in the *śāstra* within the wider cultural milieu of northern India.

By the turn of the twentieth century, to be certain, there had emerged within Indian nationalist discourse a prevalent understanding of India's Sanskritic intellectual-cultural heritage which emphasised its antiquity, rationality, scientific nature, and, generally, its 'high' civilisational status. Such an understanding, moreover, was characterised as a 'rediscovery', and utilised as evidence for India's possession of the features of modernity – a modernity which substantiated India's claim to political autonomy.[5] Within the realm of *āyurveda*, Indian writers often noted that their ancient medical system was scientific, that it 'attracted the admiration of the world', was 'the first of its kind in the world', and 'lent much towards the advancement of the medical systems of other countries'.[6] The verses of the *Veda*s were invoked as evidence of an early knowledge of the hygienic properties of water and vegetables, for example, as well as knowledge of the medicinal properties of herbs.[7] In astronomy and mathematics, nationalist scholarship of the early twentieth century, such as that of Bibhūtibhūṣaṇ Datta of Calcutta, claimed for India an early, if not the world's earliest, use of 'zero' as a numeral, evidence for which was found in the *Pañcasiddhāntikā* (ca. 505 CE).[8] Similarly, Sukumār Rañjan Dās argued for an independent genesis for Hindu astronomy, rather than a borrowing from the ancient Greek, maintaining that its 'reasonings can do credit even to modern astronomers'.[9] More famously, Praphulla Candra Rāy, in his *History of Hindu Chemistry* (first published between 1902 and 1908), established the independent, 'scientific' nature of ancient Indian endeavours within the fields of medicine and chemistry, especially.[10] Similarly, Rāy's contemporary, Brajendranāth Seal, argued that in addition to possessing an array of empirical knowledge of chemistry, ancient Hindus also understood scientific methodology. The *nyāya-vaiśeṣika*, Seal argued, 'elaborates the concepts of mechanics, physics and chemistry', while he characterised the development of the doctrine of 'cosmic evolution' in the *sāṅkhya* as being based on the principles of 'conservation, transformation, and the dissipation of energy'.[11] While the speculative character of early Indian philosophical systems devoted to the investigation of the composition and changes of matter tended to be emphasised, in contrast to the experimental methodology of contemporary practices, systems such as the *sāṅkhya* nevertheless could be seen to possess the characteristics of modern scientific hypothesising. In a later edition of Rāy and Seal's work, it was noted that the *sāṅkhya*, especially, stood 'in good comparison with some of the most recent and advanced scientific ideas of our own time, and to bear the stamp of high intellectual perfection and sublime intuition'.[12]

The parallels between early twentieth-century nationalist characterisations of 'Hindu science' (as well as Hinduism more generally), and those forged by *paṇḍits* such as Bāpūdeva Śāstrī and Viṭṭhala Śāstrī of the nature of the astronomical and philosophical aspects of the *śāstra* are striking: both emphasised India's possession of an early scientific knowledge (medical and mathematical, for example), as well as a series of philosophical systems which incorporated methodologically sound analyses of the constituents of the material world. In essence, both reflected an attempt to characterise Sanskritic knowledge in new and responsive ways to the context of claims made for the superiority of Western rationality, science, and religion, and the links forged between political power and the possession of 'truthful' knowledge. While of course many nationalist writers viewed the pursuit of 'modern' Western science as a key component to India's nationhood and liberation, the distinctive civilisational claims made on behalf of the Hindu intellectual past nevertheless served as an important feature of self-strengthening, including the corroboration of the idea that Hinduism, as a religion, maintained a consistency with the practices of science.[13] The question which needs to be posed, then, is what roles did earlier generations of so-called 'traditional' Sanskrit scholars, such as the *paṇḍits* of Benares College, play in substantiating these notions within Indian public discourse in the second half of the nineteenth century? Is it fair to view Brajendranāth Seal as the inheritor and populariser of Viṭṭhala Śāstrī's meditation on chemistry and the division of the phenomenal world as found in the *sāṅkhya*?

It has been argued by Vasudha Dalmia that, within the evolving nationalised conceptualisation of Hinduism, by the late nineteenth century the Sanskrit *paṇḍits* had suffered a 'general loss of authority' within the public realm of Indian culture, and that their scholarship was of relatively marginal importance in the emergence of national identity processes.[14] This argument has been based on a reading of a series of exchanges which took place in 1884 regarding the mandate for reopening the Anglo-Sanskrit Department of Benares College (which had been closed several years earlier). George Thibaut, who had succeeded Ralph Griffith to be principal of Benares College, had argued that any planned revival of the Anglo-Sanskrit Department should be made to answer a new set of priorities, rather than the old attempt 'to superimpose on a liberal Sanskrit education a liberal European education'. In essence, Thibaut desired to 'improve' the study of Sanskrit by reference to modern European orientalism, and convert the institution's 'old school' *paṇḍits* into 'accomplished Sanskrit scholars, in the European sense of the word'. Thibaut was concerned that the *paṇḍits* could not be said to possess a 'critical' knowledge of Sanskrit and its literature, being largely ignorant of its historical character. As such, he recommended a course of instruction whereby Sanskrit students would be exposed to English-language orientalist texts, such as John Muir's *Sanskrit Texts*, Müller's *History of Ancient Sanskrit Literature*, and Colebrooke's essays. This, he thought, would be the best way to 'enable them to form wider and more enlightened views of Indian literature, history, and antiquities'. Under the 'careful direction and guidance' of Europeans, the *paṇḍits* might then even attempt 'independent research in the wide and unexplored fields of Sanskrit literature'.[15]

Dalmia's reading of this debate essentially accepts Thibaut's argument that orientalist research had surpassed the *paṇḍits*, and that authority on the objects of orientalism – Indian history and Sanskrit literature – now rested in the higher educational institutions of Europe. The principal criteria for accepting knowledge of Sanskrit literature as authoritative, in other words, was conceived to be the possession of a 'critical' European historical methodology. There are two points one can draw from this. The first is that Indian nationalists, in particular, accepted the European paradigm of the centrality of historical understanding in the fashioning of modernity. Thus, they cited the works of European orientalists, rather than that of *paṇḍits*, in order to validate the causes they espoused in support of Hindu religion and nation. In essence, the presence of a historical consciousness in a work of scholarship was deemed as necessary for its use in the promulgation of a national consciousness.[16] The second, corollary point, is that by the end of the nineteenth century, the cultural influence of the Sanskrit *paṇḍits* had been eclipsed by a 'middle class', English-speaking, urban intelligentsia, on the one hand, and Hindu 'revivalists' such as Dayānanda Sarasvatī, the Ārya Samāj, and Svamī Vivekānanda, on the other.

Without question, Dalmia is right in that many of the representations popularised by European orientalists came to be endowed with significant cultural weight in the nineteenth century. Indeed, it is well established that colonial rule endowed European knowledge, and European ways of knowing, with social and cultural significance amongst Indians. Valorisations of ancient Indian civilisation by eighteenth-century orientalists such as William Jones and H. T. Colebrooke, as well as J.-S. Bailly and John Playfair, were often taken up by many Indian nationalist writers (including the author of *The Thoughts on India*), as proof positive of India's long possession of laws, advanced scientific knowledge, rational religion, and literature, all of which formed its own unique cultural heritage.[17] Gyan Prakash, for example, has noted that in the realm of science, especially, 'Orientalist research was reframed to position ancient India as classical India, and the culture of its early inhabitants as the heritage of modern Indians'.[18] Indeed, prominent Indian nationalists such as Lala Lajpat Rai did not invoke 'traditional' forms of Sanskrit scholarship, but rather drew on Theodor Goldstücker's lauding of the *Veda*s, in order to establish India's ancient legacy of a high spirituality and an advanced faith. This Rai used both to condemn Christian converts such as K. M. Banerjea and to underwrite the revivalist agenda of the Ārya Samāj.[19]

Yet equally, some understandings of the achievements of early Indian civilisation were forged in opposition to European claims by reference to Indian authorities, and importantly, to an Indian knowledge of the meaning of the Sanskrit *śāstra*. To return to the discussion of ancient Hindu science, Bibhūtibhūṣaṇ Datta had argued that George Rusby Kaye's scepticism (published in the *Journal of the Asiatic Society*) over the use of place value notation in ancient India, and its probable basis in a forged inscription, was ill-founded. Datta thus pointed to Sanskrit 'philosophical writings of the sixth and seventh centuries which expressly refer to the place value as an illustration of a form of philosophical category'.[20] Sāradākānta Gāṅguli, of Cuttack, also argued in the pages of *Isis* that many Europeans' interpretations of ancient Indian mathematics and astronomy were wrong, given that they were not principally 'scholars of the Sanskrit language'. George Kaye's ideas were, moreover, plainly 'erroneous', and Gāṅguli invoked his translated extracts of the works of Śaṅkarācārya, Patañjali, and Āryabhaṭṭa (the elder and younger) to substantiate claims for an Indian knowledge of place value notation and also π.[21]

More dramatically, Guru Datta Vidyārthī, leader of the militant wing of the Ārya Samāj, argued for a complete reappraisal of the *Veda*s as thoroughly scientific texts, noting that orientalist Friedrich Max Müller had mistranslated them as mythological. The principal problem, Vidyārthī noted, was that European orientalists were blind to the true meaning of the *Veda* due to their lack of knowledge of Indian religion and philosophy, their Christian prejudice, and most importantly, their ignorance of the *nirvacanaśāstra*, the Sanskrit science for determining meaning within the *Veda*s. Müller had thus interpreted the texts as *laukika*, with reference to the words' common meaning, rather than as *yaugika*, according to their etymological structure.[22] In Benares, assistant Anglo-Sanskrit professor Pramadādāsa Mittra also explicitly engaged in the critique of European representations of Hindu religious doctrine and history, taking issue, for example, with John Muir's view on the Vedic god Rudra, whom Muir had characterised as 'originally a demon worshipped by the aborigines, as the lord of evil spirits and subsequently introduced into Aryan worship'.[23] Mittra retorted that Rudra was properly understood as 'the immortal and undecaying lord of life and death as well as immortality ... the dispenser of healing medicines, the best of physicians and the father of the world', on the basis of several Vedic authorities. He thus posited that Muir had misunderstood the nature of the 'Aryan concept of the unity of the Being who variously manifests himself in the great powers of nature'.[24]

Thus knowledge of Sanskrit and the *śāstra*, and indeed, a specifically Indian understanding of them, based, for example, in religious faith, could also be productive of authority in emerging nationalist discourse. In many ways, I think that the *paṇḍit*s of Benares College should be viewed as pioneers, of a sort, in the articulation of renewed understandings of India's civilisational heritage within the colonial context, as well as in their explicit engagements with the colonial presentation of European knowledge. The forging of an epistemic place of their own making, moreover, was largely a by-product of their affiliation to the institutions of orientalism. Yet perhaps the irony is also that the facilitation of their entry into the north Indian public sphere, through the publication of Sanskritic knowledge in a variety of forms, as well as public articulations of Sanskrit learning, departed from more established and personalised (*guru-śiṣya*) methods of authoritative knowledge transmission, making access to knowledge of the *śāstra* available to a wider audience than ever before. This, then, rendered the *paṇḍit*s' claims to intellectual-cultural authority just one amongst many.[25] In the contestation of Indian national culture, in other words, claims to authority proliferated and competed for acceptance. And so while Pramadādāsa Mittra might invoke a *vyavasthā* written by the highly esteemed Benaresi *paṇḍit* Bāla Śāstrī to support his view in a debate with A. E. Gough over the latter's understanding of the concept of 'Brahma' within the *Upaniṣad*s as 'undeveloped thought',[26] many other Indian critics began to look elsewhere to substantiate their views: to their own sense of Sanskrit expertise forged outside the *pāṭhśālā*, to Hindu revivalists and *svāmī*s, or, as likely, to Europeans.[27]

But it is important to recall here that cultural authority is always in process. The projects of European orientalism had sought to institutionalise and coopt Indian forms of authority, transforming it into a resource to direct to the projects of legal codification, translation, and education. This book has consistently emphasised that such attempts to displace personalised Indian cultural authority were rarely so straightforwardly successful, and very often resulted in unexpected reversals. Thus rather than accepting the claims of colonial educators such as Thibaut at face value – claims that would relegate the *paṇḍits* to hapless bystanders in the national cultural projects of Sanskrit – it seems far more worthwhile to explore the ways in which the production of authoritative intermediary spaces as a part of orientalism continued to allow for the articulation of renewed Indian cultural identities later in the nineteenth century. Sanskrit, as an intellectual and cultural enterprise, still scowled defiance (to coopt Ballantyne's colourful phrase), though by the end of the nineteenth century, it did so in a much wider variety of ways. The historical connections between the apparently 'traditional' class of Sanskrit *paṇḍits* and the promulgation of a Sanskritised Indian national culture thus deserve further critical investigation.

Abbreviations

Libraries and Archives:

BL	British Library, London
BM	British Museum, London
OIOC	Oriental and India Office Collection, of the British Library
RAS	Royal Asiatic Society, London
UPRA	Uttar Pradesh Regional Archive, Allahabad
UPSA	Uttar Pradesh State Archive, Lucknow
WBSA	West Bengal State Archive, Calcutta

Document Sources:

BC	Board's Collection
BCJC	Bengal Criminal and Judicial Consultations
BC&S	Benares College & Seminary
BJC	Bengal Civil Judicial Consultations
BPolC	Bengal Political Consultations
BPC	Bengal Public Council
BPCon	Bengal Public Consultations
BRC	Bengal Revenue Council
BRCon	Bengal Revenue Consultations
BSC	Bengal Secret Consultations
BSDA	Bengal Sudder Dewanny Adawlut Proceedings
FDE	Files of the Director of Education, NWP
FRM	Factory Records Murshidabad
GCPI	General Committee of Public Instruction
GP	General Proceedings
HCB	Hindu College Benares
H/Misc	Home Miscellaneous Series
LCPI	Local Committee of Public Instruction
L/P&J	Letters, Public & Judicial Department
NWP	North-Western Provinces (of the Bengal Presidency)

Notes

Preface

1 'Speech of the Hon'ble James Thomason, Lt. Gov, NWP at the Opening of the Benares New College on the 11th January, 1853', BL, OIOC, V/23/128 Art. III, 27.
2 'Translation of a Hindee Address read at the opening of the New College, Benares, 10th Jan, 1853', BL, OIOC, V/23/128 Art. III, 32.
3 See, for example, the correspondence between Balvant Siṃh and the Company's government, ca. 1770, in BL, OIOC, H/Misc/202.
4 'Speech of the Hon'ble James Thomason', BL, OIOC, V/23/128 Art. III, 29.
5 Ibid., 30.
6 The English verse is Proverbs 12:19. The Hindi has not been traced. The Hindi aphorism uses an Avadhī postposition (*teṃ* or *taiṃ*), a mixture often seen in the nineteenth century.

Introduction Histories Of Empire, Histories Of Knowledge

1 Said, *Orientalism*, esp. 77–9.
2 Cannon, *Oriental Jones*, 185.
3 Kopf, *British Orientalism and the Bengal Renaissance*.
4 See also Trautmann, *Aryans and British India*, 21–4.
5 See Cannon, *Life and Mind of Oriental Jones*, esp. xiv–xvi; Kejariwal, *Asiatic Society of Bengal*; Kopf, 'The Historiography of British Orientalism'; and also the recent Irwin, *For Lust of Knowing*.
6 Dalrymple, *White Mughals*; and his 'Assimilation and Transculturation'. For a critique of this point of view, see Stoler, *Carnal Knowledge and Imperial Power*, esp. chap. 3.
7 For an extended discussion of Said and his influence within the context of South Asian history, see, for example, Moore-Gilbert, *Postcolonial Theory*; Inden, *Imagining India*; and Breckenridge & van der Veer, *Orientalism and the Postcolonial Predicament*.
8 For a critique of Inden's text, see Peabody, 'Tod's *Rajast'han*'.
9 Mani, *Contentious Traditions*.
10 Viswanathan, *Masks of Conquest*.
11 Inden, *Imagining India*, 44–5.
12 In this regard, Cooper and Stoler have emphasised the complexity of colonialism, and the tendency to treat it, as a process, as far too coherent. See their 'Between Metropole and Colony', esp. 6.
13 As such, I will use the term 'orientalism' with a small 'o' so as to differentiate it from Edward Said's usage of the term. This is not meant to imply that aspects of British orientalist scholarship in India were not Orientalist in significant ways, but just that orientalist scholarship should not automatically be equated with Said's formulation of Orientalism *per se*.

14 Of the numerous critiques of *Orientalism*, some of the most pertinent, I think, relate to the ambiguity surrounding the mechanisms by which European representations of Asian cultural forms became endowed with power within the colonial context. Nevertheless, like Terry Eagleton in a recent *New Statesman* review (13 Feb 2006), I think of *Orientalism* as a 'flawed classic', which in any case got the principal point right. For constructive reviews of Said's thesis, see, for example: Clifford, 'On *Orientalism*'; and Young, *White Mythologies*, chap. 7. For a good recent reappraisal of Said, see Marrouchi, 'Counternarratives, recoveries, refusals'.

15 On the importance of 'received knowledge' in British imperial rule, see especially Bayly, *Indian Society*; and Bayly, *Empire and Information*.

16 This is the phrase of Bayly, in his 'Orientalists, Informants and Critics', 115. The terms 'neo-orientalism' and 'practical orientalism' have often also been used synonymously.

17 See, for example, Lowe, *Critical Terrains*.

18 See, for example, Chatterjee, *Nation and its Fragments*, 98; and Dirks, *Castes of Mind*.

19 See, for example, Adas, *Machines as the Measure of Men*.

20 Chatterjee, *Nation and its Fragments*, 16.

21 For the relevance of this redemptive project to British society, see, for example, Colley, *Britons*.

22 For an overview of these historiographical movements, see Washbrook, 'Orients and Occidents'; and Drayton, 'Science, Medicine, and the British Empire'.

23 See Chatterjee, *Nation and its Fragments*, chap. 2; also, Cohn & Dirks, 'Beyond the Fringe'.

24 Cohn, *Colonialism and its Forms of Knowledge*.

25 Mani, *Contentious Traditions*.

26 See Mani, 'Production of an Official Discourse'.

27 Dirks, *Castes of Mind*, 8–9.

28 Cohn, 'The Command of Language', 16. See also, for example, Amin, 'Approver's Testimony, Judicial Discourse', and Viswanathan, *Masks of Conquest*, esp. 11–12.

29 Basalla, 'Spread of Western Science'.

30 Recent critiques of Basalla's approach, and its influence upon the study of science and empire, can be found, for example, in Raina, 'From West to Non-West?'; Chambers & Gillespie, 'Locality in the History of Science'; and Arnold, *Science, Technology and Medicine*, 9–12, 15–17.

31 Most recently, Roy MacLeod has noted that while Basalla's model lacked explanatory power, it has nevertheless 'served as a valuable heuristic device'. See MacLeod, Introduction to *Osiris*, 15 (2000), 2–3.

32 MacLeod, 'Passages in Imperial Science'.

33 See Vijay Pinch's discussion of these points in his extended review article of Bayly's *Empire and Information* and Cohn's *Colonialism and its Forms of Knowledge*: Pinch, 'Same Difference in India and Europe'.

34 Homi Bhabha has characterised understandings of the coloniser as possessing the exclusive power to create and mediate representation as a simplification of both historical actuality and theoretical possibility. See Bhabha, 'Difference, Discrimination', 200. David Arnold has made similar arguments

regarding Basalla's vision of the historiography of 'colonial science' in *Science, Technology and Medicine*, chap. 1.

35 See Bhabha, *Location of Culture*, chaps. 3, 4, 5, and esp. 6.

36 Bhabha, 'Signs Taken for Wonders' reprinted in Bhabha, *Location of Culture*, chap. 6.

37 For discussions of Bhabha's work, see Young, *White Mythologies*, chap. 8; Moore-Gilbert, *Postcolonial Theory*, chap. 4; Parry, 'Problems in Current Theories', esp. 41–3; and Parry, 'Signs of Our Times'.

38 Irschick, *Dialogue and History*, 3–12.

39 This is the central thesis of Bayly, *Indian Society*.

40 Bayly, *Empire and Information*, 9, 179.

41 Peabody, 'Cents, Sense, Census'.

42 Wagoner, 'Precolonial Intellectuals and the Production of Colonial Knowledge', 810.

43 Indeed, European science utilised 'Arabic' numerals, the concept of 'zero', and the analysis of language formation by reference to 'verbal roots' (*dhātu*), all of which were South Asian innovations. See, for example, Kumar, *Science and the Raj*, 18–31;. Baber, *Science of Empire*; and Rahman, Introduction to *Science and Technology*.

44 See, for example, Bayly, *Empire and Information*, chap. 7; Bayly, 'Orientalists, Informants and Critics', Prakash, *Another Reason*, esp. chap. 3; and Prakash, 'Science Between the Lines.'

45 Ballantyne, *Orientalism and Race*.

46 Dirks, *Castes of Mind*, 303–15.

47 Ibid., esp. 309–12. The same argument is made in Chatterjee, *Nation and its Fragments*, 27–32.

48 Mani argues that *paṇḍits*' understandings 'did not, however, challenge colonial knowledge. Officials and missionaries secured an insistence on their own view by ignoring, marginalizing, domesticating, and exceptionalizing whatever did not accord with their presumptions ... ideology literally constructs "reality"'. See Mani, *Contentious Traditions*, 193–4.

49 See Guha & Spivak, *Selected Subaltern Studies*; Chakrabarty, *Habitations of Modernity*, esp. chap. 1; and Chatterjee, *Nation and its Fragments*, for its focus upon the nationalist 'interior'.

50 Chatterjee, *Nation and its Fragments*, 27–32.

51 Scott, *Refashioning Futures*, 29.

52 Cooper & Stoler, 'Between Metropole and Colony', 3–4.

53 Gilroy, *Black Atlantic*, 2, 15.

54 See, for example, Bayly, 'Returning the British to South Asian History' for his call for a South Asian history which incorporates a more dynamic understanding of Britain and Britons.

55 In this sense, Fred Cooper has characterised colonialism as a set of 'hegemonic projects' which necessarily brought the coloniser into a series of relationships with the colonised, and which ultimately failed, for 'each ... was subverted as much by its "collaborators" as by those who "resisted" it'. See Cooper, 'Dialectics of Decolonization', 409.

56 Foucault, 'Ethics of the Concern of the Self', 298. It may also be asked to what extent the production of hybridity or creolisation can be invoked to express 'agency' in colonial contexts, especially on Bhabha's essentially linguistic model. See Moore-Gilbert, *Postcolonial Theory*, 130–40.

57 Irschick, *Dialogue and History*, 8; and Pratt, *Imperial Eyes*, 6.
58 Pratt, *Imperial Eyes*, 7. A parallel historiography is represented by analyses of inter-religious dialogue, based, for example, in the contact between 'Christianity', on the one hand, and 'Hinduism' on the other. See Young, 'Enabling Encounters'.
59 Gilroy, *Black Atlantic*, 7.
60 Wagoner, 'Precolonial Intellectuals and the Production of Colonial Knowledge'.
61 As an example-in-practice, see, for example, Spivak, 'Can the Subaltern Speak?'
62 Ballantyne, *Orientalism and Race*.
63 Foucault, 'Two Lectures', 99.
64 This is of course not intended to imply a renewed focus upon the symbolic power of the colonised, as opposed to the material power of the coloniser.
65 Bourdieu, *Logic of Practice*, 112–21; and Bourdieu, *In Other Words*, 22, 111–12. See also Swartz, *Culture and Power*, esp. 90–3.
66 Chakrabarty, *Provincializing Europe*, 20.
67 In this regard, Chakrabarty sometimes reverts to the construction of his genealogies through direct reference to Adam Smith and David Hume, for example, or the imbeddedness of Sanskrit philosophy in the vocabulary of the Bengali language. See *Provincializing Europe*, 127. See also, Guha, *Dominance Without Hegemony*, esp. chap. 1, for its invocation of the autonomous realm of the Sanskritic. For a general critique of the use of canonical thinkers in cultural history, see Mandler, 'Problem with Cultural History'.

Chapter 1 Orientalism and the Writing of World History

1 Fryer, *A New Account of East-India;* Ovington, *Voyage to Suratt.*
2 See Marshall, *Bengal*, 89–90.
3 Bayly, *Empire and Information*, 49.
4 Ibid., esp. 49–54.
5 'A Plan for the Administration of Justice' (15 Aug 1772) in *Proceedings of the Committee of Circuit*, 112–18.
6 Misra, *Central Administration*, 229–32.
7 Governor and Council in Bengal to the Court of Directors, dated 3 Nov 1772, extracted in the 'Seventh Report from the Committee of Secrecy appointed to enquire into the State of the East India Company', *Reports from Committees of the House of Commons*, vol. 4, 345–6.
8 See Cohn, 'Law and the Colonial State', 62–5. The Supreme Court was independent of the East India Company's courts, and normally applied English law to European subjects. See Misra, *Central Administration*, 234.
9 Warren Hastings to Lord Mansfield, dated 21 Mar 1774, reprinted in Gleig, *Memoirs*, vol. 1, 400.
10 Blackstone, *Commentaries on the Laws of England*.
11 See Lobban, *Common Law and English Jurisprudence*; and Lieberman, *Province of Legislation Determined*.
12 Rocher, *Orientalism, Poetry, and the Millennium*, 240; Marshall, *British Discovery of Hinduism*, 12–13; and Marshall, 'Hastings as Scholar and Patron'.
13 Marshall, *British Discovery of Hinduism*, 8; and Rocher, *Orientalism, Poetry, and the Millennium*, 240. On the compilation of the *Vivādārṇavasetu*, see Rocher, 'Overlapping Recensions'; and Rocher, 'Of Sources, Compendia, and Recasts'.

14 Halhed, *Code of Gentoo Laws*.

15 See W. Hastings to Court of Directors, dated 24 Mar 1774, BL, OIOC, H/Misc/115, 433–5; and Rocher, *Orientalism, Poetry, and the Millennium*, 54. See also Hastings' letter to Lord Mansfield, dated 21 Mar 1774, in which he refers to the Persian translation of the *Vivādārṇavasetu* as 'a specimen of the principles which constitute the right of property', in Gleig, *Memoirs*, vol. 1, 263; and the 'Translator's Preface' to the *Code*, in which Halhed claims that the text 'offers a complete confutation of the belief too common in Europe, that the Hindoos have no written laws whatever …', in Halhed, *Code of Gentoo Laws*, x. On the importance, in the eighteenth century, of the connection made between the security of property through the operation of law and the concept of 'liberty', see, for example, Dickinson, *Liberty and Property*.

16 Rocher, *Orientalism, Poetry, and the Millennium*, 241; also, Halhed, *Grammar of the Bengal Language*.

17 This is related by Halhed in his 'Preface' to *Grammar of the Bengal Language*, xxiii.

18 For Wilkins' request to be transferred to Benares, 'the grand seminary of India', see C. Wilkins to W. Hastings, n.d. [approx. Dec 1784 or Jan 1785], BL, BM Add. Ms 29,167 (Warren Hastings' Papers, General Correspondence, vol. XXXVI, Nov 1784–Jan 1785), 296–9. See also Wilkins, *Bhagvat-Geeta*.

19 Wilkins, *Heetopades of Veeshnoo-Sarma*.

20 C. Wilkins to W. Hastings, dated 6 Nov 1799, BL, OIOC, Mss Eur K178, letter #4.

21 See Dow's 'A Dissertation … Despotism in Hindostan', in which he notes that 'the mountains of Persia have not been able to stop the progress of the tide of despotism', ix; see also Cohn, 'Law and the Colonial State', 62–5.

22 Holwell, *Interesting Historical Events*, Part 2, 1–101. P. J. Marshall has observed, with regard to the content of this discussion, that Holwell 'was either remarkably credulous or remarkably inventive'. See Marshall, *British Discovery of Hinduism*, 5; and Trautmann, *Aryans and British India*, 68–9.

23 For a good discussion of Holwell's ideas, see Trautmann, *Aryans and British India*, 68–71.

24 Marshall, *British Discovery of Hinduism*, 19, 119, 130.

25 Dow, 'A Dissertation concerning … the Hindoos', lxvii.

26 Ibid., xxiii.

27 Ibid., xxix (note), xxxvii–xxxviii, xxiii.

28 Halhed, *Code of Gentoo Laws*. See, for example, xxiv, xxvii–xxx, xxxiii–xxxv, xxxix–xl, xliii.

29 For an overview, see Majeed, *Ungoverned Imaginings*, 11.

30 Marshall, *British Discovery of Hinduism*, 14; Kejariwal, *Asiatic Society of Bengal*, 29–30.

31 See, for example, Jones, *History of the Life of Nader Shah*; Jones, *Grammar of the Persian Language*.

32 See Majeed, *Ungoverned Imaginings*, 40–2.

33 See, for example, W. Jones to T. Yeates, dated 25 Apr 1782 in Cannon, *Letters*, vol. 2, 534.

34 Majeed, *Ungoverned Imaginings*, 42; Aarsleff, *Study of Language in England*, 117.

35 See Majeed, *Ungoverned Imaginings*, 42–5; note also Jones' remark, in a 'Charge to the Grand Jury' (4 Dec 1788), that 'common law ... is always clearer and generally wiser than any statute ...', 27.

36 Jones, 'Discourse on the Institution of a Society', x.

37 The close connections between the Asiatic Society and the Company's administration should not be minimised. Documents relating to the formation of the Asiatic Society are reproduced in the early pages of the first issue of the Society's journal. See *Asiatick Researches*, 1 (1788), iii–viii. The journal was in such high demand in Europe in the late eighteenth and early nineteenth centuries that it was reprinted numerous times, appearing in translation and often in pirated editions. Such reprints dropped the 'k' from Asiatick.

38 See particularly, W. Jones to C. Wilkins, dated 24 Apr 1784 in Cannon, *Letters*, vol. 2, 646–7. In addition, learning Sanskrit was not on Jones' list of desired research topics, compiled during his voyage to India. Entitled 'Objects of Enquiry', it is reproduced in Teignmouth, *Memoirs of Sir William Jones*, 228.

39 See W. Jones to P. Russell, dated 8 Sep 1785 & W. Jones to C. Chapman, dated 28 Sep 1785 in Cannon, *Letters*, vol. 2, 680 & 683–4, respectively.

40 Jones, 'Third Anniversary Discourse', 422–3. There are remarkable similarities between Jones' formulation of the relationship between these languages, and that of Halhed, as appeared both in the latter's published work and private correspondence. For a discussion on this point, see R. Rocher, 'Nathaniel Brassey Halhed'.

41 In this respect, Aarsleff has credited Jones with transforming the study of language from a philosophical discipline, to an historical one. See Aarsleff, *Study of Language in England*, 124.

42 Jones, 'Third Anniversary Discourse', 416.

43 Bryant, *A New System*, vol. 1, 9.

44 See Holwell, *Mythological, Etymological, and Historical Dictionary*, 65–6.

45 Jones, 'Third Anniversary Discourse', 416 See also Trautmann's discussion of Jones' critique of Bryant, in *Aryans and British India*, esp. 45–6.

46 Aarsleff, *Study of Language in England*, 130. Jones satirised the possible conclusions of the etymological method in his 'Discourse the Ninth' (1792), 489.

47 Jones, 'Third Anniversary Discourse', 421.

48 Ibid., 423–4.

49 This is discussed in Jones, 'Third Anniversary Discourse', esp. 424–7, and developed in greater detail in Jones, 'On the Gods of Greece, Italy, and India' (1788).

50 The affinity between Arabic and Persian was often postulated on the basis of their large shared vocabulary. See Jones, 'Sixth Discourse' (1789), 51; also Aarsleff, *Study of Language in England,* 131; Trautmann, *Aryans and British India*, 47.

51 Jones, 'Sixth Discourse', 51.

52 Jones, 'Fourth Anniversary Discourse' (1787), 5; also, Jones, 'The Sixth Discourse', 51.

53 Jones, 'Fourth Anniversary Discourse', 5–6.
54 Ibid., 6. Jones' insistence that the relationships between languages be discerned by reference to a comparison of grammatical structures would become instrumental in the advent of comparative philology in continental Europe, due to its promotion by Friedrich Schlegel, who relied heavily upon Jones' postulates in his seminal work, *Über der Sprache und Weisheit der Indier*.
55 Trautmann, *Aryans and British India*, 40.
56 Ussher, *Annals of the World*, 1.
57 Hutton, *Theory of the Earth*, 3.
58 Halhed, *Code of Gentoo Laws*, xxxvi–xxxviii. See also Marshall, *British Discovery of Hinduism*, 29–31; and Trautmann, *Aryans and British India*, 72–4. Note also Alun David's observation that 'to declare faith in biblical history, even if not necessarily in good faith, is to give oneself space, within the broadest bounds of orthodoxy, for speculative activities which might yet prove corrosive of traditional authority' in David, 'Sir William Jones', 175–6.
59 Halhed, *Code of Gentoo Laws*, xlii–xliii.
60 See Marshall, *British Discovery of Hinduism*, 31–3; also, Bailly, *Histoire de l'Astronomie Ancienne*.
61 Costard, *Letter to Nathaniel Brassey Halhed*. See also 'Appendix B' in Rocher, *Orientalism, Poetry, and the Millennium*, which contains an unpublished 1779 letter from Halhed to Costard in response, as well as a brief overview of the nature of the dispute.
62 See Trautmann, *Aryans and British India*, 42–4.
63 Jones, 'On the Gods of Greece, Italy, and India', 225. Jones reiterated this principle in 'Tenth Anniversary Discourse' (1793), 3.
64 Jones, *Institutes of Hindu Law*, 'Preface', esp. 54–6, 58.
65 Jones, 'On the Chronology of the Hindus' (1788–90), esp. 143, 145.
66 Jones, 'Discourse the Ninth', 479–80.
67 Ibid., 482.
68 Ibid., 483.
69 Ibid., 490.
70 Ibid., 491.
71 See also Majeed, *Ungoverned Imaginings*, 15.
72 See also ibid., 43.
73 Jones, 'On the Gods of Greece, Italy, and India', 221, 225–8.
74 Jones, 'On the Antiquity of the Indian Zodiack' (1790).
75 W. Jones to the second Earl Spencer, dated 4–30 Aug 1787 in Cannon, *Letters*, vol. 2, 755–6. Johannes Fabian has identified this as the 'denial of coevalness' with respect to Western ethnographic practice, in which the 'referent(s) of anthropology [are placed] in a Time other than the present of the producer of anthropological discourse'. See Fabian, *Time and the Other*, 31.
76 Edward Said has commented that the comparison of peoples is also inevitably evaluative. See Said, *Orientalism*, 149.
77 Jones, 'Second Anniversary Discourse' (1785), 411–12.
78 Jones, 'Tenth Anniversary Discourse', 2.
79 See also Trautmann, *Aryans and British India*, 59–61.

80 Wilkins, *Heetopades of Veeshnoo-Sarma*, viii.
81 See, for example, Wilford, 'On Egypt' (1792); Wilford, 'Essay on the Sacred Isles in the West' (1805). For analyses of Wilford's scholarship, see Bayly, 'Orientalists, Informants and Critics'; Leask, 'Francis Wilford and ... Hindu Geography'; and Trautmann, *Aryans and British India*, 89–93.
82 Wilford, 'On Egypt', esp. 312–14.
83 There is a good deal of overlap between the content of Maurice's various texts, not least because Maurice tended to quote his own work at some length. For Maurice's main works, see particularly, Maurice, *Indian Antiquities*; and Maurice, *History of Hindostan.*
84 Maurice, *Dissertation on the Oriental Trinities*, esp. 34–6.
85 Maurice, *Sanscreet Fragments*, 7. Maurice, *The History of Hindostan*, vol. 1, xxi.
86 Maurice referred to the 'ample and recording tablet of the skies', which provides 'the real history of the first grand family of the post-diluvian world'. See his *History of Hindostan*, vol. 1, vi.
87 For example, the Egyptians saw the constellation as the ship which carried Isis and Osiris during a worldwide flood, while the Greeks saw the ship 'Argo', which Jason and the Argonauts sailed in search of the golden fleece.
88 On Maurice, see also Young, 'The Lust of Empire and Religious Hate'.
89 'Advertisement' in *Asiatic Researches*, vol. 5 (London: 1799), iii–xi.
90 Maurice, 'Asiatic Researches; or Transactions of the Society', a review essay in *The British Critic* (1800) and reprinted in extract in Maurice, *Brahmanical Fraud Detected*, esp. 13–20.
91 Maurice, *The History of Hindostan*, vol. 2, vi; C.-F. Volney, *Les Ruins*. Volney's sceptical work appeared in English translation from 1795.
92 Jones, 'On the Chronology of the Hindus', 111. At least part of this essay is also intended to point out some of the absurdities of Hindu chronology contained in Sanskrit sources.
93 Tarkapañcānana, *A Digest of Hindu Law*. The text was reprinted in London in 1801.
94 For biographical information on Colebrooke, see Kejariwal, *Asiatic Society of Bengal*, chap. 3; and Colebrooke, *Life of H. T. Colebrooke*.
95 Colebrooke, 'On the Duties of a Faithful Hindu Widow', esp. 209. This paper was presented at the last meeting of the Asiatic Society which William Jones attended (3 Apr 1794). See Kejariwal, *Asiatic Society of Bengal*, 78. This sentiment was echoed by Alexander Hamilton with regard to French orientalists, particularly their reliance upon dubious missionary sources and, often, their ignorance of Sanskrit, in his anonymous review, '*Asiatic Researches* ... Volume the Seventh' in *The Edinburgh Review*, (1806), esp. 92–3.
96 See Colebrooke, 'On the Duties of a Faithful Hindu Widow', 209.
97 Colebrooke, 'On the Religious Ceremonies of the Hindus', esp. *Asiatic Researches*, 5, p. 345.
98 See letter from W. C. Blaquiere to C. E. Carrington, dated 15 Aug 1796, reprinted in *Asiatick Researches*, 5, p. 369; and Blaquiere, 'The Rudhiradhyaya'.
99 Bayly, *Indian Society*, 156–8; and Washbrook, 'Progress and Problems', esp. 82.

100 See Teltscher's discussion of Majeed, and more particularly his reference to David Kopf's work, in *India Inscribed*, 205–6.
101 J. Wilson, 'Empire and the Practice of Thought'.
102 Even when H. H. Wilson published his essay on Hindu funerary ceremonies (appearing some 25 years after Bentinck's 1829 abolition of *satī*), in which he sought to overthrow Colebrooke's reading of the *Ṛg Veda* verse which purported to sanction *sahamaraṇa* ('dying together'), Rādhākānt Deb wrote to Wilson to defend Colebrooke's original conclusions. See Wilson, 'On the supposed Vaidik authority'; and Rādhākānt Deb to Wilson, dated 30 Jun 1858, reprinted in Wilson, *Works*, vol. 2, 295–305.
103 This point has been made most forcefully, if somewhat derivatively, by Lata Mani in a series of articles on *satī* published primarily during the 1980s. For a synthesis, see Mani, *Contentious Traditions*.

Chapter 2 Sanskrit Erudition and Forms of Legitimacy

1 Trautmann, *Aryans and British India*, 135.
2 Metcalf, *Ideologies of the Raj*, 11–12.
3 Hatcher, 'What's Become of the Pandit?'
4 Rosane Rocher has noted in several articles the difficulties pertaining to reconstructing the most basic knowledge of the careers of these men, and that this has contributed to the under-examination of their roles in orientalist research. See, for example, Rocher, 'Weaving Knowledge'; and Rocher, 'Career of Rādhākānta Tarkavāgīśa'.
5 See Derrett, *Religion, Law, and the State*, esp. 233–7. Also, Lariviere, 'Justices and *Paṇḍitas*', though Lariviere's insistence upon maintaining an 'innocence' on the part of the Company's servants surely needs qualification.
6 For an overview of *brāhmaṇ*-hood in the South Indian context, see Price, 'Ideology and Ethnicity under British Imperial Rule', 153–5.
7 Though dated, see Ingalls, 'The Brahman Tradition'. For a contemporary North Indian treatment, see Parry, 'The Brahmanical Tradition and the Technology of the Intellect'.
8 Bernier, *History of the Late Revolution*, Tome III, 158–9.
9 O'Hanlon, *Caste, Conflict, and Ideology*, 19–20.
10 See Michaels, *The Pandit*.
11 Dow, 'A Dissertation concerning … the Hindoos', xxxvii.
12 Jones, 'Tenth Anniversary Discourse' (1793), 9.
13 Stokes, *English Utilitarians and India*, 3. On the Company's sovereignty in Bengal, more generally, see Bayly, 'British Military-Fiscal State'.
14 William Jones, for example, argued that 'good laws duly administered' by Britain in India would 'render our dominion over them a national benefit'. See his 'Charge to the Grand Jury' (10 Jun 1785), 15.
15 See Sen, 'Warren Hastings and British Sovereign Authority'.
16 Misra, *Central Administration*, 226. See also Khan, *Transition in Bengal*.
17 Misra, *Central Administration*, 226.
18 Ibid., 226–8.

19 The classic treatments of pre-colonial 'Hindu law' in India are Derrett, *Religion, Law, and the State*; and Lingat, *Classical Law of India*. Again, for the South Indian context, see Price, 'Ideology and Ethnicity under British Imperial Rule'.

20 Statement of the Comptrolling Council of Revenue at Moorshedabad, (minute of the Board & circular letter) dated 11 May 1772, BL, OIOC, FRM, G/27/7.

21 Singha, *A Despotism of Law*, 2.

22 'A Plan for the Administration of Justice' (15 Aug 1772) in *Proceedings of the Committee of Circuit*, 112–18.

23 These changes are enumerated in Misra, *Judicial Administration*; Misra, *Central Administration*; and Sinha, *Indian Civil Judiciary in Making*.

24 See, for example, the 1822 *vyavasthā* of five Benaresi *paṇḍits*, submitted to government, in Sen & Mishra, *Sanskrit Documents*, 31–3, 94–7.

25 For example, Prankishen Sing, appellant, v. Mussummaut Bhagwutee, respondent, 1793. This case revolved around the disputed inheritance of a tank. The case was appealed from the Dīvānī Adālat of Murshidabad to the Sadar Dīvānī Adālat in Calcutta, where the lower court's decision was overturned upon the basis of a *vyavasthā* from Rādhākānta Tarkavāgīśa. See MacNaghten, *Select Reports of the Sudder Dewanny Adawlut*, 4–5; also, assorted documentation in BL, OIOC, BSDA, P/152/40.

26 Marshall, *Bengal*, 50, 119.

27 Report of the Superintendent of the Khalsa Records, BL, OIOC, BRC, P/49/52 (1775), 584–6. The Council at Fort William ordered that the Superintendent of the Khalsa Records ask 'the Pundits' for their opinion on the law relative to the case in question, which concerned several aspirants to the *zamīndārī* rights of Mahomedshay, formerly held by 'Kissen Deo'.

28 P. Francis to P. Michell, dated 12 Mar 1776, with attached 'note', BL, OIOC, H/Misc/124, 61–78. The 'note' includes several *vyavasthā*s from *paṇḍits*, though these were put to the *paṇḍits* as 'general questions' in 1773. See also Marshall, *Bengal*, 120–1; and Guha, *Rule of Property for Bengal*.

29 *Papers Relating to East India Affairs, viz. Hindoo Widows, and Voluntary Imolations*, House of Commons, Parliamentary Papers, 1821.

30 See esp. Cohn, 'Law and the Colonial State in India'. See also, Rocher, 'Schools of Hindu Law'; and Derrett, *Religion, Law and the State*.

31 No. 200 (20 Dec 1771), circular letter from the Council at Fort William, dated 20 Dec 1771, BL, OIOC, BPCon, P/1/49.

32 (Consultation of 13 Apr 1772), S. Middleton to J. Cartier, Council of Fort William, dated 6 Apr 1772, BL, OIOC, BPCon, P/1/51.

33 (Consultation of 13 Apr 1772), letter from the Naib Dewan, attachment to 6 Apr 1772 letter of S. Middleton, BL, OIOC, BPCon, P/1/51.

34 No. 55 (13 Apr 1772), Council at Fort William to S. Middleton, dated 13 Apr 1772, BL, OIOC, BPCon, P/1/51. This exchange of letters is also recounted in Khan, *Transition in Bengal*, 269–71.

35 Indeed, Khān was removed from his position by the Company shortly after this exchange. See Travers, *Asiatic Empire*, chap. 3.

36 No. 114 (11 May 1772), S. Middleton to W. Hastings, dated 4 May 1772, and enclosure, undated letter from the Naib Dewan, BL, OIOC, BPCon, P/2/1.

37 Rocher, 'Shifting Ground'.
38 (Consultation of 25 Jun 1772), 'A Representation from the Naib Dewan', BL, OIOC, FRM, G/27/7.
39 For a general overview of this *paṇḍit*'s life and status, see Banerji, *Dawn of New India*, 71–91.
40 Rādhākānt Deb to H. H. Wilson, dated 5 Mar 1836, BL, OIOC, Mss Eur E301/2, 147–8.
41 Kumkum Chatterjee, personal communication dated October 16, 2002. See also her unpublished manuscript, 'Persianization of Itihasa'.
42 Rosalind O'Hanlon has commented upon the contradictory processes of the Company's early state-building activities. The Company, she argues, patronised a variety of groups, including those at odds with one another. See her 'Historical Approaches to Communalism', 250.
43 On the dynamic nature of political legitimacy in the late Mughal period, see Gordon, 'Legitimacy and Loyalty in Some Successor States'; and McLane, *Land and Local Kingship*, chap. 5.
44 Rocher, 'Career of Rādhākānta Tarkavāgīśa', 627–8.
45 Chatterjee, 'Persianization of Itihasa'.
46 On Kṛṣṇa Candra (1710–1782) and his court, see Sinha, *Pandits in a Changing Environment*, 1–4; and Adam, *Reports on Vernacular Education*, 49–50.
47 Rocher, *Orientalism, Poetry, and the Millennium*, 49.
48 W. Marriott to J. Alexander, Council of Revenue, dated 3 Jan 1772, BL, OIOC, FRM, G/27/6, 39–40; and J. Alexander to W. Marriott, dated 13 Jan 1772, ibid., 41.
49 Marshall, 'Warren Hastings as Scholar and Patron', 245.
50 Rocher, 'Career of Rādhākānta Tarkavāgīśa', 628.
51 Minute of Warren Hastings, dated 17 Apr 1781 reprinted in Sharp, *Selections from Educational Records*, 8.
52 See Freitag, *Culture and Power in Banaras*, 17–18.
53 No. 4 (17 Apr 1790), J. Duncan to Earl Cornwallis, dated 4 Apr 1790, BL, OIOC, BRCon, P/52/8, 397; 'State of Benares in 1786', BL, OIOC, H/Misc/379, 186; and 'Report of G. H. Barlow', enclosed in a letter to Government, dated 24 Aug 1787, BL, OIOC, BPCon, P/3/30, 646. See also Cohn, 'Role of Gosains in the Economy'.
54 See Bayly, *Rulers, Townsmen and Bazaars*.
55 For an overview of Benares' sacred character, see, for example, Eck, *Banaras*.
56 W. Hastings to J. Purling, dated 22 Feb 1772, reprinted in Gleig, *Memoirs*, vol. 1, 226.
57 Wink, *Land and Sovereignty in India*, 49.
58 Gordon, *The Marathas*, 146; Bayly, *Rulers, Townsmen and Bazaars*, 137.
59 Cohn, 'Political Systems in Eighteenth-Century India'.
60 For Hastings' account of the uprising, see Hastings, *Narrative of the Insurrection*.
61 Bayly, *Rulers, Townsmen and Bazaars*, 319. See also the contemporary description by the Indian sepoy Dean Mahomet, who noted that 'the people [of Benares] ... could, by no means, be reconciled to the sovereignty of the English', in Fisher, *Travels of Dean Mahomet*, 122; and, more generally, Narain, *Jonathan Duncan and Varanasi*, 164.

62 'Notification' of 12 Nov 1781, in *Calendar of Persian Correspondence*, vol. 6, item 292.
63 See Narain, *Jonathan Duncan and Varanasi*.
64 No. 13 (8 Jun 1792), J. Duncan to C. Stuart, dated 27 May 1792, BL, OIOC, BPolC, P/114/58, 432–5.
65 Resident at Benares to Lord Cornwallis, dated 1 Jan 1792, BL, OIOC, H/Misc/487, 29–38.
66 Extract of Revenue Letter from Bengal, dated 10 Mar 1792, ibid., 51–4.
67 Resident at Benares to Lord Cornwallis, dated 1 Jan 1792, ibid., 29–38.
68 Cohn, 'Law and the Colonial State in India'; and Cohn, 'The Command of Language', esp. 21.
69 Teltscher, *India Inscribed*, 200.
70 Majeed, *Ungoverned Imaginings*, 20.
71 With respect to Fort William College, see Das, *Sahibs and Munshis*. For example, William Carey published grammars of Bengali, Sanskrit, Marathi, Punjabi, Telugu and Kannada, as well as dictionaries for Marathi and Bengali in the first two decades of the nineteenth century, all under the auspices of Fort William College.
72 Wilson, *A Dictionary, Sanscrit and English*, i.
73 Majeed, for example, argues that legal codification was used to undermine the legal authority of the *paṇḍits*, in *Ungoverned Imaginings*, 20.
74 Halhed, *Code of Gentoo Laws*, xxxvi–xxxvii.
75 Ibid.
76 Halhed, *Grammar of the Bengal Language*, x–xi. See also N. B. Halhed to G. Costard, undated [1779], reprinted as 'Appendix B' in Rocher, *Orientalism, Poetry, and the Millennium*, 300.
77 W. Jones to C. Wilkins, dated 17 Sep 1785, in Cannon, *Letters*, vol. 2, 682. The *paṇḍit*'s name was Rāmalocana.
78 See, for example, Mukherji, 'European Jones and Asiatic Pandits', esp. 55.
79 See chap. 6.
80 Davis, 'On the Astronomical Computations of the Hindus', esp. 225.
81 Jones, 'Tenth Anniversary Discourse', 9; and Colebrooke, 'On the Duties of a Faithful Hindu Widow', 209. It would seem that although Halhed's 1776 *Code of Gentoo Laws* was based upon a Sanskrit compilation made by Bengal *paṇḍits*, its convoluted translation process rendered it unsuitable for inclusion in an enumeration of orientalist works considered authoritative at that time.
82 For an insightful discussion of translations made from Sanskrit into English, focussing upon the *Bhagavad Gītā*, see Majeed, 'Gandhi, Truth, and Translatability'.
83 (Consultation of 12 Nov 1781), W. Hastings to the Council at Fort William, dated 1 Nov 1781, BL, OIOC, BSC, P/A/61, 595–600.
84 C. Wilkins to W. Hastings, n.d., BL, BM Add. Ms 29,167 (Warren Hastings papers, General Correspondence, Volume XXXVI, Nov 1784–Jan 1785), 296–9.
85 Letter of H. H. Wilson, dated 28 May 1831, reprinted in 'The Boden Professorship of Sanscrit at Oxford', *The Asiatic Journal*, NS 7, 27 (Jan–Apr 1832), 242.
86 See Bayly, *Empire and Information*, 213. Two testimonials are reproduced in Sen & Mishra, *Sanskrit Documents*, 66–79. See also the 1784 Sanskrit

'ode' presented to Hastings by the *paṇḍits* of Benares, in BL, BM Add Ms 39,891 (Warren Hastings Papers, Supplement Vol. XXI, Literary Remains), 28–38, which described him as 'the chosen companion of Fortune' and offered 'the blessing of the learned men of Kasee'.

87 Rocher, 'Career of Rādhākānta Tarkavāgīśa'; and Rocher, 'Weaving Knowledge', 55.

88 W. Jones to C. Wilkins, n.d. [ca. Mar 1785], in Cannon, *Letters*, vol. 2, 666.

89 (Consultation of Nov 20 1787), 'Proposed Establishment for the Residency of Benares, to take place from the 1st of November 1787', enclosure of J. Duncan to Earl Cornwallis, dated 12 Nov 1787, BL, OIOC, BRCon, P/51/13, 325; and W. Jones to C. Wilkins, dated 1 Mar 1785, in Cannon, *Letters*, vol. 2, 665.

90 W. Jones to C. W. Boughton Rouse, dated 24 Oct 1786, in Cannon, *Letters*, vol. 2, 720.

91 W. Jones to C. Chapman, dated 28 Sep 1785, in ibid., 683–4; and W. Jones to A. Pritchard, n.d. [ca. Sep 1785], in ibid., 686.

92 W. Jones to C. Wilkins, dated 6 Jun 1785, in ibid., 677; and W. Jones to C. Wilkins, dated 17 Sep 1785, in ibid., 681–2. Jones was also concerned with what he conceived to be the widespread perjury of Hindu witnesses, and wondered in a 'Charge to the Grand Jury' (10 Jun 1787), whether they might not be made to swear 'before consecrated *fire* brought from some altar of acknowledged holiness'. See p. 21.

93 W. Jones to C. Chapman, n.d. [ca. Mar 1785], in Cannon, *Letters*, vol. 2, 667–8.

94 See Teltscher, *India Inscribed*, 199.

95 Marquis of Cornwallis to W. Jones, dated 14 Apr 1788, in Cannon, *Letters*, vol. 2, 803n.

96 No. 1 (18 Sep 1794), 'Resolution of Governor-General Sir John Shore, Peter Speke, and William Bowper', BL, OIOC, BSDA, P/152/47.

97 Regulation XII of the Regulations of 1793, reprinted in Clarke, *Regulations of the Government of Fort William*, vol. 1, 112–14.

98 Civil No. 1 (20 Jun 1794), J. Champain to G. H. Barlow, dated 9 Jun 1794, BL, OIOC, BCJC, P/128/12.

99 The Company's Resident in Benares was to oversee the conduct of examinations at Benares Sanskrit College, though allowances were made for the more sacred branches of Sanskrit literature. See Resident at Benares to Lord Cornwallis, dated 1 Jan 1792, BL, OIOC, H/Misc/487, 29–38.

100 Ibid.

101 BL, OIOC, BCJC, P/128/9 contains wide-ranging correspondence on this issue. See esp. Civil No. 7 (3 Jan 1794), Resolution of the Governor-General in Council.

102 Civil No. 3 (15 Aug 1794), J. Duncan to G. H. Barlow, dated 29 Jul 1794, BL, OIOC, BCJC, P/128/13; Civil No. 4 (15 Aug 1794) 'List of persons reported by the Chief Preceptor of the College at Benares to be qualified to fill the office of Pundit to a Court of Judicature as having studied the Dherm Shaster', ibid; and Civil No. 7 (20 Feb 1795), J. Rawlins to G. H. Barlow, dated 1 Feb 1795, BL, OIOC, BJC, P/147/17.

103 Early in the nineteenth century, the college's *paṇḍits* had collected so many manuscripts that a full-time librarian had to be appointed. These

manuscripts were commonly lent out to orientalists. See Nicholls, *Sketch of the Rise and Progress*, 20. The college also provided manuscript copies to H. H. Wilson in the 1840s. See, for example, J. R. Ballantyne to H. H. Wilson, dated 11 Mar 1846, BL, OIOC, Mss Eur E301/10, 25. See also F.-E. Hall, *Contribution Towards an Index*, which enumerates the philosophical manuscripts found in the Benares College library, as well as in other collections in the region.

104 Nicholls, *Sketch of the Rise and Progress*, 5–6; and Sen & Mishra, *Sanskrit Documents*, 54–9.

105 Nicholls, *Sketch of the Rise and Progress*, 8, 14; and Civil No. 7 (20 Feb 1795), J. Rawlins to G. H. Barlow, dated 1 Feb 1795, BL, OIOC, BJC, P/147/17.

106 Nicholls, *Sketch of the Rise and Progress*, 6.

107 Wilford, 'Essay on the Sacred Isles in the West', esp. 245–65. Note, however, that many contemporary commentators were just as liable to question Wilford's reliance upon a methodology grounded in verbal etymology and his desire to construct 'wild hypotheses'. See, for example, Hamilton's anonymous review, '*Asiatic Researches* ... Vol. VI', in *The Edinburgh Review* (1802), esp. 39–40.

108 Wilford, 'Essay on the Sacred Isles in the West', 249–52.

109 Colebrooke, 'On the Vedas, or Sacred Writings of the Hindus'.

110 Bentley, 'On the Hindu Systems of Astronomy'; and [Hamilton], review article, '*Asiatic Researches* ... Vol. VIII', in *The Edinburgh Review* (1808).

111 Mill, *History of British India*, vol. 1, 131–2, 389–90.

112 Ibid., 397.

113 Robertson, *Historical Disquisition*, 330–1.

114 Stewart, *Elements of the Philosophy of the Human Mind*, vol. 3. See Trautmann, *Aryans and British India*, 124–8.

115 Ward, *View of the History, Literature, and Mythology*, vol. 1, 69, 88.

116 Maurice, *Brahmanical Fraud Detected*.

Chapter 3 An Empire of the Understanding

1 On the relation of 'Providence' to British imperialism, more generally, see Drayton, *Nature's Government*.

2 This is stressed by Bayly in his 'Orientalists, Informants and Critics'.

3 Mill, *History of British India*, in three volumes. There have been many good studies published on Mill's body of thought and his influence in imperialism. See, for example, Majeed, *Ungoverned Imaginings*; Trautmann, *Aryans and British India*; Stokes, *English Utilitarians and India*; Zastoupil, *John Stuart Mill and India*, chap. 1; and Mehta, *Liberalism and Empire*, chap. 3.

4 Mill held several important positions with the East India Company, including the executive position of Examiner of correspondence from 1830, when he became responsible for the drafting of the Company's despatches to India in all of its administrative departments. See Zastoupil, *John Stuart Mill and India*, 7; Stokes, *English Utilitarians and India*, 48–9.

5 Mill, *History of British India*, vol. 1, 391.

6 Berry, *Social Theory of the Scottish Enlightenment*, esp. 64.
7 See Hopfl, 'From Savage to Scotsman'.
8 For an overview, see Smith, 'Report of 1762–3', esp. 13–23.
9 Stewart, 'Account of the Life and Writings and Adam Smith'. Stewart also noted that 'conjectural history' approximated what David Hume had called 'natural history'.
10 Millar, *Origin of the Distinction of Ranks*, 3rd ed.
11 Mill, *History of British India*, vol. 1, xiii. See also, Majeed, *Ungoverned Imaginings*, 138–40. Mill valued the critical distance which he gained from perusing a wide variety of tracts in European languages.
12 Robertson, *Historical Disquisition*, 2nd ed., 229–30.
13 See the 'Appendix' to Robertson's *Historical Disquisition*, 227–334.
14 Ibid., 283.
15 Ibid., 282–7.
16 Ibid., 295.
17 Ibid., 295–8.
18 Ibid., 332–3.
19 Smith, 'History of Astronomy', 26–7.
20 See Mill, *History of British India*, vol. 1, 480.
21 Ibid., 428.
22 Ibid., 310.
23 Ibid., 431–3.
24 Ibid., 429.
25 Mehta, *Liberalism and Empire*, 81, 95; Majeed, *Ungoverned Imaginings*, 136, 144.
26 See Majeed, *Ungoverned Imaginings*, 146–9.
27 Mill, 'Education', 52.
28 Mehta, *Liberalism and Empire*, chap. 3.
29 Mill, *History of British India*, vol. 1, 389.
30 Ibid., 391.
31 Ibid., 362.
32 See Chapter 5.
33 Mill, *History of British India*, vol. 1, 362–75. See also Mehta, *Liberalism and Empire*, 82–7.
34 Though, of course, the extent and nature of the evaluation differed substantially between Jones and Mill. See Majeed, *Ungoverned Imaginings*, 16.
35 Mill, *History of British India*, vol. 1, 398.
36 Bentley, 'Remarks on the Principal Æras' (1798); and Bentley, 'On the Antiquity of the Surya Siddhanta' (1799).
37 [Hamilton], review article, '*Asiatic Researches* ... Vol. VI' (1802); and [Hamilton], review article, '*Asiatic Researches* ... Vol. VIII' (1808). See also Bentley's responses to Hamilton's critique, in Bentley, 'On the Hindu Systems of Astronomy' (1805); and the full-length treatise, in which Bentley's irritation with Hamilton's reviews dominates much of the discussion: Bentley, *Historical View of the Hindu Astronomy*.
38 Colebrooke believed that the *Sūrya Siddhānta* dated to ca. 600 BC. See Colebrooke, 'Hindu Astronomy'.
39 Mill, *History of British India*, vol. 1, 395–404, esp. 397.

40 Playfair, 'Questions and Remarks on the Astronomy of the Hindus'. Playfair had earlier read a paper entitled 'Remarks on the Astronomy of the Bramins' at the Royal Academy in Edinburgh, in which, drawing upon the work of French astronomers, he claimed that Indian astronomy was both unique and ancient, by demonstrating that descriptions of astronomical phenomena attributed to the onset of the *Kali Yuga* (ca. 3102 BC) were necessarily based upon direct observation rather than retrospective calculation. See esp. 186.

41 Davis, 'On the Astronomical Computations of the Hindus' (1790), esp. 228.

42 Playfair, 'Questions and Remarks on the Astronomy of the Hindus', 159–60; see also Davis, 'On the Astronomical Computations of the Hindus', 245–7.

43 Robertson, *Historical Disquisition*, 294.

44 Playfair, 'Remarks on the Astronomy of the Bramins', 136, 187.

45 Mill, *History of British India*, vol. 1, 436–7.

46 Ibid., 399.

47 Smith, 'Astronomy of the Hindus' in the *Calcutta Review* (1844).

48 This is Robertson's term. See his *Historical Disquisition*, 300.

49 Mehta, *Liberalism and Empire*, 81.

50 'Despatch to the Government of India, on the Subject of General Education in India', dated 19 Jul 1854, BL, OIOC, Mss Eur F78/12.

51 G. Nicholls to J. C. C. Sutherland, Secretary GCPI, dated 12 Jan 1836, WBSA, GCPI Corresp. BC&S, Vol. 9, 357–9.

52 The 'preamble' of East India Company Charter Act of 1813, quoted in Laird, *Missionaries and Education*, 67.

53 Section 43 of the East India Company Charter Act of 1813 (53 Geo. III, c. 155, s. 43), reprinted in Zastoupil & Moir, *Great Indian Education Debate*, 91.

54 Zastoupil & Moir, *Great Indian Education Debate*, 5; see also, Embree, *Charles Grant and British Rule*. Grant was Chairman of the Company several times early in the nineteenth century.

55 Grant, *Observations on the State of Society*.

56 Importantly, H. T. Colebrooke was a member of the Governor-General's Council from 1807 to 1811, and may have had an influence upon Lord Minto's thinking in this respect. See Zastoupil & Moir, *Great Indian Education Debate*, 90–1, esp. note 1.

57 The minute of Governor-General Lord Minto, dated 6 Mar 1811, is reprinted in Adam, *Reports on Vernacular Education*, 308–9; also in Sharp, *Selections from Educational Records*, 19–21. Minto also suggested the establishment of traditional Islamic colleges at Bhagalpur and Jaunpur.

58 Brooke, Hamilton, Bird & Wilson to H. Mackenzie, dated Mar 17, 1820, WBSA, GCPI Corresp. HCB, Vol. 7, 21–45.

59 'Public Disputations of the Students of the Hindu College of Benares in the year 1821', WBSA, GCPI Corresp. HCB, Vol. 7, 129.

60 H. H. Wilson & Capt. E. Fell to W. A. Brooke, F. Hamilton, W. W. Bird & H. H. Wilson, Committee of the Hindu College Benares, dated 3 Mar 1820, WBSA, GCPI Corresp. HCB, Vol. 7, 9–20; and Brooke, Hamilton, Bird, & Wilson to H. Mackenzie, dated 17 Mar 1820, ibid., 21–45. See also 'Obituary of Captain Fell', *The Asiatic Journal*, 18 (1824), 265.

61 Wilson, *The Megha Duta*; and Wilson, *Dictionary, Sanscrit and English*.
62 For an overview of Wilson's career, see 'The Late Professor H. H. Wilson', *The Times*, 23 May 1860.
63 No. 26 (21 Aug 1821), enclosure to letter of H. H. Wilson to H. Mackenzie, dated 17 Jul 1821, BL, OIOC, BRCon, P/59/1; also, see Minto, 'Minute of 6 March 1811', in Adam, *Reports on Vernacular Education*, 308–9.
64 No. 26 (21 Aug 1821), enclosure to letter, H. H. Wilson to H. Mackenzie, dated 17 Jul 1821, BL, OIOC, BRCon, P/59/1.
65 Resolution of the Bengal Government, dated 17 Jul 1823, reprinted in Sharp, *Selections from Educational Records*, 53; and Zastoupil & Moir, *Great Indian Education Debate*, 108–9.
66 A. Stirling to GCPI, dated 31 Jul 1823, reprinted in Sharp, *Selections from Educational Records*, 56.
67 No. 27 (21 August 1821), Resolution of the Governor-General, BL, OIOC, BRCon, P/59/1. Similarly, in a minute of 1815 the Governor-General wrote of his scepticism over the efficacy of Benares Sanskrit College in accomplishing anything other than rendering a student 'more dextrous in those crooked practices which the depraved habitudes of the community would offer to his imitation'. See Minute of 2 Oct 1815, reprinted in Adam, *Reports on Vernacular Education*, 310–11.
68 Resolution of the Bengal Government, dated 17 Jul 1823, reprinted in Sharp, *Selections from Educational Records*, 53.
69 GCPI to A. Stirling, dated 6 Oct 1823, reprinted in Sharp, *Selections from Educational Records*, 87.
70 No. 25695, GCPI to Governor-General Lord Amherst, dated 18 Aug 1824, BL, OIOC, BC, F/4/909, 981–93.
71 Ibid., para. 11.
72 No. 26 (21 Aug 1821), enclosure to letter, H. H. Wilson to H. Mackenzie, dated 17 Jul 1821, BL, OIOC, BRCon, P/59/1.
73 J. H. Harington, 'Observations suggested by the provision in the late Act of Parliament for the promotion of science and literature amongst the inhabitants of the British possessions in India', quoted in Adam, *Reports on Vernacular Education*, 310.
74 Lushington, *The History, Design, and Present State*, 134.
75 Despatch of the Court of Directors, dated 18 Feb 1824, reprinted in Sharp, *Selections from Educational Records*, 91–3; and Zastoupil & Moir, *Great Indian Education Debate*, 115–17 (esp. para. 83). See also Majeed, *Ungoverned Imaginings*, 141.
76 Harington, 'Observations' in Adam, *Reports on Vernacular Education*, 310.
77 No. 26 (21 Aug 1821), enclosure to letter, H. H. Wilson to H. Mackenzie, dated 17 Jul 1821, BL, OIOC, BRCon, P/59/1.
78 The GCPI advocated the study of philosophy in English at Calcutta Sanskrit College, for example, in its letter to A. Stirling, dated 6 Oct 1823, reprinted in Sharp, *Selections from Educational Records*, 88.
79 Minault, 'Qiran al-Sa'ādain', 261.
80 E. Fell to H. H. Wilson, dated 18 Jun 1823, BL, OIOC, Mss Eur E301/1, 122–4.

81 Capt. Thoresby to H. H. Wilson, Secretary GCPI, dated 25 Mar 1829, WBSA, GCPI Corresp. BC&S, Vol. 8, 99–108; and Capt. Thoresby to H. H. Wilson, dated 9 Nov 1829, ibid., 209–16.

82 Capt. Thoresby to H. H. Wilson, dated 18 Jul 1830, BL, OIOC, Mss Eur E301/1, 196–7.

83 C. Thoresby to H. H. Wilson, Secretary GCPI, dated 3 Mar 1831, WBSA, GCPI Corresp. BC&S, Vol. 8, n.p; and G. Nicholls to Benares LCPI, dated 7 Apr 1838, WBSA, GCPI Corresp. BC&S, Vol. 10, 401–3. Note that the attendance of a low-caste *camār* at the seminary later in 1838 was unlikely to have improved the situation, as numerous petitions were received from 'respectable' families which were opposed to the seminary's non-discriminatory admittance policies. See the translations of two Bengali & Persian letters, WBSA, GCPI Corresp. BC&S, Vol. 10, 527–9.

84 Laird, *Missionaries and Education*, 71–2.

85 Middleton, *Statutes of the Missionary Institution*, 3, 5. Also, Kay, *Some Account of the Foundation*, 11, Appendix 'D'.

86 See Laird, *Missionaries and Education*, 101–9. See also the *Reports of the Calcutta School Book Society*. See, for example, Goldsmith, *Abridgement of the History of England*; and Joyce, *Dialogues illustrative of the first principles*.

87 See Rauch, *Useful Knowledge*, esp. 40–6; and Bayly, *Empire and Information*, 215.

88 Yates, *Padārthavidyāsāra* (Sanksrit, 1828); and Yates, *Padārthavidyāsāra*, 2nd ed. (1834). The 1st edition was published in 1825.

89 See, Jacob, *Scientific Culture*, 149–50; and van Berkel, 'Science in the Service of the Enlightenment', 79–80.

90 Yates, 'Advertisement' in his *Padārthavidyāsāra*, 2nd ed.

91 For an overview of Carey's career, see Young, *Resistant Hinduism*, 33–7.

92 W. Carey to J. Sutcliffe, dated 10 Oct 1798, cited in Young, *Resistant Hinduism*, 34; and Carey, 'On the Importance of Sungskrita'.

93 Laird, *Missionaries and Education*, 233, 235–6. Note, however, that Trevelyan also adopted at times a more conciliatory tone, advocating the use of vernacular languages, enriched by English, to promote Western 'useful knowledge'. See Trevelyan, *On the Education of the People of India*.

94 J. Tytler to H. H. Wilson, dated 3 Jul 1833, BL, OIOC, Mss Eur E301/1, 38–41.

95 J. Tytler to H. H. Wilson, dated 14 Mar 1834, BL, OIOC, Mss Eur E301/2, 70–2.

96 No. 77633, Minute of T. B. Macaulay, dated 2 Feb 1835, BL, OIOC, BC, F/4/1846, 127–46.

97 Ibid., esp. 144.

98 No. 77633, Resolution of the Governor-General of India in Council in the General Department, dated 7 Mar 1835, BL, OIOC, BC, F/4/1846, 161–3.

99 The Benares Sanskrit College, for example, received a stipulated income enshrined in treaty, as well as interest from its excess income. Moreover, the *rāja* of Benares contributed an ongoing measure of funding, in addition to an original donation of land and money for its establishment. See Chapter 6.

100 No. 77633, Resolution of the Governor-General, dated 7 Mar 1835, BL, OIOC, BC, F/4/1846, 162. See also Rādhākānt Deb to H. H. Wilson, dated 5 Mar 1836, BL, OIOC, Mss Eur E301/2, 147–8.

101 G. Nicholls to Benares LCPI, dated 15 Feb 1838, WBSA, GCPI Corresp. BC&S, Vol. 10, 229–31; and G. Nicholls to T. A. Wise, Secretary GCPI, dated 4 Feb 1841, WBSA, GCPI Corresp. BC&S, Vol. 11, 395–7. Note also that the number of Sanskrit students receiving a stipend during approximately this same time was reduced from something over 105 to 32.

102 'Propositions adopted by the General Committee of Public Instruction, 11th April 1835' in Sharp, *Selections from Education Records*, 142; and Thoresby to J. C. C. Sutherland, Secretary GCPI, dated Mar 28 1835, WBSA, GCPI Corresp. BC&S, Vol. 9, 183.

103 Jones, Religious Tract Society, to G. Nicholls, dated 1 Jul 1837, WBSA, GCPI Corresp. BC&S, Vol. 10, 343; 'list of books received from the Religious Tract Society' dated 27 Feb 1838, ibid., 337; and GCPI to G. Nicholls, dated 17 May 1838, ibid., 345–7.

104 F. J. Shore to C. E. Trevelyan, dated 23 May 1834, BL, OIOC, H/Misc/790, 199–202.

105 Rādhākānt Deb to H. H. Wilson, dated 5 Mar 1836, BL, OIOC, Mss Eur E301/2, 147–8.

106 J. Tytler to T. B. Macaulay (copy), dated Jan 26 1835, BL, OIOC, Mss Eur E301/2, 103–9.

107 Hodgson's first two letters, dated Aug and Sep 1835, were then republished in 1837 as B. H. Hodgson, *Preeminence of the Vernaculars; or the Anglicists Answered.* All references to a further reprinting in Hodgson, *Miscellaneous Essays*, vol. 2.

108 Hodgson, *Preeminence of the Vernaculars* (letter #2), 292.

109 Ibid.

110 On the Munro School, see Zastoupil, *John Stuart Mill and India*, chap. 3; and Stokes, *English Utilitarians and India*, 5–25.

111 Malcolm, *Political History of India*, vol. 1, 82. Also, Bayly, *Empire and Information*, 2.

112 Wilson, 'Education of the Natives of India', a letter to the editor dated 5 Dec 1835, *The Asiatic Journal*, N.S. 19, 73 (1836), 1–16. Reprinted in Zastoupil & Moir, *Great Indian Education Debate*, 206–23. Further references to the reprinted edition.

113 Ibid., 216 (reprint).

114 Mill wrote to Wilson in January of 1836 to 'say how much pleasure I have derived from your letter in this month's *Asiatic Journal*'. He also noted that the Government of India had defied instructions from London on educational policy. See J. S. Mill to H. H. Wilson, dated 5 Jan 1836, BL, OIOC, Mss Eur E301/2, 143.

115 Draft Despatch of J. S. Mill, BL, OIOC, H/Misc/723, para. 20. This despatch was never sent by the Directors.

116 Wilson, 'Education of the Natives of India', 217 (reprint).

117 Draft Despatch of J. S. Mill, BL, OIOC, H/Misc/723, para. 16.

118 Ibid, para. 17.

119 Wilson, 'Education of the Natives of India', 221 (reprint).

120 Hodgson, *Pre-eminence of the Vernaculars* (letter #1), 270. More will be said about the conceived 'power of language' and its role in translation in Chapter 5.
121 For example, No. 25695, GCPI to Governor-General Lord Amherst, dated 18 Aug 1824, BL, OIOC, BC, F/4/909, para. 11.
122 Wilson, 'Education of the Natives of India', 220 (reprint).
123 Tytler, 'On native education and the study of Sanscrit, Arabic and Persian'.
124 No. 25695, GCPI to Governor-General Lord Amherst, dated 18 Aug 1824, BL, OIOC, BC, F/4/909, para. 11.
125 J. Tytler to T. B. Macaulay (copy), dated 26 Jan 1835, BL, OIOC, Mss Eur E301/2, 103–9.
126 The article referred to is Wilkinson, 'On the Use of the Siddhantas' (1834).
127 Wilson, 'Education of the Natives of India', 220 (reprint).
128 Hodgson, *Pre-eminence of the Vernaculars* (letter #2), 293, emphasis in original.
129 See, for example, Bayly, *Empire and Information*, chap. 7; Prakash, 'Science Between the Lines'; and Minkowski, 'The Pandit as Public Intellectual'.
130 For an overview, see [Muir], *Brief Notice of the Late Mr Lancelot Wilkinson*.
131 Wilkinson, 'On the Use of the Siddhantas', 505.
132 Ibid., 505–6. See also Wilkinson's edited *Siddhānta* texts, for example: Wilkinson, *The Gunitadhia*.
133 Wilkinson, 'On the Use of the Siddhantas', 509.
134 Ibid., 506.
135 Ibid., 509.
136 Ibid., 507.
137 J. Prinsep to H. H. Wilson, dated 2 Nov 1836, BL, OIOC, Mss Eur E301/2, 184–5.
138 Adam, *Reports on Vernacular Education*, esp. 314–17.
139 Ibid., 317–19.
140 'Minutes of the LCPI, Benares, upon the Annual Examination of the English Seminary, Dec 1838', WBSA, GCPI Corresp. BC&S, Vol. 10, 863–78.
141 No. 77638, Minute of Governor-General Lord Auckland, dated 24 Nov 1839, BL, OIOC, BC, F/4/1846, 5–76, esp. para. 5.
142 Ibid., para. 10.
143 Despatch of the Honorable the Court of Directors to the Governor General of India in Council, dated 20 Jan 1841, BL, OIOC, L/P&J/3/1015 (Public Department No. 1 of 1841); also, *Report of the General Committee of Public Instruction, 1839–40,* cli–cliv.
144 Anonymous, 'Native Education in India', 207.

Chapter 4 Enlisting Sanskrit on the Side of Progress

1 Bhardwaj, *Hindu Places of Pilgrimage*, 41; and Eck, *Banaras*.
2 Bernier, *History of the Late Revolution*, Tome III, 158.

3 Benares was both a 'brahmanical' city, and a 'representative' city, in that it attracted communities of *brāhmaṇs* from all over the subcontinent. When James Prinsep conducted his survey of Benares in the late 1820s, he found amongst the city's population of 180,000 at least 32,000 *brāhmaṇs* from a wide variety of India's regions. See Prinsep, 'Census of the Population'; also, Shastri, 'Dakshini Pandits at Benares'.

4 Sherring, *Benares*, v.

5 Chunder, *Travels of a Hindoo*, vol. 1, 236.

6 Sherring, *Benares*, vi.

7 'Speech of the Hon'ble James Thomason, Lt. Gov, NWP at the Opening of the Benares New College on the 11th January, 1853', BL, OIOC, V/23/128, Art. III, 30.

8 See Nicholls, *Sketch of the Rise and Progress*, 79.

9 No. 77638, Minute of Governor-General Lord Auckland, dated 24 Nov 1839, BL, OIOC, BC, F/4/1846, 5–76. See also Chapter 3.

10 Capt. Marshall to T. A. Wise, dated 3 May 1841, WBSA, GCPI Corresp. BC&S, Vol. 11, 679–93. This is reprinted in *General Report ... 1840–41 & 1841–42*, xcv–cxi.

11 See Muir, 'Memorandum on the State of the Sanscrit College at Benares, and the means of its improvement', dated 2 Apr 1844, in *General Report on Public Instruction... 1843–44*, Appendix 'Q'. Also, No. 59 (Apr 1844), BL, OIOC, NWP GP, P/214/63.

12 L. Wilkinson to T. A. Wise, dated Aug 1841, WBSA, GCPI Corresp. BC&S, Vol. 11, 927–9. See also [Muir], *Brief Notice of the Late Mr. Lancelot Wilkinson*, 9.

13 *General Report on Public Instruction ... 1843–44*, 1.

14 Stokes, *English Utilitarians and India*, 28.

15 J. Thomason to H. H. Wilson, 20 Apr 1848 & 26 Jan 1849, BL, OIOC, Mss Eur E301/11, 26, 80 respectively. See also the relevant correspondence on village education in Saletore, *Banaras Affairs*. For secondary works, see: Bayly, *Empire and Information*, 219–20; Young, *Resistant Hinduism*, 50–2; and Muir, *Honourable James Thomason*.

16 Muir, *Mataparīkṣā* (1839). This text also went through several more editions. For an overview of John Muir, his attack on Hinduism, and the resultant Indian 'responses', see Young, *Resistant Hinduism*, esp. 49–80.

17 See J. Muir to G. Nicholls, dated 8 Feb 1838, WBSA, GCPI Corresp. BC&S, Vol. 10, 351.

18 J. Thornton, Secretary to Govt NWP, to J. Muir, dated 13 Apr 1844, reprinted in *General Report on Public Instruction ... 1843–44*, ci.

19 Muir, 'Memorandum on the State of the Sanscrit College at Benares', in *General Report on Public Instruction ... 1843–44*, cii. Muir had also issued an earlier, preliminary report. See No. 133 (Apr 1844), J. Muir, 'Memo on the Benares Sanskrit College', dated 24 Mar 1844, BL, OIOC, NWP GP, P/214/63.

20 See Chapter 6. See also, Prior, 'British Administration of Hinduism', esp. 100–40.

21 Muir, 'Baconian Philosophy Applicable to the Mental Regeneration of India', 125–6.

22 See also, Young, 'Church Sanskrit'.

23 Muir, 'Memorandum on the State of the Sanscrit College at Benares', in *General Report on Public Instruction ... 1843–44*, ciii, cv.
24 See, for example, Reed, *From Soul to Mind*, 36–7.
25 Muir, *Vyavahārāloka*.
26 Muir, *Vyavahārāloka*, Speech to Students and Paṇḍits, Apr 1844 ('*Kāśīsthavidyālayādhyakṣasya śrīmajjānmyūrasāhibasya vidyālayīyān śrīmatpaṇḍitāñ chātrāṃśca prati vijñāpanam*'), 3.
27 Ibid., 4.
28 Muir, *Vyavahārāloka*, vi.
29 Muir, 'Memo on the Benares Sanskrit College', BL, OIOC, NWP GP, P/214/63, para. 4.
30 Muir, 'Memorandum on the State of the Sanscrit College at Benares', in *General Report on Public Instruction ... 1843–44*, civ.
31 Ibid.
32 Muir, 'Memo on the Benares Sanskrit College', BL, OIOC, NWP GP, P/214/63, para. 7.
33 Muir, 'Baconian Philosophy Applicable to the Mental Regeneration of India', 124.
34 A similar methodology was also followed by Muir's contemporary and friend in Benares, the Revd William Smith, who attempted an 'appeal to the head' in which he would point out the logical inconsistencies in Hinduism, and compare them with what he believed were the philosophically sound tenets of Christianity. See Sherring, *Missionary Life and Labours*, esp. 90–1.
35 Muir, 'An Address to the Students of the Benares College', dated 10 Feb 1845, in *General Report on Public Instruction ... 1844–1845*, xcv–xcix.
36 See Muir, 'Benares Sanskrit College'. Muir signed this article 'J. M.'
37 See, for example, Ballantyne, *Principles of Persian Caligraphy*; Ballantyne, *Practical Oriental Interpreter*.
38 J. R. Ballantyne to Mrs. H. Siddons, dated 5 Sep 1839, BL, OIOC, Mss Eur E301/4, 81; and J. R. Ballantyne to H. H. Wilson, dated 24 Jan 1845, Mss Eur E301/9, 7. Also, see Ballantyne's obituary in the *Journal of the Royal Asiatic Society*, N.S. 1 (1865), v–vii. See also the entry for J. R. Ballantyne in *Edinburgh Academy Register*.
39 J. R. Ballantyne to Mrs. H. Siddons, dated 5 Sep 1839, BL, OIOC, Mss Eur E301/4, 81.
40 J. R. Ballantyne to H. H. Wilson, dated 24 Jan, 19 Feb, and 20 Mar 1845, BL, OIOC, Mss Eur E301/9, 7, 19, & 46, respectively. See also Ballantyne's obituary in the *Journal of the Royal Asiatic Society*, N.S. 1 (1865), v–vii.
41 See Ballantyne, *Discourse on Translation*, 7. While this reference dates to the latter half of his tenure as Superintendent, it is his clearest statement on the 'proposed end' of his pedagogy. The sentiment is also echoed in earlier publications, see for instance [Ballantyne], 'Prospects of India' (1849). Ballantyne wrote in *Benares Magazine* under the pseudonym 'K'. Given the nature of these articles, his wider publications, and location in Benares, it must have been quite straightforward to identify him as the author.
42 Cosslett, Introduction to *Science and Religion*. See also, for example, Pratt, *Scripture and Science not at Variance*, published in London in 1859, and also in Calcutta.

43 J. R. Ballantyne to H. H. Wilson, dated 11 Mar 1846, BL, OIOC, Mss Eur E301/10, 25. See also Ballantyne, *Shakespeare's Play of MacBeth*.

44 While there is no definitive evidence of the level of Ballantyne's expertise in Sanskrit at this time, a notebook of his dated 1847 with a very partial translation of Pāṇini's difficult grammatical text, the *Aṣṭādhyāyī*, is suggestive that he was learning the grammar at the college, and that his level of competency was only fair. See BL, OIOC, Mss Eur D357.

45 Muir, 'On the Best Mode of Reasoning', 365. This sentiment is also expressed in [Ballantyne], 'Prospects of India', 347.

46 Ballantyne, *Laghu Kaumudi*, v. Ballantyne also later published a Sanskrit grammar on a 'European model'. See Ballantyne, *First Lessons in Sanskrit Grammar*.

47 *General Report on Public Instruction ... 1846–1847*, 26.

48 Ballantyne, *Lectures on the Nyaya Philosophy* (1848); Ballantyne, *Lecture on the Sankhya Philosophy* (1850); Ballantyne, *Lecture on the Vedanta (*1851).

49 Ballantyne also edited an English translation of a part of the important *nyāya* text, the *Bhāṣā-Pariccheda*. This was also to be used by the English Department of the college.

50 By 1844, for example, there were 246 students attached to the English Department, all of whom were studying elements of English, Hindi, and Urdu. See *General Report on Public Instruction ... 1843–44*, 17–24.

51 *General Report on Public Instruction ... 1846–1847*, 31–2; and J. R. Ballantyne to H. H. Wilson, dated 1 Sep 1846, BL, OIOC, Mss Eur E301/10, 74.

52 [Ballantyne], 'The Prospects of India', 344–6. See also, Hodgson, *Pre-eminence of the Vernaculars*, 292–3. Ballantyne and Hodgson became friends while in India. See, for example, J. R. Ballantyne to B. H. Hodgson, dated 1 Sep 1856; RAS, 'Hodgson Papers'; and J. R. Ballantyne to H. H. Wilson, dated 2 Mar 1848, BL, OIOC, Mss Eur E301/11, 14.

53 [Ballantyne], 'The Prospects of India', 346.

54 *Report on Public Instruction ... 1846–47*, 35–6.

55 Ibid., 36.

56 It should be noted that Ballantyne's ideas here correspond closely with the sentiment expressed by H. H. Wilson in a series of lectures delivered at Oxford in 1840: 'the whole tendency of Brahmanical education is to enforce dependence upon authority' (36). There are other points of connection with Ballantyne's thought, as well, including, the notion that *brāhmaṇs* are indifferent to truth (37). See Wilson, *Two Lectures*.

57 *General Report on Public Instruction ... 1846–47*, 36–8.

58 Ballantyne, *Lectures on the Sub-Divisions of Knowledge*, Part 1, 'Preface'.

59 Ibid., 1–2.

60 See also No. 404 (26 April 1855), J. R. Ballantyne, 'Scheme of a set of Sanskrit and Vernacular Treatises for the use of the Colleges and Schools in India', dated Nov 1848, BL, OIOC, NWP GP, P/215/43.

61 Ballantyne, *Lectures on the Sub-Divisions of Knowledge,* Part 4, p. 21 (Sanskrit, p. 22).

62 Ballantyne, *Discourse on Translation*, 7.

63 Quoted in the introduction to Ballantyne, *Christianity Contrasted*, vii–x. See also Penrose, *Attempt to Prove the Truth of Christianity*.

64 Ballantyne, *Bible for Pandits*, xxi.

65 [Ballantyne], 'The Prospects of India', 347–8.

66 Ballantyne, *Discourse on Translation,* 7.

67 Ibid.

68 J. R. Ballantyne to H. H. Wilson, dated 11 Aug 1848, BL, OIOC, Mss Eur E301/11, 55–7.

69 [Ballantyne], 'The Prospects of India', 347.

70 Ibid.

71 *General Report on Public Instruction ... 1846–1847,* 35.

72 Extract from a report by Dr. Ballantyne, Principal of the Benares College, dated 9 Dec 1847, BL, OIOC, Mss Eur E301/10, 204–5; and No. 403 (26 Apr 1855), J. R. Ballantyne, 'Report of the Annual Examination of the Benares College 1854', BL, OIOC, NWP GP, P/215/43, para. 45.

73 Ibid., para. 36.

74 Ballantyne, 'Advertisement' in *Synopsis of Science,* xii. (all references in this chapter will be to the 2nd edition of 1856).

75 BL, OIOC, Mss Eur F384, undated pamphlet.

76 [Ballantyne], 'On the Nyaya System of Philosophy'. See also, Ballantyne, *Synopsis of Science,* ix–x.

77 Ballantyne, *Synopsis of Science,* xii.

78 [Ballantyne], 'On the Nyaya System of Philosophy', 9 (reprint).

79 Ballantyne, *Synopsis of Science,* vi.

80 Ibid., 1.

81 Ibid., 7.

82 Ibid., 2–3.

83 Ibid., 62.

84 Ibid., 150.

85 Ibid., 151. See also Ballantyne, *Discourse on Translation,* 31. A version of this essay also appears at the beginning of *A Synopsis of Science.*

86 Ballantyne's final two major publications before returning to England in 1861 were *Christianity Contrasted with the Hindu Philosophy (*1859), and *The Bible for Pandits (*1860). These discussed specifically the 'Special Revelation' of God, in the form of the Christian Scriptures. Neither text was utilised in Benares College, as this would have contravened educational policy. See below.

87 For example, all edited by Ballantyne: (#3) *The Method of Induction* (extracted from J. S. Mill's *System of Logic*); (#4) *Metaphysics and Mental Philosophy, Vol. 1* (Berkeley's *Treatise Concerning the Principles of Human Knowledge*), and *Metaphysics and Mental Philosophy, Vol. II* (D. Stewart's *Elements of the Philosophy of the Human Mind*); (#5) *An Explanatory Version of Bacon's Novum Organum;* (#8) *Chapters on Political Economy* (adapted from Whatley & DeQuincey); (#10), *Physical Geography* (extracted from the work of Mrs. M. Somerville).

88 Viṭṭhala Śāstrī was Assistant Professor of *nyāya* at Benares College from 1853, a position he held jointly with Veṅkaṭa Rāma Śāstrī, and Professor of *sāṅkhya* from 1856 until his death in 1867. See Govindadeva Śāstrī, 'Notice of Viṭṭhala Śāstrī, *paṇḍit*' (in Sanskrit). Prior to 1853 Viṭṭhala Śāstrī was a celebrated student in Ballantyne's '*paṇḍit* class'. See Chapter 6.

89 For reference to this class, see for example, J. R. Ballantyne to H. H. Wilson, dated 11 Aug 1848, BL, OIOC, Mss Eur E301/11, 55–7; Ballantyne, *Synopsis*

of Science, ii; and, see also the annual reports on the college, such as No. 451 (31 May 1854), J. R. Ballantyne, 'Report of the Annual Examination of the Benares College, 1853', BL, OIOC, NWP GP, P/215/34, para. 15–16, 20–6.

90 Ballantyne, *Explanatory Version of Bacon's Novum Organum (*Reprint for the Pandits 5).

91 Ballantyne, *Synopsis of Science*, vii.

92 Macaulay, *Life and Writings of Francis Bacon*, 69. This is a review of Basil Montagu's 16 vol. *Works of Francis Bacon*.

93 Ballantyne, *Synopsis of Science*, v.

94 Ibid. See also Wilson, *Two Lectures*, 37.

95 [Ballantyne], 'Pandits and Their Manner of Teaching', 60–1 (reprint).

96 Muir, 'Baconian Philosophy Applicable to the Mental Regeneration of India', 124.

97 Ballantyne, *The Method of Induction (*Reprints for the Pandits 3); and Ballantyne, *Elements of Logic* (Reprints for the Pandits 6).

98 Reprints for the Pandits No. 9 was a work on chemistry, and particularly, the adapted lectures of R. Griffith (presented before Queen Victoria) and Farraday's lectures 'On the Non-Metallic Elements'. See No. 47 (14 Nov 1853), BL, OIOC, NWP GP, P/215/27; and No. 451 (31 May 1854), 'Report of the Annual Examination of the Benares College, 1853', BL, OIOC, NWP GP, P/215/34, para. 22.

99 No. 147 (23 Jan 1851), J. Thornton to J. R. Ballantyne, dated 23 Jan 1851, BL, OIOC, NWP GP, P/215/9.

100 No. 88 (9 May 1854), J. R. Ballantyne to W. Muir, dated 19 Apr 1854, BL, OIOC, NWP GP, P/215/33.

101 Ballantyne & Viṭṭhala Śāstrī, *Heliographic Rules and Reasons* (*Ravikiraṇkūrcikayā citralekhana, prakriyopapattivarṇanaṃ*).

102 No. 404 (26 Apr 1855), J. R. Ballantyne to J. Thomason, Lt-Governor, NWP, dated 20 Oct 1852, BL, OIOC, NWP GP, P/215/43, para. 11. See also, No. 134 (21 Feb 1851), 'Report of the Annual Examination for the Benares College for 1850', BL, OIOC, NWP GP, P/215/9. In this report, Ballantyne states: 'we shall, I hope, be able to employ the telescope frequently to demonstrate the accuracy of the astronomical predictions of Europe ...' See para. 25. A surveying class was also added to the curriculum of Benares College during the mid-1850s.

103 Ballantyne, *Lectures on the Sub-Divisions of Knowledge*, 'Preface' to Part 1, n.p., also *Synopsis of Science*, ix.

104 Reid, *General Report on Public Instruction ... 1854–55*, 30–1, 38.

105 This text, which appeared under the Hindi name of *Nyāyakaumudi*, was translated into Hindi by Bāpūdeva Śāstrī, and went through several printings. See, for example, No. 119 (18 Aug 1853), BL, OIOC, NWP GP, P/215/26. Also, see the following Hindi tract which appears to have been based heavily on the *Synopsis of Science*: Hall & Tivarī, *Siddhānt Saṅgrah Bhāṣā*.

106 A Hindi version of the treatise on 'physical science' was being prepared by Govindadeva Śāstrī in 1852. See No. 69 (7 April 1852), J. R. Ballantyne to W. Muir, dated 1 Apr 1852, BL, OIOC, NWP GP P/215/16.

107 Ballantyne, *Hindi Version of the Hitopadesha*.

108 No. 228 (19 Apr 1856), F.-E. Hall, 'Memo on Hindi', dated 4 Dec 1854, BL, OIOC, NWP GP, P/215/54. Ballantyne explicitly concurred in the content of Hall's memorandum.
109 This notion is intimated throughout Ballantyne's *Discourse on Translation.*
110 'Speech of the Hon'ble James Thomason, Lieutenant-Governor, NWP, at the Opening of the Benares New College on the 11th January 1853', BL, OIOC, V/23/128, Art. III, 26–31.
111 Williams, *Dictionary, English and Sanskrit*, iii.
112 'Education, first draft', BL, OIOC, Mss Eur F78/12, 43–93. Explicit references to Ballantyne, though not Benares, were removed in the official despatch, dated 19 July 1854.
113 Smith, 'Dr. Ballantyne and Government Education'.
114 [Kay], 'The Benares College.' See also the positive reviews of Ballantyne's *Christianity Contrasted with Hindu Philosophy*, and *Bible for Pandits*, which appeared in the *Calcutta Review*, 33, 66 (Dec 1859) and *Calcutta Review*, 35, 69 (Sep 1860), respectively.
115 Ballantyne, *Synopsis of Science*, xv.
116 Quoted in Ballantyne, *Bible for Pandits*, xvii.
117 J. R. Ballantyne to the Council of Education, n.d., WBSA, Council of Education, Correspondence 1853, No. I.
118 E. C. Śarman to F. I. Mouat, dated Sep 1853, WBSA, Council of Education, Correspondence 1853, No. II. On Īśvaracandra Vidyāsāgar, see Hatcher, *Idioms of Improvement.*
119 Banerjea's criticisms led to a lengthy riposte from Ballantyne. See No. 404 (26 Apr 1855), J. R. Ballantyne to J. Thomason, dated 20 Oct 1852, BL, OIOC, NWP GP, P/215/43.
120 See J. R. Ballantyne to H. H. Wilson, dated 11 Mar 1846, BL, OIOC, Mss Eur E301/10, 25; and *General Report on Public Instruction ... 1845–1846*, 23.
121 Wallis, *Notes on Books and Proceedings*, 14–15, 20, 30, 41, 45–7, 73–6.
122 Sherring, *Missionary Life and Labours*, 91.
123 Ballantyne, *Bible for Pandits*, lxxxix–xc.
124 Ibid., xc.
125 Ibid., xxi.
126 Ibid., iv.
127 Ballantyne, *Synopsis of Science*, 151.
128 Ballantyne, *Christianity Contrasted*, 14.
129 Ibid., 20–59.
130 Ibid., 91.
131 See Young, *Resistant Hinduism*. It should be noted here that Ballantyne's argument is in no way innovative, and indeed, is consistent with many of the points made by Muir in his much earlier text, *Mataparīkṣā* (1839).
132 Ballantyne, *Christianity Contrasted*, 111.
133 No. 193 (24 Apr 1852), 'Report of the Annual Examination of the Benares College, 1851', dated 20 Jan 1852, BL, OIOC, NWP GP, P/215/16, para. 35.
134 [Ballantyne], 'On the Ontology of the Vedānta', esp. 103 (reprint).

135 [Ballantyne], 'Gist of the Vedānta', esp. 83 (reprint).
136 See Ballantyne, *Christianity Contrasted*, xxxi–xxxvii.
137 [Ballantyne], 'Gist of the Vedānta', 92 (reprint).
138 [Ballantyne], 'On the Ontology of the Vedānta', 93–4 (reprint).
139 Ibid., 100–2 (reprint).
140 Ibid., 102 (reprint).
141 Ibid., 105 (reprint).
142 Ballantyne, *Metaphysics and Mental Philosophy* (Reprints for the Pandits 4).
143 Ballantyne, *Christianity Contrasted*, esp. 38–52.
144 Colebrooke, 'On the Philosophy of the Hindus'. See also, Kennedy, *Nature and Affinities of Ancient and Hindu Mythology*; and Haughton, *Exposition of Vedanta Philosophy by H. T. Colebrooke vindicated.*
145 See, for example, Kopf, *Brahmo Samaj*; and Hatcher, 'Contemporary Hindu Thought.'
146 Gore, *Rational Refutation*, esp. 158–69. See also the positive review of a pamphlet authored by Nīlakaṇṭha, entitled *The Consideration of the Vedant Doctrines and an Epitome of the Christian Doctrine*, printed in *The Missionary*, 3, 9 (Sep 1853), 247–8. Nīlakaṇṭha is reported to have argued that the *vedānta* is 'unreasonable', 'inconsistent', and 'fallacious'.
147 *British and Foreign Evangelical Review*, 9, 31 (Jan 1860), 136–52, esp. 147–8.
148 Ballantyne, *Bible for Pandits*, xxxix–xl.

Chapter 5 On Language and Translation

1 See, for example, Cheyfitz, *Poetics of Imperialism*.
2 Cohn, 'Command of Language'.
3 See, for example, Niranjana, *Siting Translation*.
4 See Teltscher, *India Inscribed*, 211–15; and Bassnett & Trivedi, Introduction to *Post-Colonial Translation*.
5 This term is adapted from Venuti, *Translator's Invisibility*, 19–20.
6 Bassnett & Trivedi, Introduction.
7 Aarsleff, 'Locke's Influence', 271.
8 Ibid., 272–3.
9 I will quote from Thomas Nugent's English translation: de Condillac, *Essay on the Origin of Human Knowledge*.
10 von Humboldt, *On Language*, 49. See also Foucault, *The Order of Things*, chap. 8, esp. 290.
11 See Nugent's preface in Condillac, *Essay on the Origin of Human Knowledge*, for an overview. Aarsleff describes Condillac as 'by all odds the most important figure [of eighteenth-century scholarship on language], both as a theorist and by virtue of his influence'. See Aarsleff, *From Locke to Saussure*, 107.
12 Condillac, *Essay on the Origin of Human Knowledge*, 169–71. Condillac here argues against William Warburton's notion in *The Divine Legation of Moses Demonstrated*, that Adam and Eve were given a language 'very poor and narrow' by God, which they then expanded upon.
13 Ibid., 173–4.

14 Ibid., 228–9.
15 Ibid., 234–5, 282.
16 Ibid., 249–50.
17 For example, ibid., 242–9.
18 Ibid., 254.
19 Ibid., 255–6.
20 Ibid., 282–3.
21 Ibid., 285.
22 Ibid., 182.
23 Ibid., 228, 282.
24 Ibid. 228.
25 Ibid., 288–90.
26 Ibid., 248–9, 288–9.
27 Jones, 'Essay on the Poetry of the Eastern Nations', 533.
28 Ibid., 527–8.
29 Ibid., 527.
30 For example, Majeed, *Ungoverned Imaginings*, 48; and Teltscher, *India Inscribed*, 204.
31 Jones, *Poems*, 404.
32 Carey, *Grammar of the Sungskrit Language*, iii.
33 Colebrooke, 'On the Sanscrit and Pracrit Languages', 200.
34 Wilson, *Dictionary, Sanscrit and English*, 'Dedication'.
35 Halhed, *Grammar of the Bengal Language*, iii.
36 Carey, *Grammar of the Sungskrit Language*; Colebrooke, *Grammar of the Sanscrit Language*; and Wilkins, *Grammar of the Sanskrita Language*. Wilkins, in particular, pointed out that the study of Sanskrit should appeal to those interested in the 'structure and affinity of languages', as well as those interested in the ancient history, literature, and philosophy of India. See his 'Preface'.
37 See [Hamilton], review article, 'Grammar of the Sanskrita Language' in *The Edinburgh Review* (1809), esp. 367.
38 Wilkins, *Grammar of the Sanskrita Language*, 1.
39 Jones, 'Third Anniversary Discourse' (1786), 422.
40 Carey, *Grammar of the Sungskrit Language*, iv.
41 See Wilson's 1819 *Dictionary, Sanscrit and English*. Also, Colebrooke's 1808 translation of the Sanskrit lexicon, the *Amerakośa*, for use at the College of Fort William: Colebrooke, *Cosha*.
42 Jones, 'Third Anniversary Discourse', 422.
43 Colebrooke substantiated his argument by reference to etymology. For example, he noted that the word *sat* in Sanskrit means 'existent', from which can be derived in Sanskrit the word *satya*, meaning 'true' or 'truth'. The Hindi word for this is *sac*, which Colebrooke argued is derived from *satya* by dropping the final vowel, substituting 'j' for 'y', and then transforming 'tj' to the more harmonious 'ch'. See Colebrooke, 'On the Sanscrit and Pracrit Languages', 221–3. See also Wilson, *Introduction to the Grammar of the Sanskrit Language*, x.
44 Colebrooke, 'On the Sanscrit and Pracrit Languages', 222–3.
45 Hamilton used this analogy in his review article, 'Grammar of the Sanskrita Language', 369.
46 Carey, *Dictionary of the Bengalee Language*, 'Preface'.

47 Ibid., viii–ix.
48 Wilkins, *Grammar of the Sanskrita Language*, x–xi.
49 Liu, *Translingual Practice*, 3–6.
50 Ibid., 4.
51 Breton, *Vocabulary of the Names*. Breton was assisted in making this compilation by H. H. Wilson, who had originally come to India on the Company's medical service.
52 Ibid., 'Preface', n.p. Yet somewhat incongruously, Breton also noted that despite the 'inadequate knowledge of medical science and Anatomy', the 'natives' were still able to perform 'admirable cures and delicate operations' with great success.
53 Tytler, 'On Native Education', *The Calcutta Literary Gazette*, NS 1, 25, esp. 382.
54 Moore, 'Proposal for Printing by Subscription', 8.
55 Wilkinson, 'On the Use of the Siddhantas', 514.
56 See 'Report of the Sub-Committee, Appointed at the Meeting of the General Committee of Public Instruction, Held on the 29th July, 1841, for Collecting and Arranging the Information Necessary for the Preparation of the Scheme of Vernacular School Books' in *General Report ... 1840–41 and 1841–42*, xxxv–li. See also No. 77638, Minute of Governor-General Lord Auckland, dated 24 Nov 1839, BL, OIOC, BC, F/4/1846, para. 12.
57 Indeed, by late-1843, with the imminent devolution of educational responsibilities from the central government at Calcutta, it was decided that the responsibility for preparing all vernacular textbooks in Urdu and Hindi was to be transferred to the NWP Government at Agra. See C. Beadon to R. N. C. Hamilton, dated 20 Nov 1843, quoted in *General Report on Public Instruction ... 1843–44*, 3–4.
58 No. 77633, Minute of T. B. Macaulay, dated 2 Feb 1835, BL, OIOC, BC, F/4/1846, 144.
59 *General Report on Public Instruction ... 1843–44*, 7.
60 Minute of F. Boutros on Delhi College, dated 1 Jul 1842 in *General Report ... 1840–41 and 1841–42*, cxxv–xvi.
61 Ibid.
62 *General Report on Public Instruction ... 1843–44*, 7.
63 Ibid.
64 Minute of F. Boutros, dated 10 Jan 1844 in *General Report on Public Instruction ... 1843–44*, lxxii–xix.
65 The yearly *General Report on Public Instruction* normally listed in an appendix titles that had been published in the previous year, either at Delhi College or by the Agra School Book Society. See, for example, *General Report on Public Instruction ... 1844–45*, Appendix A.
66 This is not to say that Hindi books were not published, nor widely available, for they were. The number of Hindi books available for educators in NWP, however, tended to be much smaller than Urdu books, and sometimes also of a much older vintage. Adam's translation of *Stewart's Historical Anecdotes*, which first appeared under the Hindi title *Upadeśa Kathā* in an 1825 publication from Calcutta, was still being offered in 1844 as a standard Hindi text in NWP. See 'List of Books in Hindi Generally Used in Schools and Colleges of the

North Western Provinces', *General Report on Public Instruction ... 1843–44*, Appendix S.

67 The Revd J. J. Moore, the Urdu Translator to Government, and Secretary of the Agra School Book Society, was appointed Curator of School Books in September 1844. See *General Report on Public Instruction ... 1844–45*, 2–3; and J. Thornton to Revd J. J. Moore, dated 2 Sep 1844 reprinted in ibid., ii–iii.

68 The publication of this journal is discussed in Minault, 'Qiran al-Sa'ādain'. It was first suggested by Boutros in a minute dated 10 Jan 1844, reprinted in *General Report on Public Instruction ... 1843–44*, lxxii–lxxix.

69 *General Report on Public Instruction ... 1845–1846*, 5.

70 Rājendralāl Mitra notes that Boutros' translations 'never were touched beyond the four walls of the college premises'. See Mitra, *Scheme for the Rendering of European Scientific Terms*, 4.

71 See Chapter 4.

72 Ballantyne, *Discourse on Translation*, 5.

73 Hodgson, *Preeminence of the Vernaculars*, letter #1, 267.

74 *General Report on Public Instruction ... 1847–1848*, 21.

75 Ballantyne, *First Lessons in Sanskrit Grammar*, 105.

76 Ballantyne, *Synopsis of* Science, i. (all references in this chapter will be to the 2nd edition of 1856 unless otherwise noted).

77 No. 404 (26 Apr 1855), J. R. Ballantyne to J. Thomason, Lt Governor of NWP, dated 20 Oct 1852, BL, OIOC, NWP GP, P/215/43, para. 2.

78 Ballantyne, *Discourse on Translation*, 12–13.

79 Ballantyne, *Christianity Contrasted*, v–vi.

80 Ibid., 194.

81 *General Report on Public Instruction ... 1850–51*, 52.

82 Mill, *Proposed Version of Theological Terms*, 1, 25–6.

83 Ibid., 4, 29.

84 Ballantyne, *Bible for Pandits*, 3.

85 Ballanynte's use of the term *diva* for 'heaven' is even more 'neutral' than that of Mill, who wished to 'Christianise' the Sanskrit term *svarga* away from its association with 'the third heaven of Indra and the gods'. H. H. Wilson, in contrast, preferred the use of the term *dyu*, which is a derivation of *diva*. See Mill, *Proposed Version of Theological Terms*, 23, 37.

86 Ballantyne, *Lectures on the Sub-Divisions of Knowledge*, Part 1, 'Preface', n.p.

87 Ballantyne, *Discourse on Translation*, 11.

88 Ibid., 15.

89 Ballantyne, *Synopsis of Science*, ix. Also, *General Report on Public Instruction ... 1850–51*, 52.

90 Yates, *Padārthavidyāsāra* (1828). Technical terms included *lavaṇamaya* ('consisting of salt') for 'saline', and *tārapinākhya* ('one with the name *tārapina*') for 'turpentine'.

91 Mack, *Principles of Chemistry*.

92 Anonymous, *Rasāyan Prakāś*.

93 Ballantyne, *Discourse on Translation*, 15–16.

94 Ballantyne, *Christianity Contrasted*, 213–15. This section does not appear in earlier versions of his discussion of translation, either in *A Synopsis of Science* or *A Discourse on Translation*.

95 Ballantyne, 'Preface' to *Synopsis of Science*, vol. 2 (1852 ed.); and Ballantyne, *Discourse on Translation*, 16–18.
96 Ibid.
97 See No. 119 (18 Aug 1853), regarding the 'Hindee Synopsis of Science', BL, OIOC, NWP GP, P/215/26.
98 Ballantyne reports on the progress made in the 'Hindi Version of the Treatise on Physical Science' in No. 69 (7 Apr 1852), J. R. Ballantyne to W. Muir, dated 1 Apr 1852, BL, OIOC, NWP GP, P/215/16.
99 No. 46 (13 Aug 1851), J. Thornton to J. R. Ballantyne, dated 13 Aug 1851, BL, OIOC, NWP GP, P/215/12. See also Bāpūdeva Śāstrī, *Bījagaṇita*; and Bāpūdeva Śāstrī, *Vyaktagaṇita*.
100 Bāpūdeva Śāstrī, *Bhūgolavarṇana*. See also Rām Jasan, *Bhūgola-Candrikā*.
101 Bāpūdeva Śāstrī, *Trikoṇamiti*.
102 Mathurā Prasāda Miśra, *Vāhyaprapañca-darpaṇa*; and Ballantyne, *Laghu Kaumudi*, Mathurā Prasāda Miśra, transl. (this version is in Hindi).
103 Mathurā Prasāda Miśra, *Trilingual Dictionary*; and Rām Jasan, *Sanskrit and English Dictionary*.
104 See also Dalmia, *Nationalization of Hindu Traditions*, 190–1.
105 Miśra, *Trilingual Dictionary*, 4.
106 *General Report on Public Instruction ... 1846–1847*, 33–4.
107 No. 226 (24 Mar 1853), W. Muir to J. R. Ballantyne, dated 24 Mar 1853, BL, OIOC, NWP GP, P/215/23.
108 Ibid.
109 No. 228 (19 Apr 1856), 'Memo' by F.-E. Hall, dated 4 Dec 1854, BL, OIOC, NWP GP, P/215/54.
110 No. 205 (22 Mar 1853), W. Muir to LCPI Agra, Bareilly, Ajmere, and Saugor, Secretary Roorkee College, and Visitor General NWP Schools, dated 22 Mar 1853, BL, OIOC, NWP GP, P/215/23.
111 No. 270 (27 May 1853), J. Middleton (Secretary Agra LCPI) to W Muir, dated 1 Apr 1853, BL, OIOC, NWP GP, P/215/24; and No. 272 (27 May 1853), J. Cargill (Secretary Delhi LCPI) to W. Muir, dated 4 April 1853, ibid.
112 Sevaka Rāma, *Śabda Prabandāvalī*.
113 Śivdayāl Upādhyāy, *Hindī kī Dūsrī Kitāb*.
114 Mitra, *Scheme for the Rendering of European Terms*, esp. 19–27.
115 Śyām Sundar Dās, *Hindi Scientific Glossary*, 151–2.
116 'Padārth bād', *Hindī Pradīp* 1, 6 (Feb 1878).
117 On this point see also Rai, *Hindi Nationalism*.
118 In addition to a consideration of the process of language codification, and the lexical separation of Hindi from Urdu necessitated by the practical demands of education and official communication. See Dalmia, *Nationalization of Hindu Traditions*, chap. 4.
119 Rājā Śiva Prasād, *Vidyankur*, 'Preface'.

Chapter 6 *Paṇḍits*, Sanskrit Learning, and Europe's 'New Knowledge'

1 Kane, *History of Dharmaśāstra*.
2 Pollock, 'Death of Sanskrit'.

3 Indeed, the Sanskrit Knowledge-Systems on the Eve of Colonialism Project declares that by 1750, the coming of colonialism was concomitant with a 'decline' that 'ended the age-old power of Sanskrit thought to shape Indian intellectual history'. While this project very usefully explicates the dynamicism of Sanskrit scholarship 1550–1750, its very terms of reference occlude a meaningful discussion of the uses made of Sanskrit erudition by Indians during the colonial period. See Pollock, 'Introduction'.

4 Hatcher, 'Sanskrit Pandits Recall Their Youth'.

5 On this point, see Kaviraj, 'Sudden Death of Sanskrit Knowledge'.

6 See also Hatcher, 'What's Become of the Pandit?'

7 Some significant exceptions being the work of Brian Hatcher, Rosane Rocher, and several others. See Chapter 2.

8 See, for example, the voluminous and interesting, but ultimately problematic Upādhyāy, *Kāśī kī Pāṇḍitya Paramparā*; also, Sinha, *Pandits in a Changing Environment*. Michaels' edited collection, *The Pandit*, while certainly not hagiography, does to some extent trade on Sanskrit nostalgia.

9 Kumar, 'Sanskrit Pandits and Modernisation', esp. 55–6.

10 Leask, 'Francis Wilford and ... Hindu Geography'.

11 Bayly, 'Orientalists, Informants and Critics'.

12 On this point, in a different context, see Said, *Culture and Imperialism*, 30, 38.

13 See, for example, Bayly, *Empire and Information*, 2; Cooper, 'Dialectics of Decolonization', 406–7; and Gilroy, *Black Atlantic*, 1–5.

14 No. 26 (21 Aug 1821), enclosure to H. H. Wilson to H. Mackenzie, dated 17 Jul 1821, BL, OIOC, BRCon, P/59/1, para. 17–18.

15 C. Wilkins to Rt. Hon. J. Sulivan, dated 25 Aug 1813, BL, BM Add Ms 29,234 (Warren Hastings' Papers, Copies of Essays, etc.), 204–11.

16 Adam, *Reports on Vernacular Education*, 49–53.

17 Ibid., 119.

18 No. 104 (23 Mar 1850), 'Memorandum regarding village schools in the district of Benares and indigenous and other schools in the city cantonments and civil station', by D. F. McLeod, dated Dec 1849, and No. 105 (23 Mar 1850), D. Tresham to D. F. McLeod, dated 31 Mar 1849, BL, OIOC, NWP GP, P/215/3. See also, Thornton, *Memoir on the Statistics of Indigenous Education*, 90–4.

19 G. Nicholls to J. C. C. Sutherland, dated 8 Aug 1838, WBSA, GCPI Corresp. BC&S, Vol. 10, 561–4; and G. Nicholls to J. C. C. Sutherland, dated 30 Aug 1838, ibid., 569–72.

20 Lutgendorf, 'Ram's Story in Shiva's City', 40–1.

21 I owe most of these references to conversations with Candradhar Prasād Nārāyaṇ Siṃh of Varanasi. See also Upādhyāy, *Kāśī kī Pāṇḍitya Paramparā*, 113–33, 791–815; Lutgendorf, *Life of a Text*, 146–7; and Dalmia, *Nationalization of Hindu Traditions*, 79–80.

22 See Upādhyāy, 123–4.

23 Tārācaraṇa Tarkaratna, *Tarkaratnākara*. See also Upādhyāy, *Kāśī kī Pāṇḍitya Paramparā*, 123–4.

24 See below.

25 See Chapter 2. Also, Mukherji, 'European Jones and Asiatic Pandits', 55.

26 Rocher, 'Career of Rādhākānta Tarkavāgīśa', 629.
27 'Petition of Jagannatha Sharma', BL, OIOC, BPC, P/4/18, 78.
28 Adam, *Reports on Vernacular Education*, 119–20.
29 Ibid., 49–50.
30 Cited in Sen & Mishra, *Sanskrit Documents*, 56.
31 See, for example, reports of *paṇḍits* attached to G. Nicholls to LCPI, Benares, dated Aug 1839, WBSA, GCPI Corresp. BC&S, Vol. 10, 1001–16. One of the college's *paṇḍits* noted that 20–25 students attended his house for instruction, while another stated 'pupils come to my house in the afternoon, and each of them read by me two hours, after which they go home about 8 o'clock in the night ... by which they make a great deal of improvement ...' (emphasis in original).
32 See also Rocher, 'British Orientalism in the Eighteenth Century', esp. 220–5.
33 Halhed, *Code of Gentoo Laws*, 4–5.
34 Ibid., 39–61.
35 'Translation of a Cubbitt, or Ode, written in the Sanscritt Language, and presented in March 1784', BL, BM Add Ms 39,891 (Warren Hastings Papers, Supplement Vol. XXI, Literary Remains), 28–38.
36 See also Sen & Mishra's discussion of the *paṇḍits*' possible motivations in petitioning on behalf of Warren Hastings during his trial, in the introduction to their *Sanskrit Documents*, 2–6.
37 Adam, *Reports on Vernacular Education*, 119, 316.
38 See, for example, Dalmia, 'Sanskrit Scholars and Pandits', 324–6. Dalmia's article relies heavily upon George Nicholls' account of the college, *Sketch of the Rise of Progress of the Benares Patshalla*.
39 See below for a discussion of this point.
40 See 'Translation of a Baousta', BL, BM Add Ms 39,892 (Warren Hastings Papers, Supplement Vol. XXII, Papers relating to India), 128–30; attachment to G. Nicholls to J. C. C. Sutherland, dated 9 Dec 1836, WBSA, GCPI Corresp. BC&S, Vol. 9, 633–40; Sen & Mishra, *Sanskrit Documents*, *passim*; and Gabriel, 'Learned Communities and British Educational Experiments', 70–3, 82–5. See also Chapter 2.
41 Including: Nārāyaṇa Śāstrī (*vyākaraṇa*), Kāśīnātha Śāstrī (*sāṅkhya*), Hīrānanda Paṇḍit (*sāhitya*), Umārāma Paṇḍit (*vedānta*), Viṭṭhala Śāstrī (assistant *nyāya*), Lajjāsaṅkara Śarmā (*jyotiṣa*), Bāpūdeva Śāstrī (natural philosophy), Nandalāl Śarmā (*jyotiṣa*), Kālīprasād Śarmā (*nyāya*), Rām Jasan Paṇḍit (Anglo-Sanskrit), and Gulzār Śarmā (*dharmaśāstra*).
42 Undated *vyavasthā* (Sanskrit and Urdu), BL, OIOC, Mss Eur F384. The list of names indicates that it must have been signed at the earliest in 1853.
43 See, for example, extract of Revenue Letter to Bengal, dated 25 Jun 1793, BL, OIOC, H/Misc/487, 55–7; and No. 3134A of 1867, R. Simson to E. C. Bayley, dated 12 Sep 1867, UPRA (Allahabad), FDE, SL 17. The 1794 treaty confined the *rāja*'s official power to a separate Benares estate. See *Imperial Gazetteer of India*, 187–9.
44 H. Mackenzie to Committee for Superintending the Hindu College, Benares, dated 8 Feb 1822, WBSA, GCPI Corresp. HCB, Vol. 7, 133–6; Capt Thoresby to H. H. Wilson, dated 19 Mar 1829, WBSA, GCPI Corresp.

BC&S, Vol. 8, 75–8; Capt Thoresby to H. H. Wilson, dated 15 Mar 1832, ibid., n.p.; and Nicholls, *Sketch of the Rise and Progress*, 49, 64.

45 G. Nicholls to J. C. C. Sutherland, dated 29 Jan 1836, WBSA, GCPI Corresp. BC&S, Vol. 8, 391–4; and G. Nicholls to J. C. C. Sutherland, dated 24 Mar 1836, ibid., 413–14.

46 Attachment to G. Nicholls to LCPI Benares, dated 5 Dec 1846, WBSA, GCPI Corresp. BC&S, Vol. 9, 641–3.

47 See, for example, the list enumerated in *General Report on Public Instruction ... 1845–1846*.

48 It was noted, for example, in 1841 that 'the pandits have always been permitted to pursue their own plans of instruction'. In this document there is also a list of texts which composed this curriculum for *vyākaraṇa*, *jyotiṣa*, *nyāya*, *dharmaśāstra*, *purāṇa*s, *vedānta*, *mīmāṃsā*, and *sāṅkhya*. See 'Report on the System of Instruction followed in the Sanscrit College at Benares', WBSA, GCPI Corresp. BC&S, Vol. 11, 547–54.

49 See rules 8–10, which restrict European superintendence over the 'secret' and 'too sacred' branches of Sanskrit learning. 'Extract from the Proceedings of the Resident at Benares dated 1st December 1791', BL, OIOC, H/Misc/487, 38–49.

50 For example, see 'Report on the System of Instruction Followed in the Sanskrit College at Benares' dated 8 Mar 1841, WBSA, GCPI Corresp. BC&S, Vol. 11, 547–54; also, Nicholls, *Sketch of the Rise and Progress*, 32–3.

51 G. Nicholls to J. C. C. Sutherland, dated 12 Feb 1837, WBSA, GCPI Corresp. BC&S, Vol. 9, 733–6; G. Nicholls to J. C. C. Sutherland, dated 4 Feb 1837, ibid., 737–40; and Sanskrit petition (damaged), undated, ibid., 741. The petition was unsuccessful, however.

52 Petition of Jānakīprasād Paṇḍit to J. A. Loch, dated 24 May 1841 (English), WBSA, GCPI Corresp. BC&S, Vol. 11, 981–4; and petition of Jānakīprasād Paṇḍit to GCPI, dated 1841 (translation), ibid., 1009–12.

53 Attachment to G. Nicholls to J. C. C. Sutherland, dated 9 Dec 1836 (Hindi, with English translation), WBSA, GCPI Corresp. BC&S, Vol. 9, 633–40.

54 G. Nicholls to J. C. C. Sutherland, dated 27 May 1837, WBSA, GCPI Corresp. BC&S, Vol. 9, 817–18; and testimonials, ibid., 821–2.

55 Madhusūdana Tarkālaṅkāra to H. H. Wilson, dated 28 Jun 1839 (Sanskrit), BL, OIOC, Mss Eur E301/1, 224–5.

56 Petition of Rajeev Lochun Pandita, dated 11 July 1828 (Sanskrit, damaged), WBSA, GCPI Corresp. HCB, Vol. 7, 791–2; and summary of same, ibid., 797–800.

57 The case revolved around the *jāgīr* of 'Bissumbhur Pandit'.

58 W. H. Macnaughten, Secretary to the Govt of India, to R. D. Mangles, dated 13 Mar 1837, reprinted in 'appendix C' to Ramchunder Surmoona, *Memorial*; J. Thomason to G. Mainwaring, dated 15 Apr 1837, WBSA, GCPI Corresp. BC&S, Vol. 9, 807–8; and G. Nicholls to J. C. C. Sutherland, dated 4 May 1837, ibid., 803–4.

59 Ramchunder Surmoona, *Memorial*, 3, 'appendix D'.

60 Pandit Eshwur Duttu Pandey, Late Professor of Law, to G. Nicholls, dated May 1837 (translation), WBSA, GCPI Corresp. BC&S, Vol. 9, 825–8.

61 Resolution of the Right Honorable the Governor-General in Council, dated 27 Sep 1837, reprinted in Ramchunder Surmoona, *Memorial*, 'appendix E'.
62 Ramchunder Surmoona, *Memorial*, 6–7.
63 Ibid., 4, 7.
64 Ibid., 'appendix A'.
65 Ibid., esp. 7–15.
66 Sumboo Chunder Mittra to H. H. Wilson, dated 31 Jul 1839, BL, OIOC, Mss Eur E301/4, 69–70.
67 Sumboo Chunder Mittra to H. H. Wilson, dated 15 Sep 1840, BL, OIOC, Mss Eur E301/5, 146–7.
68 Rāmcandra Śarmā to H. H. Wilson, dated Sep 17 1840 (Sanskrit), BL, OIOC, Mss Eur E301/5, 130–1.
69 Cited in Sen & Mishra, *Sanskrit Documents*, 37–42, 113–15.
70 Assorted papers, BL, OIOC, Mss Eur F384, n.p.
71 This is obviously a different Viṭṭhala Śāstrī than the *vyākaraṇa paṇḍit*, discussed earlier, who died in 1836.
72 See Young, 'Receding from Antiquity'.
73 See Chapter 3.
74 L. Wilkinson to T. A. Wise, dated Aug 1841, WBSA, GCPI Corresp. BC&S, Vol. 11, 927–9.
75 Ballantyne, *Lectures on the Sub-Divisions of Knowledge*, 'Preface', n.p. See also J. R. Ballantyne to H. H. Wilson, dated 11 Aug 1848, BL, OIOC, Mss Eur E301/11, 55–7.
76 Ballantyne, *Synopsis of Science*, 2nd ed., ix. See also No. 403 (26 Apr 1855) 'Report of the Annual Examination of the Benares College 1854', dated 5 Jan 1855, BL, OIOC, NWP GP, P/215/43, para. 18.
77 Ballantyne, *Discourse on Translation*, 12–13.
78 No. 96 (19 Sep 1851), J. R. Ballantyne to J. Thornton, dated 26 Aug 1851, with attachment, Bapu Deva Tonkekar to J. R. Ballantyne, dated 25 Aug 1851, BL, OIOC, NWP GP, P/215/12; and No. 97 (19 Sep), J. Thornton to J. R. Ballantyne, dated 19 Sep 1851, ibid.
79 No. 134 (21 Feb 1851), 'Report of the Annual Examination of the Benares College for 1850' dated 4 Jan 1851, BL, OIOC, NWP GP, P/215/9, para. 27.
80 See, for example, Bāpūdeva Śāstrī, *Elements of Plane Trigonometry* (Sanskrit); and Bāpūdeva Śāstrī & Ballantyne, *Hindi Geography*.
81 Bāpūdeva Śāstrī, *Translation of the Surya Siddhanta*; and Bāpūdeva Śāstrī, *Siddhanta Shiromani*.
82 L. Wilkinson to T. A. Wise, Secretary GCPI, dated August 1841, WBSA, GCPI Corresp. Vol. 11, 927–30; also, J. Muir, 'An Address to the Students of the Benares College' in *General Report on Public Instruction … 1844–45*, xcvii.
83 Owen, 'On Hindu Neology', 202–5.
84 Whitney, 'Reply to the Strictures of Prof. Weber', 395.
85 Discussed in greater detail below.
86 Bāpūdeva Śāstrī, *Phalit kā Vicār* [Reflections on Astrology].
87 Bāpūdeva Śāstrī, 'The Practice of Astrology by Hindus and Mohammedans', 151–3.

88 Ibid., 154–6.
89 Ibid., 156.
90 In this regard, note Bayly's observation that Bāpūdeva's edition of the *Sūrya Siddhānta* and its commentary, the *Siddhānta Śiromaṇi*, supported Bhāskarācārya against Wilkinson's critique of inconsistency. See Bayly, *Empire and Information*, 263; and Bayly, 'Orientalists, Informants and Critics'.
91 Owen's 'On Hindu Neology' is printed together with Bāpūdeva Śāstrī, 'On the Sidereal and Tropical Systems' in *Memoirs Read Before the Anthropological Society of London*.
92 Bāpūdeva Śāstrī, 'On the Sidereal and Tropical Systems', 206–7.
93 Ibid., 209.
94 Bāpūdeva Śāstrī, 'Bhaskara's Knowledge of the Differential Calculus'.
95 Bāpūdeva Śāstrī, 'On the Sidereal and Tropical Systems', 209–10.
96 Ibid., 211.
97 Ibid., 215.
98 Muir, 'An Address to the Students of the Benares College', dated 10 Feb 1845 in *General Report on Public Instruction ... 1844–45*, xcv–xcix.
99 Basic biographical information can be found in Govindadeva Śāstrī, 'Notice of Viṭṭhala Śāstrī, *paṇḍit*' (Sanskrit).
100 See *General Report on Public Instruction... 1849–50*, 52; and *General Report on Public Instruction ... 1851–52*, 50. Note that *A Dialogue Concerning Art* was the first in the 'Reprints for the Pandits' series.
101 Viṭṭhala Śāstrī & Ballantyne, *Bekanīyasūtravyākhyāna*.
102 Ballantyne had conceived of the *nyāya* chair as the 'nucleus and centre of the whole Sanskrit department', given the special position which that school of philosophy enjoyed in his pedagogy. See *General Report on Public Instruction... 1851–52*, 47–50; and *General Report on Public Instruction ... 1852–53*, 60.
103 No. 403 (26 Apr 1855), 'Report of the Annual Examination of the Benares College 1854', dated 5 Jan 1855, BL, OIOC, NWP GP, P/215/43, para. 37.
104 See also *General Report on Public Instruction ... 1853–54*, 63–4.
105 J. R. Ballantyne to H. H. Wilson, dated 25 Oct 1856, BL, OIOC, Mss Eur E301/13, 171.
106 Hall, *Contribution Towards an Index*, ii.
107 BL, OIOC, Mss Eur F384.
108 *General Report on Public Instruction ... 1853–54*, 63.
109 No. 403 (26 Apr 1855), 'Report of the Annual Examination of the Benares College 1854' dated 5 Jan 1855, incl. 'Report of Pandit Vitthala Shastri', BL, OIOC, NWP GP, P/215/43, para. 48.
110 Ballantyne & Viṭṭhala Śāstrī, *Heliographic Rules and Reasons*.
111 See *General Report on Public Instruction ... 1853–54*, 63.
112 Roer, *Division of the Categories of the Nyāya Philosophy*.
113 Roer's translation of *pariccheda* as 'division' in this context is also quite poor; 'clarification' is closer.
114 The example given is: Mūṣikā is a word; Mūṣikā eats grain; therefore, a word eats grain.
115 Viṭṭhala Śāstrī, note entitled 'Dr Roer on Bhāshā', dated 11 Dec 1860, BL, OIOC, Mss Eur F384 (English & Sanskrit).

116 Ballantyne & Viṭṭhala Śāstrī, *Pañcabhūtavādārtha*. Note that despite Ballantyne's claim to authorship here, this text is an English translation of an original Sanskrit composition of Viṭṭhala Śāstrī. The text is published in a side-by-side dual-language edition.
117 Viṭṭhala Śāstrī, *Bekanīyasūtravyākhyāna*.
118 *'Bhāratavarṣīyapaṇḍitavidyārthibhyo yuropīyapaṇḍitānāṃ bhūtapañcakaviṣayakaṃ mataṃ jñāpayituṃ'*.
119 Having its origin in the *Brāhmaṇas*, the notion of *pañcabhūta* is a generally accepted one in most Sanskrit-based philosophical systems, including the *sāṅkhya* and *nyāya-vaiśeṣika*.
120 Viṭṭhala Śāstrī, *Pañcabhūtavādārtha*, 4–5.
121 Ibid., 5.
122 Viṭṭhala Śāstrī, *Bekanīyasūtravyākhyāna*, 11–12 (English), 17–19 (Sanskrit).
123 Viṭṭhala Śāstrī, *Bekanīyasūtravyākhyāna*, 29–31 (English), 47–51 (Sanskrit).
124 Anonymous, 'Pandit Prema Chandra Tarkabāgīs'.
125 See Orsini, 'Pandits, Printers and Others'; also, Bayly, *Empire and Information*, 241.
126 The *Benares Recorder* was edited by a German, and owned by Bābū Prasād Nārāyaṇ Siṃh, whom E. A. Reader described as 'an old gentleman, who could not read a word of English, but was proud to show his friends a newspaper of his own on his own table'. See Reade, *Contributions to the Benares Recorder*, 'Preface'.
127 See Miśra, *Saṃskṛt Patrakāritā kā Itihās*, [History of Sanskrit Journalism], 225. The listing of Sanskrit journals found in Miśra's work shows that both *Kāśīvidyāsudhānidhi* and *Pratnakamranandinī* were the first journals published in Sanskrit in India. These were quickly followed by several journals in Agra, Lahore, Allahabad, Pune, Patna, and Calcutta.
128 Satyavrata Sāmaśramī, *Sāma Veda Saṅhitā*. Satyavrata was later elected an associate member of the Asiatic Society of Bengal in 1893. See *Proceedings of the Asiatic Society of Bengal, January to December 1893* (1894), 32; also, Griffith, *Hymns of the Samaveda*, 'Preface'.
129 See *The Hindu Commentator* (*Pratnakamranandinī*), 6, 1 (Saṃvat 1930). Also, ' Pratnakamranandinī: A Review', *The Pandit*, 2, 17 (Oct 1867), 116.
130 Much of the content of *The Pandit* has now been reprinted. Some of the English-language material appears in Miśra, *Paṇḍit Revisited*; while the Sanskrit material can be found in Miśra, *Paṇḍitaparikramā*, multiple volumes.
131 R. Griffith to H. S. Reid, dated 12 Nov 1861, UPRA (Allahabad), FDE, SL 6, File 178.
132 No. 62 of 1862, R. Griffith to M. Kempson, dated 4 Jun 1862, UPRA (Allahabad), FDE, SL 12, File 420.
133 Quoted in *The Pandit*, NS 1, 1 (June 1876), 'note', n.p.
134 Bāla Śāstrī, *Bhāmatī: Brahmasūtraśāṅkarabhāṣya-vyākhyā*. Note also that a large number of Sanskrit works were edited and published by the college under the supervision of Griffith and Thibaut in the 'Benares Sanskrit Series'. Many *paṇḍit*s of the college were involved in this, though not exclusively.
135 For example, Viṭṭhala Śāstrī's index of topics covered in the *'nyāya-cintāmaṇi'*, *'Cintāmaṇiprakaraṇasūcīpatra'*.

136 Keśava Śāstrī, *'Ātmasopānaprastāvanā'* [an introduction to the staircase to the soul]; and Keśava Śāstrī, *'Ātmasopānaṃ nāma vedāntaprakaraṇaṃ'* [a treatise on the *vedānta* named staircase to the soul]. Upādhyāy praises this work as being a 'great achievement'. See *Kāśī kī Pāṇḍitya Paramparā*, 298.

137 BL, OIOC, SV/412, Statement of the Particulars Regarding Books, Maps, etc. Published in the North Western Provinces (3rd Quarter, 1867).

138 Kempson, *Report on the Progress of Education*, 11.

139 For biographical information, see Upādhyāy, *Kāśī kī Pāṇḍitya Paramparā*, 297–9. Thibaut was particularly indebted to Keśava Śāstrī for his help in translating Śaṅkarācārya's *Śārīrakabhāṣya*. See ibid., 99.

140 Revd K. M. Banerjea taught at Bishop's College in Calcutta. See his *Dialogues on the Hindu Philosophy* (also published in India).

141 Keśava Śāstrī, *Jñānasiddhāntacandrikā*.

142 These appeared in the New Series of *The Pandit* from 1877 onwards. The *Yoga Sūtras* were also published separately in Benares by the Medical Hall Press in 1884.

143 Keśava Śāstrī, 'Letter to the Editor of The Pandit', *The Pandit*, 10, 109 (Jun 1875), 23–4.

144 Śivaprasād was an inspector in the NWP Department of Public Instruction. For biographical details, see Dalmia, *Nationalization of Hindu Traditions*, 132n.

145 Śivaprasād, letter to the editor, *The Pandit*, 5, 55 (Dec 1870), 158 (Sanskrit).

146 'A Hindu', letter to the editor, *The Pandit*, 5, 56 (Jan 1871), 207.

147 *'Bhiṣagvaro Bhāūdājī'*, *The Pandit*, 2, 24 (May 1868), 271–2 (Sanskrit).

148 See Mainkar, *Writings and Speeches of Dr Bhau Daji*.

149 Arnold, *Science, Technology and Medicine*, 70.

150 *The Pandit*, 2, 24 (May 1868), 271–2 (Sanskrit).

151 See *Transactions of the Benares Institute*; also Dalmia, *Nationalization of Hindu Tradition*, 114–17.

152 Sherring, 'Benares and its Antiquities'.

153 Ṭhākur Dāss, 'On the Commentaries of Ramanuja Acharya and Sankara Acharya'.

154 Rājārāma Śāstrī, 'Essay on the Prabodha Chandroday'.

155 See *Transactions of the Benares Institute*, 91–5.

156 Information on the Literary Society of Benares Paṇḍits is sketchy. See, however, *The Theosophist*, 1, 5 (Feb 1880), 132.

157 I owe this reference to Francesca Orsini.

158 Olcott, *Old Diary Leaves*, 128.

159 'Our "American Pandit"', *The Theosophist*, 1, 6 (Mar 1880), 151.

160 See Rāma Miśra Śāstrī, 'The Vedant Darsana'.

161 Including: Bāla Śāstrī, Gaṅgādhara Śāstrī, Ḍhuṇḍirāja Śāstrī, Keśava Śāstrī, Govindadeva Śāstrī, and others. For an account, in Sanskrit, see *'atha māghaśuklapratipadi saṃvṛttāyāḥ saṃskṛtasamājanāmnyāḥ sabhāyāḥ prathamopastaraṇasya varṇanaṃ'* [a description of the first meeting of the organisation known by the name of the Sanskrit Samāj ...], *The Pandit*, N.S. 1 (Jun 1876), 45–51.

162 *The Theosophist*, 2, 4 (Jan 1881), 86; and Olcott, *Old Diary Leaves*, 277–9.

163 The Theosophical Society was founded in New York in 1875, by Henry Olcott and Helena P. Blavatsky. The Society was soon headquartered in Bombay (then later in Madras), and in 1898 Annie Besant opened the Society's Central Hindu College in Benares. The Society's mandate was, quite simply, to promote the 'universal brotherhood of humanity', but was largely devoted to the utilising a variety of occultist and spiritualist practices in a quest for spiritual insight. See, for example, van der Veer, *Imperial Encounters*, 75–7.

164 *Paṇḍits* were closely involved in other Dharma Sabhās across northern India. For an overview of Hindu 'revivalism' and 'reformism', see not only Dalmia, *Nationalization of Hindu Traditions*, but also Jones, *Socio-Religious Reform Movements*.

165 For an overview of the Dharma Sabhā, see Śītalaprasāda Tripāṭhī, *'Śrīkāśirājasaṃsthāpitakāśīdharmmasabhāyaḥ saṅkṣiptaṃ vṛttaṃ'* [a description of the establishment of the Kāśī Dharma Sabhā]. Dalmia also discusses the establishment of this organisation in her *Nationalization of Hindu Traditions*, esp. 355–8.

166 See Sītalaprasāda Tripāṭhī, *'Śrīkāśīdharmmasabhā – Prakāśitaparīkṣāviṣayādi-vyavasthitipratipādakapatrasaṅkṣepaḥ'* [an exposition of the documents which explain the decisions on various topics of investigation made known by the Kāśī Dharma Sabhā].

167 Note also, for example, the publication in 1869 of an extensive commentary by Bāla Śāstrī on an 1855 *vyavasthā* by Rājārāma Śāstrī, which had pronounced the invalidity of widow remarriage at the request of a group of Bengalis in Calcutta. See Bāla Śāstrī, *Vidhavodvāhaśaṅkāsamādhi'* [a proof on the subject of widow remarriage].

168 Dayānanda was the founder of the Ārya Samāj, and sought to establish a 'scientific' and 'modern' form of Hinduism within the sole confines of the *Vedas*. See, for example, Jordens, *Dayananda Sarasvati*; and Prakash, *Another Reason*, esp. chap. 3 & 4.

169 Among the reports of the *śāstrārtha* of 1869 which I have been able to locate, one may enumerate: an original report in *Pratnakamranandinī* (1869); and a Hindi version, Dīkṣita, *Kāśīke Vidvānoṅkā aur Dayānandajīkā Saccā Kāśī Śāstrārth*. See also Dalmia, *Nationalization of Hindu Traditions*, 384–5; and Jordens, *Dayananda Sarasvati*, 67–9.

Afterword Sanskrit, Authority, National Culture

1 Anonymous, *Thoughts on India*.

2 Ibid., 8–9.

3 Ibid., 311–12.

4 Ibid., 301–2.

5 See Prakash, *Another Reason*, esp. chap. 4; Arnold, *Science, Technology and Medicine*.

6 'Antiquity of the Hindu Medical System' in *The Oriental: a monthly journal devoted to the resuscitation of Indian literature*, 1, 1 (Oct 1898): 8–9.

7 Ibid., see also, for example, the *Journal of Ayurveda, or the Indian System of Medicine*, whose honorary editor-in-chief was Kavirāj Gaṇanāth Sen, a

prominent promoter of *āyurveda*. It was noted that this journal represented 'a good example of the use of the history of science for nationalistic purposes. The Ayurveda movement is a revolt ... against the intellectual domination of an alien race ...' See Sarton, 'Twenty First Critical Bibliography', 555.

8 Datta, 'Early Literary Evidence'. In the late 1930s Datta became a *saṃnyāsī*, and took the name Svāmī Vidyāranya.

9 Dās, 'Some Notes on Indian Astronomy'.

10 Rāy, *History of Hindu Chemistry*.

11 Seal, 'Physicochemical Theories of the Ancient Hindus', 243–4. See also, Seal, *Positive Sciences of the Ancient Hindus*.

12 Rāy, *History of Chemistry in Ancient and Medieval India*, 40.

13 For an overview, see Arnold, *Science, Technology and Medicine*, esp. 172–4.

14 Dalmia, 'Sanskrit Scholars and Pandits of the Old School'; also, but with further qualifications, Dalmia, *Nationalization of Hindu Traditions*, 103–7.

15 'Memorandum on the proposed reestablishment of an Anglo-Sanskrit Department in the Benares College' by G. Thibaut, dated 25 Mar 1884, UPSA (Lucknow), Education Block, Box 4, SL 17, File 35, No. 2. Also reprinted in Nicholls, *Sketch of the Rise and Progress*, 109–13.

16 Dalmia, 'Sanskrit Scholars and Pandits of the Old School'; and Dalmia, *Nationalization of Hindu Traditions*, 103–7.

17 See Chatterjee, *Nation and its Fragments*, 98; Bhatt, *Hindu Nationalism*, 9–12.

18 Prakash, *Another Reason*, 101.

19 Lala Lajpat Rai, 'Introduction', 400–3. Of course, that the *paṇḍits* vehemently opposed 'purification' movements such as the Ārya Samāj was likely significant in this case, but the point that European orientalist understandings had served to displace elements of former subjectivities in India is well taken.

20 Datta, 'Literary Evidence of the Use of Zero', 449–50.

21 Gāṅguli, 'Notes on Indian Mathematics: A Criticism of Georgey Rusby Kaye's Interpretation', *Isis*, 12, 1 (1929): 132–45.

22 Guru Datta Vidyārthī, 'The Terminology of the Vedas and European Scholars'. On the *nirvacanaśāstra*, see Kahrs, *Indian Semantic Analysis*.

23 Muir, 'Relations of the Priests to Other Classes', *The Pandit*, 2, 14 (Jul 1867), 45.

24 Pramadādāsa Mittra, letter to the editor, *The Pandit*, NS 1 (Nov 1876): 382–6.

25 In the Islamic context, see Robinson, 'Technology and Religious Change'.

26 Pramadādāsa Mittra, 'Brahma, Iswara and Maya'.

27 See also my forthcoming 'Contesting Translations: Orientalism and the Interpretation of the *Vedas*', *Modern Intellectual History*, 4, 1 (2007).

Bibliography

Archival Sources

British Library, London

Bengal Civil Judicial Consultations (BJC)
Bengal Criminal and Judicial Consultations (BCJC)
Bengal Political Consultations (BPolC)
Bengal Public Consultations (BPCon)
Bengal Public Council (BPC)
Bengal Revenue Consultations (BRCon)
Bengal Revenue Council (BRC)
Bengal Secret Consultations (BSC)
Bengal Sudder Dewanny Adawlut Proceedings (BSDA)
BM Add. Mss (Warren Hastings' Papers)
Board's Collection (BC)
Factory Records Murshidabad (FRM)
General Proceedings, North-Western Provinces (NWP GP)
Home Miscellaneous Series (H/Misc)
Letters, Public & Judicial Department (L/P&J)
Mss Eur D357 (Notebook of J. R. Ballantyne)
Mss Eur E301 (Letters to H. H. Wilson)
Mss Eur F384 (Ballantyne Papers)
Mss Eur F78 (Papers of Sir Charles Wood)
Mss Eur K178 (Some Correspondence of Charles Wilkins)
SV/412 (Statement of the Particulars Regarding Books, Maps, etc. Published in the North Western Provinces, 3rd Quarter, 1867)
V/23/128 Art. III (Papers Regarding the Benares College)

West Bengal State Archive, Calcutta

SL/No. 55/1–2, GCPI Correspondence Vol. 7, Hindu College Benares (1820–28)
SL/No. 56–59, GCPI Correspondence Vol. 8–11, Benares College & Seminary (1828–42)
SL/No. 166, Council of Education, Copies of Correspondence ... relating to Sanskrit Education 1853

Uttar Pradesh State Archive, Lucknow

SL/No. 17, Box 4, File 35 of the Education Block, NWP

Uttar Pradesh Regional Archive, Allahabad

SL/No. 6, 12, 17, Files of the Director of Education, NWP (FDE)

Royal Asiatic Society, London

Brian Houghton Hodgson Papers

Periodicals

The Asiatic Journal
Asiatick Researches (Calcutta)
Asiatic Researches
Benares Magazine
British and Foreign Evangelical Review
The British Critic
Calcutta Christian Observer
The Calcutta Literary Gazette
Calcutta Review
Edinburgh Review
Friend of India
Hindī Pradīp
Journal of Ayurveda
Journal of the American Oriental Society
Journal of the Asiatic Society of Bengal
Journal of the Royal Asiatic Society
The Missionary
The Oriental: a monthly journal devoted to the resuscitation of Indian literature
The Pandit [or] Kāśīvidyāsudhānidhi
Pratnakamranandinī
Proceedings of the Asiatic Society of Bengal
The Theosophist
The Times
Transactions of the Royal Asiatic Society
Transactions of the Royal Society of Edinburgh

Official Published Government Sources

Adam, W. *Adam's Reports on Vernacular Education in Bengal and Behar, submitted to Government in 1835, 1836, and 1838*. Calcutta: Home Secretariat Press, 1868.

Calendar of Persian Correspondence, being letters which passed between some of the Company's servants and Indian rulers and notables, vol. 6. Delhi: Manager of Publications, 1938.

Clarke, R., ed. *The Regulations of the Government of Fort William in Bengal, in force at the end of 1853*, vol. 1. London: J & H Cox, 1854.

General Report of the Late General Committee of Public Instruction, for 1840–41 & 1841–42. Calcutta: William Rushton & Co., 1842.

General Report on Public Instruction in the North Western Provinces of the Bengal Presidency for 1843–44. Agra: Agra Ukhbar Press, n.d.

General Report on Public Instruction in the North Western Provinces of the Bengal Presidency for 1844–45. Agra: Secundra Orphan Press, 1846.

General Report on Public Instruction in the North Western Provinces of the Bengal Presidency for 1845–1846. Agra: Secundra Orphan Press, 1847.

General Report on Public Instruction in the North Western Provinces of the Bengal Presidency for 1846–1847. Agra: Secundra Orphan Press, 1848.

General Report on Public Instruction in the North Western Provinces of the Bengal Presidency for 1847–1848. Agra: Secundra Orphan Press, 1849.

General Report on Public Instruction in the North Western Provinces of the Bengal Presidency for 1849–50. Agra: Secundra Orphan Press, 1850.
General Report on Public Instruction in the North Western Provinces of the Bengal Presidency for 1850–51. Agra: Secundra Orphan Press, 1852.
General Report on Public Instruction in the North Western Provinces of the Bengal Presidency for 1851–52. Agra: Secundra Orphan Press, 1853.
General Report on Public Instruction in the North Western Provinces of the Bengal Presidency for 1852–53. Agra: Secundra Orphan Press, 1853.
General Report on Public Instruction in the North Western Provinces of the Bengal Presidency for 1853–54. Agra: Secundra Orphan Press, 1854.
Great Britain, House of Commons. *Papers Relating to East India Affairs, viz. Hindoo Widows, and Voluntary Imolations. Parliamentary Papers*. London: 1821.
Great Britain, House of Commons. *Reports from Committees of the House of Commons*, vol. 4. London: 1776.
The Imperial Gazetteer of India, new ed., vol. 7. Oxford: Clarendon Press, 1908.
Kempson, M. *Report on the Progress of Education in the North Western Provinces for the year 1866–67*. Allahabad: Government Press, 1867.
MacNaghten, W. H. *Select Reports of the Sudder Dewanny Adawlut, from 1791 to 1803*, vol. 1, part 1. Calcutta: Sreenaught Banerjee and Brothers, 1866.
Proceedings of the Committee of Circuit at Krishnagar and Kasimbazar, Vols. I, II, & III, 10 June to 17 September 1772. Calcutta: Bengal Secretariat Book Depot, 1926.
Reid, H. S. *General Report on Public Instruction in the North Western Provinces for 1854–55*. Agra: Secundra Orphan Press, 1856.
Report of the General Committee of Public Instruction, of the Presidency of Fort William in Bengal, for the Year 1839–40. Calcutta: Bengal Military Orphan Press, 1841.
Reports of the Calcutta School Book Society. Calcutta: School Book Society's Press, 1817–1833.
Saletore, G. N., ed., *Banaras Affairs 1811–1858, Vol. II*. Allahabad: Central Record Office, 1959.
Sharp, H., ed. *Selections from Educational Records, Part 1, 1781–1839*. Calcutta: Superintendent Government Printing, 1920.
Thornton, R. *Memoir on the Statistics of Indigenous Education within the North Western Provinces of the Bengal Presidency*. Calcutta: Baptist Mission Press, 1850.

Contemporary Published Sources

Anonymous. 'Native Education in India.' *Asiatic Journal*, NS 36, 144 (1841): 201–9.
Anonymous. 'Pandit Prema Chandra Tarkabāgīs: an Obituary.' *The Pandit*, 1, 12 (May 1867): 184–5.
Anonymous. *Rasāyan Prakāś: Conversations on Chemistry in Hindi*. Calcutta: Baptist Mission Press, 1847.
Anonymous. *The Thoughts on India, by a Brahman*. Benares: Arya Press, 1881.
Bailly, J.-S. *Histoire de l'Astronomie Ancienne, depuis son origine, jusqu' à l'éstablishment de l'école d'Alexandrie*. Paris: 1775.
Ballantyne, J. R., ed. *The Bhasha Parichchheda and its commentary the Siddhanta Muktavali, an exposition of the Nyaya Philosophy*. Calcutta: Encyclopædia Press, 1851.

——. *The Bible for Pandits, the First Three Chapters of Genesis, Diffusely and Unreservedly Commented, in Sanskrit and English.* Benares: Medical Hall Press, 1860.

——, ed. *Chapters on Political Economy, Vol. 1.* Reprints for the Pandits 8. Allahabad: Presbyterian Mission Press, 1854.

——. *Christianity Contrasted with Hindu Philosophy: an essay, in five books, Sanskrit and English: with practical suggestions tendered to the missionary among the Hindus.* London: James Madden, 1859.

——. *A Discourse on Translation, with reference to the educational despatch of the Hon. Court of Directors, of the 19th July 1854.* Mirzapore: Orphan School Press, 1855.

——, ed. *Elements of Logic, extracted from the work of Richard Whately, D. D., Archbishop of Dublin.* Reprints for the Pandits 6. Allahabad: Presbyterian Mission Press, 1853.

——, ed. *An Explanatory Version of Bacon's Novum Organum.* Reprints for the Pandits 5. Mirzapore: Orphan School Press, 1852.

——, ed. *First Lessons in Sanskrit Grammar.* Mirzapore: Orphan Press, 1851.

[——.] 'The Gist of the Vedānta – as a Philosophy.' *Benares Magazine*, 4 (Nov 1850): 325–33. Reprinted in *Paṇḍit Revisited, Part One*, ed. B. N. Miśra. Varanasi: Sampurnanand Sanskrit University, 1991.

——, ed. *Hindi Version of the Hitopadesha: Book 1, retaining as many as possible of the original Sanskrit expressions.* Mirzapore: Orphan School Press, 1851.

——, ed. *The Laghu Kaumudi, a Sanskrit Grammar, by Varadarāja, with an English version, commentary, and references.* Mirzapore: Orphan Press, 1849.

——, ed. *Laghu Kaumudi*, Mathurā Prasāda Miśra, transl. Benares: 1856.

——. *A Lecture on the Sankhya Philosophy, Embracing the Text of the Tattwa Samasa.* Mirzapore: Orphan School Press, 1850.

——. *A Lecture on the Vedanta, Embracing the Text of the Vedanta-Sara.* Allahabad: Presbyterian Mission Press, 1851.

——. *Lectures on the Nyaya Philosophy, Embracing the Text of the Tarka Samgraha.* Benares: 1848.

——. *Lectures on the Sub-Divisions of Knowledge, and their Mutual Relations. Delivered in the Benares Sanskrit College.* Printed in four parts. Part 1: Mirzapore: Orphan School Press, 1848; Part 2: Mirzapore: Orphan School Press, 1849; Part 3: Calcutta: Encyclopaedia Press, 1849; Part 4: Allahabad: Presbyterian Mission Press, 1849.

——, ed. *Metaphysics and Mental Philosophy*, 2 vols. Reprints for the Pandits 4. Allahabad: Presbyterian Mission Press, 1852–3.

——, ed. *The Method of Induction.* Reprints for the Pandits 3. Mirzapore: Orphan Press, 1852.

[——.] 'On the Nyaya System of Philosophy, and the Correspondence of its Divisions with those of Modern Science.' *Benares Magazine*, 1 (Feb 1849): 276–93. Reprinted in *Paṇḍit Revisited, Part One*, ed. B. N. Miśra. Varanasi: Sampurnanand Sanskrit University, 1991.

[——.] 'On the Ontology of the Vedānta.' *Benares Magazine*, 6, 30 (Dec 1851): 994–1009. Reprinted in *Paṇḍit Revisited, Part One*, ed. B. N. Miśra. Varanasi: Sampurnanand Sanskrit University, 1991.

[——.] 'The Pandits and Their Manner of Teaching.' *Benares Magazine*, 2 (Oct 1849): 355–62; *Benares Magazine*, 3 (Mar 1850): 213–21; *Benares Magazine*,

4 (Dec 1850): 432–40. Reprinted in *Paṇḍit Revisited, Part One*, ed. B. N. Miśra. Varanasi: Sampurnanand Sanskrit University, 1991.

——, ed. *Physical Geography*. Reprints for the Pandits 10. Mirzapore: Orphan School Press, 1855.

——. *The Practical Oriental Interpreter; or, Hints on the Art of Translating Readily from English into Hindustani and Persian, etc.* London: Madden & Co., 1843.

——. *Principles of Persian Caligraphy*. London: Madden & Co., 1839.

[——.] 'The Prospects of India – Religious and Intellectual.' *Benares Magazine*, 1 (March 1849): 344–74.

——, ed. *Shakespeare's Play of MacBeth, with an explanatory preface*. Mirzapore: Orphan Press, 1848.

——. *A Synopsis of Science from the Standpoint of the Nyāya Philosophy, Sanskrit and English*, vol. 2. Mirzapore: Orphan Press, 1852.

——. *A Synopsis of Science, in Sanskrit and English, Reconciled with the Truths to be Found in the Nyaya Philosophy*, 2nd ed. Mirzapore: Orphan Press, 1856.

——. & Viṭṭhala Śāstrī. *Heliographic Rules and Reasons, in Sanskrit, Hindi, and English [or] Ravikiraṇkūrcikayā Citralekhana, Prakriyopapattivarṇanaṃ*. Benares: Medical Hall Press, 1857.

——. & Viṭṭhala Śāstrī. *Pañcabhūtavādārtha: Lectures on the Chemistry of the Five Hindu Elements*. Benares: Medical Hall Press, 1859.

Banerjea, K. M. *Dialogues on the Hindu Philosophy, comprising the Nyaya, the Sankhya, the Vedant; to which is added a discussion of the Authority of the Vedas*. London: Williams and Norgate, 1861.

Bentley, J. *A Historical View of the Hindu Astronomy, from the earliest dawn of that science in India, down to the present time*. Calcutta: Baptist Mission Press, 1823.

——. 'On the Antiquity of the Surya Siddhanta, and the Formation of the Astronomical Cycles Therein Contained.' *Asiatick Researches*, 6 (1799): 537–88.

——. 'On the Hindu Systems of Astronomy, and their Connection with History in Ancient and Modern Times.' *Asiatick Researches*, 8 (1805): 193–244.

——. 'Remarks on the Principal Æras and Dates of the Ancient Hindus.' *Asiatick Researches*, 5 (1798): 315–43.

Bernier, F. *The History of the Late Revolution of the Empire of the Great Mogol*. London: Pitt, Miller, Starkey, 1761.

Blackstone, W. *Commentaries on the Laws of England*. 4 vols. Oxford: Clarendon Press, 1765–1769.

Blaquiere, W. C., transl. 'The Rudhiradhyaya, or sanguinary Chapter, translated from the Calica Puran.' *Asiatick Researches*, 5 (1798): 371–91.

Breton, P. *A Vocabulary of the Names of the Various Parts of the Human Body and of Medical and Technical Terms in English, Arabic, Persian, Hindee and Sanscrit, for the Use of the Members of the Medical Department in India*. Calcutta: Government Lithographic Press, 1825.

Bryant, J. *A New System; or, an Analysis of Ancient Mythology: wherein an attempt is made to divest tradition of fable; and to reduce the truth to its original purity*, 2nd ed. 2 vols. London: 1775.

Carey, W. *A Dictionary of the Bengalee Language, in which the Words are Traced to Their Origin, and Their Various Meanings Given*. Serampore: Mission Press, 1815.

——. *A Grammar of the Sungskrit Language, Composed from Works of the Most Esteemed Grammarians, to which are Added Examples for the Exercise of the*

Student, and a Complete List of the Dhatoos, or Roots. Serampore: Mission Press, 1806.

——. 'On the Importance of Sungskrita to the Future Improvement of India.' *Friend of India*, 2 (1819), 373–82, 426–42.

Chunder, B. *The Travels of a Hindoo to Various Parts of Bengal and Upper India*. 2 vols. London: Trübner & Co., 1869.

Colebrooke, H. T., transl. *Cosha, or Dictionary of the Sanscrit Language, by Amera Sinha. With an English Interpretation, and Annotation*. Serampoor: 1808.

——. *Essays on the Religion and Philosophy of the Hindus*. London: Williams and Norgate, 1858).

——. *A Grammar of the Sanscrit Language*. Calcutta: Honorable Company's Press, 1805.

——. 'Hindu Astronomy. Mr. Colebrooke's reply to the attack of Mr. Bentley.' *The Asiatic Journal*, 21, 123 (Mar 1826): 360–6.

——. 'On the Duties of a Faithful Hindu Widow.' *Asiatick Researches*, 4 (1795): 209–19.

——. 'On the Philosophy of the Hindus, Part IV.' *Transactions of the Royal Asiatic Society*, 2 (1830): 1–39.

——. 'On the Religious Ceremonies of the Hindus, and of the Brahmens Especially.' *Asiatick Researches*, 5 (1798): 345–68; *Asiatick Researches*, 7 (1801): 232–85, 288–311.

——. 'On the Sanscrit and Pracrit Languages.' *Asiatick Researches*, 7 (1801): 199–231.

——. 'On the Vedas, or Sacred Writings of the Hindus.' *Asiatick Researches*, 8 (1805): 369–476.

Colebrooke, T. E. *The Life of H. T. Colebrooke*. London: Trübner & Co., 1873.

Costard, G. *A Letter to Nathaniel Brassey Halhed, Esquire, Containing Some Remarks on his Preface to the Code of Gentoo Laws Lately Published*. Oxford: 1778.

Dās, S. R. 'Some Notes on Indian Astronomy.' *Isis*, 14, 2 (1930): 388–402.

Dās, Ś. S., ed. *The Hindi Scientific Glossary, Containing the Terms of Astronomy, Chemistry, Geography, Mathematics, Philosophy, Physics and Political Economy, and Their Hindi Equivalents*. Benares: Medical Hall Press, 1906.

Datta, B. 'Early Literary Evidence of the Use of the Zero in India.' *The American Mathematical Monthly*, 33, 9 (1926): 449–54.

Davis, S. 'On the Astronomical Computations of the Hindus.' *Asiatick Researches*, 2 (1790): 225–87.

de Condillac, E. B. *An Essay on the Origin of Human Knowledge, being a Supplement to Mr Locke's Essay on the Human Understanding*, T. Nugent, transl. London: J. Nourse, 1756.

Dīkṣita, M. P. *Kāśīke Vidvānoṅkā aur Dayānandajīkā Saccā Kāśī Śāstrārth*. Benares: Hitcintak Press, 1916.

Dow, A. 'A Dissertation concerning the Customs, Manners, Language, Religion and Philosophy of the Hindoos.' In A. Dow, *The History of Hindostan, from the Earliest Account of Time, to the Death of Akbar; translated from the Persian of Mahummud Casim Ferishta of Delhi*, vol. 1. London: T. Becket & P. A. DeHondt, 1768.

——. 'A Dissertation concerning the Origin and Nature of Despotism in Hindostan.' In A. Dow, *The History of Hindostan, from the death of Akbar, to the complete settlement of the empire under Aurungzebe*, vol. 3. London: T. Becket & P. A. DeHondt, 1772.

——. *The History of Hindostan, from the death of Akbar, to the complete settlement of the empire under Aurungzebe. ...* vol. 3. London: T. Becket & P. A. DeHondt, 1772.

——. *The History of Hindostan, from the Earliest Account of Time, to the Death of Akbar; translated from the Persian of Mahummud Casim Ferishta of Delhi. ...* 2 vols. London: T. Becket & P. A. DeHondt, 1768.

Fryer, J. *A New Account of East-India and Persia, in eight letters, being nine years travel*. London: Chiswell, 1698.

Gāṅguli, S. 'Notes on Indian Mathematics: A Criticism of Georgey Rusby Kaye's Interpretation.' *Isis*, 12, 1 (1929): 132–45.

Gleig, G. R. *Memoirs of the Life of the Right Honourable Warren Hastings, in Three Volumes*. London: Richard Bentley, 1841.

Goldsmith, O. *An Abridgement of the History of England*, transl. F. Carey. Serampore: Calcutta School Book Society, 1820.

Gore, N. N. S. *A Rational Refutation of the Hindu Philosophical Systems*, transl. F.-E. Hall. London & Madras: The Christian Literature Society for India, 1897 [1862 orig.].

Grant, C. *Observations on the State of Society among the Asiatic Subjects of Great Britain, Particularly with Respect to Morals; and on the means of improving it. Written chiefly in the year 1792* (House of Commons, 15 June 1813).

Griffith, R. T. H., ed. & transl. *Hymns of the Samaveda, Translated with a Popular Commentary*. Benares: E. J. Lazarus, 1893.

Halhed, N. B. *A Code of Gentoo Laws, or, Ordinations of the Pundits, from a Persian Translation, made from the Original, written in the Shanscrit Language*. London: 1776.

——. *A Grammar of the Bengal Language*. Hoogly, Bengal: 1778.

Hall, F.-E. *A Contribution Towards an Index to the Bibliography of the Indian Philosophical Systems*. Calcutta: Baptist Mission Press, 1859.

—— & Śītalāprasāda Tivarī. *Siddhānt Saṅgrah Bhāṣā* [a collection of philosophical doctrines in the vernacular]. Agra: Sikander Press, 1882.

[Hamilton, A.] '*Asiatic Researches: or Transactions of the Society instituted in Bengal, ...* Vol. VI.' *The Edinburgh Review*, 1, 1 (Oct 1802): 26–43.

[——.] '*Asiatic Researches: or Transactions of the Society instituted in Bengal, ...* Vol. VIII.' *The Edinburgh Review*, 12, 23 (Apr 1808): 36–50.

[——.] '*Asiatic Researches: or, Transactions of the Society instituted in Bengal,...* Volume the Seventh. London: 1804.' *The Edinburgh Review*, 9, 17 (Oct 1806): 92–101.

[——.] 'A Grammar of the Sanskrita Language, by Charles Wilkins, London, 1808.' *The Edinburgh Review*, 13, 26 (Jan 1809): 366–81.

Hastings, W. *A Narrative of the Insurrection which happened in the Zemeendary of Banaris in the month of August 1781*. Calcutta: 1782.

Haughton, G. C. *The Exposition of Vedanta Philosophy by H. T. Colebrooke vindicated, being a refutation of certain published remarks of Colonel Vans Kennedy*. London: 1835.

Hodgson, B. H. *Pre-eminence of the Vernaculars, or the Anglicists Answered*. Reprinted in B. H. Hodgson, *Miscellaneous Essays Relating to Indian Subjects*, Vol. II. London: Trübner & Co., 1880.

Holwell, J. Z. *Interesting Historical Events, Relative to the Provinces of Bengal and the Empire of Indostan. ...* 3 parts. London: T. Becket & P. A. DeHondt, 1765–1771.

Holwell, W. *A Mythological, Etymological, and Historical Dictionary; extracted from the Analysis of Ancient Mythology*. London: 1793.

Hutton, J. *Theory of the Earth with Proofs and Illustrations*. Edinburgh: 1795.

Jones, W. 'Charge to the Grand Jury, at Calcutta, December 4, 1788.' In W. Jones, *The Works of Sir William Jones*, vol. 3. London: 1799.

——. 'Charge to the Grand Jury, at Calcutta, June 10, 1785.' In W. Jones, *The Works of Sir William Jones*, vol. 3. London: 1799.

——. 'Charge to the Grand Jury, at Calcutta, June 10, 1787.' In W. Jones, *The Works of Sir William Jones*, vol. 3. London: 1799.

——. 'A Discourse on the Institution of a Society, for inquiring into the History, Civil and Natural, the Antiquities, Arts, Sciences, and Literature, of Asia, by the President.' *Asiatick Researches*, 1 (1788): ix–xvi.

——. 'Discourse the Ninth, on the Origin and Families of Nations, delivered 23 February, 1792.' *Asiatick Researches*, 3 (1792): 479–92.

——. 'An Essay on the Poetry of the Eastern Nations.' Reprinted in W. Jones, *The Works of Sir William Jones*, vol. 4. London: 1799.

——. 'The Fourth Anniversary Discourse, delivered 15 February, 1787, by the President.' *Asiatick Researches*, 2 (1790): 1–17.

——. *Grammar of the Persian Language*. London: 1771.

——. *The History of the Life of Nader Shah, King of Persia*. London: T. Cadell, 1773.

——, transl. *Institutes of Hindu Law: or, The Ordinances of Menu, according to the Gloss of Culluca, comprising the Indian system of duties, religious and civil*. In W. Jones, *The Works of Sir William Jones*, vol. 3. London: 1799.

——. 'On the Antiquity of the Indian Zodiack.' *Asiatick Researches*, 2 (1790): 289–306.

——. 'On the Chronology of the Hindus. Written in January, 1788.' *Asiatick Researches*, 2 (1790): 111–47.

——. 'On the Gods of Greece, Italy, and India, written in 1784, and since revised.' *Asiatick Researches*, 1 (1788): 221–75.

——. *Poems, Consisting Chiefly of Translations from the Asiatick Languages*. Reprinted in W. Jones, *The Works of Sir William Jones*, vol. 4. London: 1799.

——. 'The Second Anniversary Discourse, delivered 24 February, 1785, by the President.' *Asiatick Researches*, 1 (1788): 405–14.

——. 'The Sixth Discourse; on the Persians, delivered 19 February, 1789.' *Asiatick Researches*, 2 (1790): 43–66.

——. 'The Tenth Anniversary Discourse, delivered 28 February 1793, by the President, on Asiatic History, Civil and Natural.' *Asiatick Researches*, 4 (1795): 1–17.

——. 'The Third Anniversary Discourse, delivered 2 February, 1786, by the President.' *Asiatick Researches*, 1 (1788): 415–31.

——. *The Works of Sir William Jones*. 6 vols. London: 1799.

Joyce, J. *Dialogues illustrative of the first principles of mechanics and astronomy, designed to form a prize-book in schools and a help to natives desirous of scientific knowledge*. Calcutta: School Book Society's Press, 1819.

Kane, P. V. *History of Dharmaśāstra*, vol. 1. Poona: Bhandarkar Oriental Research Institute, 1930.

Kay, W. *Some Account of the Foundation, History, and Purposes of Bishop's College, Calcutta*. Calcutta: Bishop's College Press, 1859.

[——.] 'The Benares College.' *The Missionary*, 3, 9 (Sep 1853): 236–46.

Kennedy, V. *Researches on the Nature and Affinities of Ancient and Hindu Mythology*. London: Longman, Rees, Orme, Brown & Green, 1831.

Lushington, C. *The History, Design, and Present State of the Religious, Benevolent and Charitable Institutions founded by the British in Calcutta and its Vicinity*. Calcutta: 1824.

Macaulay, T. B. *The Life and Writings of Francis Bacon, Lord Chancellor of England*. Edinburgh: 1837.

Mack, J. *Principles of Chemistry*. Serampore: Serampore Press, 1834.

Malcolm, J. *The Political History of India, 1784–1823*. 2 vols. London: J. Murray, 1826.

Maurice, T. 'Asiatic Researches; or Transactions of the Society ... Volume the Fifth. Printed, verbatim, from the Calcutta edition.' *The British Critic*, 16 (Aug 1800): 147–60.

——. *Brahmanical Fraud Detected: or the attempts of the sacerdotal tribe of India to invest their fabulous deities and heroes with the honours and attributes of the Christian Messiah, Examined, Exposed, and Defeated,...* London: 1812.

——. *A Dissertation on the Oriental Trinities: extract from the fourth and fifth volumes of Indian Antiquities*. London: 1800.

——. *The History of Hindostan, its arts and sciences, as connected with the history of the other great empires of Asia, during the most ancient periods of the world*. 2 vols. London: 1795–1798.

——. *Indian Antiquities: or, Dissertations, relative to ... Hindostan. ...* 7 vols. London: 1793–1800.

——. *Sanscreet Fragments, or Interesting Extracts from the Sacred Books of the Brahmins, on subjects important to the British Isles*. London: 1798.

Middleton. *Statutes of the Missionary Institution of the Incorporated Society for the Propagation of the Gospel in Foreign Parts; to be called and known as Bishop's College, near Calcutta*. London: 1825.

Mill, J. 'Education.' Reprinted in *James Mill and Education* ed. W. H. Burston. Cambridge: Cambridge University Press, 1969.

——. *The History of British India*. 3 vols. London: Baldwin, Cradock, and Joy, 1817.

Mill, W. H. *Proposed Version of Theological Terms, with a View to Uniformity in Translations of the Holy Scriptures etc. Into the Various Languages of India*. Calcutta: Bishop's College Press, n.d. [1828].

Millar, J. *The Origin of the Distinction of Ranks: or, an inquiry into the circumstances which give rise to influence and authority, in the different members of society*, 3rd ed. London: J. Murray, 1781.

Miśra, Mathurā Prasāda. *A Trilingual Dictionary; Being a Comprehensive Lexicon in English, Urdu, and Hindi, ...* Benares: E. J. Lazarus and Co., 1865.

——. transl. *Vāhyaprapañca-darpaṇa, or, Mann's Lessons in General Knowledge rendered into Hindi*. Benares: Medical Hall Press, 1859.

Mitra, R. *A Scheme for the Rendering of European Scientific Terms into the Vernaculars of India*. Calcutta: Thacker Spink & Co., 1877.

Mittra, Pramadādāsa. 'Brahma, Iswara and Maya.' *The Theosophist*, 1, 1 (Oct 1879): 13–18.

Moore, J. J. 'Proposal for Printing by Subscription, the Following Sanscrit Works, Recommended for Publication by L. Wilkinson, Esq., of Sehore.' In *The Gunitadhia, or A Treatise on Astronomy, with a Commentary Entitled The*

Mitacshara, Forming the Third Portion of the Siddhant Shiromuni, by Bhaskara Acharya, ed. L. Wilkinson. Calcutta: Baptist Mission Press, 1842.
Muir, J. 'The Baconian Philosophy Applicable to the Mental Regeneration of India.' *Calcutta Christian Observer*, 7, 70 (March 1838): 123–6.
——. 'The Benares Sanskrit College.' *Benares Magazine*, 5, 25 (Feb 1851): 94–108.
[——.] *A Brief Notice of the Late Mr. Lancelot Wilkinson of the Bombay Civil Service, with his opinions on the education of natives of India, and on the state of native society*. London: Smith, Elder & Co., 1853.
——. *Mataparīkṣā: a sketch of the argument for Christianity and against Hinduism*. Calcutta: Bishop's College Press, 1839.
——. 'On the Best Mode of Reasoning on the Subject of Religion with Educated Hindus and Mahomedans; and on the Qualifications Necessary for the Purpose.' *The Christian Intelligencer* (Oct–Nov 1845): 363–73, 403–10.
——. 'Relations of the Priests to Other Classes of Indian Society in the Vedic Age.' *The Pandit*, 1 (1866–67): 150 ff. Originally printed in *The Journal of the Royal Asiatic Society of Great Britain and Ireland*, NS 2 (1866): 257–302.
——. *Vyavahārāloka: Brief Lectures on Mental Philosophy and Other Subjects; delivered in Sanskrit to the Students of the Banares Sanskrit College, with an address to the pandits and students*. Allahabad: Presbyterian Mission Press, 1845.
Muir, W. *The Honourable James Thomason, Lieutenant-Governor, N.-W.P., India, 1843–1853 A.D.* Edinburgh: T & T Clark, 1897.
Nicholls, G. *Sketch of the Rise and Progress of the Benares Patshalla or Sanskrit College, now forming the Sanskrit Department of the Benares College*. Allahabad: Government Press, United Provinces, 1907 [1848 orig.].
Olcott, H. S. *Old Diary Leaves, the Only Authentic History of the Theosophical Society*, second series 1878–83, 2nd ed. Madras: Theosophical Publishing House, 1928.
Ovington, J. *A Voyage to Suratt, in the year 1689*. London: Jacob Tonson, 1696.
Owen, S. R. I. 'On Hindu Neology.' *Memoirs Read Before the Anthropological Society of London*, 2 (1865–1866): 202–5.
Penrose, J. *An Attempt to Prove the Truth of Christianity from the Wisdom Displayed in its Original Establishment, and from the History of False and Corrupted Systems of Religion* ... Oxford: University Press, 1808.
Playfair, J. 'Questions and Remarks on the Astronomy of the Hindus.' *Asiatick Researches*, 4 (1795): 159–63.
——. 'Remarks on the Astronomy of the Bramins.' *Transactions of the Royal Society of Edinburgh*, 2 (1790): 135–92.
Pratt, J. H. *Scripture and Science not at Variance; with remarks on the Historical Character, Plenary Inspiration, and Surpassing Importance of the Earlier Chapters of Genesis*, 3rd ed. London: Thomas Hatchard, 1859.
Prinsep, J. 'Census of the Population of the City of Benares.' *Asiatic Researches*, 17 (1832): 470–98.
Rām Jasan, transl. *Bhūgola-Candrikā: Geography of the World*. Benares: 1859.
——. *A Sanskrit and English Dictionary, Being an Abridgment of Professor Wilson's Dictionary, with an Appendix Explaining the Use of Affixes in Sanskrit*. Benares: E. J. Lazarus and Co., 1870.
Rai, Lala Lajpat. Introduction to *Maharshi Swami Dayananda Saraswati and His Work* (1898). Reprinted in *The Collected Works of Lala Lajpat Rai*, vol. 1, ed. B. R. Nanda. Delhi: Manohar, 2003.

Rāy, P. C. *A History of Hindu Chemistry from the Earliest Times to the Middle of the Sixteenth Century AD*, 2 vols. Calcutta: 1902–1909.

Reade, E. A. *Contributions to the Benares Recorder, in 1852*. Agra: Government Press, 1858.

Robertson, W. *An Historical Disquisition concerning the Knowledge which the Ancients had of India*, 2nd ed. London: A. Strahan & T. Cadell, 1794.

Roer, E., ed. & transl. *Division of the Categories of the Nyāya Philosophy*. Bibliotheca Indica 8. Calcutta: Baptist Mission Press, 1850.

Sāmaśramī, Satyavrata, ed. *Sāma Veda Saṅhitā, with the commentary of Sāyana Āchārya*. Bibliotheca Indica New Series. 5 vols. Calcutta: Asiatic Society of Bengal, 1871–1878.

Sarton, G. 'Twenty First Critical Bibliography of the History and Philosophy of Science and of the History of Civilization.' *Isis*, 9, 3 (1927): 491–604.

Śāstrī, Bāla, ed. *Bhāmatī: Brahmasūtraśāṅkarabhāṣya-vyākhyā* [an exposition of the commentary of Śaṅkara on the *Brahmasūtra*]. Benares: Benares Printing Press, 1880.

——. *Vidhavodvāhaśaṅkāsamādhi* [a proof on the subject of widow remarriage]. Benares: Medical Hall Press, 1869.

Śāstrī, Bāpūdeva. 'Bhaskara's Knowledge of the Differential Calculus.' *The Journal of the Asiatic Society of Bengal*, 27, 3 (1858): 213–16.

——. *Bhūgolavarṇana: Geography of the World, Consisting Chiefly of the Geography of India*. Mirzapore: Orphan Press, 1853.

——. *Bījagaṇita: the Elements of Algebra*. Bombay: 1850.

——. *Elements of Plane Trigonometry*. Agra: Secundra Orphan Press, 1855.

——. 'On the Sidereal and Tropical Systems.' In *The Transactions of the Benares Institute for the Session 1864–65*. Benares: Medical Hall Press, 1865. Reprinted in *Memoirs Read Before the Anthropological Society of London*, 2 (1865–1866): 205–15.

——, ed. *The Siddhanta Shiromani (Ganitadhyaya and Goladhyaya), a treatise on astronomy, by Bhaskaracharya. With his own exposition, the Vasanabhashya*. Benares: Medical Hall Press, 1866.

——, transl. *Translation of the Surya Siddhanta by Pundit Bapu Deva Shastri, and of the Siddhanta Shiromani by the late Lancelot Wilkinson, revised by Pundit Bapu Deva Shastri, from the Sanskrit*. Bibliotheca Indica 32. Calcutta: Baptist Mission Press, 1861.

——. *Phalit kā Vicār* [Reflections on Astrology]. Benares: Medical Hall Press, 1870.

——. 'The Practice of Astrology by Hindus and Mohammedans and the Influence which it exerts upon them.' In *The Transactions of the Benares Institute for the Session 1864–65*. Benares: Medical Hall Press, 1865.

——. *Trikoṇamiti*, Venī Śaṅkara Vyāsa, transl. Benares: Medical Hall Press, 1859.

——. *Vyaktagaṇita: Elements of Arithmetic*. Benares: 1875.

—— & J. R. Ballantyne. *Hindi Geography*. Mirzapore: Orphan School Press, 1855.

Śāstrī, Govindadeva. 'Notice of Viṭṭhala Śāstrī, *paṇḍit*.' *The Pandit*, 1, 12 (May 1867): 177–8.

Śāstrī, Keśava. *'Ātmasopānaṃ nāma vedāntaprakaraṇaṃ'* [a treatise on the *vedānta* named staircase to the soul]. *The Pandit*, N.S. 4 (1882): 146–76, 177–89.

——. *'Ātmasopānaprastāvanā'* [an introduction to the staircase to the soul]. *The Pandit*, N.S. 4 (1882): 145.

——. *'Jñānasiddhāntacandrikā.' The Pandit*, 8, 87 (Aug 1873): 68–71, ff.

Śāstrī, Rājārāma. 'Essay on the Prabodha Chandroday.' In *Transactions of the Benares Institute for the Session 1864–65*. Benares: Medical Hall Press, 1865.

Śāstrī, Rāma Miśra. 'The Vedant Darsana.' *The Theosophist*, 1, 6 (Mar 1880): 158–9, ff.

Śāstrī, Viṭṭhala. '*Cintāmaṇiprakaraṇasūcīpatra*' [index of the treatise *Cintāmaṇi*]. *The Pandit*, 1, 5 (Oct 1866): 64–5.

—— & J. R. Ballantyne. *Bekanīyasūtravyākhyāna: An Explanatory Version of Bacon's 'Novum Organum' in Sanskrit and English*. Benares: Recorder Press, 1852 (Section 1 of Book 1 only).

Seal, B. 'The Physicochemical Theories of the Ancient Hindus.' Reprinted in *History of Chemistry in Ancient and Medieval India, incorporating the History of Hindu Chemistry*, ed. P. Rāy. Calcutta: Indian Chemical Society, 1956.

Seal, B. *The Positive Sciences of the Ancient Hindus*. London: Longmans, Green, 1915.

Sevaka Rāma. *Śabda Prabandāvalī*. Allahabad: Government Press, 1873.

Shastri, M. H. 'Dakshini Pandits at Benares.' *Indian Antiquary*, 41 (Jan 1912): 7–13.

Sherring, M. A. 'Benares and its Antiquities.' In *Transactions of the Benares Institute for the Session 1864–65*. Benares: Medical Hall Press, 1865.

——. *Benares: The Sacred City of the Hindus in Ancient and Modern Times*. Delhi: Low Price Publications, 1990 [1868 orig.].

——. *The Missionary Life and Labours of the Rev. William Smith*. Benares: Medical Hall Press, 1879.

Śiva Prasād, Rājā. *Vidyankur, or an Adoption from Chamber's 'Rudiments of Knowledge', and the first few pages of 'Introduction to the Sciences'*, 4th ed. Allahabad: Government Press, 1881.

Smith, A. 'The History of Astronomy.' In A. Smith, *Essays on Philosophical Subjects*. London: T. Cadell & W. Davies, 1795.

——. 'Report of 1762–3.' In A. Smith, *Lectures on Jurisprudence*, eds. R. L. Meek, D. D. Raphael, & P. G. Stein. Oxford: Clarendon Press, 1978.

Smith, G. 'Dr. Ballantyne and Government Education.' *Calcutta Review*, 25, 50 (1855): 305–22.

Smith, T. 'Astronomy of the Hindus.' *Calcutta Review*, 1, 1 (1844): 257–89.

Stewart, D. 'Account of the Life and Writings and Adam Smith, L. L. D.' In A. Smith, *Essays on Philosophical Subjects*. London: T. Cadell & W. Davies, 1795.

——. *Elements of the Philosophy of the Human Mind*. 3 vols. London: John Murray, 1792–1827.

Surmoona, Ramchunder. *Memorial, to the Honorable the Court of Directors of the East India Company*. [Calcutta?], n.p., n.d., ca. 1838.

Tarkapañcānana, J., ed. *A Digest of Hindu Law on Contracts and Successions, with a Commentary*, transl. H. T. Colebrooke. Calcutta: 1798.

Tarkaratna, Tārācaraṇa. *Tarkaratnākara: Nyāya Śāstra kā Sār* [the essence of the *nyāya*]. Benares: Light Press, 1868.

Teignmouth. *Memoirs of the Life, Writings and Correspondence of Sir William Jones*. London: 1804.

Ṭhākur Dāss. 'On the Commentaries of Ramanuja Acharya and Sankara Acharya.' In *Transactions of the Benares Institute for the Session 1864–65*. Benares: Medical Hall Press, 1865.

The Edinburgh Academy Register, a record of all those who have entered the school since its foundation in 1824. Edinburgh: Edinburgh Academical Club, 1914.

The Transactions of the Benares Institute for the Session 1864–65. Benares: Medical Hall Press, 1865.

Trevelyan, C. E. *On the Education of the People of India*. London: Longman, Orme, Brown, Green & Longmans, 1838.

Tripāṭhī, Śītalaprasāda. *'Śrīkāśīdharmmasabhā – Prakāśitaparīkṣāviṣayādivyavasthiti-pratipādakapatrasaṅkṣepaḥ'* [an exposition of the documents which explain the decisions on various topics of investigation made known by the Kāśī Dharma Sabhā]. *The Pandit*, 5, 57 (February 1871): 232–3.

——. *'Śrīkāśirājasaṃsthāpitakāśīdharmmasabhāyaḥ saṅkṣiptaṃ vṛttaṃ'* [a description of the establishment of the Kāśī Dharma Sabhā]. *The Pandit*, 5, 56 (Jan 1871): 205–6.

Tytler, J. 'On native education and the study of Sanscrit, Arabic and Persian.' *The Calcutta Literary Gazette* (14 June 1834): 371.

——. 'On Native Education.' *The Calcutta Literary Gazette*, NS 1, 25 (June 21 1834): 381–3

Upādhyāy, Śivdayāl. *Hindī kī Dūsrī Kitāb: Second Hindi Reader, Containing Literature, Grammar, Arithmetic, Geography and Science Lessons, with English and Persian Equivalents for Its Technical Terms*. Benares: Medical Hall Press, 1881.

Ussher, J. *The Annals of the World*. London: 1658.

Vidyārthī, Guru Datta. 'The Terminology of the Vedas and European Scholars.' In *The Wisdom of the Rishis, or, Complete Works of Pandita Guru Datta Vidyarthi*, ed. Svamī Vedānanda Tīrtha. Lahore: Arya Pustakalaya, n.d..

Volney, C.-F. *Les Ruins, ou Méditation sur les Révolutions des Empires*. Paris: 1791.

von Humboldt, W. *On Language: On the Diversity of Human Language Construction and Its Influence on the Mental Development of the Human Species*, ed. M. Losonsky, transl. P. Heath. Cambridge: Cambridge University Press, 1999 [1836].

Wallis, A. W. *Notes on Books and Proceedings in the Educational Department of Bengal; with an Appendix, from the German of Dr Max Müller*. Calcutta: Bishop's College Press, 1853.

Ward, W. *A View of the History, Literature, and Mythology of the Hindoos: including a minute description of their manners and customs, and translations form their principal works*, 3 vols. London: Kingsbury, Parbury & Allen, 1822.

Whitney, W. D. 'Reply to the Strictures of Prof. Weber upon an Essay Respecting the Asterismal Systems of the Hindus, Arabs, and Chinese.' *Journal of the American Oriental Society*, 8 (1866): 382–98.

Wilford, F. 'On Egypt and Other Countries adjacent to the Cali River, or Nile of Ethiopia, from the ancient books of the Hindus.' *Asiatick Researches*, 3 (1792): 295–468.

——. 'An Essay on the Sacred Isles in the West, and other essays connected with that work.' *Asiatick Researches*, 8 (1805): 245–367.

Wilkins, C., transl. *The Bhagvat-Geeta, or Dialogues of Kreeshna and Arjoon; in eighteen lectures; with notes. Translated from the original, in the Sanskreet, or ancient languages of the Brahmans*. London: 1785.

——. *A Grammar of the Sanskrita Language*. London: W. Blumer and Co., 1808.

——, transl. *The Heetopades of Veeshnoo-Sarma*. Bath: 1787.

Wilkinson, L., ed. *The Gunitadhia, or A Treatise on Astronomy, with a commentary entitled The Mitacshara, forming the third portion of the Siddhant Shiromuni: by Bhaskara Acharya*. Calcutta: Baptist Mission Press, 1842.

——. 'On the Use of the Siddhantas in the work of Native Education.' *Journal of the Asiatic Society of Bengal*, 3 (1834): 504–19.

Williams, M. *A Dictionary, English and Sanskrit*. London: W. H. Allen, 1851.

Wilson, H. H. *A Dictionary, Sanscrit and English: translated, amended and enlarged, from an original compilation prepared by learned natives for the College of Fort William*. Calcutta: Hindostanee Press, 1819.

——. 'Education of the Natives of India.' *The Asiatic Journal*, N.S. 19, 73 (1836): 1–16. Reprinted in *The Great Indian Education Debate: Documents Relating to the Orientalist-Anglicist Controversy, 1781–1843*, ed. L. Zastoupil & M. Moir. London: Curzon Press, 1999.

——. *An Introduction to the Grammar of the Sanskrit Language, for the Use of Early Students*. London: J. Madden and Co., 1847.

——, transl. *The Megha Duta; or Cloud Messenger; a poem, in the Sanscrit Language: by Calidasa. Translated into English verse, with notes and illustrations*. London: Black, Perry, and Co., 1814 [1813 orig.].

——. 'On the supposed Vaidik authority for the burning of Hindu widows, and on the funeral ceremonies of the Hindus.' *Journal of the Royal Asiatic Society*, 16 (1854): 201–14.

——. *Two Lectures on the Religious Practices and Opinions of the Hindus; delivered before the University of Oxford, on the 27th and 28th of February*. Oxford: 1840.

——. *Works*. 12 vols. ed. R. Rost. London: Trübner & Co., 1862–1871.

Yates, W. *Padārthavidyāsāra: Elements of Natural Philosophy and Natural History; in a series of familiar dialogues. Translated into the Sungscrit language, under the superintendence of Rev. W. Yates*. Calcutta: School Book Society's Press, 1828.

——. *Padārthavidyāsāra: Elements of Natural Philosophy and Natural History, in a series of familiar dialogues. Designed for the Instruction of Indian Youth*, 2nd ed. Calcutta: School Book Society's Press, 1834.

Secondary Works

Aarsleff, H. *From Locke to Saussure, Essays on the Study of Language and Intellectual History*. Minneapolis: University of Minnesota Press, 1982.

——. 'Locke's Influence.' In *The Cambridge Companion to Locke*, ed. V. Chappell. Cambridge: Cambridge University Press, 1994.

——. *The Study of Language in England, 1780–1860*. Minneapolis: University of Minnesota Press, 1983.

Adas, M. *Machines as the Measure of Men: Science, Technology, and Ideologies of Western Dominance*. Ithaca: Cornell University Press, 1989.

Amin, S. 'Approver's Testimony, Judicial Discourse: the Case of Chauri Chaura.' In *Subaltern Studies*, vol. 5, ed. R. Guha. Delhi: Oxford University Press, 1987.

Arnold, D. *Science, Technology and Medicine in Colonial India, 1760–1947*. New Cambridge History of India, III, 5. Cambridge: Cambridge University Press, 2000.

Baber, Z. *The Science of Empire: Scientific Knowledge, Civilization, and Colonial Rule in India*. Delhi: Oxford University Press, 1998.

Ballantyne, T. *Orientalism and Race: Aryanism in the British Empire*. Basingstoke: Palgrave Macmillan, 2002.
Banerji, B. *Dawn of New India*. Calcutta: M. C. Sarkar & Sons, 1927.
Basalla, G. 'The Spread of Western Science.' *Science*, 156 (5 May 1967): 611–22.
Bassnett, S. & H. Trivedi. Introduction to *Post-Colonial Translation: Theory and Practice*, eds. S. Bassnett & H. Trivedi. London: Routledge, 1999.
Bayly, C. A. 'The British Military-Fiscal State and Indigenous Resistance: India 1750–1820.' Reprinted in C. A. Bayly, *Origins of Nationality in South Asia: Patriotism and Ethical Government in the Making of Modern India*. New Delhi: Oxford University Press, 1998.
——. *Empire and Information: Intelligence Gathering and Social Communication in India, 1780–1870*. Cambridge: Cambridge University Press, 1996.
——. *Indian Society and the Making of the British Empire*. New Cambridge History of India, II, 1. Cambridge: Cambridge University Press, 1988.
——. 'Orientalists, Informants and Critics in Banaras, 1790–1860.' In *Perspectives of Mutual Encounters in South Asian History, 1760–1860*, ed. J. Malik. Leiden: Brill, 2000.
——. *Origins of Nationality in South Asia: Patriotism and Ethical Government in the Making of Modern India*. New Delhi: Oxford University Press, 1998.
——. 'Returning the British to South Asian History: The Limits of Colonial Hegemony.' Reprinted in C. A. Bayly, *Origins of Nationality in South Asia: Patriotism and Ethical Government in the making of Modern India*. Delhi: Oxford University Press, 1998.
——. *Rulers, Townsmen and Bazaars: North Indian Society in the Age of British Expansion, 1770–1870*. Delhi: Oxford University Press, 1992 [1983 orig.].
Berry, C. J. *The Social Theory of the Scottish Enlightenment*. Edinburgh: Edinburgh University Press, 1997.
Bhabha, H. K. 'Difference, Discrimination, and the Discourse of Colonialism.' In *The Politics of Theory*, eds. F. Barker, et al. Colchester: University of Essex, 1983.
——. *The Location of Culture*. London: Routledge, 1994.
Bhardwaj, S. M. *Hindu Places of Pilgrimage in India*. Berkeley: University of California Press, 1983 [1973 orig.].
Bhatt, C. *Hindu Nationalism: Origins, Ideologies and Modern Myths*. Oxford: Berg, 2001.
Bourdieu, P. *In Other Words: Essays Towards a Reflexive Sociology*, transl. M. Adamson. Stanford: Stanford University Press, 1990.
——. *The Logic of Practice*, transl. R. Nice. Stanford: Stanford University Press, 1990.
Breckenridge, C. A. & P. van der Veer, eds. *Orientalism and the Postcolonial Predicament*. Philadelphia: University of Pennsylvania Press, 1993.
Cannon, G., ed. *The Letters of Sir William Jones*. 2 vols. Oxford: Clarendon Press, 1970.
——. *The Life and Mind of Oriental Jones*. Cambridge: Cambridge University Press, 1990.
——. *Oriental Jones: A Biography of Sir William Jones, 1746–94*. London: Asia Publishing House, 1964.
Chakrabarty, D. *Habitations of Modernity: Essays in the Wake of Subaltern Studies*. Chicago: Chicago University Press, 2002.
——. *Provincializing Europe: Postcolonial Thought and Historical Difference*. Princeton: Princeton University Press, 2000.

Chambers, D. W. & R. Gillespie. 'Locality in the History of Science: Colonial Science, Technoscience, and Indigenous Knowledge.' *Osiris*, 15 (2000): 221–40.

Chatterjee, K. 'The Persianization of Itihasa: Performance-Narratives and Mughal Political Culture in 18th Century Bengal.' Unpublished manuscript in author's possession.

Chatterjee, P. *The Nation and its Fragments: Colonial and Postcolonial Histories*. Princeton: Princeton University Press, 1993.

Cheyfitz, E. *The Poetics of Imperialism: Translation and Colonization from the Tempest to Tarzan*. Oxford: Oxford University Press, 1991.

Clifford, J. 'On *Orientalism*.' Reprinted in J. Clifford, *The Predicament of Culture: Twentieth-Century Ethnography, Literature, and Art*. Cambridge, Mass: Harvard University Press, 1988.

Cohn, B. S. *Colonialism and its Forms of Knowledge: The British in India*. Princeton: Princeton University Press, 1996.

——. 'The Command of Language and the Language of Command.' Reprinted in B. S. Cohn, *Colonialism and its Forms of Knowledge: The British in India*. Princeton: Princeton University Press, 1996.

——. 'Law and the Colonial State in India.' Reprinted in B. S. Cohn, *Colonialism and its Forms of Knowledge: The British in India*. Princeton: Princeton University Press, 1996.

——. 'Political Systems in Eighteenth-Century India: The Benares Region.' Reprinted in B. S. Cohn, *An Anthropologist Among the Historians and Other Essays*. Delhi: Oxford University Press, 1987.

——. 'The Role of Gosains in the Economy of Eighteenth and Nineteenth Century Upper India.' *The Indian Economic and Social History Review*, 1, 4 (1964): 175–82.

——. & N. B. Dirks. 'Beyond the Fringe: The Nation-State, Colonialism, and the Technologies of Power.' *Journal of Historical Sociology*, 1 (1988): 224–9.

Colley, L. *Britons: Forging the Nation, 1707–1837*. New Haven: Yale University Press, 1992.

Cooper, F. 'The Dialectics of Decolonization: Nationalism and Labor Movements in Postwar French Africa.' In *Tensions of Empire: Colonial Cultures in a Bourgeois World*, eds. F. Cooper & A. L. Stoler. Berkeley: University of California Press, 1997.

——. & A. L. Stoler. 'Between Metropole and Colony: Rethinking a Research Agenda.' In *Tensions of Empire: Colonial Cultures in a Bourgeois World*, eds. F. Cooper & A. L. Stoler. Berkeley: University of California Press, 1997.

Cosslett, T. Introduction to *Science and Religion in the Nineteenth Century*, ed. T. Cosslett. Cambridge: Cambridge University Press, 1984.

Dalmia, V. *The Nationalization of Hindu Traditions: Bhāratendu Hariśchandra and Nineteenth-Century Banaras*. Delhi: Oxford University Press, 1997.

——. 'Sanskrit Scholars and Pandits of the Old School: The Benares Sanskrit College and the Constitution of Authority in the Late Nineteenth Century.' *Journal of Indian Philosophy*, 24 (1996): 321–37.

Dalrymple, W. 'Assimilation and Transculturation in Eighteenth-Century India: A Reply to Pankaj Mishra.' *Common Knowledge*, 11, 3 (2005): 445–85.

——. *White Mughals: Love and Betrayal in Eighteenth-Century India*. London: HarperCollins, 2002.

Das, S. K. *Sahibs and Munshis: An Account of the College of Fort William*. Calcutta: Orion Publications, 1978.

David, A. 'Sir William Jones, Biblical Orientalism and Indian Scholarship.' *Modern Asian Studies*, 30, 1 (1996): 173–84.

Derrett, J. D. M. *Religion, Law, and the State in India*. London: Faber & Faber, 1968.

Dickinson, H. T. *Liberty and Property: Political Ideology in Eighteenth-Century Britain*. London: Weidenfeld & Nicholson, 1977.

Dirks, N. *Castes of Mind: Colonialism and the Making of Modern India*. Princeton: Princeton University Press, 2001.

Dodson, M. S. 'Contesting Translations: Orientalism and the Interpretation of the *Vedas*.' *Modern Intellectual History*, 4, 1 (2007), forthcoming.

Drayton, R. *Nature's Government: Science, Imperial Britain, and the "Improvement" of the World*. New Haven: Yale University Press, 2000.

——. 'Science, Medicine, and the British Empire.' In *The Oxford History of the British Empire, Vol. V, Historiography*, ed. R. W. Winks. Oxford: Oxford University Press, 1999.

Eck, D. *Banaras: City of Light*. New Delhi: Penguin, 1993 [1983 orig.].

Embree, A. T. *Charles Grant and British Rule in India*. London: Allen & Unwin, 1962.

Fabian, J. *Time and the Other: How Anthropology Makes its Object*. New York: Columbia University Press, 1983.

Fisher, M. H., ed. *The Travels of Dean Mahomet: An Eighteenth-Century Journey Through India*. Berkeley: University of California Press, 1997.

Foucault, M. 'The Ethics of the Concern of the Self as a Practice of Freedom.' In M. Foucault, *Ethics: Subjectivity and Truth*, The Essential Works of Foucault 1, ed. P. Rabinow. New York: The New Press, 1997.

——. *The Order of Things: An Archaeology of the Human Sciences*. London: Routledge, 1970.

——. 'Two Lectures.' In M. Foucault, *Power/Knowledge: Selected Interviews and Other Writings 1972–1977*, ed. C. Gordon. New York: Pantheon Books, 1980.

Freitag, S. B., ed. *Culture and Power in Banaras: Community, Performance, and Environment, 1800–1980*. Berkeley: University of California Press, 1989.

Gabriel, R. 'Learned Communities and British Educational Experiments in North India: 1780–1830.' Ph.D. dissertation, University of Virginia, 1979.

Gilroy, P. *The Black Atlantic: Modernity and Double Consciousness*. Cambridge, Mass.: Harvard University Press, 1993.

Gordon, S. 'Legitimacy and Loyalty in Some Successor States of the Eighteenth Century.' In *Kingship and Authority in South Asia*, ed. J. F. Richards. Delhi: Oxford University Press, 1998 [1978 orig.].

——. *The Marathas, 1600–1818*. New Cambridge History of India, II, 4. Cambridge: Cambridge University Press, 1993.

Guha, R. *Dominance Without Hegemony: History and Power in Colonial India*. Cambridge, Mass.: Harvard University Press, 1998.

——. *A Rule of Property for Bengal: An Essay on the Idea of Permanent Settlement*. Paris: Mouton & Co., 1963.

——. & G. C. Spivak, eds. *Selected Subaltern Studies*. New York: Oxford University Press, 1988.

Hatcher, B. A. 'Contemporary Hindu Thought.' In *Contemporary Hinduism: Ritual, Culture, and Practice*, ed. R. Rinehart. New York: ABC–CLIO, 2004.

——. *Idioms of Improvement: Vidyasagar and Cultural Encounter in Bengal*. New York: Oxford University Press, 1996.

——. 'Sanskrit Pandits Recall Their Youth: Two Autobiographies from Nineteenth-Century Bengal.' *Journal of the American Oriental Society*, 121, 4 (2001): 580–92.

——. 'What's Become of the Pandit? Rethinking the History of Sanskrit Scholars in Colonial Bengal.' *Modern Asian Studies*, 39, 3 (2005): 683–723.

Hopfl, H. M. 'From Savage to Scotsman: Conjectural History in the Scottish Enlightenment.' *The Journal of British Studies*, 17, 2 (1978): 19–40.

Inden, R. *Imagining India*. London: C. Hurst & Co., 2000 [1990 orig.].

Ingalls, D. 'The Brahman Tradition.' In *Traditional India: Structure and Change*, ed. M. Singer. Philadelphia: The American Folklore Society, 1959.

Irschick, E. F. *Dialogue and History: Constructing South India, 1795–1895*. Berkeley: University of California Press, 1994.

Irwin, R. *For Lust of Knowing: The Orientalists and Their Enemies*. London: Allen Lane, 2006.

Jacob, M. C. *Scientific Culture and the Making of the Industrial West*. Oxford: Oxford University Press, 1997.

Jones, K. W. *Socio-Religious Reform Movements in British India*. New Cambridge History of India, III, 1. Cambridge: Cambridge University Press, 1989.

Jordens, J. T. F. *Dayananda Sarasvati: His Life and Ideas*. Delhi: Oxford University Press, 1978.

Kahrs, E. G. *Indian Semantic Analysis: The 'nirvacana' tradition*. Cambridge: Cambridge University Press, 1998.

Kaviraj, S. 'The Sudden Death of Sanskrit Knowledge.' *Journal of Indian Philosophy*, 33 (2005): 119–42.

Kejariwal, O. P. *The Asiatic Society of Bengal and the Discovery of India's Past, 1784–1838*. Delhi: Oxford University Press, 1988.

Khan, A. M. *The Transition in Bengal, 1756–1775: A Study of Saiyid Muhammad Reza Khan*. Cambridge: Cambridge University Press, 1969.

Kopf, D. *The Brahmo Samaj and the Shaping of the Modern Indian Mind*. Princeton: Princeton University Press, 1979.

——. *British Orientalism and the Bengal Renaissance*. Berkeley: University of California Press, 1969.

——. 'The Historiography of British Orientalism, 1772–1992.' In *Objects of Enquiry: The Life, Contributions, and Influences of Sir William Jones (1746–1794)*, eds. G. Cannon & K. R. Brine. New York: New York University Press, 1995.

Kumar, D. *Science and the Raj, 1857–1905*. Delhi: Oxford University Press, 1997.

Kumar, N. 'Sanskrit Pandits and the Modernisation of Sanskrit Education in the Nineteenth to Twentieth Centuries.' In *Swami Vivekananda and the Modernization of Hinduism*, ed. W. Radice. Delhi: Oxford University Press, 1998.

Laird, M. A. *Missionaries and Education in Bengal, 1793–1837*. Oxford: Clarendon Press, 1972.

Lariviere, R. W. 'Justices and *Paṇḍitas*: Some Ironies in Contemporary Readings of the Hindu Legal Past.' *The Journal of Asian Studies*, 48, 4 (1989): 757–69.

Leask, N. 'Francis Wilford and the Colonial Construction of Hindu Geography, 1799–1822.' In *Romantic Geographies: Discourses of Travel 1775–1844*, ed. A. Gilroy. Manchester: Manchester University Press, 2000.

Lieberman, D. *The Province of Legislation Determined: Legal Theory in Eighteenth-Century Britain*. Cambridge: Cambridge University Press, 1989.

Lingat, R. *The Classical Law of India*, transl., J. D. M. Derrett. Berkeley: University of California Press,1973.

Liu, L. *Translingual Practice: Literature, National Culture, and Translated Modernity – China, 1900–1937*. Stanford: Stanford University Press, 1995.

Lobban, M. *The Common Law and English Jurisprudence, 1760–1850*. Oxford: Clarendon Press, 1991.

Lowe, L. *Critical Terrains: British and French Orientalisms*. Ithaca: Cornell University Press, 1991.

Lutgendorf, P. *The Life of a Text: Performing the Rāmcaritmānas of Tulsidas*. Berkeley: University of California Press, 1991.

——. 'Ram's Story in Shiva's City: Public Arenas and Private Patronage.' In *Culture and Power in Banaras: Community, Performance and Private Patronage, 1800–1980*, ed. S. B. Freitag. Berkeley: University of California Press, 1989.

MacLeod, R. Introduction to *Osiris*, 15 (2000): 2–3.

——. 'Passages in Imperial Science: From Empire to Commonwealth.' *Journal of World History*, 4, 1 (1993): 117–50.

Mainkar, T. G., ed. *Writings and Speeches of Dr Bhau Daji*. Bombay: University of Bombay, 1974.

Majeed, J. 'Gandhi, Truth, and Translatability.' *Modern Asian Studies*, 40, 2 (2006): 303–32.

——. *Ungoverned Imaginings: James Mill's* The History of British India *and Orientalism*. Oxford: Clarendon Press, 1992.

Malik, J., ed. *Perspectives of Mutual Encounters in South Asian History, 1760–1860*. Leiden: Brill, 2000.

Mandler, P. 'The Problem with Cultural History.' *Cultural and Social History*, 1 (2004): 94–117.

Mani, L. *Contentious Traditions: The Debate on Sati in Colonial India*. Berkeley: University of California Press, 1998.

——. 'Production of an Official Discourse on *Sati* in Early Nineteenth Century Bengal.' *Economic and Political Weekly*, 21, 17 (26 April 1986): 32–40.

Marrouchi, M. 'Counternarratives, recoveries, refusals.' In *Edward Said and the Work of the Critic: Speaking Truth to Power*, ed. P. A. Bové. Durham: Duke University Press, 2000.

Marshall, P. J. *Bengal: The British Bridgehead, Eastern India 1740–1828*. New Cambridge History of India, II, 2. Cambridge: Cambridge University Press, 1987.

——, ed. *The British Discovery of Hinduism in the Eighteenth Century*. Cambridge: Cambridge University Press, 1970.

——. 'Warren Hastings as Scholar and Patron.' In *Statesmen, Scholars and Merchants: Essays in Eighteenth-Century History presented to Dame Lucy Sutherland*, eds. A. Whiteman, J. S. Bromley & P. G. M. Dickson. Oxford: Clarendon Press, 1973.

McLane, J. R. *Land and Local Kingship in Eighteenth-Century Bengal*. Cambridge: Cambridge University Press, 1993.

Mehta, U. S. *Liberalism and Empire: A Study in Nineteenth Century British Liberal Thought*. Chicago: University of Chicago Press, 1999.

Metcalf, T. R. *Ideologies of the Raj*. New Cambridge History of India, III, 4. Cambridge: Cambridge University Press, 1995.

Michaels, A., ed. *The Pandit: Traditional Scholarship in India*. New Delhi: Manohar, 2001.

Minault, G. 'Qiran al-Sa'ādain: The Dialogue Between Eastern and Western Learning at Delhi College.' In *Perspectives of Mutual Encounters in South Asian History, 1760–1860*, ed. J. Malik. Leiden: Brill, 2000.

Minkowski, C. Z. 'The Pandit as Public Intellectual: The Controversy over *Virodha* or Inconsistency in the Astronomical Sciences.' In *The Pandit: Traditional Scholarship in India*, ed. A. Michaels. Delhi: Manohar, 2001.

Misra, B. B. *The Central Administration of the East India Company, 1773–1834*. Manchester: Manchester University Press, 1959.

——. *The Judicial Administration of the East India Company in Bengal, 1765–1782*. Delhi: Motilal Banarsidass, 1961.

Miśra, B. N., ed. *Paṇḍit Revisited, Part One*. Varanasi: Sampurnanand Sanskrit University, 1991.

——, ed. *Paṇḍitaparikramā*. Mult. vols. Varanasi: Sampurnanand Sanskrit University, 1991.

Miśra, R. M. *Saṃskṛt Patrakāritā kā Itihās* [History of Sanskrit Journalism]. Delhi: Vivek Prakāśan, Saṃvat. 2033.

Moore-Gilbert, B. *Postcolonial Theory: Contexts, Practices, Politics*. London: Verso, 1997.

Mukherji, A. 'European Jones and Asiatic Pandits.' *Journal of the Asiatic Society*, 27, 1 (1985): 43–58.

Narain, V. A. *Jonathan Duncan and Varanasi*. Calcutta: Firma K. L. Mukhopadhyay, 1959.

Niranjana, T. *Siting Translation: History, Post-Structuralism, and the Colonial Context*. Berkeley: University of California Press, 1992.

O'Hanlon, R. *Caste, Conflict, and Ideology: Mahatma Jotirao Phule ad Low Caste Protest in Nineteenth-Century Western India*. Cambridge: Cambridge University Press, 1985.

——. 'Historical Approaches to Communalism: Perspectives from Western India.' In *Society and Ideology: Essays in South Asian History*, ed. P. Robb. Delhi: Oxford University Press, 1993.

Orsini, F. 'Pandits, Printers and Others: Publishing in Nineteenth-Century Benares.' In *Print Areas: Book History in India*, eds. S. Chakravorty & A. Gupta. Delhi: Permanent Black, 2004.

Parry, B. 'Problems in Current Theories of Colonial Discourse.' *Oxford Literary Review*, 9, 1–2 (1987): 27–58.

——. 'Signs of Our Times: Discussion of Homi Bhabha's *The Location of Culture*.' *Third Text*, 28/29 (1994): 5–24.

Parry, J. 'The Brahmanical Tradition and the Technology of the Intellect.' In *Reason and Morality*, ed. J. Overing. London: Tavistock Publications, 1985.

Peabody, N. 'Cents, Sense, Census: Human Inventories in late Precolonial and Early Colonial India.' *Comparative Studies in Society and History*, 43, 4 (2001): 819–50.

——. 'Tod's *Rajast'han* and the Boundaries of Imperial Rule in Nineteenth-Century India.' *Modern Asian Studies*, 30, 1 (1996): 185–220.

Pinch, W. 'Same Difference in India and Europe.' *History and Theory: Studies in the Philosophy of History*, 38, 3 (1999): 389–407.

Pollock, S. 'The Death of Sanskrit.' *Comparative Studies in Society and History*, 43, 2 (2001): 392–426.

——. 'Introduction: Working Papers on Sanskrit Knowledge-Systems on the Eve of Colonialism.' *Journal of Indian Philosophy*, 30 (2002): 431–9.

Prakash, G. *Another Reason: Science and the Imagination of Modern India*. Princeton: Princeton University Press, 1999.

——. 'Science Between the Lines.' In *Subaltern Studies: Writings on South Asian History and Society*, vol. 9, eds. S. Amin & D. Chakrabarty. Delhi: Oxford University Press, 1996.

Pratt, M. L. *Imperial Eyes: Travel Writing and Transculturation*. London: Routledge, 1992.

Price, P. G. 'Ideology and Ethnicity under British Imperial Rule: 'Brahmans', Lawyers and Kin-Caste Rules in Madras Presidency.' *Modern Asian Studies*, 23, 1 (1989): 151–77.

Prior, K. 'The British Administration of Hinduism in North India, 1780–1900.' Ph.D. dissertation, University of Cambridge, 1990.

Rahman, A. Introduction to *Science and Technology in India, Pakistan, Bangladesh, and Sri Lanka*, ed. A. Rahman. Harlow: Longman, 1990.

Rai, A. *Hindi Nationalism*. New Delhi: Orient Longman, 2001.

Raina, D. 'From West to Non-West? Basalla's Three-stage Model Revisited.' *Science as Culture*, 8, 4 (1999): 497–516.

Rauch, A. *Useful Knowledge: The Victorians, Morality, and the March of Intellect*. Durham: Duke University Press, 2001.

Reed, E. S. *From Soul to Mind: The Emergence of Psychology, from Erasmus Darwin to William James*. New Haven: Yale University Press, 1997.

Robinson, F. 'Technology and Religious Change: Islam and the Impact of Print.' *Modern Asian Studies*, 27, 1 (1993): 229–51.

Rocher, L. 'Schools of Hindu Law.' In *India Maior*, eds. J. Ensink & P. Gaeppke. Leiden: E. J. Brill, 1972.

Rocher, R. 'British Orientalism in the Eighteenth Century: The Dialectics of Knowledge and Government.' In *Orientalism and the Postcolonial Predicament: Perspectives on South Asia*, eds. C. A. Breckenridge & P. van der Veer. Philadelphia: University of Pennsylvania Press, 1993.

——. 'The Career of Rādhākānta Tarkavāgīśa, an Eighteenth-Century Pandit in British Employ.' *Journal of the American Oriental Society*, 109, 4 (1989): 627–33.

——. 'Nathaniel Brassey Halhed, Sir William Jones, and Comparative Indo-European Linguistics.' In *Recherches de Linguistique Hommages à Maurice Leroy*. Brussels: Université de Bruxelles, 1980.

——. 'Of Sources, Compendia, and Recasts: Competent Witnesses in the *Vivādārṇavasetu*.' In *Indology and Law: Studies in Honour of Professor J. Duncan M. Derrett*, eds. G. D. Sontheimer & P. K. Aithal. Wiesbaden: Franz Steiner Verlag, 1982.

——. *Orientalism, Poetry, and the Millennium: The Checkered Life of Nathaniel Brassey Halhed, 1751–1830*. Delhi: Motilal Banarsidass, 1983.

——. 'Overlapping Recensions and the Composing Process: Ceilings of Interest in the *Vivādārṇavasetu*.' *Journal of the American Oriental Society*, 105, 3 (1985): 531–41.

——. 'Shifting Ground: H. T. Colebrooke and Indian Pandits.' Paper presented at the Annual Conference on South Asia, University of Wisconsin, Madison, Oct 7, 2005.

——. 'Weaving Knowledge: Sir William Jones and Indian Pandits.' In *Objects of Enquiry: The Life, Contributions, and Influences of Sir William Jones (1746–1794)*, eds. G. Cannon & K. R. Brine. New York: New York University Press, 1995.

Said, E. W. *Culture and Imperialism*. New York: Vintage Books, 1994.

——. *Orientalism*. New York: Vintage Books, 1979.

Scott, D. *Refashioning Futures: Criticism after Postcoloniality*. Princeton: Princeton University Press, 1999.

Sen, N. 'Warren Hastings and British Sovereign Authority in Bengal, 1774–1780.' *The Journal of Imperial and Commonwealth History*, 25, 1 (1997): 59–81.

Sen, S. & U. Mishra, eds. *Sanskrit Documents, Being Sanskrit Letters and Other Documents Preserved in the Oriental Collection at the National Archives of India*. Allahabad: Ganganatha Jha Research Institute, 1951.

Singha, R. *A Despotism of Law: Crime and Justice in Early Colonial India*. Delhi: Oxford University Press, 1998.

Sinha, C. *Indian Civil Judiciary in Making*. Delhi: Motilal Banarsidass, 1971.

Sinha, S. *Pandits in a Changing Environment*. Calcutta: Surat Book House, 1993.

Spivak, G. C. 'Can the Subaltern Speak?' In *Marxism and the Interpretation of Cultures*, eds. C. Nelson & L. Grossberg. Urbana: University of Illinois Press, 1988.

Stokes, E. *The English Utilitarians and India*. Delhi: Oxford University Press, 1989 [1959].

Stoler, A. L. *Carnal Knowledge and Imperial Power: Race and the Intimate in Colonial Rule*. Berkeley: University of California Press, 2002.

Swartz, D. *Culture and Power: The Sociology of Pierre Bourdieu*. Chicago: University of Chicago Press, 1997.

Teltscher, K. *India Inscribed: European and British Writing on India, 1600–1800*. Delhi: Oxford University Press, 1995.

Trautmann, T. R. *Aryans and British India*. Berkeley: University of California Press, 1997.

Travers, T. R. *Ideology and Empire in Eighteenth-Century India: The British in Bengal*. Cambridge: Cambridge University Press, forthcoming.

Upādhyāy, B. *Kāśī kī Pāṇḍitya Paramparā*, 2nd ed. Vārāṇasī: Viśvavidyālaya Prakāśan, 1994.

van Berkel, K. 'Science in the Service of the Enlightenment, 1700–1795.' In *A History of Science in the Netherlands: Survey, Themes and Reference*, eds. K. van Berkel, L. C. Palm, A. van Helden. Leiden: Brill, 1999.

van der Veer, P. *Imperial Encounters: Religion and Modernity in India and Britain*. Princeton: Princeton University Press, 2001.

Venuti, L. *The Translator's Invisibility: A History of Translation*. London: Routledge, 1995.

Vishwanathan, G. *Masks of Conquest: Literary Study and British Rule in India*. London: Faber and Faber, 1990.

Wagoner, P. B. 'Precolonial Intellectuals and the Production of Colonial Knowledge.' *Comparative Studies in Society and History*, 45, 4 (2003): 783–814.

Washbrook, D. A. 'Orients and Occidents: Colonial Discourse Theory and the Historiography of the British Empire.' In *The Oxford History of the British Empire, Vol. V, Historiography*, ed. R. W. Winks. Oxford: Oxford University Press, 1999.

——. 'Progress and Problems: South Asian Economic and Social History, ca. 1720–1860.' *Modern Asian Studies*, 22, 1 (1988): 57–96.

Wilson, J. 'Empire and the Practice of Thought: Classifying and Codifying Law in Early Colonial Bengal.' Seminar paper presented at Tufts University, Boston, 8 Apr 2005.

Wink, A. *Land and Sovereignty in India: Agrarian Society and Politics under the Eighteenth-Century Maratha Svarajya*. Cambridge: Cambridge University Press, 1986.

Young, B. '"The Lust of Empire and Religious Hate": Christianity, History, and India, 1790–1820.' In *History, Religion, and Culture: British Intellectual History 1750–1950*, eds. S. Collini, R. Whatmore, & B. Young. Cambridge: Cambridge University Press, 2000.

Young, R. *White Mythologies: Writing History and the West*. London: Routledge, 1990.

Young, R. F. 'Church Sanskrit: An Approach of Christian Scholars to Hinduism in the Nineteenth Century.' *Wiener Zeitschrift für die Kunde Südasiens*, 23 (1979): 222–7.

——. 'Enabling Encounters: Transformative Experiences on the Edges Between Hinduism and Christianity.' Lectures presented at the University of Cambridge in November 2002. http://www.martynmission.cam.ac.uk/CRFoxYoung.pre.htm

——. 'Receding from Antiquity: Responses to Science and Christianity on the Margins of Empire, 1800–1850.' In *Christians and Missionaries in India: Cross-Cultural Communication Since 1500*, ed. R. E. Frykenberg. Grand Rapids: Wm. B. Eerdmans Publishing Co., 2003.

——. *Resistant Hinduism: Sanskrit Sources on Anti-Christian Apologetics in Early Nineteenth Century India*. Vienna: De Nobili Research Library, 1981.

Zastoupil, L. *John Stuart Mill and India*. Stanford: Stanford University Press, 1994.

——. & Moir M., eds. *The Great Indian Education Debate: Documents Relating to the Orientalist-Anglicist Controversy, 1781–1843*. London: Curzon Press, 1999.

Index